The Secret Gospel of Mark Unveiled

PETER JEFFERY

The Secret Gospel of Mark Unveiled

IMAGINED RITUALS OF SEX, DEATH, AND MADNESS IN A BIBLICAL FORGERY

Yale University Press
New Haven &
London

Published with assistance from the Kingsley Trust Association Publication Fund established by the Scroll and Key Society of Yale College.

Set in Sabon type by Keystone Typesetting, Inc.
Printed in the United States of America by Sheridan Books.

Library of Congress Cataloging-in-Publication Data
Jeffery, Peter, 1953–
The secret Gospel of Mark unveiled : imagined rituals of sex, death, and madness in a biblical forgery / Peter Jeffery.
p. cm.
Includes bibliographical references and index.
ISBN-13: 978-0-300-11760-8 (cloth : alk. paper)
ISBN-10: 0-300-11760-4 (cloth : alk. paper)
1. Secret Gospel according to Mark. I. Title.
BS2860.S42J44 2006
229'8—dc22

2006014035

A catalogue record for this book is available from the British Library.

For those who didn't know

I was a problem for which there was no solution.
— *Oscar Wilde*

Contents

Acknowledgments

This book started out as a longish footnote in a more serious mono-graph: *They Saw His Glory: How Judaism and Christianity Grew Apart, as Told in Their Most Ancient Hymns*. I had always had my doubts about the Secret Gospel of Mark, but it was only in 2003, when the *Journal of Early Christian Studies* published a forum of three articles about it, that I realized how seriously this other Marcan gospel was being taken in some quarters. At that point I expanded my footnote into an independent article, which the *Journal* accepted on the condition that I enlarge the section on ancient homo-sexuality. That article was never published, however; before long it had grown into two articles, then into this book. As a result, I never found my way back to the book I had been trying to write: the more moving tale that is told in the psalms of Torah and Temple, the hymns of the Pseudepigrapha and the Qum-ran community, the spiritual songs of the New Testament, the liturgies of early church and synagogue.

I wish to express my gratitude to all those known and anonymous readers who helped me along the way — especially my hilarious wife, Margot, and her many merry friends. Harold Attridge, Adela Yarbro Collins, Elizabeth A. Clark, Michael Moses, Simon Morrison, and Wayne Heisler were particularly helpful. I can't thank you enough. And I pray for the late Morton Smith — may God rest his anguished soul.

A Note on Psalm Numbering

The Psalter contains 150 psalms, but in ancient times there was more than one way to number them. Most English Bibles follow the Hebrew numbering, which is therefore the one most familiar to English readers. Coptic and Latin Bibles, as well as modern vernacular translations from the Latin, follow the Greek numbering. The Syriac Bible had a third way of numbering the Psalms. In this book, because it deals with ancient Christian texts, the psalms are identified first by their Greek/Latin number and then by the Hebrew/English number in square brackets.

"A Discovery of Extraordinary Importance"

*The whole story spans more than thirty years, from 1941 to the present. I am
shocked to find how much of it I have already forgotten. No doubt if the past,
like a motion picture, could be replayed, I should also be shocked to find how
much of the story I have already invented. Memory is perhaps more fallacious
than forgetfulness.*
— Morton Smith

An Ancient Monastery

East of Bethlehem in the Judean desert, on a cliffside overlooking the
Kidron Valley, halfway between Jerusalem and the Dead Sea, stands one of the
most ancient monasteries in the Christian world, the Great Laura of Mar
Saba. It is named in Aramaic for its founder, St. Sabbas,[1] a Greek from Cae-
sarea, in Asia Minor, who began building the first structure in the year 483.[2]
Sabbas lived a long life (439–532), which was well documented by Cyril of
Scythopolis, who was able to interview many people who had known him
personally. Cyril's life of Sabbas forms the largest section of Cyril's *Lives of the
Monks of Palestine*, one of the core texts of monastic historiography.[3]

The Great Laura has been a major center of Eastern Orthodox Christianity
ever since. Some of its monks were important authors and theologians,[4] and
many became bishops, martyrs, and saints. Most eminent of them all was St.

John of Damascus (eighth century), the great systematic theologian of Eastern Christianity, who formulated the Orthodox theology of the icons and perhaps the first Christian theological response to Islam.[5] His prolific writings counterbalance the reticence of another St. John, called "the Silent," who had fled an Armenian bishopric to become one of St. Sabbas's original disciples, then chose to live in deliberate isolation, not speaking for many years.[6]

As the area was conquered by the Persians in 614 and the Muslims in 638, Mar Saba began to experience violent attacks, which continued for centuries. Many monks are remembered as martyrs, their bones still venerated at the monastery. But as Greek culture began to recede from the area, Mar Saba became a major center for the translation of Christian texts and ideas: many writings were rendered from Greek into Georgian and Arabic, a smaller number from Syriac into Greek.[7] In the ninth century, Theōdūrus Abū Qurra was the first author to write original Christian works in Arabic,[8] while St. Theodore of Edessa reputedly converted a Caliph of Baghdad.[9]

Over the centuries, as Mar Saba evolved from a laura (a cluster of individual hermitages around a common church) to a coenobium (an organized monastic community with an abbot), its way of life was codified in the Sabaite monastic typikon (customary), which exerted far-reaching influence in Palestine,[10] throughout Greek-speaking Christianity,[11] in the Slavic world,[12] and even in Rome.[13] Still more influential was its liturgical typikon, one of the central sources of the tradition we now call the Byzantine rite.[14] Mar Saba was also a leading center for hymnody, beginning in the early eighth century with a remarkable generation of hymnographers. The Oktoechos, or book of the eight musical modes, may have originated there, and is traditionally ascribed to St. John of Damascus.[15] Numerous hymns of the *kanon* genre, based on the nine biblical odes, are ascribed to St. John, and to his reputed adoptive brother St. Kosmas, who later became bishop of Maiuma in Gaza. The genre is said to have been invented by St. Andrew, who later became bishop of Crete.[16] Later in the eighth century, the *kanonarchos* or song-leader at Mar Saba was St. Stephen the Sabaite, known as the Thaumaturge or miracle-worker.[17] Other hymnographers followed in succeeding centuries down to the present.[18]

A YOUNG VISITOR

"Monasteries are never without guests," as the great St. Benedict wrote in the sixth century.[19] So it was in 1941 that Morton Smith first visited Mar Saba. A twenty-six-year-old graduate student on a traveling fellowship from Harvard Divinity School, he had been stranded in the Holy Land (of all places!) when the Second World War made it impossible for American ships to cross the Mediterranean Sea. Smith used his time well, though, pursuing a second doctorate at Hebrew University. A chance acquaintance with a high official in the Greek Orthodox Patriarchate brought him the rare opportunity to stay at Mar Saba as an honored guest. By his own account, published decades later in 1973, Smith "spent almost two months there," from "after the Christmas season" to "early in Lent," and during that time he was shown many cells and caves, containing artworks and artifacts that outsiders rarely see:[20] "Here were many of the most beautiful icons, and here, I was told, had occurred the great fire, sometime in the eighteenth century, when many of the finest icons, manuscripts, and vestments . . . were destroyed. Most of the remaining manuscripts had been carried off to Jerusalem in the late nineteenth century, at the order of the Patriarch, but there were still a few stored in the great tower, and there was a good library of old editions of the Church fathers in a room over the porch of the new church."[21]

But in 1941 Smith had little interest in the libraries he saw — or so he claimed in his 1973 memoir: "I was shown the two libraries, as I was the other sights of the monastery, but at the time I paid them little attention. My main interest was in the services, which gave me a new understanding of worship."[22] What this "new understanding" was, and what he did with it, will be a major theme in this book. But for now we must stay with the libraries and the manuscripts.

"Supposed Scholarly Labors"
SMITH'S WORK AT MAR SABA

After the war, Smith returned to Harvard to complete his doctorate in theology. It was only then, he reported in 1973, that "I became interested in Greek manuscripts and manuscript hunting." After teaching posts at Brown and Drew universities, Smith arrived in 1957 at the history department of Columbia University in New York, where he would spend the rest of his career. The itinerant life of a young professor can be draining, and Smith felt that "by the spring of 1958 I was ready for a rest and remembered the tranquillity of Mar Saba." A sabbatical, and the permission of the new Greek Patriarch in Jerusalem, enabled him to spend three weeks there, searching out and cataloguing whatever manuscript material the monastery still possessed.[23] As Smith recalled in 1973, he focused his work on the tower library but was permitted to take books back to his room overnight. His published catalogue, however, describes a few manuscripts that were not kept in the tower, but elsewhere in the monastery.[24]

> Every morning except Sunday, after the services, a monk would climb with me the long stairways that led to the old tower — they must have amounted to a dozen or fifteen stories — and sit by patiently while I went through volume after volume of the books and manuscripts piled every which way on the floor

and in the bookcases that lined the side walls of the topmost room. I first cleared one shelf of a bookcase and then began lining up there the printed books I had inspected. When a volume turned out to contain manuscript material, I set it aside. When I had found three or four manuscripts we called it a day. The room was locked and I took the manuscripts down to my cell for study. Next morning I returned them, worked through another pile or two of volumes, found another few manuscripts, and so continued. Little by little the chaos of old books was reduced to order, and, as the line of printed texts grew along one side of the room, a much smaller line of catalogued manuscripts began to grow along the other.[25]

If we compare this with Smith's description of the daily schedule at Mar Saba, the implications are that he and the monk would climb the stairs shortly after 6 a.m., when the six-hour night vigil service ended. Seemingly they worked until noon, when Smith says the only full meal of the day was served.[26] However, Smith seems to have misremembered the timing of the daily meal, for other sources say that in those days it was served about 10:00 or 10:30 in the morning.[27] If the library was only open four hours a day (roughly 6 to 10 a.m.), that would not be atypical for an old-world monastery.

The timing of the religious services interests us because it structured Smith's workday. But it seems to have been a factor only because it determined the availability of the monk librarian. By 1958, Smith claimed, he had lost interest in the liturgical celebrations that so fascinated him in 1941, and so he had stopped attending them.

> Never revisit a place that fascinated you when you were young — you discover not only its changes, but your own. . . . Electricity had been introduced, and not even the Byzantine liturgy can survive direct illumination. Perhaps that was just as well; it enabled me to blame the lighting for my own failure to respond at forty-three as I had at twenty-six. Six hours of a service to which one is not responding are a bit too much, but as a guest of the Patriarch I was under no obligation to attend. I soon made my supposed scholarly labors an excuse for spending most of my time in my cell, enjoying the solitude and the silence for which the monastery had been founded.[28]

It would appear, then, that Smith and the monk worked in the tower from about 6 to 10 o'clock in the morning, six days a week. Smith would then retire to his own room with the day's manuscript finds, and presumably work there until he retired in the evening. The monk, on the other hand, would have gone to the afternoon service from 1:30 to 2:30 p.m. — actually a sequence of services comprising Nones, Vespers, and the Office of the Dead or a Paraklesis honoring the saint of the day. Compline (Apodeipnon) followed at about 4:00 p.m. The monk would have retired to bed not long after, for at midnight or 1:00 a.m. he would have to be up again for the marathon night vigil, encompassing the rest of the daily round or cursus: Mesonyktikon, Orthros, Prime, Terce, Sext, the Typika, and the eucharistic Divine Liturgy (or Mass) of the day.[29] When all that was over, about 6:00 or 6:30 a.m., he and Smith would climb the stairs to the tower again. Smith would presumably return the previous day's manuscripts and begin searching for more. Three or four manuscripts per day for three six-day weeks would be fifty-four to seventy-two volumes; indeed, Smith's published catalogue describes seventy-one manuscripts in Greek.[30]

Not everything was catalogued, however.[31] By his own account, Smith omitted about twenty-five non-Greek manuscripts (in Turkish, Romanian, and Slavic languages), twenty Greek liturgical manuscripts of the nineteenth and twentieth centuries, a paper folder containing fragments of relatively recent liturgical manuscripts, and a leather folder containing older fragments of more varied content.[32] And Smith acknowledged in his catalogue that there could well be other, undiscovered manuscripts hidden away in parts of the monastery.[33] In an article Smith published in 1960, he wrote that out of some "four or five hundred volumes in the tower library alone . . . the examination yielded some ninety items which could be catalogued as manuscripts, and two folders full of loose manuscript material."[34] This enumeration evidently included the seventy-one Greek manuscripts he catalogued and the twenty liturgical manuscripts he did not, but omitted the manuscripts in other languages. To examine four or five hundred volumes in eighteen workdays, Smith would have had to look at about twenty-five books each four-hour day—about ten minutes per volume. But for the three or four manuscripts he took back to his room each day, he could have had from about noon (or whenever the meal ended) until he retired to bed, perhaps a total of about ten hours.

MISGIVINGS

So the numbers add up, pretty much, though they show Smith was working on a tight schedule. Other aspects of Smith's account do not add up, however. Given the limited amount of time for onsite work, some of the choices Smith made are hard to explain. His decision not to catalogue the twenty recent liturgical manuscripts is consistent with the fact that he was no longer the young seminarian whose "main interest was in the services." Yet most of the other material didn't interest Smith either. His 1973 memoir expresses surprising ambivalence about the entire cataloguing project, even though it had been his own idea.

> I had not expected much from the Mar Saba manuscripts, since I knew that almost all of them had been carried off to Jerusalem in the past century and were listed in the catalogue of the Patriarchal library. But there was always the chance that something had been missed, or that other manuscripts had been

brought in by monks coming from other monasteries. In any event it would be helpful to know what was in the library. So I patiently listed manuscript copies of prayer books and hymns and sermons and lives of saints and anthologies from the Church fathers and so on — the proper and predictable reading of a monastic community.[35]

If Smith "had not expected much," why had he chosen to devote valuable sabbatical time to this effort? Was it worth traveling all the way from North America on the mere "chance that something had been missed"? The claim that "it would be helpful to know what was in the library" seems a weak justification, considering that the "predictable reading" — the liturgical, hagiographical, and patristic literature — was of so little interest that it tried his patience to catalogue it.

Indeed, Smith seems to have had a somewhat distant relationship with his own catalogue, which he slightingly called "my notes on the collection."[36] He never published the original English text; it appeared only in a modern Greek translation made by a Mar Saba monk, in a journal of the Jerusalem Patriarchate not widely available in Western libraries. This implies that only Greek Orthodox monks and clergy were expected to have much interest in the material. But why would Smith have wanted to write for that audience, given his lack of enthusiasm for their worship and their "predictable reading"?

Scholars who write catalogues are usually interested in the manuscripts they spend so much time working on. More than that, they also tend to be interested in the history of the libraries that house these manuscripts.[37] The library of a 1,450-year-old monastery like Mar Saba holds obvious appeal for a person with such interests. But whatever motivated Smith, it was certainly not the history of the Mar Saba library. He referred to it only in sketchy and incomplete ways and did not ask the kinds of questions that a library historian usually would have asked. For example, Smith rarely speculated on how long any particular item had been at Mar Saba. He reveals no curiosity about how or when there came to be two distinct collections: one in the tower, the other "over the porch of the new church." He mentioned the eighteenth-century fire in the caves, but not the 1834 earthquake that provoked widespread looting and forced extensive rebuilding — the reason why there is a new church at Mar Saba.[38] The last manuscript listed in Smith's article is a 1910 catalogue of Mar Saba's books, but "this catalogue was discovered on the last day of my stay at the monastery and I did not have time to examine it."[39] That could well be true, but Smith did not even photograph it, and he never returned to Mar Saba to read it. Nor, apparently, did he ever visit the library of the Greek Patriarchate, though he surely realized that some of the handwritings and fragments he found at the monastery were likely to have counterparts among the 706 Mar

Saba manuscripts that were relocated to Jerusalem in 1887. Smith never even speculated about the many former Mar Saba manuscripts that have migrated to other libraries throughout the world; today at least 55 are known.[40]

If Smith was like many Western scholars of that era, he would have been interested primarily in finding early manuscripts, good textual witnesses to important ancient texts. On that score, it is true, the collection offers relatively little. Most of the seventy-one items he catalogued (at least fifty) were written during the nineteenth or twentieth century, with sixteen more dating from the eighteenth or nineteenth. But if Smith wanted early sources, why didn't he devote his time to the fragments in the leather folder, many of which he judged to be older than the seventeenth century?[41] He knew that fragments removed from old bindings (which is what such folders frequently consist of) will often be of earlier date than any of the intact manuscripts in a library.[42]

Smith also seems to have cared little for the three oldest items he did catalogue, which he dated to the tenth or eleventh century. Two were fragments of liturgical texts,[43] and we know how he felt about those. The other was a parchment fragment of an unidentified "sermon or ascetic work," to which he really should have given more attention. Originally addressed to monks, it contains an admonition Smith would have done well to ponder: "Remember the eternal fire each evening when you go to sleep and when you get up, and indolence [*rhathymia*] will never overcome you at the time of psalmody."[44] As we will see, this mysterious text points obscurely to the dark heart of the problem, for the fear of Hell and the purpose of psalmody are the twin enigmas that veil, or rather shroud, the mystery of Morton Smith.

MANUSCRIPT HUNTING

If Smith had "not expected much," if he did not try to reconstruct the history of the library, if he wasn't particularly interested in the three early fragments or the contents of the leather folder — what drew him to Mar Saba? When he went there in 1958, he already had a lot of experience searching Greek ecclesiastical libraries for manuscripts and must have had some notion of what he was likely to find. His publications about those other libraries help to clarify his modus operandi; in fact, they show that the Mar Saba project was in some ways atypical. To begin with, Mar Saba was the only place for which Smith (or rather a monk-translator) published an entire catalogue. For all the other collections he systematically explored, Smith kept most of his notes unpublished and wrote articles describing only the manuscripts he thought were worthwhile. It is best to think of Smith, then, not as a cataloguer (interested in entire collections and library history), but as someone engaged in what he himself called "manuscript hunting."

Three themes tend to recur in Smith's articles on Greek libraries, permitting us to construct a picture of him as a "manuscript hunter." First, what he was most excited about finding, or most disappointed at not finding, were unknown manuscripts of the church fathers, the Apocrypha (ancient religious writings that were not included in the Bible), and the Pseudepigrapha (writings attributed pseudonymously to biblical personages).[45] Evidently his dream scenario was to discover the lost Greek original of a major pseudepigraphical work that had been thought to survive only in ancient translations: "Who knows?" he once wrote. "Perhaps as this is being written (or read) the last Greek manuscript of the Odes of Solomon is being eaten by a worm in a little monastery somewhere in Greece."[46] Certainly the Greek original of this very early Christian hymnal (it is certainly not by King Solomon!) would be a discovery of major importance — scholars know it now mainly from the Syriac translation.[47] But if that was the kind of treasure Smith hoped to find, why did he go to Mar Saba, if it was a place where he "had not expected much"?

According to one of his students, Smith was looking for manuscripts of Isidore of Pelusium, on whom he had already published two articles.[48] Yet Smith knew there was an unidentified text ascribed to Isidore in one of the Mar Saba manuscripts that had gone to Jerusalem — why did he never visit the Patriarchate to try to identify it?[49] He could hardly have gone to Mar Saba without passing through Jerusalem.

The second recurring theme in Smith's writings is represented by his long, plaintive lists of all the kinds of manuscripts he did not care about.

> . . . the sort of content expectable from the manuscripts in the collections here discussed . . . does a good deal to explain why so little attention has been paid to these texts. The history of the music and the liturgical and devotional literature of the Greek Orthodox Church from 1453 to 1953 is probably among the least fashionable of academic disciplines; modern Greek canon law is another subject that excites little enthusiasm; another is the after-life of medieval Aristotelianism in the Turkish empire; finally, a fair number of the anonymous works on profane topics, the treatise[s] on theology, and the catechisms are elementary texts, presumably of no significance.[50]

To each his own, but one would never guess from this that Smith had once preferred the Mar Saba music and liturgy over its libraries. The story of how his views changed will turn out to be very revealing, as we will see — for in his 1973 memoir, Smith claimed to have developed a profound understanding of Byzantine hymnody, despite his resolute refusal to learn anything specific about it.

As for the third theme, Smith would emphasize the importance of searching printed books for handwritten material and argue that such late manuscripts can have real value for the textual criticism even of much earlier writers. For example, in 1960 he wrote:

> At present, copying is generally done on ordinary paper. But formerly paper was rare and expensive, so every spare page of available books was pressed into use. Thus a seventeenth-century edition of the Ignatian epistles, in Mar Saba, had copied onto its last pages, probably in the early eighteenth century, a passage allegedly from the letters of Clement of Alexandria. Since the letters of Clement are almost unknown, the manuscript has considerable importance if the attribution is correct, and not least as an illustration of the fact that persons hunting for manuscript material should not neglect printed books. Not only end papers and blank pages, but even margins often contain considerable manuscript additions.[51]

By this standard, Smith should have considered his Mar Saba project a modest success, rather than the disappointment he described it to be. Glued inside the covers of a 1746 edition of prayers for Vespers and Matins, he found two leaves of a fifteenth-century commentary on Sophocles.[52] A collection of pieces removed from other book covers included "pages of a fifteenth-century manuscript of 'St. Macarius of Egypt' — a name used to disguise a collection of tracts by ancient Syrian heretics."[53] As it happened, these pages "turned out to contain fragments of texts unknown to the standard editions."[54] Smith's 1960 article mentioned other items of potential interest: "the collection contains one or two early patristic and ascetic excerpts which may be of importance. For the rest, there is the usual predominance of liturgical material. Some of the *hagiographica* [lives of the saints] may be of interest as evidence of the particular tradition of the monastery, which was influential in its day."[55]

This, it seems to me, is a not unreasonable description of the material Smith catalogued. But something happened between 1960 and 1973 — so that, for some reason, Smith's later account is more bipolar.[56] Though the Smith of 1960 recognized several items that "may be of importance" or "may be of interest," the Smith of 1973 would say, "I was gradually reconciling myself to my worst expectations and repeating every day that I should discover nothing of importance."[57] Yet somehow, finding the unknown letter from Clement of Alexandria shot him suddenly to the other extreme. It was so miraculous, apparently, that it even revived his interest in attending monastic liturgies. As he wrote in 1973:

> Then, one afternoon near the end of my stay, I found myself in my cell, staring incredulously at a text written in a tiny scrawl I had not even tried to read in the tower when I picked out the book containing it. But now that I came to

puzzle it out, it began, "From the letters of the most holy Clement, the author of the Stromateis. To Theodore," and it went on to praise the recipient for having "shut up" the Carpocratians. The Stromateis, I knew, was a work of Clement of Alexandria, one of the earliest and most mysterious of the great fathers of the Church — early Christian writers of outstanding importance. I was reasonably sure that no letters of his had been preserved. So if this writing was what it claimed to be, I had a hitherto unknown text by a writer of major significance for early Church history. Besides, it would add something to our knowledge of the Carpocratians, one of the most scandalous of the "gnostic" sects, early and extreme variants of Christianity. Who Theodore was, I had no idea. I still don't. But Clement and the Carpocratians were more than enough for one day. I hastened to photograph the text. . . . Then the bell rang for vespers, and I went off, walking on air.[58]

Researchers in all kinds of fields have written about the excitement they felt at making important new discoveries. The "discovery story" is a fairly common genre, despite its relative neglect by the anthologizers and literary critics. But compared with more typical examples, Smith's discovery story seems positively fishy. For example, when Constantin von Tischendorf, another young man working in another Greek monastery, discovered the Codex Sinaiticus — one of the earliest manuscripts of the entire Greek Bible — he stayed up all night studying it, for "it really seemed a sacrilege to sleep."[59] When Smith discovered the letter of Clement, he experienced a sudden mood swing from "worst expectations" to "walking on air." Yet he got up and went to Vespers instead of staying to investigate his discovery, even though his time at the monastery was almost over — or so he says. Smith seems to have forgotten what he told us earlier — that he had stopped attending the religious services because he no longer "responded" to them; "I soon made my supposed scholarly labors an excuse for spending most of my time in my cell." There is also the question of which service Smith meant by the word "vespers." Was this the afternoon service (1:30–2:30), which actually incorporated None, Vespers, and Paraklesis? Or did Smith mean Compline at 4 p.m., using the word "vespers" in a casual sense to mean "evening service"? The terminological inexactitude, in the context of an inherently implausible story, suggests to me that Smith's account is to some extent fictionalized, aimed more at selling a book in 1973 than at reporting what he actually remembered from 1958.

For almost three weeks, that is, Smith had been excusing himself from services to study manuscripts in his room — manuscripts that only discouraged him, that fulfilled his "worst expectations," in which he "discover[ed] nothing of importance." Yet when he finally found something genuinely interesting, with his stay at the monastery almost over, he left the book on his desk and floated off to church, so excited by his discovery that he forgot he didn't go to church anymore. We will meet this strange combination of euphoria and amnesia again, at important junctures throughout Smith's tale—a weird, giddy forgetfulness that punctuates his narrative with eerie predictability, and points —as memory lapses often do—to even larger denials. In the end we will be forced to conclude that Smith's memoir of 1973 is simply not a reliable account of what happened at Mar Saba in either 1941 or 1958.

"A HITHERTO UNKNOWN TEXT"

An unknown letter by St. Clement of Alexandria, who lived at the end of the second century (ca. 150–ca. 215), would indeed be an exciting find—at least as exciting as the recent discoveries of new letters and sermons by St. Augustine.[60] New information about the Carpocratians would be welcome within the relatively small field of those who study ancient Gnostic and more-or-less Christian sects. But what really made Smith's discovery so intriguing, to him and to everyone else, was the fact that it also included quotations from an unknown apocryphal gospel—or rather two of them: one is stated to have been read (but secretly) in the church at Alexandria, where it was believed to have been authored by the same evangelist who wrote the familiar Gospel according to Mark; the other is described as a Carpocratian redaction of this secret gospel, which the author of the letter ("Clement") considered corrupt. Though several apocryphal gospels survive from ancient times (wholly or in part), and many more are mentioned by ancient writers, scholars had had no idea that these two gospels—the Secret Gospel of Mark and its Carpocratian expansion—ever existed.

> Even before I finished transcribing the text, I began to think it was too good to be true. Here was new information about Jesus, a new miracle story, a quotation from a secret Gospel by St. Mark, and the information that Mark had written a second, secret Gospel, and that Clement's church, as well as the Carpocratians, had used it! If the letter was really by Clement I had a discovery of extraordinary importance. But if it was a fake of some sort and I rushed into print with an announcement of a "great discovery," I could make myself an internationally conspicuous fool. So I kept my mouth shut.[61]

Actually, Smith didn't completely keep his mouth shut, but we'll get to that later.

Morton Smith was a prolific scholar who knew many languages. Ultimately the author of seven books and 120 articles, he was effectively an expert in four difficult fields: (1) the Old Testament and ancient Israel, (2) the New Testament and early Christianity, (3) the Mishnah and early post-biblical Judaism, and (4) ancient Greek magic.[62] Some of his research was groundbreaking, and much of it offered original perspectives and exciting new approaches. Yet the Mar Saba discovery of 1958 would become Smith's best-known achievement, the focal point of much of his scholarly oeuvre, the thing that made him truly famous even outside the world of scholarship. In the ensuing decades, Mark's Secret Gospel has generated a huge bibliography, as scholars and others have reacted to the text and argued about how to interpret it. A number of experts on the New Testament have accepted both the letter and the gospel as genuine, even important, documents of the early Christian period. Others have agreed with Smith's original impression that it is "too good to be true,"[63] implying that it is a modern forgery, perhaps even by Smith himself.[64] A significant number have remained noncommittal, waiting for definitive proof to emerge.

Reputation-destroying accusations of forgery or fraud should not be made lightly, of course, even after the accused individual has died (Smith died in 1991). But since the charge has already been made, and more than once, it is worth pointing out that, if true, it would explain a lot. If the real purpose of Smith's journey was to plant a spurious manuscript in an ancient monastery library, so that he could then "discover" it in a plausible environment — that could explain why he made too short a visit to a library whose history he didn't care about, spent too much of his brief time looking at manuscripts that didn't interest him, didn't finish cataloguing all the available manuscripts, never attempted to compare his material with the main collection in Jerusalem, and ultimately left his catalogue for someone else to publish. Prior knowledge of what he would discover might explain why Smith had time to go to Vespers once it turned up, if in fact he did go. And if Smith really was engaged in the kind of massive deception that a forgery of this magnitude would entail, it would be no wonder that he describes every memory lapse as an emotionally liberating experience.

Again, if it was Smith who wrote the letter of "Clement," this might explain why, in his 1973 account of the discovery, he was so eager to emphasize its importance by denigrating the rest of the collection in which he "found" it. It might also explain why he became such an advocate of searching printed books for recent manuscript material. If the Mar Saba fragment really was penned by an eighteenth-century hand in a seventeenth-century book, it is even more recent than the fifteenth-century Sophocles; yet if the text really was composed by Clement of Alexandria, it would be even earlier than the fourth- or fifth-century "Macarius." As a previously unknown patristic writing that cites two unknown apocryphal gospels, this short text of Clement amounts to at least three discoveries in one. Does all this add up to dramatic vindication of the practice of looking for manuscripts hidden in printed books? Or did Smith champion such late manuscripts as a way of legitimating the one he "discovered"?

In the context of so many questions, Smith's playful bantering that "I soon made my supposed scholarly labors an excuse for spending most of my time in my cell" takes on an ominous demeanor: "supposed"? Was Smith engaged in something that wouldn't usually be considered "scholarly labors"? What was he really doing all those hours by himself while the monks were at prayer?

Clement of Alexandria and a Secret Gospel of Mark

Upon his return to the United States in 1958, Smith didn't quite keep his mouth shut but took the unusual step of immediately publishing the Greek text and a translation in a private edition for limited circulation. Copies of this first edition are very difficult to find; I have not seen any myself and do not know for whom they were intended.[65] In his 1973 memoir, Smith claimed that he spent two years studying every word in the text and writing out a detailed commentary, which he then mailed to fourteen experts on "late classical and patristic Greek."[66] After collecting their replies, in 1960 Smith read a paper on his discovery, at a meeting of the Society for Biblical Literature, the leading organization for biblical scholars.[67] But for the next fifteen years, Smith seems to have been a model of scholarly caution, withholding full publication while he researched his discovery. During that period he also produced many other publications and obtained tenure at Columbia.

In 1973 the material was finally made available to the world—but in an unusual way, for Smith published both a scholarly edition and a popular account in the same year. The book for scholars, *Clement of Alexandria and a Secret Gospel of Mark,* was published by Harvard University Press.[68] It includes meticulous analyses of the paleography, the Greek vocabulary and literary characteristics, the historical background, interrelationships with other gospels and other works of Clement, and the known data on the Carpocratians. The level of detail is intimidating, especially for a text as short as Clement's letter is; there are even analyses of Clement's rhythmic cadences and the Secret Gospel's apparent oral formulas—all of it quite fascinating if one is willing to invest the time and effort to read the book carefully.[69] A curious feature of Smith's exhaustive commentary is that it quotes with unusual frequency from the private conversations and personal correspondence he engaged in with other scholars, as if he felt a powerful need to demonstrate that his discovery had been taken seriously by all the right people. At least nineteen of these individuals are even listed in the bibliography by their initials—a very uncommon practice. As a result, one gets the impression that the new text was examined and found legitimate by virtually the entire pantheon of classicists and biblical scholars who were active at elite English-speaking universities during the 1960s. If any of these worthies expressed any doubts about the date or authenticity of the purported letter of Clement, however, we will never know, for we have only the excerpts Smith chose to publish. Their original letters no longer survive, for Smith's papers were destroyed after his death in accordance with his instructions.[70]

For a more general audience, Smith published *The Secret Gospel: The Discovery and Interpretation of the Secret Gospel According to Mark* with Harper & Row.[71] The title emphasizes that it is the new gospel, not the letter of Clement or the Carpocratians, that is the most interesting element in Smith's discovery. This book, since it is for popular consumption, begins with the lively memoir of Smith's visits to Mar Saba, from which I have been quoting throughout this chapter. It then proceeds to a summary of the arguments and interpretations Smith propounded in his more scholarly book. But instead of parading famous academic names, as in the Harvard book, Smith suggested similarities between his discovery and the Dead Sea Scrolls,[72] even though (as he well knew) Clement of Alexandria lived too late and too far away to have had anything to do with the Jewish Qumran community that owned the scrolls.

The simplicity and clarity of the Harper book offer a welcome contrast to the dense complexity of the Harvard book, so that a scholar who really wants to understand Smith should read both. But there is another reason to read both of them: the scholarly Harvard book was essentially completed in 1966, though not published until 1973. The popular Harper book was written second[73] and clearly incorporates some advances in Smith's interpretation of what he discovered. Some of the differences between the two books, in fact, will become significant clues in unraveling the mystery of the Secret Gospel. An interesting question I will not be able to answer is this: Was the publication of the two books deliberately synchronized so that they would be released in the same year, as if to maximize the notoriety of the new gospel? Scholarly books can take a long time to work their way through the publication process, but (in my experience) deliberate delay in order to coincide with a book for the general public would be unheard of.

THE TEXT

It is to the scholarly Harvard book, of course, that one looks for the original Greek text of Clement's letter.[74] Smith's translation into English was published in both books, but with slight differences in wording and punctuation.[75] Here I reproduce the translation from the popular Harper book, on the theory that it represents Smith's later and more considered preferences. But I note the variants of the Harvard book in footnotes (even though they are of minimal significance). In the popular book, Smith put square brackets around some words that have no exact counterpart in the Greek original, but are only implied.[76] None of these bracketings occurs in the scholarly book, where of course one can examine the Greek text for oneself. I myself have taken the liberty of adding, in parentheses, the locations of direct quotations from the Bible. (For the readers' convenience, this translation of the letter also appears in the appendix at the back of the book.)

From the letters of the most holy Clement, author of the *Stromateis*.[77] To Theodore:

You did well in silencing the unspeakable teachings of the Carpocratians. For these are the "wandering stars" (Jude 13) referred to in the prophecy, who wander from the narrow road of the commandments into a boundless abyss of the carnal and bodily sins. For, priding themselves in knowledge, as they say, "of the deep [things] of Satan" (Revelation 2:24), they do not know that they are casting themselves away into "the nether world of the darkness" (Jude 13) of falsity, and, boasting that they are free, they have become slaves of servile desires. Such [men] are to be opposed in all ways and altogether. For, even if they should say something true, one who loves the truth should not, even so, agree with them. For not all true [things] are the truth, nor should that truth which [merely] seems true according to human opinions be preferred to the true truth, that according to the faith.

Now of the [things] they keep saying about the divinely inspired Gospel according to Mark, some are altogether falsifications, and others, even if they do contain some true [elements], nevertheless are not reported truly. For the true [things], being mixed with inventions, are falsified, so that, as the saying [goes], even the salt loses its savor (Luke 14:34).

[As for] Mark, then, during Peter's stay in Rome he wrote [an account of] the Lord's doings, not, however, declaring all [of them], nor yet hinting at the secret [ones], but selecting those[78] he thought most useful for increasing the faith of those who were being instructed. But when Peter died as[79] a martyr, Mark came over to Alexandria, bringing both his own notes and those of Peter, from which he transferred to his former book the things suitable to whatever makes for progress toward knowledge [*gnosis*]. [Thus] he composed a more spiritual Gospel for the use of those who were being perfected. Nevertheless, he yet did not divulge the things not to be uttered, nor did he write down the hierophantic teaching of the Lord, but to the stories already written he added yet others and, moreover, brought in certain sayings of which he knew the interpretation would, as a mystagogue, lead the hearers into the innermost sanctuary of that truth hidden by seven [veils]. Thus, in sum, he prearranged[80] matters, neither grudgingly nor incautiously, in my opinion, and, dying, he left his composition to the church in Alexandria, where it even yet is most carefully guarded, being read only to those who are being initiated into the great mysteries.

But since the foul demons are always devising destruction for the race of men, Carpocrates, instructed by them and using deceitful arts, so enslaved a certain presbyter of the church in Alexandria that he got from him a copy of the secret Gospel, which he both interpreted according to his blasphemous and carnal doctrine and, moreover, polluted, mixing with the spotless and holy words utterly shameless lies. From this mixture is drawn off the teaching of the Carpocratians.

To them, therefore, as I said above, one must never give way,[81] nor, when they put forward their falsifications, should one concede that the secret Gospel is by Mark, but should even deny it on oath. For, "Not all true [things] are to be said to all men."[82] For this [reason] the Wisdom of God, through Solomon, advises, "Answer the fool from his folly" (Proverbs 26:5), teaching that the light of the truth should be hidden from those who are mentally blind. Again it says, "From him who has not shall be taken away" (Matthew 25:29), and, "Let the fool walk in darkness" (Ecclesiastes 2:14). But we are "children of light" (1 Thessalonians 5:5), having been illuminated by "the dayspring" of the Spirit[83] of the Lord "from on high" (Luke 1:78), and "Where the Spirit of the Lord is," it says, "there is liberty" (2 Corinthians 3:17), for "All things are pure to the pure" (Titus 1:15).

To you, therefore, I shall not hesitate to answer the [questions] you have asked, refuting the falsifications by the very words of the Gospel. For example, after "And they were in the road going up to Jerusalem" (Mark 10:32), and what follows, until "After three days he shall arise" (Mark 10:34), [the secret Gospel] brings the following [material] word for word:

"And they come into Bethany, and a certain woman, whose brother had died, was there.[84] And, coming, she prostrated herself before Jesus and says to him, 'Son of David, have mercy on me.' But the disciples rebuked her. And Jesus, being angered, went off with her into the garden where the tomb was, and straightway a great cry was heard from the tomb. And going near Jesus rolled away the stone from the door of the tomb. And straightway, going in where the youth was, he stretched forth his hand and raised him, seizing his hand. But the youth, looking upon him, loved him and began to beseech him that he might be with him. And going out of the tomb they came into the house of the youth, for he was rich. And after six days Jesus told him what to do and in the evening the youth comes to him, wearing a linen cloth over [his] naked [body]. And he remained with him that night, for Jesus taught him the mystery of the kingdom of God. And thence, arising, he returned to the other side of the Jordan."

After these [words] follows the text, "And James and John come to him" (Mark 10:35), and all that section. But "naked [man] with naked [man]" and the other things about which you wrote are not found.

And after the [words], "And he comes into Jericho" (Mark 10:46), [the secret Gospel] adds only, "And the sister of the youth whom Jesus loved and his mother and Salome were there, and Jesus did not receive them." But the many other [things about] which you wrote both seem to be and are falsifications.

Now the true explanation and that which accords with the true philosophy . . .

There the text breaks off incomplete.

Obviously this short text is extremely complicated and raises all sorts of questions. There are, to begin with, the issues of whether this is indeed a lost letter of Clement, and who the addressee Theodore could have been. Many questions could be asked about what is said concerning the Carpocratians, the nature of the controversy in which Clement and Theodore were involved, and the remarks about truth, falsification, and lying under oath. The traditions about Mark and his second (secret) gospel have already spawned considerable scholarly discussion — but no less problematic are "the great mysteries," apparently clandestine initiation rites that provided the only occasions on which the Secret Gospel was read, or its existence even acknowledged. Something needs to be understood here: the Greek word *mysterion,* from which we get the English word "mystery," can also mean "secret," so that the Secret Gospel in Greek is *mystikon evangelion,* which could also be translated "the mystic gospel" or "the mystical gospel." In Greek Orthodox Christianity the word *mysterion* corresponds to the Western Christian term "sacrament," so that "those who are being initiated into the great mysteries" are presumably experiencing the three sacraments of Christian initiation: (1) baptism (water immersion), (2) chrismation, sealing, or confirmation (anointing with oil), and (3) Eucharist (receiving the consecrated bread and wine for the first time).[85]

How these early Christian sacraments were actually administered, therefore, ought to be a central issue in the debate over what to make of the Mar Saba fragment. But in fact, most of the scholarly discussion has focused on a question that New Testament scholars are more interested in, namely the interrelationships among the three recensions of Mark's gospel — the familiar one and its Alexandrian and Carpocratian expansions. Smith himself, however, made the initiatory sacraments a central issue in his own writings, since his primary interpretive claim is that the Secret Gospel reveals how Jesus initiated his disciples. According to an elaborate argument that Smith constructed from a wide range of evidence, Jesus carried out secret, nocturnal initiation rites, with each disciple individually, utilizing magical practices that may have included homosexual intercourse. Even without the homosexuality, however, Smith's reconstruction is well outside of mainstream thinking and highly debatable on many points. But once Smith raised the possibility of a sexual element, it became much more difficult to discuss the Mar Saba discovery calmly. Are those who remain unconvinced really assessing the evidence objectively, or are they letting their disapproval of homosexuality color their historical judgment? Are some people overly inclined to accept the discovery as genuine out of a desire to find a Christian justification for homosexuality? In the chapters to follow I will propose a whole new approach to the study of the Mar Saba fragment. But first it will be helpful to summarize, as briefly as possible, what the main issues have been and what is already known or has been said about each of them in turn.

Summary

In this chapter I offer a careful reading of Morton Smith's 1973 account of his visits to Mar Saba in 1941 and 1958. During the latter visit he allegedly discovered the letter of Clement of Alexandria that quotes from the Secret Gospel of Mark. His memoir includes some odd features that raise questions about its veracity: Smith tried too hard to emphasize the contrast between the importance he ascribed to the letter of Clement and the other manuscripts in the library, which he excessively denigrates as uninteresting. He showed surprisingly little interest in the history of the Mar Saba library, given the time he spent cataloguing it. His claim to have been fascinated by the liturgy at the monastery contrasts with his neglect of the liturgical manuscripts in the library. After discovering the fragment, he showed too much interest in obtaining endorsements from famous scholars. Smith also described extreme mood swings and bouts of amnesia that raise doubts about his truthfulness.

Questions

The schedule of my trip took me off to Istanbul. By the time I got there I was badly upset. Moments of wild excitement alternated with spells of profound pessimism and even resentment. The thing just couldn't be true; it was too important! Why had nobody else ever mentioned the secret Gospel of Mark, if there was one? And why did it have to be my luck to walk into this trap? I couldn't suppress it; I'd already told Scholem. — But then, why shouldn't it be genuine? The handwriting of the manuscript must be, roughly, of the eighteenth century. Who, at that time, in a Greek monastery devoted to the devotional life, could have made up such a thing? What monk knew anything about Carpocrates? What motive could there possibly be for the invention of such a document? — But if it were genuine, then . . . ! And so off again into excitement, and then back to depression.   *— Morton Smith*

The Manuscript

The authentication of any document must begin with its physical characteristics, and the manuscript Smith discovered is certainly unusual. Not all the writings of Clement of Alexandria have survived, but those that have are preserved in parchment codices of the tenth and eleventh centuries (and later).[1] The Mar Saba letter, on the other hand, was written on the rear flyleaves of a book printed in 1646, containing the letters of St. Ignatius of Antioch, a church father who died in the early second century, about three generations before Clement. Smith, with more or less agreement from the paleographers he consulted, determined the handwriting to belong to the mid-eighteenth century. Comparison with the writing of Callinicus III, who was Patriarch of Constantinople around 1760, led Smith to conclude that "we may suppose with some probability that the writer of the present letter had been trained in the Patriarchal Academy in Constantinople" — without verifying that Callinicus himself was trained there![2] But if the hand of the Clementine letter belonged to a Mar Saba monk (a strong likelihood for a document found in the Mar Saba library) it could well reappear — perhaps even with a name or a date — somewhere among the forty-six eighteenth-century manuscripts that were relocated from Mar Saba to Jerusalem.[3] There is no indication that Smith ever checked.

Could a letter written in the late second century be preserved only in one partial copy of the eighteenth century? The gap of sixteen centuries is not impossible, but it is unusually long. The extant writings of St. Justin Martyr, who lived in the second century between Ignatius and Clement, survive in only one manuscript from the year 1364, plus a fifteenth-century copy of it.[4] The works of the important Roman historian Tacitus, who died in the early second century CE, are very poorly preserved despite a tradition that they were copied four times a year by imperial mandate.[5] In particular the *Germania* — now his best-known work — survives only in fifteenth-century copies of a lost medieval manuscript.[6] The poems of Catullus, who lived in the first century BCE, are known to us from copies of the late fourteenth century, even though several classical and medieval authors are known to have read earlier manuscripts that no longer exist — including one in Petrarch's hand.[7]

The Fight at Finnsburg, an Anglo-Saxon poem comparable to *Beowulf* (thus presumably written down about 1000 CE), survived the Middle Ages in a single fragment that has since been lost. Its contents, therefore, are known only from a transcription published in 1705.[8] The world record may belong to the collection of ancient Sanskrit hymns known as the Rig-Veda — thought to have been composed before the year 1000 BCE; its earliest manuscripts date from the seventeenth century CE.[9]

Thus Smith's proposed explanation for the gap has to be considered plausible, even if unprovable. Letters by Clement evidently did circulate at one time, for the *Sacra Parallela,* a work ascribed to John of Damascus, quotes from Clementine letters that don't otherwise survive.[10] This implies that John (or whoever wrote the *Sacra Parallela*) had access to a copy of Clement's letters, a manuscript that no longer exists (as far as we know). If indeed the author was John, then this manuscript existed in the eighth century, and one may suppose that he saw it in the library at Mar Saba.[11] If all these assumptions are true, then the gist of Smith's argument is that John's manuscript of Clement, or a later copy of it, remained at Mar Saba until the eighteenth-century fire, when it largely perished, leaving behind an "isolated leaf" that someone copied onto the flyleaves of the book Smith found and catalogued.[12] Having survived a major fire, the isolated leaf may have been in very fragile condition; at any rate it disappeared, so that only the eighteenth-century copy remains today.

In support of this theory, Smith was eager to persuade us that "the life of the monastery seems to have been continuous — or practically continuous" from John's time down to the early modern era: "The buildings were occasionally pillaged or even 'destroyed,' but the monks seem never to have been driven away for long."[13] Smith's quotation marks around the word "destroyed" seem meant to emphasize that much of the monastery consists of stone buildings and caves, yet he was apparently unaware of the history of earthquakes at Mar Saba and did not recall that manuscripts are more fragile than stone.

Moreover, the pillages weren't exactly occasional. Endless attacks were carried out by various marauding tribes and non-Christian groups, which repeatedly drove the monastic community almost to extinction and were still causing problems as recently as the nineteenth century.[14] Herman Melville, who visited Mar Saba in January 1857, describes a situation in which violent gangs seem to have permanently loitered near the gates of the monastery, threatening or robbing everyone who passed through.[15] When Mark Twain visited a decade later, it was customary for travelers to hire armed guards, who, however, actually worked hand in glove with the marauders.[16] Later still, according to an experienced American Protestant missionary: "Cases have occurred in the experience of missionaries, in which the robbers have been known and identified; but on complaint being made to the authorities, the sufferers have been advised to let the matter quietly drop. This of course refers to the towns and villages; but the Arab robbers who scour the deserts defy all authority."[17] Yet the travelers and missionaries had fewer problems than the monks, who regularly had to bribe both the authorities and the competing outlaw groups for protection. One nineteenth-century monk historian gives the impression that raising and borrowing money for such payoffs was practically the only thing the Christian groups in the Holy Land ever did, except for occasional breaks to dispute with each other and/or celebrate Easter. On the rare occasions when no particular horde was ravaging the area, Mar Saba would be plundered by its own Muslim slaves, who evidently thought nothing of knocking holes in the walls for this purpose.[18] It is no wonder that the bulk of the library was eventually moved to the Patriarchate inside the city.

Thus it is not so easy to dismiss the fact that, in 1547, a Russian monk named Sophronius reported to the bishop of Moscow that murderous raids had left Mar Saba uninhabited for about a century, until it was reopened in 1540 by Greek monks and a Wallachian (i.e., Romanian) abbot from Mount Athos.[19] Smith asks us to accept that Sophronius's allegation has been "refuted" in the major Greek history of the monastery, without giving us the book's actual arguments.[20] But since reports of Romanian or Slavic occupancy may have served the purposes of the Russian czars in their efforts to control the Christian holy sites, it is possible that the monastery's Greek historians have leaned too sharply to the contrary view—with political disagreements, the truth is often somewhere in between.

Hence an important question: Is the Mar Saba library, in fact, an ancient collection with a continuous history going back to John of Damascus or before? Or was it mostly assembled at some later point (such as the 1540 reopening), with older manuscripts brought in from elsewhere? The obvious way to explore this issue would be through a study of the library stamps, bookplates, and other ownership marks in the main collection of Mar Saba manuscripts at Jerusalem. But I have seen no evidence that Smith ever considered this question, or ever even visited the Jerusalem collection.

However, even if we could accept that Clement's letters survived from the eighth century (when John of Damascus read them) into the eighteenth (when a portion was copied into the book where Smith found it), we would still have to explain the thousand-year gap, during which we have no record that a copy of Clement's letters existed anywhere, at Mar Saba or anyplace else. To meet this objection, Smith offered a creative argument from silence, proposing that "the fact that nobody referred to it . . . suggests that it did not circulate, but lay neglected in some corner of a single library."[21] This too is perfectly possible, but is it more likely than the alternative, that no one referred to the manuscript because it no longer existed? It was Smith who wrote (in a different context), "What usually requires explanation is not the disappearance of an ancient work, but its preservation."[22]

Smith's closing peroration seems to amount to an inarticulate outburst that any line of reasoning will do, as long as it persuades us that the Clement letter is genuine: "All this history is merely plausible, and plausibility is not proof. Things probably happened thus, though they may have happened otherwise. History, however, is by definition the search for the *most* probable explanations of preserved phenomena. When several explanations are possible, the historian must always choose the most probable one. But the truth is that improbable things sometimes happen. Therefore truth is necessarily stranger than history."[23] Necessarily?

Is the Letter by Clement?

Dozens of scholars have offered opinions on Smith's discovery — at first in book reviews, then in their own articles and books. Smith himself summed up the early results in two articles published in 1982: one in *Harvard Theological Review*,[24] the other in the postscript to a 1982 reprint of his popular Harper book.[25] The better-known one, in the Harvard journal, is subtitled "the score at the end of the first decade," and indeed it is all about keeping score: "when I sent the text with a first draft of my commentary to fourteen outstanding scholars, all but two . . . thought Clement had written the letter. . . . Of the scholars listed in the bibliography here following, twenty-five have agreed in attributing the letter to Clement, six have suspended judgement . . . , and only four have denied the attribution. . . . In sum, most scholars would attribute the letter to Clement, though a substantial minority are still in doubt."[26] The postscript to the 1982 reprint contains the identical bibliography, but is less reserved in tone. There, scholars who doubted the authenticity of the Mar Saba text are called "liars" and their writings "worthless," "useless," and deserving of contempt.[27] Comparison of the postscript with the *Review* article makes for an interesting study of the differences between refereed and unrefereed publications.

The strongest argument for authenticity is that the vocabulary and literary style are very much like Clement's, so that some scholars "see no reason to doubt the authenticity of Clement's letter."[28] Others, however, think it is too good: "it is *more* like Clement than Clement ever was . . . as if someone knew Clement's rare words . . . and wanted to use a number of them to show the Clementine distinctive vocabulary (but overdoing it), while fearing to use words occurring nowhere else in Clement lest one suspect a non-Clementine style."[29]

It has also been questioned whether the contents reflect Clement's time and place, or his religious or philosophical views. According to one summary of objections, "The description of a church archive containing secret writings, the recommendation of a falsehood to be fortified by a false oath on polemical grounds, the idea of two stages of secret teaching of Jesus, and the report of Mark's migration to Alexandria contradict everything that we know from Clement."[30] "Moreover," comments another writer, "the letter presupposes a conception of the Church which is more strongly institutionalized than it appears elsewhere in Clement,"[31] whose organizational environment might be described better as "a school for training in virtue" or "a Christian study circle."[32]

It would be most accurate to say that the case for Clement's genuine author-ship is inconclusive. The Greek text was added to the critical edition of Clem-ent's works, but "provisionally . . . to further discussion."[33] In the most author-itative bibliography of patristic writings, the Mar Saba letter is listed among the "doubtful and spurious" works of Clement.[34] The excerpts from the Secret Gospel have frequently been included in anthologies of ancient apocryphal writings,[35] but sometimes with an editorial preface explaining the uncertainty.

Who Were the Carpocratians?

As Smith understood it, the Carpocratians were "one of the most scan-dalous of the 'gnostic' sects, early and extreme variants of Christianity. . . . Carpocrates was said to have taught that sin was a means of salvation. Only by committing all possible actions could the soul satisfy the demands of the rulers of this world and so be permitted to go on to the heavens, its true home."[36] This is derived from *Against the Heresies,* by St. Irenaeus of Lyons (ca. 115–ca. 202 CE). The earliest of the so-called "heresy catalogues," it amounts to an encyclopedia of ancient sects and what (in Irenaeus's view) was wrong with their practices and beliefs. Irenaeus wrote quite a bit about the Carpocratians; the passage Smith was referring to seems to say that their views on good and evil were connected with their belief in reincarnation and the transmigration of souls.

> They have fallen into such unbridled madness that they boast of having in their power and of practicing every kind of impious and godless deed. For they claim that deeds are good or bad only because of human opinion. There-fore, they say that the souls must have experience in every kind of life and in every act by means of transmigration from one body to another, unless some soul would preoccupy itself once and for all, and in an equivalent manner do in one coming [into this world, i.e., one lifetime] all the deeds — deeds which it is not only wrong for us to speak of and listen to, but which we may not even think or believe that such things are done among people who live in our cities. The purpose of this, according to their writings, is that the souls, having had every experience in life, may at their departure not be wanting in anything; moreover, they must take care lest they be again sent forth into a body because something was wanting to their liberation. For this reason they assert that Jesus [taught] . . . that no one will escape from the power of the Angels who made the world, but will always transmigrate from one body to another until he has had experience in absolutely every kind of action that exists in the world. And when nothing is wanting to him, his soul, having been liberated, escapes to the God who is above the Angels, the makers of the world. In this manner all souls are saved — whether in one coming [into this world] they

preoccupy themselves in being mixed up in every kind of action, whether they transmigrate from one body to another, or, what is the same, whether they have been sent into every kind of life. And having fulfilled the requirements and paid the debts, they are liberated, so that they no longer have to operate in a body.

Now, whether these impious, unlawful, and forbidden acts are really practiced by them, I would hardly believe. But in their writings it is so written, and they also explain it so. Jesus, they assert, spoke privately in mystery to his disciples and apostles and commissioned them to hand down privately these things to those who are worthy and believe; for they are saved by faith and love. But the other things are indifferent, some good, some bad, according to the view of men, inasmuch as nothing is bad by nature.[37]

It is difficult to assess Irenaeus's report. He seems to have derived his information from reading Carpocratian books rather than talking to actual Carpocratians; he is unsure how they put their writings into practice. One wonders whether Irenaeus fully understood what he was reading, especially if the Carpocratians also had secret teachings that were handed down "privately" to members only. Since we do not know what books Irenaeus read, and do not have any Carpocratian writings in complete form, we cannot read the Carpocratian side of the story for ourselves and thus form our own opinion of their religion. But if early Christian leaders like Clement of Alexandria and Theodore (whoever he was) actually believed that the Carpocratians taught and practiced "impious, unlawful, and forbidden acts" (Irenaeus) it is not surprising that they disparaged their "blasphemous and carnal doctrine" (Mar Saba letter).

Opposition between Clement's church and the Carpocratians, whatever it was actually about, does seem to provide the historical context for the Mar Saba letter. It appears that the Carpocratian version of Mark's gospel contained words and passages that were not in Theodore's Bible, so that Theodore wrote to Clement asking what to make of this extra material. Clement's reply is that most of the extra passages "seem to be and are falsifications" with which the Carpocratians have "polluted" the gospel text. What no one in the twentieth century would have expected is the information that Clement's church, too, had an alternate gospel, with additional material believed to be by the same Mark who wrote the original gospel. For some unclear reason, this expanded text was kept quiet and read only at secret ceremonies. It was so secret that those who knew of its existence were expected to "deny it on oath." Yet the Carpocratians had obtained a copy and used it as the basis for their own version. Thus one purpose of Clement's letter was to tell Theodore which interpolations were found in the secret Alexandrian recension (assumed to be by Mark himself) and which were not (assumed to be false additions made by Carpocrates).

Unfortunately, Clement did not quote any of the Carpocratian variants, except one. He simply referred back to "the other things about which you wrote" in Theodore's original letter, which we don't have. The one exception is highly provocative, however: the two Greek adjectives *gymnos gymnō*, which Smith translates as "naked [man] with naked [man]." The word "man" is not given in the Greek but implied by the masculine singular endings. Much the same is true of the preposition "with"; it is not explicitly stated, but only implied by the dative ending of *gymnō*. A translator who supplied a different preposition, such as "to," "on," or "in," would not be wrong grammatically. It all depends on what we imagine those two naked [men] were doing. Since the Carpocratians, whose gospel contains this wording, are said to have had a reputation for "carnal and bodily sins," one infers that Jesus and the young man were up to no good, hence Theodore's consternation and Clement's outrage. Or perhaps the whole thing is an adventure in reader-response criticism. Are we reading more into the text than is really there? What would that say about us?

Is the Secret Gospel by Mark?

On one level, the question of Mark's authorship of the gospel is similar to the one about Clement's authorship of the letter. The style and vocabulary are very much like the canonical gospel of Mark — to such a degree that some would call it "too Marcan to be Mark."[38] On another level, however, the question itself would be regarded as too simplistic. Since the nineteenth century some scholars have believed that the second gospel (like some other texts in our New Testament) was not completed in a single act of composition but went through a series of revisions on its way to achieving the form in which we know it.[39] Some of the reasons for thinking this have to do with its relationships to the first and third gospels.

The vast majority of New Testament scholars believe that Matthew and Luke used material from Mark when they were writing their own gospels. This would explain why the first three gospels have so much wording in common that they can be placed in parallel columns and read synoptically. But it also leads to new questions, such as, what about the passages in Mark's gospel that Matthew and Luke *did not* use? One possible explanation for some of these gaps is the hypothesis that Matthew and Luke used an earlier form of the gospel of Mark, which did not yet contain the material Matthew and Luke "omitted."[40] Other discrepancies involve material that may have been difficult for Matthew and Luke to make sense of—notably the story of a young man, clad only in a white linen cloth (the Greek word is *sindōn*), who ran away naked when Jesus was arrested (Mark 14:51–52).[41] But the presence of this story has also been taken as evidence that "the text of canonical Mark . . . is not the original Mark used by Matthew and Luke, but an abbreviated version of the *Secret Gospel of Mark*."[42] That would mean that Clement was wrong. Mark did not write the canonical gospel first, and then add further material to it at a second stage. The Secret Gospel with its extra material existed first, but some subsequent editor shortened it to produce the canonical gospel we know.

The Clement letter seems to support the speculations of those who think that the gospel of Mark anciently circulated in more than one form, since it shows not only that the Carpocratian heretics had their own version, but that the church of Alexandria even had two, the familiar gospel and the Secret Gospel. However, those who would appeal to Clement's letter disagree among themselves as to the specifics. Some believe that canonical Mark was the earlier text, and that Secret Mark was produced later, by adding material to create "an amplification of the canonical Gospel."[43] Others have thought that the Secret Gospel, with the extra material quoted by Clement, was compiled first, then shortened to produce canonical Mark by removing the material Clement quoted. To emphasize the variability of the gospel texts without presupposing their interrelationships, some have found it more convenient to call Clement's Secret Gospel "the longer text" and canonical Mark "the shorter text," following Smith's own usage.[44] Others still would "affirm that the text itself does not warrant the construction of such bold hypotheses."[45] The role of theological disputes between the Carpocratians and other groups and the difficulty of establishing the dates at which all these things happened leave the whole subject open to a wide range of opinions.[46]

Morton Smith's own theory is one of the more complicated ones. Indeed he admitted that "the mass of factual data that had to be dealt with in evaluating the letter of Clement and Secret Mark was such that my full presentation, *Clement,* is a dreadfully complex book."[47] One of his central proposals was that an early gospel, written in the Aramaic language (the Semitic tongue actually spoken by Jesus and the first disciples), lay behind the gospels of both Mark and John. It contained a story of Jesus raising a young man from the dead that ultimately took shape in both traditions, as the story of the young man in Clement's Secret Mark and the story of Lazarus in John 11:1–44. As Smith summarized in 1982:

> Essentially I conjectured that an original Aramaic gospel had been twice translated into Greek; John had used one translation, Mark another. (This

accounts for their agreement in outline, but difference in wording.) Each left out some elements and added many. Mark was then variously expanded—by Matthew, by Luke, and by the author of Secret Mark, who imitated Mark's style, but added episodes from the old Greek translation, inserting them where they had stood in the original outline. (Hence the Lazarus story has the same location, vis-à-vis the outline, in Secret Mark as in John.) According to Clement, the Carpocratians, too, got hold of Secret Mark and expanded ("corrupted") it yet further.[48]

According to this theory, therefore, Secret Mark is both earlier and later than canonical Mark; though the story of the young man is an interpolation, it incorporates old material that Mark himself knew but didn't use in his first recension.

Actually, Smith's theory as a whole was even more complicated than this, as he himself pointed out in a footnote: "Canonical Mark seemed to have been cut down from a longer text; Clement's secret gospel shows some signs of censorship; in sum, there seem to have been many minor alterations and we can grasp securely only the main outlines."[49] The upshot: "the explanation finally proposed is complex—so complex that most critics did not try to present it, and several of those who did, got it wrong."[50]

Now it seems to me that the real reason Smith's argument was so complex was that he was committed less to a particular thesis than to a particular conclusion—the conclusion that the Secret Gospel transmits very early traditions about Jesus, as early as one can get. When his statements to this effect are removed from their context and arranged in a simple list, they appear to contradict each other, except for the fact that they all converge on an early date:

> If the resurrection story was in Mark's source it was probably in the earliest form of Mark. If so, the canonical text of Mark would have been produced by abbreviation; the secret text would have been earlier.[51]

> Even if the secret Gospel passages were expansions of Mark, they were expansions made very early, in the style and by the school of the original author; they must have had the same tradition behind them. Whether they were written down fifteen years earlier or ten years later would not make great difference to their historical value.[52]

> Once it is admitted that all Gospels alike are abstracts from the traditions of the early churches, then the fact that one was written down ten or fifteen years before or after another does not make much difference; the later document can easily contain the more important tradition—as Clement said the later text of Mark did.[53]

And whatever it was that happened, exactly, must have happened mostly before the time of Carpocrates, who was active about the year 125, bringing the dating of Secret Mark, as Smith notes, "close to the canonical gospels, commonly dated about 70 to 100."[54] Elsewhere Smith put it even earlier — the story of the young man was added to Mark's gospel even before the composition of Matthew's and Luke's.[55] The postscript to the 1982 reprint goes earlier still, referring to the "original Aramaic gospel (about A.D. 50?)."[56] That could make it earlier than any of the writings preserved in the New Testament.[57] When all of Smith's proposals are knit together to produce something that looks like a comprehensive theory — with the help of scholarly jargon, the usual professions of caution, and long lists of data — the result is "a dreadfully complex book." But time and again, the complexity boils down to the claim that in the Secret Gospel we have access to very early, unusually reliable information about Jesus.

A funny thing about all this is that, as Smith recounts the process of how he arrived at his very complex theory, he blacks out again, exhibiting the same kind of dizzy memory lapse we saw before at Mar Saba, when right after discovering the Clement letter he "went off" to "vespers" (whatever that was), "walking on air":

> Curiously, I have no memory of the days when all this became clear. The experience I shall never forget — it was probably the high point of my life. But the other things that must have been happening at the same time are simply gone, hidden by the blaze of the facts, like stars in the day. I know it happened in the spring of 1963. I think I remember the strange feeling of walking around the unchanged world, doing the usual things, unnoticed and unnoticeable, with all of this going on inside my head.[58]

Dissociative episodes like this are a persistent and troubling feature of Smith's literary persona, whether or not they have anything to do with the man himself. They hardly inspire confidence in what his books aim to tell us — particularly since, as we shall see, Smith made many bizarre and irresponsible statements identifying Christianity with mental illness, even while he repeatedly denigrated the value of psychiatry.

Does the Secret Gospel Have Historical Value?

"Even if the secret Gospel passages were expansions of Mark, . . . [w]hether they were written down fifteen years earlier or ten years later would not make great difference to their historical value," Smith wrote. That would certainly be true if their historical value is zero. But is it? Smith professed agnosticism on such questions: "it would be naive to ask whether or not the events reported in the longer text 'really happened.' "[59] Yet he also concluded that the new text "would seem to be of the highest historical value."[60] In less guarded moments, Smith always wrote as if the Secret Gospel does report reliable historical facts. When he began to decipher the manuscript at Mar Saba, and wonder whether it was too good to be true, he thought, "Here was new information about Jesus."[61] In response to a negative book review by a clergyman, Smith sneered, "Why those who worship Jesus should think further information about him 'alarming' is an interesting question."[62]

This degree of assurance is actually quite unusual in New Testament studies. Although Christians without technical education tend to read the gospels as stenographic records of what Jesus did and said, scholars have recognized for a long time that each gospel is a theological document, synthesizing oral traditions that developed over at least a generation since Jesus' lifetime. Thus Smith quoted with approval a statement by C. H. Dodd: "The early Church was not such a bookish community as it has been represented. It did its business primarily through the medium of the living voice, in worship, teaching and missionary preaching, and out of these three forms of activity — liturgy, didache [teaching], kerygma [preaching] — a tradition was built up, and this tradition lies behind all literary production of the early period, including our written gospels."[63] The transition from oral teaching, preaching, and worship to written gospel has been outlined by Raymond E. Brown as "the three stages of gospel formation":

> (1) The public ministry or activity of Jesus of Nazareth (first third of the first century)
> (2) The (apostolic) preaching about Jesus by his followers (second third of the first century)
> (3) The written gospels (last third of the first century).[64]

As a result, each gospel records traditions that have been shaped within a particular early Christian community, informed by a generation of reflection on the identity and message of Jesus and shaped by situations that emerged after his lifetime — situations such as the translation of Jewish concepts and Aramaic terminology into the wider Hellenistic language and culture, persecutions, conflicts with other religious groups, and the destruction of the Jerusalem Temple in 70 CE. "Rather than depending on a personal memory of events," Brown continues, "each evangelist has arranged the material he received in order to portray Jesus in a way that would meet the spiritual needs of the community to which he was addressing the Gospel. . . . The evangelists emerge as authors, shaping, developing, pruning the transmitted Jesus material, and as theologians, orienting that material to a particular goal."[65]

For Christian believers nowadays, this does not imply that the gospels are unreliable, for the entire process was guided by the Holy Spirit. The gospels themselves show that the apostles did not fully understand Jesus until after his resurrection (Mark 9:8–9, Luke 24:25–32), and they also show Jesus promising that, as Christians faced new situations, they would have divine assistance in reaching new formulations of the gospel truth.[66] As orthodox Christians understand it, this does not mean that there would be new revelations in the future, but that the complete revelation of Jesus to the apostles would, with the passage of time, be comprehended more fully, a process theologians call "the development of doctrine."[67]

But historians, unlike philosophers, are often more interested in where an idea came from and how it spread than whether it is true. From this perspective, the "three stages of gospel formation" pose a massive research problem: how to strip away all the theological developments to recover the original historical individual that Jesus was. This huge area of research is often referred to by the title of a classic book by Albert Schweitzer, "the quest of the historical Jesus."[68]

But Morton Smith seems to have wanted to leapfrog the entire "quest." His high valuation of the tradition transmitted by the Secret Gospel seems to say that, for once, we have something genuinely early and reliable. Thus Smith is asking quite a lot from his readers. Faithful Christians fear they are being asked to believe that this unheard-of fragment is effectively the same kind of material as the canonical gospels, and therefore as trustworthy as they, if not more so. Historians who are familiar with the complexities and uncertainties of historical Jesus research — and who know that Smith was, too — find themselves being urged to conclude that, of all the vast library of Christian and quasi-Christian writings that survive from ancient times — orthodox, proto-orthodox, and otherwise — this eighteenth-century scrawl on a seventeenth-century flyleaf brings us as close to the historical Jesus as it is possible to get. This is no small demand, especially when we consider what — according to Smith — this highly reliable gospel actually tells us about Jesus.

What Does the Secret Gospel Say?

Smith's interpretation of the Secret Gospel excerpts leads to the most incendiary issue of all: "I had shown that the gospel fragments represented Jesus as practicing some sort of initiation, and I had argued that this initiation was a baptism supposed to admit the recipient into the kingdom of God and free him from the Mosaic law, this being effected by an illusory ascent to the heavens, of the sort described in the magical papyri, and by union with Jesus, also magical."[69] Later in this book we will take a close look at Smith's ex-

tended argument that the earliest form of Christian initiation, the kind practiced by Jesus himself, was a secretive, magical rite that each disciple went
through individually — and that it involved altered states of consciousness
("an illusory ascent to the heavens"), liberation from the moral law, magical
practices, and a "union with Jesus," which (Smith strongly implied) was actually an act of homosexual intercourse. According to Smith, this was "the
mystery of the kingdom of God" of Mark 4:11, the same mystery that Jesus
taught one night to the barely dressed young man whom he loved, and who
loved him. Smith seems never to have wondered whether Jesus had any female
disciples and how they might have been baptized, even though, as we will see,
his exegesis gives a central place to a female character who arguably was a
disciple.

How Smith arrived at these conclusions will be traced fully in the rest of this
book. But for now it should be noted that they never met with much acceptance. As Smith assessed it in 1982:

> Of course nobody accepted the proposed explanation. I was amazed that so
> many went so far as to concede that Jesus might have had some secret doctrines
> and some initiatory ceremonies, or to recognize, even if unwillingly and with
> reservations, that magic did have a role in the first-century Church. The most
> violent abuse (from scholars) came from two circles, one, the *dévots* . . . ,[70] the
> other, the adherents of current exegetic cliques (form criticism, redaction
> criticism, etc.) who were outraged that I had not given their literature of
> mutually contradictory conjectures the attention they thought it deserved.[71]

Thus it could be said that Smith evaded the issue of why his theory wasn't
accepted, by changing the subject to the abuse he felt he had unjustly suffered,
both from "the devout" (scholars with Christian religious beliefs) and from
the "adherents of current exegetic cliques" or methodologies. The implication
seems to be that the two groups are not very different, each unable to evaluate
evidence objectively because it is blinded by its own received orthodoxy. Thus
Smith went on to lament that his scholarly book had "overestimated the professional readers for whom the book was written," while his popular book
"suffered even more from the same misjudgement,"[72] whatever that means.
Smith's riposte was his next book, *Jesus the Magician,* wherein he offered
considerable further evidence that Jesus had indeed practiced magic.[73] As for
"mutually contradictory conjectures," we will soon have occasion to observe
that Smith's opponents held no monopoly on that.

The general rejection of Smith's magical and sexual interpretation contrasts
sharply with the widespread acceptance of the Secret Gospel as a genuine
ancient writing. Two scholars who offer very different readings of the material
are nevertheless close to agreement on where Smith went wrong. Marvin

Meyer, who "assume[s] the authenticity of the Mar Saba letter as a copy of an ancient text," has argued that "instead of using the fragments to formulate conjectures about the historical Jesus, after the manner of Smith, we may rather interpret the fragments within the redactional history of the Markan tradition." This means that, when the Secret Gospel is read in conjunction with the stories about young men in canonical Mark, "a subplot" is "expose[d]" that "communicates" a "vision of the life and challenge of discipleship, as that is exemplified in the career" of the young man.[74] Thus all the youths in all the Marcan stories are taken as effectively one character, whose developing understanding of Jesus somewhat parallels that of the Beloved Disciple in the Gospel of John: "Just as the youth in *Secret Mark* embodies Mark's vision of the life of discipleship, so also Lazarus as Beloved Disciple illustrates the ideal of the follower of Christ who has been raised to new life. This symbolic disciple is depicted in a less developed manner in Mark and in a more expanded and historicized fashion in John."[75] There is nothing particularly sexual about either of these characters, as Meyer sees them, even when he is drawing comparisons with naked youths in pagan rituals, such as the clearly sexual Dionysiac mysteries.[76]

On the other hand Theodore W. Jennings, in *The Man Jesus Loved,* which seems to derive its title from the second excerpt of the Secret Gospel, proposes a multilevel "gay-affirmative rereading" of the entire New Testament, finding support in many passages for his contention "that the Jesus tradition contains a good deal that is relevant to the discussion of same-sex erotic relationships, and that all of it is positive."[77] Yet he too thinks that "serious questions may however be raised about Smith's interpretation of Secret Mark when we consider it within the context of canonical Mark where it allegedly belonged."[78] Like Meyer, Jennings would read the Secret Gospel passages in light of the rest of Mark's gospel. Contextual reading, he finds, leads to increased credibility for the Secret Gospel, but not for Smith's exegesis of it:

> Although these reflections suffice to show that Smith's interpretation of Secret Mark is inadequate, they do not discredit Secret Mark. To be sure, some scholars at first supposed that Smith might have invented the letter of Clement with the fragments of Secret Mark in order to bolster his own views of baptismal initiation into magical identification with Jesus. But, as our reflections show, if this had been Smith's intention, then the material in Secret Mark is singularly ill suited to further Smith's own interpretive strategies. The critique of his interpretation then only serves to strengthen the credibility of Secret Mark itself.[79]

The similarities and differences between Meyer's and Jennings's interpretations could be taken as showing that what is really hard to believe is not the

Mar Saba text, but what Smith made of it. Without Smith's presuppositions, the Secret Gospel excerpts can be read as closely related to canonical Mark and as having no more of a sexual character than the rest of the New Testament—even though people may disagree over what the New Testament actually says about sexuality. This demonstration makes it seem more plausible that Smith discovered the text rather than composed it himself, but it tells us nothing about who composed it and when. The most it can be said to prove is that the Secret Gospel texts closely resemble the style of canonical Mark, which we knew already.

Just as the manuscript of this book was nearing completion, a new book appeared that expands upon and replies to the statements with which I ended the last paragraph. According to Scott G. Brown, the Secret Gospel was not written in a Marcan "school" or by an ancient imitator of Mark. It was written by the very same man who wrote the canonical gospel of Mark. This he argues because the "Markan vocabulary, style, and literary techniques," as well as "Markan redactional interests and theology," are so close to those of the familiar Mark. Brown writes that "the notion that someone other than Mark would try to think exactly like Mark is contradicted" by the fact that we do not find such slavish imitation elsewhere in ancient and biblical literature, even in many situations where it might be reasonable to expect it. He continues: "Another author would probably have had no interest in propagating Markan theology and no reason to do so. A different author who wished to expand Mark's gospel would probably have imitated Mark's style but pursued his own theological agenda." For anyone other than Mark to mimic Mark's way of writing so exactly, he would have to have "read the gospels like a late-twentieth-century narrative critic."[80]

This, of course, invites the obvious retort: "Maybe he *was* a late-twentieth-century narrative critic." I see Brown's reply to this as falling into two parts. First, Brown has systematically considered and rejected every point made by the major reviewers who considered the Mar Saba text a "modern forgery."[81] Then, he offers two reasons why it would be unreasonable to accuse Smith. First, Smith's publications from before 1958 show that his views on the gospel of Mark changed after he discovered the fragment. Surely Smith would not have forged something that contradicted his own opinions. Second, the "longer text" or Secret Gospel, as Jennings observed, actually doesn't support Smith's theories very well. "Clearly, if Smith wanted to create a text that gave firm support for his revolutionary views about Jesus," Brown points out, "he did a really poor job."[82] Thus the true author would have to be Mark himself, and the Secret Gospel would be a unique case of a newly discovered work by a biblical author, which sharpens the urgency of the next question.

Is the Secret Gospel Holy Scripture?

In portraying himself as the victim of "violent abuse," Smith hinted at two other issues. First, is there a role for ad hominem arguments in the academy, or should we assume that a scholar's personal behavior or misbehavior has no bearing on the authenticity of his discoveries or the quality of his publications? Episodes of manic forgetfulness alternating with angry feelings of abuse and persecution make for a worrisome combination, but armchair psychoanalysis dressed up as objective scholarship is not much better. Therefore I will leave this issue aside, with the mere observation that "Smith was famous for giving as well as he received."[83]

The other and more interesting issue arises from Smith's assertion that most of his opposition came from religious people and the (evidently no less pious) "adherents of current exegetic cliques."[84] Can religious or academic orthodoxies make a person more resistant to new evidence that points in an unexpected direction? Does a lack of allegiances make a person more open-minded? There are some who would answer these questions affirmatively. According to Shawn Eyer, "Secret Mark's plight constitutes a warning to all scholars as to the dangers of allowing sentiments of faith to cloud or prevent critical examination of evidence. When seen in light of the massive literature which has been produced by the other major manuscript finds of our century, the Dead Sea Scrolls, Nag Hammadi codices, the comparative dearth of good studies on this piece in particular can only be explained as a stubborn refusal to deal with information which might challenge deeply-held personal convictions."[85]

I would argue, however, that people who are secure in their religious beliefs are among the least likely to feel threatened by something like the Secret Gospel. A conventional believer who holds the traditional Christian positions that magic is a form of idolatry, that freely chosen homosexual acts are always sinful, and that Jesus never sinned, will be convinced from the outset that Smith's interpretation is absurd and that the Secret Gospel—if it really says what Smith asserts it does—must be some sort of fraud. Better to ignore it than to lend it credibility by attacking it. However a Christian scholar—one who is qualified to review Smith's books in a professional publication—will understand that the Mar Saba text is bound to reveal something about the historical context in which it was written and thus shed some sort of light, however unusual, on whatever period in the history of Christianity it belongs to. If it is a genuine artifact from the first century, therefore, the devout Christian scholar will welcome whatever historical information it reveals about first-century Christianity. If it was composed at some later time, such as the twentieth century, then it is bound to reveal something about how Christianity was perceived at that historical point. A Christian scholar who is critical of Smith's publications, then, is not necessarily writing out of fear that the Secret Gospel will somehow contradict or overthrow the canonical gospels. Modern Christian historians do not, for example, get upset about or try to suppress Jewish texts that say Jesus was conceived in adultery,[86] docetic texts that deny he was human,[87] or Muslim texts that deny he was divine.[88]

Moreover, even if the Secret Gospel really was written in Aramaic around 50 CE, by someone who had known Jesus well, that would be no reason to add it to the Christian Bible. New additions to the scriptural text are precluded by two doctrines that almost all Christian denominations uphold. The first is the doctrine of divine inspiration, that "all Scripture is inspired by God" or "God-breathed [*theopneustos*]" (2 Timothy 3:16). This means, as the Second Vatican Council explains it, that the Holy Scriptures "have God as their originator" or "author [*auctorem*]":[89] "In the process of composition of the sacred books God chose and employed human agents, using their own powers and faculties, in such a way that they wrote as authors in the true sense, and yet God acted in and through them, directing the content entirely and solely as he willed. It follows that we should hold that whatever the inspired authors or 'sacred writers' affirm, is affirmed by the Holy Spirit."[90] But this does not apply to everything those "human agents" wrote during their lifetimes—only the texts that were divinely inspired. If someone were to discover an unknown writing that was indisputably composed by Mark, or Paul, or any other New Testament writer—even an epistle from Jesus himself—this newfound text would be of extraordinary historical interest, but it would not be Scripture. This is because of the second doctrine, which answers questions like: How do we know which writings are divinely inspired? How can we say that the familiar Gospel According to Mark was revealed by God acting "in and through" its human author, while the Secret Gospel—ostensibly by the same historical personage—was not? The response to such questions is "canonicity." That is, only those writings are reckoned as canonical scriptures that the Church has continually read as such in its worship, teaching, and preaching since the earliest times.

Most Christian groups regard this Canon of Scripture as closed.[91] No further writings can be added to it, no matter how ancient or truth-filled they may be, even if the human author insisted that he wrote it in miraculous circumstances or was guided by the Holy Spirit. This is consistent with the Christian belief that, even though God "has spoken in many and various ways," he has been uniquely and fully revealed in the person of Jesus Christ, "the radiance of God's glory and the exact representation of God's nature," so that no further revelation is necessary for human salvation (Hebrews 1:1–3).

The New Testament itself, after all, frankly admits that there were other writings about Jesus that circulated in ancient times.[92] Why should anyone be surprised if some of these noncanonical writings have survived, or been rediscovered, even though they were not included in the Bible? It is not impossible that such a writing may record something that the historical Jesus actually said or did, even something not recorded in any other text. But to insert it into the Bible now would imply that the faith of the Church has somehow been incomplete or deficient for all those centuries since Jesus' time.

Thus there are two factors in assigning the status of canonical scripture to any text: the belief that it was inspired by God, and the experience and acknowledgement of the Christian community across the centuries that God's living word is indeed encountered in these particular writings. Of course, any community or organization that does not feel committed to these Christian doctrines is free to read the Secret Gospel, or any other text, as it sees fit. To my knowledge, the only group that has accorded religious authority to the Secret Gospel is one that stands well outside the historical Christian mainstream. It was this group that issued the 1982 reprint of Smith's popular book, *The Secret Gospel,* through Dawn Horse Press, one of many organizations associated with a religious leader who was known at the time as Da Free John.[93] Smith clearly approved the publication, since he added the postscript and cited it in the *Harvard Theological Review* article.[94] But if Smith thought he was bringing scholarship to a wider public, the publisher clearly had a different aim: the reprint includes a full-page advertisement for a book titled *Call for the Radical Reformation of Christianity* by (who else?) Da Free John, giving the impression that Smith's book, or at least the Secret Gospel, can be read as supporting the "Daist" agenda. According to the ad, "Jesus . . . instructed people within his native tradition, but he Taught [*sic*] them how to transcend themselves and their religious conventionality via a direct and radical process of God-Communion. . . . Christians must surrender themselves, one by one, to the Living Spiritual and Transcendent God, and so enter the Great Way nakedly, free of all self-armor, superiority, moral righteousness, and conflict with other lovers of the Truth."[95] Evidently the radical reformation being called for would not be so different from Smith's take on the Secret Gospel, in its ambiguously stated demand for Christians to surrender nakedly, one by one, to a direct and radical process of communion, transcending any religious conventionality, "self-armor," or moral righteousness that might lead to "conflict with other lovers." The whole advertisement resembles what folklorists call an "extended double entendre," a popular type of humor in twentieth-century North America. That is to say, the double meaning is not limited to a single word but extends through the entire text.[96] We will encounter this genre again — it has a peculiar tendency to keep reappearing in the vicinity of the Mar Saba text.

Da Free John may have endorsed the Secret Gospel, but he has made no secret of his own teachings; in fact he has published numerous books (under various names) explaining them — far more than I have had time to read. But when I searched the Internet looking for a concise summary of his religious views, it was easier to find allegations about sexual goings-on on his private island in the Pacific. Why Smith chose to work with this particular publisher I have no clue, but I suspect it was initially the publisher's idea.

As for the "adherents" of the various scholarly orthodoxies, it seems to me Smith had little to complain about. If a doctrinaire application of form criticism, redaction criticism, or any other kind of criticism leads to a different interpretation of the Secret Gospel, that is the way scholarship works. The new interpretation may tell us something important about the material, or it may tell us more about the scholar who propounded it. In either case, further discussion will eventually sort out whatever has enduring value and is worth building upon. As long as scholars care more about the truth than about their personal reputations, I for one will always be confident that things will ultimately move in the right direction. In the free marketplace of ideas, the best defense against a bad idea is a better idea.

If any group of people is likely to react uncritically to Smith's discoveries, it is the general public, or at least those large segments of it that lack training in the academic study of history and have little or no Christian faith, so that they are compelled to get their gospel from the news media. But these are the same people that Smith, in the two editions of his popular book, has worked so hard to persuade. Therefore I see little justification for the claim that Smith's discovery is being rejected out of hand, without serious consideration of the vast quantity of evidence he has put forward in its defense.

From Firestorm to Stalemate

Nevertheless, suspicion continues in some quarters. In an article subtitled "Stalemate in the Academy," Charles W. Hedrick has recently argued that "*Secret Mark* has yet to be given a full and impartial hearing." It "appears to have been discredited and shunted aside, to a great degree for other than scholarly reasons."[97] These reasons had to do with discomfort about Smith's theory that Jesus practiced magical rites, particularly the hint that these rites may have included homosexual acts.

> Smith's critical study argued that the early Christian movement began in Palestine as a mystery religion, specifically with a baptismal initiation administered by Jesus to each of his closest followers. This initiation, Smith notes

(but only in passing, I might add), may have included a physical union between Jesus and the initiate. At least, a physical encounter could not be excluded, Smith avers. Smith never develops this concept any further in the
book, but it is the one line in the book that most disturbed reviewers. Smith
argues that the Christian church in the second and third centuries covered up
this baptismal founding rite of Christianity, a rite initiated by Jesus himself.

   . . . In the firestorm of criticism that followed his publications, he was
vilified personally and even accused of forging the Clement letter himself . . .
Thirty years later, the reviews of Smith's books are almost embarrassing to
read — not embarrassing to Smith, though I am sure they must have bothered
him immensely at the time, but embarrassing to the academy. From my later
perspective, the personal attacks on Smith were entirely unwarranted. . . . I
have been asked in public gatherings, after presenting papers on *Secret Mark*,
whether the negative reaction in the academy was due to homophobia. I
cannot answer that question — I seriously doubt that anyone can. But the
question is natural enough, in light of the strong response to Smith's one line
about homosexuality in both his books.[98]

Hedrick went on to quote liberally from the reviews he considered most
embarrassing. After arguing that "Smith simply could not have pulled off a
forgery under the conditions at the monastery in 1958,"[99] he proceeded to
point out some areas where accepting the authenticity of the Secret Gospel
would enable fruitful debate. First of all, "homosexual acts by Jesus should be
a non-issue for a historian. . . . The historian's questions are different: for
example, did Jesus baptize or not? . . . The whole issue needs to be revisited in
the light of the claims made that *Secret Mark* reflects a baptismal tradition."[100]
The Secret Gospel should also be valued as a "witness to the instability of
gospel texts in the first and second centuries," and because it "encourages us to
think of an undifferentiated tradition" underlying both the gospel of Mark
(hence also Matthew and Luke) and that of John.[101] Finally, Hedrick "com-
mended" scholars whose publications "bypass the stalemate and push the
academy to deal with specific issues of interpretation in *Secret Mark*." Ignoring new discoveries, or "deliberately eliminating them from the discussion, is
not a historian's solution."[102]

   In a response, Guy G. Stroumsa largely concurred: "Since I have been interested in early Christian esoteric traditions for many years, the idea of a secret
gospel in the Alexandrian Church never really surprised me. Smith's analysis of
the secret gospel seemed to me as far-fetched as it was brilliant, but the continuous skepticism about the very existence of Clement's letter, and accusations of
forgery, perhaps by Smith himself, have always seemed to me to stem from quite
unscholarly grounds, more often than not implicitly rather than explicitly

stated."[103] Stroumsa thought his personal sense that "Smith's account of his important discovery" deserved "total trust"[104] could be confirmed from the extensive correspondence between Smith and Gershom Scholem (an expert on Jewish mysticism), which is still preserved at the National and University Library in Jerusalem. These documents illuminate Smith's relationship with his most important teacher at Hebrew University, and they

> reveal . . . , perhaps for the first time, the real drive under Smith's evolving perception of Jesus and the very beginnings of Christianity. . . . Ancient Jewish magic, mystical ascents to heaven, and the antinomian figure of the seventeenth-century false Messiah from Smyrna, Shabbatai Zvi, all profoundly marked Smith. With the loss of his faith (he had begun his career as an Episcopalian minister) he eventually came to see Jesus as an antinomian figure, once the discovery of *Secret Mark* permitted him gradually to build a sustained thesis in this direction. . . . In his sustained search for the Jewish background of earliest Christianity, he went into a path too little trodden: that of early Jewish esotericism. . . .
>
> Like his mentor Scholem, Smith was fascinated throughout his life with old manuscripts, bringing new evidence on ancient religious history, in particular on magical, mystical, and heretical trends. His unexpected discovery of the Mar Saba document put him on the track of an interpretation of Jesus similar, *mutatis mutandis,* to Scholem's interpretation of Shabbatai Zvi. Moreover, like Scholem had done for Kabbalah in Judaism, Smith attempted to emphasize the centrality of esoteric traditions and rituals in early Christianity, traditions and rituals later suppressed or transformed by emerging orthodoxy. That in this attempt he was not as successful as he wished seems obvious. Probably he overplayed his hand. But no one can seriously deny that his discovery of the Clementine letter was genuine, and that he did with it exactly what a scholar working in a library should do: photograph the text, publish a list of the documents analyzed, and put the book back on the shelf afterwards. I can only concur with Hedrick's conclusion: once the absurd and slanderous discussion of the genuine character of Smith's find is behind us, we will be able to discuss seriously the real implications of the text.[105]

In a second response, however, Bart Ehrman argued that "the jury is still out."[106] While emphasizing that he was not accusing Smith, Ehrman listed a number of unresolved issues regarding the authenticity of the Mar Saba document — issues that he classified into three categories as "hard to understand," "hard to explain," and "hard not to find amusing." Most of these had already been raised by other scholars but, in Ehrman's opinion, never satisfactorily answered:

> What is hard to understand involves the circumstance that Smith knew a lot about Greek manuscripts and ancient forgeries, and must have known full well

that in order to detect a forger at work, one needs to examine carefully the physical evidence itself, the manuscript, in hand, under microscope if possible, looking for characteristics of the pen, stray marks, ink bleeding into lines, hard-to-detect smudging. . . . But given everything Smith knew or came to know about manuscripts and their forgeries, why did *he* show no interest in going back to examine the manuscript? He himself admits that at the time of the discovery he was rushed, and so he took his pictures and put the book back on the shelf. But why would he spend fifteen years of his life reading and analyzing the words in the photographs knowing full well that the clues to forgery could not be found in the photographs but only in the physical specimen?[107]

Unfortunately, this type of forensic examination will have to be postponed indefinitely, for in 1976 or 1977 the book was taken from Mar Saba to the Jerusalem Patriarchate for safekeeping. There the two leaves were removed from the back of the book, photographed in color, and then promptly lost.[108] Hedrick suspects that "homophobia may well have contributed to the disappearance."[109]

Erhman's category of "things that are hard to explain" includes three questions: First, "Why does this letter contradict in content what Clement says elsewhere?" Though Clement wrote of "gnosis" or spiritual knowledge, this was never "a matter of hidden texts with arcane instruction," but of "deeper understanding of readily available texts." Nor would Clement have advocated lying or swearing false oaths.[110] Second, "Why is the style of the letter *so* much like Clement's style . . . *more* like Clement than Clement ever was"? The author of the text seems to be trying to emulate "the Clementine distinctive vocabulary (but overdoing it)."[111] Third, this alleged eighteenth-century copy of a medieval manuscript contains no copying mistakes or "transmissional errors," but "must be an autograph."[112]

The last category consists of the "interesting, even amusing, aspects of the whole business." It includes the fact that the letter breaks off just as it is about to reveal "the true explanation and that which accords with the true philosophy . . . ," and the "brilliant irony" that the letter was inserted into an early modern edition of a highly interpolated ancient author, St. Ignatius of Antioch, facing a page on which the editor inveighed against "theologically motivated scribes" who falsify ancient texts.[113] Most remarked-upon in this category are the dedications in Smith's two books. The scholarly one published by Harvard University Press was dedicated to Smith's Harvard mentor Arthur Darby Nock, who is widely asserted to have been unconvinced that the Mar Saba letter was genuine.[114] The popular Harper book, however, bears the strange dedication, "For the One Who Knows," inviting speculation that there is a hidden secret behind all this, which Smith shared with an unidentified confederate.[115] Is this whole thing actually a very complex and esoteric joke?

One observer who is convinced he has gotten the joke is Donald Harman Akenson, a professor of Irish Studies who sees much to criticize in contemporary New Testament scholarship:

> Anyone who could not spot it as a forgery from a height of 3,000 feet should not be allowed to make authoritative pronouncements on the authenticity of texts that relate to [Jesus] of Nazareth. . . . Any country-road antiques dealer would recognize the signs at once.
>
> But, as a test of the competence of the allegedly leading-edge North American scholars, what makes this simultaneously frightening and revealing is that *even if one knew nothing of its diagnostically-fraudulent provenance,* one still would immediately recognize it not only as inauthentic, but as part of a very nasty, but very funny, knife-sharp joke . . . a nice ironic gay joke at the expense of all the self-important scholars who not only miss the irony, but believe that this alleged piece of gospel comes to us in the first-known letter of the great Clement of Alexandria. . . .
>
> Whoever set this skilled and amusing bit of post-modern scholarly theatre in train must have been immensely diverted by the way it played.[116]

But not even Akenson is able to say who the joker was. Was Smith a perpetrator or a victim? And if it is all a joke: Why?

A Different Approach

I think Hedrick's word "stalemate" is not a bad description, though it may somewhat oversimplify the situation. The text discovered at Mar Saba is like some exotic toy—a puzzle within a puzzle within a puzzle—with at least one of the puzzles being the man who discovered it. If the interlocking puzzles have not been solved so far, I would say it is because the whole problem has been investigated too narrowly. Almost all the discussion has been focused on the Secret Gospel and its relationship to canonical Mark, perhaps the very place where the forger (if there was a forger) wanted us to look, like a thimblerigger playing the shell game. I am convinced that a narrow discussion of this particular issue will keep the mystery unsolved because biblical studies in its current form does not have the capability to solve it. At least thirty years of erudite discussion have not yet done so.

Forensic study of the ink, the handwriting, and other physical characteristics might do the job, but only if the original manuscript resurfaces.[117] However, a forger with a high level of expertise in Greek manuscripts and New Testament studies (the level of expertise that Smith had) might conceivably be able to create a document that was almost impervious to detection. The flyleaves on which the document was written are probably genuine pieces of seventeenth-century paper, and it is possible to reproduce eighteenth-century ink. An expert scholar would know exactly what his fellow experts would look for and therefore know just how to fool them.

It is when forgers venture into areas where they *lack* expertise that they tend to get caught. The British physician Harold Shipman (1946–2004) poisoned more than two hundred patients over the course of his thirty-year career but evaded detection by forging medical records to make the deaths look natural. As a doctor he knew just how to do that, and he did it so well he was even exonerated by a police investigation, which found all the records in order. He was caught only when he forged a transparently amateurish will for his richest and most famous victim that would have left all her money to him. The lawyers (one of whom was the victim's daughter) saw through it immediately, and the jig was finally up.[118]

Looking at the Mar Saba document, then, from unaccustomed perspectives, from outside New Testament studies, might reveal a mistake in some area where the author did not know enough, and did not know enough to hide what he did not know. Or it might reveal knowledge that only a first- or second-century author could possibly have known, confirming that the Mar Saba artifact is what it appears to be. We will not find such an alternative perspective by focusing on the well-worn question "Is the Clement letter a forgery?" We need a new and different approach.

PROFILES IN FORGERY

Forgeries are not uncommon; historians deal with them all the time. A remarkably large proportion of the documents historians work with are of dubious or questionable origin, and it is part of the historian's job to determine whether this is due to deliberate deception, subsequent misunderstanding, or simple confusion. The reason it matters, however, is not because of ethical considerations, but because the historian needs to read the text against the background of its proper historical context, the time and place in which it was actually written. A forged banknote may be worthless as currency, but even the cruelest and most outrageous forgery can be a goldmine of information about the historical circumstances of the person who created it, because even the most ingenious forger is inevitably a person of his or her time. As Anthony Grafton notes: "The forger imposes personal values and period assumptions and idioms on his evocation of the past; that is why his work must eventually cease to seem credible as what it once purported to be, and becomes instead a document of its own time."[119] But it is precisely these "personal values and period assumptions and idioms" that the historian is interested in, because they reveal both the forger's relationship to his own present and "his evocation of the past," not to mention his imagined future. Thus the historical work of textual criticism somewhat resembles psychoanalysis, as researchers seek to escape their own "personal values and period assumptions" in order to temporarily acquire (for the sake of understanding) the perspectives of the original writer. "Like the psychoanalyst," Grafton continues, "the critic sets out to fight the monsters that crowd about us in the long sleep of reason that is human history. Like the psychoanalyst, the critic wields fragile weapons and is constantly betrayed by his own subjectivity."[120] But these fragile weapons have been improved and sharpened by centuries of historical research, to the advantage of forgers and critics alike. They include the study of physical artifacts like watermarks and ink chemistry, of cultural conventions like form and genre, and of individual quirks like vocabulary and "stylometry."[121]

But they also include techniques for establishing an author's identity through certain psychological characteristics — something that should be compared less with psychoanalysis than with profiling, a term borrowed from crime detection. A trained police profiler can walk through a crime scene, look around, and then tell fellow officers, "OK, we're looking for a short Caucasian male, probably unemployed, about thirty-five years old, who still lives with his mother."[122] The historical study or criticism of texts aims at a similar specificity, but it is applicable to any mystery, whether or not a crime is suspected. Indeed it is often most useful with ancient and medieval texts, where the chances of identifying a specific individual as the author are limited, unless it is an author from whom we also have extensive, undisputed writings. Harold Love writes in *Attributing Authorship*:

> In establishing an attribution, profiles will be necessary for both the author of the anonymous or pseudonymous work and the principle suspect or suspects. . . . Such a profile will extend beyond ethos to consider all aspects of the text which have any bearing on personality, including singularities of style. The method naturally works best with the more personal kinds of writing: one would have to proceed with great caution in attempting to profile a dramatist through his or her characters (which has not stopped many attempts). . . .
>
> In medieval studies such a method is often the only kind of attribution that can be attempted. We can profile the Gawain-poet (or poets) but not identify him (or them). William Langland's name is given to us as the author of *Piers Plowman,* but, apart from a few sketchy details, what we know of him is derived from his poem. Much critical writing is in effect a form of profiling: the critic attempts to define the particular sensibility or world-view of the author and to distinguish it from that of other authors. . . . It goes without saying that the reader needs to be convinced that the affinities proposed are really individual. One would expect two Augustinian friars of the fifteenth

century or two eighteenth-century French philosophers to show similarities of self-presentation as well as knowledge. We must also be aware of the phenomenon of authors' close modelling of themselves on a revered elder or predecessor. Lastly, we must never forget that the "author in the work" is always a textual performance.[123]

Besides "profiling," other metaphors that have been proposed include the more forensic "fingerprinting" and the more bookish "finding a literary voice."[124] In any case the important question for the historian is not "Is this genuine?" but "Who wrote this? What kind of person was he or she, and in what historical period can we find people like that?"

To take a very simple example, we can look at a text that is easily recognized as a fake. This would be the brief writing known as *Cidade Calenixness, or The Dialogue of Jesus and John,* in which Jesus teaches John the doctrines of Mary Baker Eddy (1821–1910), the founder of Christian Science. Allegedly translated from a Latin papyrus in the British Museum, the text has circulated for about a century in Christian Science circles; rumor has it that both the British Museum and the Mother Church in Boston continue to receive inquiries about it. But any well-informed person can see that it is not what it appears to be. There is, first of all, the highly anachronistic content, which requires a date after the founding of Christian Science in the late nineteenth century. Second, the gobbledygook name looks more like Anglicized Portuguese than like Latin or any biblical language, implying that the forger was not even capable of the relatively simple task of creating a Latin title.[125] Most early Christian papyri are in Greek or Coptic anyway, rather than Latin. Finally, the British Museum insists that the alleged papyrus does not exist in its collections.[126]

Even from this brief look, however, we can tell a lot about the unidentified author. He or she (let's say "she") lived in the twentieth century and seems to have wanted to show that the teachings of Christian Science are identical to the teachings of Jesus. She was probably an English speaker, not only because the document is in English, but because she regarded the British Museum as the most impressive repository of ancient documents, the kind of place where unknown sayings of Jesus would most likely be discovered. Yet she also seems to have known Portuguese. She did not know Latin — in fact she seems to have regarded Latin with some awe as the paradigmatic ancient language, the language in which important new teachings of Jesus are most likely to be preserved and discovered. Closer analysis of the text, fully informed by twentieth-century controversies surrounding Christian Science, may well make it possible to narrow down the possibilities of when and by whom this text could have been written. With time and effort, after rooting out considerably more information, it might eventually be possible to fit this profile to a specific historical individual and determine exactly who the true author was.

There is one kind of person, however, who might resist the suggestion that *Cidade Calenixness* is a modern creation: the Christian Scientist who sincerely believes that the teachings of Mary Baker Eddy are in close continuity with the teachings of Jesus. The more closely the author's worldview confirms our own, that is, the easier it is for us to accept a text as what it claims to be. Hence the extraordinary seriousness with which some people in our time—both appreciative readers and worried ecclesiastics—take *The Da Vinci Code: A Novel*. The book frankly admits, in its title, to being fiction, yet it also claims to be based on a series of "accurate" historical "facts," which many readers today find easy to believe though they are instantly recognizable as fallacious by professional historians.[127] The "facts" boil down to a claim that official Christianity suppressed the memory that Jesus married and fathered a child with Mary Magdalene, but that this knowledge was preserved by secretive heterodox groups and handed down by means of arcane texts and mystical symbols. Since so many in our culture view Christianity as a repressive, male-dominated, antiquated institution with bizarre and irrational neuroses about sex, many find these claims very reasonable, easier to accept than conventional Christianity as they know it. The credibility of these non-facts is enhanced all the more because some of them were not invented by the author of *The Da Vinci Code* but had already been circulated by the authors of other popular books, some of whom have even sued for copyright infringement.

This does not mean, however, that cultural stories and attitudes, like those expressed in *The Da Vinci Code,* should be simply dismissed as "wrong." On the contrary, they reveal a lot about the culture that produced them. A critical scholar of the twenty-sixth century, for instance, working from the only surviving copy of *The Da Vinci Code,* which has lost its copyright page, would be able to tell that it must have been written at the beginning of the twenty-first century: the kind of paper, the English vocabulary, the mystery-story genre all fit that time frame, and so (more particularly) does its portrait of a misogynistic Christianity, a cultlike Opus Dei, a sexually active Jesus, an ersatz-feminist primordial mother-goddess fertility religion.[128] From the very different perspective of twenty-sixth century cultural concerns, it will be obvious that these are early twenty-first century characteristics.

Similarly, the approach to take with the Mar Saba text is not to ask, "Was this written by Clement of Alexandria or Morton Smith?" but a more open-ended, "Where and when could this have been written?" And we must remain open to the possibility (until it can be ruled out) that the Mar Saba text was written within the culture of twentieth-century "academia." A professor of ancient Greek or biblical studies would know just how to flatter the concerns of his or her own colleagues, putting them in the same position as an Anglo-Portuguese Christian Scientist to whom *Cidade Calenixness* looks like a fascinating and important ancient document.

Life Situations

Students of ancient literature and religious texts do quite a lot of profiling, though they have other terms for it. Biblical scholars, with their penchant for German terminology, look for the *Sitz im Leben* or "life situation," the historical circumstances that shaped the author's thinking.[129] For example, the New Testament includes a gospel, three epistles, and an apocalypse (i.e., the book of Revelation), all of which are ascribed to authors named John. Over the centuries, Christians have often assumed that all these authors were the same person, to be identified with the apostle John, the son of Zebedee and brother of James. Moreover, since the gospel claims to derive its authority from an unnamed figure called "the disciple whom Jesus loved" (John 13:23, 19:26, 21:20), this character too has been identified as John, and nicknamed the Beloved Disciple.

There are, however, a number of reasons to doubt that all these books were written by the same author. One reason is that they presuppose different life situations. The gospel of John was written in a context of severe tension between the followers of Jesus and another group called "the Jews." It seems to reflect a time when Judaism and emerging Christianity were separating antagonistically, and the Christians were starting to lose sight of their Jewish background. Believers in Christ were being expelled from synagogues (John 9:22) or hiding their faith so as not to be expelled (John 19:38), and the Christian movement was starting to attract Samaritans and other marginal and non-Jewish people (John 4:39–42, 12:20–23). The epistles, however, do not seem concerned with this problem, as if they were written after that crisis had passed. The burning issue in the epistles is the eruption of conflict and division within the Christian community itself.[130] In the apocalypse, however, the major problem seems to be persecution from without, more specifically from the Roman empire.[131] This author's group seems to have maintained a Jewish self-identification, in opposition to "those . . . who say that they are Jews and are not" (Revelation 3:9). Thus the various works ascribed to John point to three distinct historical situations, not one.

Of course an early Christian leader might have lived through a variety of situations, especially if he lived a long time, as St. John is reputed to have done.

So the Sitz im Leben may not be enough by itself to establish an author's identity. As authors react to their life situations, however, they take some sort of philosophical or theological position regarding the issues they are dealing with. Even when a writing incorporates traditional ideas, narratives, or themes, these will have been shaped to support the author's theological vision. Now the gospel, epistles, and apocalypse of John are shaped by theologies that are similar in many respects, but there are important differences. For example, each presents a different *ecclesiology*, or concept of how the church is structured. The author of 2 John (1) calls himself a presbyter or elder, an ecclesiastical title that does not occur in the gospel of John. He personifies the community he is writing to as "the elect lady and her children," an imagery that is also lacking in the gospel.

The John of Revelation, on the other hand, thinks of himself as a prophet (Revelation 1:3); he writes "in the spirit" (Revelation 1:10) to seven churches but personifies each (or its leader) as an "angel" (which in Greek originally meant "messenger"). And since this John is a prophet, he passes on words from Jesus himself: "And to the angel of the church in Thyatira write: 'The words of the Son of God'" (Revelation 2:18). John the elder, on the other hand, writes in his own voice. Thus it is fair to say that these two Johns, the elder and the prophet, seem to assume different models of the Christian community (a lady versus an angel) and of authority within that community (an elder versus a prophet). They seem to reflect two different but later, more developed states of affairs than the relatively unstructured community gathered around the disciple Jesus loved in the gospel of John.

There are other ancient writings ascribed to John, which were not accepted into the New Testament, and they illustrate further ways that scholars can distinguish one author from another. The Acts of John differs from the New Testament writings in its *Christology*, its theology of who Christ was. The Christ depicted in the Acts of John does not really have a material body. When he walks he leaves no footprints. On the cross he only seems to suffer.[132] This is what specialists call a "docetic" Christology, from the Greek word for "seem" (*dokeō*). We know that docetic Christologies were already circulating while the New Testament was being written because some New Testament authors expressly opposed them (2 John 7). The gospel of John, for example, emphasizes that Jesus had a material human body. The Beloved Disciple saw blood and water flow from his side at the crucifixion (John 19:34–35). Even after the resurrection, Jesus ate food and invited Doubting Thomas to touch his wounds (John 20:27–29, 21:12–15). Thus the Acts of John expresses a Christology that is incompatible with the gospel and epistles of John.

Yet another ancient work, discovered in modern times and called the Secret

Book (Apocryphon) of John, also claims to be by John the son of Zebedee.[133] But it cannot have been written by the same author as any of the other works ascribed to John because it takes place in a Gnostic universe, full of unfamiliar mystical beings and with a nonbiblical understanding of human nature. As one scholar points out, "The book is a veritable epitome of Gnostic ideas about the origins of the world, the false God worshipped by Jews and ordinary [non-Gnostic] Christians, the coming of Christ and the destiny of those who awaken to *gnosis* [knowledge] of their indestructible, eternal self."[134] In other words, it is unlike the New Testament writings and the Acts of John in having both a different cosmology (theory of the universe) and a different anthropology (theory of the human person). It could not possibly have been written by any of the New Testament authors, or by the author of the Acts of John.

To take a fresh look at the Mar Saba document, then, we should ask how its author or authors conceptualized what they perceived to be the major issues at the time. The letter ascribed to Clement, with its fulminations against the Carpocratian heretics, certainly reflects an ecclesiology. Can we tease it out in enough detail to ascertain who this author could have been, or if he really was Clement of Alexandria? The fragments of the Secret Gospel certainly express some sort of Christology: can we discern its outlines clearly enough to recover the theological views of the person who wrote it, the religion of the Secret Evangelist? Two themes stand out as being of particular interest, as Hedrick's "Stalemate" article indicates: the question of homosexuality and the secret initiatory rites. Therefore they are likely to offer the best starting points in our quest for the historical author. And as it happens, both sexuality and liturgy offer long and complex histories, with many places where one could locate a wayward text.

HOMOPHOBIA?

It seemed to Hedrick that some of the negative reaction to Smith's publications is motivated by "homophobia" (a pseudo-Greek term of recent coinage for prejudice against homosexuals). Such attitudes are out of place in scholarly research, he thought: "Homosexual acts by Jesus should be a non-issue for a historian."[135] He meant, of course, that ethical judgments about the behavior attributed to Jesus are outside the historian's domain, that we cannot decide the date or authenticity of a document on the basis of whether we approve of what it describes.

But if there are textual allusions or references to homosexual behavior, these could, on the contrary, be of great interest to the historian: they could help identify the period and milieu of the author, ancient or modern, just as any of the other concerns or interests revealed in the text might point to its time and place of origin. And as Ehrman emphasized, "much of Smith's entire work on the Secret Gospel does indeed move towards the homoerotic aspects of the historical 'facts' he has uncovered about Jesus. . . . It was precisely the libertine character of the material that struck Smith at the outset. . . . The homoerotic emphasis was not imported into Smith's view from the outside, by homophobic voyeurs in the guild. It is all right there, plain to see, at the climactic moment of the narrative."[136]

The significance of homosexuality for the historian is that, like heterosexuality, celibacy, and much of "human nature," it is multivalent, encompassing a wide spectrum of behaviors and attitudes that are variously constructed in different historical periods and cultures.[137] Therefore, just as the Christology, ecclesiology, or cosmology expressed in a text may point to the historical period or community of its redactor — or eliminate alternative possibilities — so too a clearly delineated "sexology" or construction of human sexuality (if we can find one) can tell us much about the views of the original author and his audience. This, in turn, can only help us locate the correct historical setting. Eventually it will be clear that the Clement letter does reveal an identifiable sexology, one which expresses a coherent message that is easy to understand and which fits perfectly into a certain modern strain of thought and a popular modern — even modernist — hagiography. Viewed from that angle, the characters are clearly seen to be acting out a coherent if tendentious portrayal of human sexuality, narrating a tale of "sexual preference" that could only have been told by a twentieth-century Western author, whether or not this author was Morton Smith. The multivalence of human sexuality is the key to a secret that, as we shall see, is itself multiveiled.

"GREAT MYSTERIES"

Although the hints of homosexuality in the Secret Gospel are ambiguous, there can be little doubt that the story of Jesus raising the youth from the dead and teaching him the mystery of the kingdom somehow represents the process of coming to faith as the Secret Evangelist conceived it. This is made more explicit in the letter of Clement, which says that the Secret Gospel had acquired a place in the liturgy of the Alexandrian church, where it was "read only to those who are being initiated into the great mysteries." Thus no analysis of the Mar Saba text can be complete without some consideration of its relationship to early Christian initiation ceremonies. As Hedrick put it, "the whole issue" of early Christian initiation practices "needs to be revisited in the light of the claims made that *Secret Mark* reflects a baptismal tradition."[138] Just as important as the document's sexology, then, is its liturgiology, or conception of the Christian liturgy. Since liturgical traditions vary greatly across the history and geography of the Christian world, the liturgical aspect of the Mar Saba document is likely to offer the most important clues as to its provenance.

When the Mar Saba fragment is viewed through the binocular optic of its sexology and its liturgiology, it is easier to see that it exhibits many strange features that (considered individually) *could* have been written by an ancient author but (taken together) produce a textual whole that is very difficult to locate in any identifiable Sitz im Leben in the ancient world. To get to that point, however, is a journey of many steps, for the letter of Clement to Theodore, though short, is actually extremely complicated. Indeed it describes no less than five traditions of oral or written doctrine or practice, each of which may reflect a different authorial profile or life situation — each of which, therefore, demands historical investigation on its own terms.

Five Streams of Tradition

If we could put aside our heretofore exclusive concern with the nature of the Secret Gospel, we would probably judge that the most striking feature of the Mar Saba text is its many references to initiation ceremonies, the liturgical rites by which new adult converts were admitted to the ecclesial communities mentioned in the document. Thus Clement states that Mark, while writing his original gospel in Rome, "select[ed] those" stories about Jesus that "he thought most useful for increasing the faith of those who were being instructed."[139] Then Mark relocated to Alexandria "bringing both his own notes and those of Peter, from which he transferred to his former book the things suitable to whatever makes for progress toward knowledge [*gnōsis*]. [Thus] he composed a more spiritual Gospel for the use of those who were being perfected." So far, there are two Marcan gospels, connected to two distinct stages of an initiation process: "being instructed" and "being perfected."

Besides Mark's two gospels, however, the Mar Saba letter also describes oral instruction of some sort, using vocabulary that originated in the non-Christian mystery religions: "Nevertheless, he yet did not divulge the things not to be uttered,[140] nor did he write down the hierophantic teaching of the Lord, but to the stories already written he added yet others and, moreover, brought in certain sayings of which he knew the interpretation would, as a mystagogue, lead the hearers into the innermost sanctuary of that truth hidden by seven [veils]." Thus Clement knew about three stages or levels of teaching that he traced back to Mark: (1) the original gospel, (2) a longer and more spiritual gospel, and (3) an oral teaching that provided interpretations of these written gospels. His description of the oral teaching evokes an atmosphere trembling with the solemn language of the ancient mystery religions, of hierophancy and the unutterable, of a mystagogy that leads to an innermost sanctuary hidden by seven veils. In his commentary on the word "hierophantic," Smith summarized a long letter he received from Werner Jaeger, stating, "Most striking is the consistent use throughout the letter of terminology derived from the mysteries; this is found in Clement's other works as well, but is more concentrated in this letter than elsewhere."[141]

Mark's two gospels, along with his oral, mystagogical interpretation, were handed down (we are told) to the time of Clement, when they were utilized in an initiation liturgy that constitutes, as it were, a fourth layer of tradition. For when Mark died, "he left his composition to the church in Alexandria, where it even yet is most carefully guarded, being read only to those who are being initiated into the great mysteries." No doubt these initiation rites had evolved since Mark's time, and in this liturgical context the more spiritual gospel came to be treasured as the mystical or Secret Gospel. A historically acute reading, therefore, should be alert to possible differences — among the three traditions that allegedly originated with Mark and the developed liturgical tradition that Clement practiced.

But the Mar Saba document also reports a fifth kind of doctrine, "the unspeakable teachings of the Carpocratians," which involve both oral interpretations and a different recension of the Secret Gospel. Carpocrates, "instructed by [demons] and using deceitful arts, so enslaved a certain presbyter of the church in Alexandria that he got from him a copy of the secret Gospel, which he both interpreted according to his blasphemous and carnal doctrine and, moreover, polluted, mixing with the spotless and holy words utterly shameless lies. From this mixture is drawn off the teaching of the Carpocratians." It was Theodore's uncertainty about the Carpocratian gospel and teachings that had prompted him to send questions to Clement of Alexandria, apparently; the letter discovered at Mar Saba is a portion of Clement's response.

To unravel what the Mar Saba writer is really saying, then, we must be able to keep track of five distinct layers or streams of transmission, involving varying amounts of oral and written content: (1) the gospel for those being instructed, presumably canonical Mark, (2) the longer, "more spiritual" gospel for those being perfected, which Mark wrote in Alexandria and which leads mystagogically to Gnosis or spiritual knowledge, (3) the unwritten interpretations of these documents, the "hierophantic teaching of the Lord" and "things not to be uttered" that were also traced back to Mark, (4) the Alexandrian rites of initiation, in which the more spiritual gospel was read as the Secret Gospel and the hierophantic teachings handed on, and (5) the Carpocratian gospel, with its associated teachings and interpretations. Only through this five-sided prism can we expect to read correctly the two stories that are all we actually have from the extra material written by Mark: one in which a young man becomes a disciple of Jesus, the other in which Jesus refuses to meet with some women.

Taken as a whole, however, this fivefold tradition is difficult to explain. The two-stage initiation is enough by itself to raise questions about what kind of Christianity the Mar Saba text represents. Clement, in fact, criticized the Valentinians for teaching that, after baptism, the believer needed to undergo a second stage of being perfected.[142] Small wonder, then, that we have been unable to solve the Mar Saba riddle by investigating only two of the five strands of tradition: the relationship between canonical Mark and the "more spiritual" gospel. If the Mar Saba material actually is what it appears to be, then the secret teachings, the initiation rites, and the rival Carpocratian church were all essential parts of the ecclesiastical environment that preserved these multiple Marcan gospels, and none can be safely ignored if we wish to determine where and when that was.

Besides, each of the five streams of tradition should, in principle, have left historical traces that can be corroborated by, or are at least consistent with, other surviving evidence from ancient Alexandria. For example, the obvious way to corroborate the historicity of the Secret Gospel would be to find another manuscript of it. If none is known to survive (and as a secret text it would probably have been restricted to a small number of copies), then we should look for other evidence that the Alexandrian church possessed and used a secret gospel. It would probably be difficult to trace the historical trajectory of the third stream, Mark's unwritten teaching, precisely because it was unwritten. But we could still look for evidence that some tradition of unwritten teaching was cultivated in Alexandria and attributed to Mark. Investigating the fifth stream might be hampered by our limited knowledge of Carpocratian beliefs and practices; indeed, if we had more data, we could probably separate this into multiple streams, distinguishing the transmission of the written gospel from the oral teachings and interpretations connected with it.

But the fourth stream, the initiation liturgy of the Alexandrian church, is less obscured by such difficulties. If something like the Secret Gospel were ever read in the Alexandrian initiation rites, it should have left traces somewhere in the Greek literature of Christian Egypt, or in the traditions of the Coptic and Ethiopian Orthodox Churches, which preserve a huge amount of textual, artistic, and archaeological material relevant to liturgical practices and initiation ceremonies. It is with the fourth stream, then—the most neglected yet potentially the most fruitful—that the effort to authenticate and understand the Mar Saba text should begin.

Summary

In this chapter I review the major issues that have been aired in the scholarly discussion of the Mar Saba fragments. Is the manuscript authentic? Is the letter really by Clement of Alexandria? Who were the Carpocratians? Is the Secret Gospel by Mark? Does the gospel have historical value? (Smith considered it very early and reliable.) What does the gospel really say, and should it be regarded as Holy Scripture? What about Smith's theory that the Secret Gospel shows Jesus engaging in ritualized homosexual acts? Instead of revisiting all that others have written about these questions, I propose a different approach to the Secret Gospel. Every document from the past can be analyzed to determine its author's "profile," his or her historical situation and beliefs about the world he or she lives in. Techniques for this have been developed by many different kinds of researchers. If we read the Mar Saba document with the suspicions of a profiler, the first thing we notice is that it seems to report five distinct streams of tradition, each of which would presumably have its own profile: (1) the familiar gospel of Mark, (2) the Secret Gospel, (3) the oral teaching ascribed to Mark that was not written down, (4) the secretive initiation liturgies in the church of Alexandria, where the Secret Gospel was read, and (5) the Carpocratian form of the gospel. If the Mar Saba text is what it appears to be, it ought to be possible to find historical corroboration for each of the five streams of tradition. The place to begin is with the fourth stream, the Alexandrian liturgy, as the one where confirming evidence is most likely to be found.

The Secret Gospel and the
Origins of Christian Liturgy

*I was amused to see how many times I had thought the same thing, and each
time with the enthusiasm that accompanies an original idea. Many compare
the human mind to a computer, but I fear it is more like a tape recorder. This
makes the question of what you put in so important; the first step toward
higher learning is to limit your intake. . . . Work at a problem too long and you
find yourself unable to see anything but the arguments you have already
seen. . . . Historians usually find what they are looking for — a fact that makes
me uneasy. But anyhow, I saw what I think I see, and it amounts to substantial
New Testament evidence for the existence and nature of Jesus' baptismal rite.*
— Morton Smith

Liturgy in Three Dimensions

Reconstructing religious ceremonies from long ago is no simple task;
scholarly literature is rife with self-satisfied but unrecognized failures. The
basic problem is that rituals subsist in three dimensions, while many academics — particularly if they have little personal experience with worship
themselves — work mainly in one. Those who are trained as historians (or text
critics), to work primarily with texts, tend to assume that a liturgy is essen-

tially a specific kind of text, and this perception seems all the more obvious in situations where texts are all that survive. But a rite is not a text. It is primarily an action (to use a Christian theological term) or a performance (to use an anthropological term) — even when the main activity is the reading, recitation, singing, or writing of texts.[1] Action is primary over text, both logically and chronologically, because human beings learn to use their bodies before they learn to use language.

Every ritual is the action of a human individual or community; therefore, it is essential to look "beyond the text,"[2] or beyond the textual dimension, into the dimension of liturgical acts. Historians can use many kinds of evidence for this purpose. Archeological evidence can include ritual objects and spaces, and artistic depictions of ritual acts, be they "realistic" or symbolic. Travelogues and descriptions of rites by uncomprehending outsiders can be very helpful. It is no accident that the most informative text we have on early Christian worship practices is the letter of Pliny the Younger to Trajan, asking how to prosecute Christians who refuse to participate in the imperial cult.[3] If a ritual tradition has persisted into recent times, one can learn something from the living practice, provided that its historical development in the intervening centuries is adequately documented and understood. There are often cases of "invented tradition" that look to an unsophisticated observer more ancient than they actually are.[4]

Thus text and act constitute two of the three dimensions a historian of liturgies must investigate. And just as there are well-known processes of textual transmission, there are also less-understood processes by which actions and movements are transmitted from one generation to another, across time and space. The third dimension might be called "ritual criticism"[5] or ritual theory. In every ritual community, there is some sort of ongoing debate about what the rites mean and how to perform them correctly. Elements of this discussion become accessible to historians when they are enshrined in any enduring medium, such as a text. Early Christian ritual criticism survives, first of all, in the kinds of documents we call "church orders," going back to the second-century *Didache* or "Teaching of the Twelve Apostles."[6] Beginning in the fourth century we also have the mystagogical sermons, in which the rites of Christian initiation were first explained to the newly baptized, not before but after they had actually gone through them.[7] There is a certain logic in this apparently inverted ordering: ritual criticism can and does shape ritual texts and actions, but it emerges as a reaction to texts and actions that are already in use. Liturgical reformers begin by articulating principles they assert to be foundational, and then demand that the rites be adjusted to express these principles more clearly. But more usually it is the acts and texts that come first, leaving the commentators and theorists to figure out what they really mean and provide historical explanations of how they emerged, explaining and upholding practices and texts of which no one remembers the actual origin, despite the reformer's insistence that in fact he does.

Sermons, commentaries, laws, and theological tracts continue throughout Christian history to preserve elements of ritual criticism. But ritual criticism need not be textual. Private prayer, "paraliturgical" worship, and unofficial practices of all kinds may encode perceptions of what is valuable or inadequate about the formal communal liturgy. The ultimate in ritual criticism staged as ritual action is the widespread destruction of medieval shrines and cult objects that took place in the early modern period, whether inspired by the Protestant Reformation, the Enlightenment, or the French Revolution and other political upheavals.

Modern academics find it relatively easy to construct their own ritual criticism, using insights from psychology, anthropology, and the other human sciences. The results will often seem intellectually exciting, identifying apparent universal human traits and desires that enable fascinating comparisons across religions, cultures, and historical periods. But much of it will actually be fanciful and irrelevant when it substitutes for, rather than supplements, close study of the theology and ritual criticism that is internal to the tradition in question. Anyone with a Ph.D. can write a brilliant essay showing that the Christian rite of Holy Communion is really a kind of sublimated cannibalism, that pilgrimage is a return to a womb that isn't there, that commitment ceremonies enact unacknowledged societal tensions. But writings like that do little to illuminate the really important subject, which is what the rite means and how it functions for the people who practice it, or who practiced it long ago. For that, a scholar has to do the really hard work of learning to listen to and understand the conversations that are or were going on within the worshiping community. Only with that knowledge can one introduce meaningful parallels and contrasts from outside the community's symbolic universe.

Thus responsible scholarly treatment of any liturgical or ritual tradition should aim, even when the surviving evidence is limited, to give full attention to all three dimensions of worship: the textual, the practical or actional, and the theoretical or critical. We know we are approaching success when we can explain the more-or-less perennial dialectic between the theoretical and practical dimensions, between which (at least in Christian traditions) the textual dimension is often the hallowed and bloodied battleground. Thus we can learn a lot about a church by studying its hymnal (the textual dimension). But we can learn even more by attending its worship and observing that these people rarely use their hymnal—they rely instead on photocopied pamphlets that are distributed each week and then discarded (the practical dimension). It is only when we have identified and interviewed the decision-makers, and gotten them to explain the critique of the hymnal that the disposable photocopies embody (the critical dimension), that we will begin to understand who this community is before its god. The ideal is the same when we are dealing with rituals that have not been celebrated in many centuries, even though (because of loss of evidence) the goal may not be fully attainable. Since we can no longer question the ritual leaders (or followers), we must do what we can with imaginative and exhaustive analysis of whatever evidence does exist. That is why "the study of the history of the liturgy and its texts is probably the most complex and least accessible of the humanistic disciplines."[8] And that is why, in my opinion, it is not enough for a would-be liturgical historian to be thoroughly trained in textual criticism and historical methodologies. She or he must also have ethnographic skills and the ability to observe and interpret actual rituals as they are being carried out, to "read" performances as they are happening, and to learn from living people as much as from books.[9]

Agnostic historians who think their only creed is objectivity are not the only ones who have difficulty working in all three dimensions. During the twentieth century, the major Christian denominations experienced the liturgical renewal movement, a wave of ritual criticism that resulted in extensive reforms of the liturgical rites. But since the most potent critics were historically trained theologians, experts in the interpretation of texts but uninformed about ritual action and the performing arts, they assumed that reforming a liturgy was principally a matter of revising its texts, after which everything else would naturally fall into place. They were completely unprepared for the fact that many worshippers, including much of the clergy, were more attuned to the actional, nontextual dimension of worship, where emotional and imagistic logic trumps the verbal, rationalistic logic that prevails in the textual dimension. Although much good was intended, and some good achieved, the overall result was a mess, and the official leaders and scholars of today — students of the original reformers — are now wondering how to face a new wave of ritual criticism that they shudder to view as a "conservative restoration."[10] Things will only improve when both sides learn to take a critical stance toward their own criticism. For conflict between competing ideals, criticism fighting practice over texts, is not an aberration but the normal state of affairs, what the history of a liturgy is usually like, a major cause of the temporal, geographic, religious, and cultural differences between worshipping groups within the same religion. Historians and theologians who don't know this get away with it mainly because they write for other historians and theologians who don't know it either.

Morton Smith himself did not know any of this. For someone who wrote as much as he did about early Christian worship, it is remarkable how little he read, even of what was considered required reading in his time. But besides being uninformed, he approached this subject with a strong methodological bias that made objective liturgical study impossible. It has been described thus:

> Certain themes and concerns unite all of Smith's work[, including] . . . scorn for pseudo-scholarship, that is, pronouncements and opinions born of religious faith and confessional conviction but masquerading as "objective scholarship." Smith argued that "the Bible" is a theological category inherited from Judaism and Christianity, and as such is an obstacle to a proper understanding of ancient Judaism and Christianity. Smith had only scorn for those who believed that any truth might somehow be lurking in the New Testament miracle stories (except insofar as the cures allegedly effected by Jesus might have been psycho-somatically induced cures of psycho-somatically induced illnesses). Smith had only scorn too for those who saw any truth in the prophetic experiences of either the Old Testament or the New Testament, as if God or any god would ever or did ever communicate in such a way with humans. For Smith the ideal of scholarly objectivity could be met only through atheism or Epicureanism, that is, the assumptions that if the gods exist, they intervene not at all in human affairs. . . . (Whether Smith actually was an atheist or an Epicurean, I do not know.)[11]

But doctrinaire atheism is no more objective than doctrinaire Calvinism or Hinduism. A student of ritual who insists that communication with gods is impossible is like a physicist who insists that magnetism is impossible — he will always be trying to explain the evidence away. The truly objective stance is what might be called "procedural agnosticism." The scientist in the laboratory must assume that the phenomena she observes are to be explained solely by knowable scientific laws, without supposing miraculous intervention by a force outside the laws. She must work from that assumption because otherwise she will never discover the scientific laws. But she works this way even though, after leaving the laboratory, she may (or may not) belong to a group that prays for the sick or that celebrates the Exodus from Egypt every year. For the same reason, the researcher in the humanities has to assume that what he is observing is to be explained by sociological, psychological, or other knowable principles that operate on the level of observable human reality. He must make that assumption if he is ever to find out what the principles are, and he makes it even though, on his own time, he may (or may not) meditate every day or weep at the chanting of the Quran.

To study people at worship, then, one does not have to believe what they believe. One may well believe that the things they do are primarily caused by political or economic factors the worshippers themselves do not fully perceive. But one must grant in principle the validity of their experiences; otherwise, one has no hope of understanding what they are doing or of making legitimate comparisons with other cultures or historical periods. If the only explanation I will accept is that these people are deluded, I will never understand them but will spend all my time trying to prove it is they who are deluded, not I. And what is the right word for someone who aims to prove that everyone but himself is deluded? Such an approach will inevitably take the researcher where it took Morton Smith: into an attitude of persistent and inexorable scorn for the people whose behavior he was claiming to elucidate.

To profile the liturgiology of the Mar Saba text, then, we do not begin with questions like "Could Jesus really raise people from the dead?" or even "Did Jesus claim to raise people from the dead?" Instead we begin with the axiom that the Carpocratians, the Secret Evangelist, Clement (or whoever), and those who participated in the "great mysteries" all had experiences and understandings of what worship meant to them and how it was to be done. Our job is to try to figure out what these experiences felt like and what these understandings were — how the textual, the practical, and the critical interacted to form the religious lives of these different people. This kind of three-dimensional examination will take a good four chapters. But in the long run, our effort to locate this liturgiology in early Christian Alexandria will result in the very opposite of corroboration. On one issue after another, the letter of Clement proves to be so out of place that (we must conclude) it cannot be describing the liturgy Clement knew, or any later form of it that might have been attributed to Clement posthumously or pseudonymously. In fact, the more closely we examine the Mar Saba letter from a liturgical vantage point, the more difficult it is to see how it could be an early Christian writing at all. By the end of this book it will be clear that the Mar Saba document fits perfectly into its true historical context — but that context is not the world of the New Testament.

An Easter Baptism?

The story of Jesus and the young man is, of course, the most extensive and most-discussed of the two excerpts from the Secret Gospel. Its obvious similarity to the story of the raising of Lazarus (John 11:1–45) was among the reasons Smith concluded (among other things) that it was not an addition to canonical Mark (as Clement says) but "was probably in the earliest form of Mark," witnessing to a common source shared with John, though it was eventually excised in the process that produced the familiar canonical text of Mark.[12]

And they come into Bethany, and a certain woman, whose brother had died, was there. And, coming, she prostrated herself before Jesus and says to him, "Son of David, have mercy on me." But the disciples rebuked her. And Jesus, being angered, went off with her into the garden where the tomb was, and straightway a great cry was heard from the tomb. And going near Jesus rolled away the stone from the door of the tomb. And straightway, going in where the youth was, he stretched forth his hand and raised him, seizing his hand. But the youth, looking upon him, loved him and began to beseech him that he might be with him. And going out of the tomb they came into the house of the youth, for he was rich. And after six days Jesus told him what to do and in the evening the youth comes to him, wearing a linen cloth over [his] naked [body]. And he remained with him that night, for Jesus taught him the mystery of the kingdom of God. And thence, arising, he returned to the other side of the Jordan.

We have only one variant from the Carpocratian recension, the phrase *gymnos gymnō*, and we do not know exactly where it fits into the text. Clement informs Theodore only, "But 'naked [man] with naked [man]' and the other things about which you wrote are not found."

Apart from statements in the Mar Saba letter, three features in the Secret Gospel are suggestive of an initiation rite: both (1) the weeklong period of teaching that ends with a nocturnal vigil and (2) the naked body covered by a linen cloth would seem to be items from the performance dimension, while (3) the raising from the dead of a young man who becomes a disciple seems to offer an interpretation from the critical dimension. This particular threesome suggests a marked emphasis on the themes of death and resurrection. If "after six days" refers to the period of Monday through Saturday, both the raising of the youth and his meeting with Jesus would have occurred on the first day of the week, or Sunday; the nocturnal meeting could have begun Saturday evening and lasted until "very early" Sunday morning, the time of the resurrection in Mark (16:2). The linen cloth or *sindōn* could suggest a towel used in conjunction with a water immersion, or a shroud or burial cloth. As we will see, Smith also sought to connect it with the white garments that, in some early Christian traditions, the neophytes or newly baptized would put on after emerging naked from the baptismal pool, though the word "sindōn" was not typically used to designate such postbaptismal clothing. Themes of death and resurrection are further underlined by the fact that the whole episode was interpolated into Mark's gospel right after Jesus predicts his own resurrection (10:34).

And yet, if this story does reflect an early Christian initiation rite, it was a very odd one, lacking many of the ritual elements that occur in other early liturgical sources:[13] Instead of a lengthy period of fasting, exorcisms, preaching and instruction in the Bible, renunciations of sin, and professions of faith, Jesus' six days in the youth's house sound almost like a holiday of sensual pleasure, "for he was rich." No immersions or anointings are mentioned that would require the removal of clothing — yet when the youth comes to Jesus at night, he is naked but for a linen sheet. There is none of the vocabulary of light or illumination, or sealing or crowning, that typically occurs in early Christian references to initiation rites. There are no references to milk and honey, no imagery of entering the Promised Land (even though Jesus crosses the Jordan!), no obvious banquet or Eucharistic motifs. By contrast, the initiation stories in some of the apocryphal acts of the apostles are easy to connect to early Christian liturgical practices, even as scholars continue to disagree over what exactly they tell us about the developmental history of the initiation rites.[14]

The obvious explanation for this paucity of elements is, of course, the presumed early date of the text: if Clement (at the end of the second century) thought the Secret Gospel had been written by Mark (in the first century), then it could not have been written much later than 150 CE. Surely the initiation rites of that time were in a primitive state of development and had not yet acquired all the familiar features we find in post-Nicene sources![15] But this explanation does not satisfy, because the three ritual items it does mention are precisely the wrong ones for the second century: resurrection themes, a preparation period leading to a vigil, and white garments are much easier to place in the fourth or fifth century than in the second. Like the Piltdown hoax, which joined an apelike jaw to a humanlike cranium when all other extant fossils exhibit the opposite combination,[16] the Secret Gospel threatens to turn liturgical history on its head. If it were genuine it would be extraordinary.

In fact, if we scour the known history and bibliography of Christian initiation practices, looking for any context in which these and only these three elements could plausibly be found, a very curious thing happens: we find ourselves drawn away from the early Christian period altogether, toward the writings of Anglican liturgiologists who were active in the middle of the twentieth century — right about the time the Mar Saba text was allegedly discovered, and in the same Christian denomination to which the discoverer had once belonged. In that part of the Christian world, and at that time, the Secret Gospel would have seemed a very plausible witness to early Christian initiation practices, for it includes just what Anglicans of the mid-twentieth century were taught to expect: resurrection symbolism, a period of instruction ending in a night vigil, and a white garment. Today, after another fifty years of ecumenical scholarship, it all seems far less credible. This is easiest to see if we begin about

1950 and work forward to the scholarship of today, which in turn brings us closer to the early Christian period than was possible half a century ago.

THE SHAPE OF THE LITURGY

Before the liturgical renewal that began in the 1960s, the Book of Common Prayer, used in various editions throughout the Anglican Communion, contained three proper texts for Easter Even, as the day before Easter was called. The epistle (1 Peter 3:17–22) presents baptism as a sharing in the resurrection: "baptism doth also now save us, . . . by the resurrection of Jesus Christ." The gospel (Matthew 27:57–66) gives us the evening time frame and the sindōn or cloth: "When the even was come," Joseph of Arimathea took the body of Jesus, "wrapped it in a clean linen cloth, and laid it in his own new tomb." The collect, or prayer of the day, alludes to Romans 6:3–11 in associating baptism with death and burial as a preparation for resurrection. It asks "that as we are baptized into the death of thy blessed Son . . . , so by continual mortifying our corrupt affections we may be buried with him; and that through the grave, and gate of death, we may pass to our joyful resurrection."[17] It is a particularly interesting assemblage of texts. On the one hand, it dates back only to the Reformation: the epistle and gospel were selected by Thomas Cranmer for the first Prayer Book of 1549, while the collect was composed in the seventeenth century.[18] On the other hand, the texts seem intended to recall (some aspects of) the pre-Reformation liturgy, as it was practiced in the late medieval English regional Uses of Sarum or Salisbury, Hereford, Bangor, York, and Lincoln — all of which were local variants of the Roman rite.[19] In these traditions, as at Rome itself, the day before Easter (known as Holy Saturday) was the preeminent time for baptisms, recalling the pre-medieval period when the catechumenate leading to adult baptism had been the norm. The adult baptisms took place during the Paschal Vigil, a long service that originally began after dark on Saturday evening and ended with the first Mass of Easter itself, very early Sunday morning.[20] It included blessings of a new fire and of a special candle, twelve readings from the Old Testament, then a blessing of the baptismal water, followed by the baptism itself. As the neophytes, or newly baptized, emerged from the baptismal pool, they donned white clothing, heard the epistle (Colossians 3:1–4), sang their first alleluia as Christians, listened to the first resurrection gospel (Matthew 28:1–7), and received first communion.[21] The white robes, however, were real garments, not flat linen cloths resembling burial shrouds. The neophytes wore them for an entire week of liturgies full of Promised Land symbolism, then returned to ordinary clothing on the eighth day, Quasimodo Sunday (so called after the Latin of 1 Peter 2:2, which supplied the text of the introit antiphon).[22]

Over the centuries, however, two developments changed the significance of the Paschal Vigil. Understandable anxiety about infant mortality led to a situation in which most people were baptized as infants, shortly after birth, so that the Paschal Vigil was usually celebrated with no adult converts to baptize. While this was happening, other developments were tending to make the celebration of Mass a daily event, though it had originally been celebrated less often. Thus the Paschal Vigil crept backward from Saturday evening to Saturday morning and effectively became the Mass of the day, though a Mass with strong baptismal themes, celebrating the resurrectional theology of baptism in commemoration of the adult baptisms that had once been an essential part of this service. Action passed into text. In the different ways that liturgical reformers have dealt with these developments, we can witness some of the ways by which ritual criticism interacts with the dimensions of action and text to help shape paths of further growth.

Twentieth-century liturgical reformers, since they were trained as historical theologians, were particularly interested in reconstructing the origins of liturgical traditions. They also recognized that, in our post-Christian culture, it is again possible and desirable to seek adult converts who will need to be baptized. Thus in the twentieth-century liturgical renewal, many denominations restored the original practice of baptizing adults during a vigil on Easter night. The reformers of the sixteenth and seventeenth centuries, however, saw things differently, and as a result took three different approaches. The authors of the Prayer Book, since they continued the practice of infant baptism, did away with the Paschal Vigil altogether. In its place, they substituted new texts that preserved the traditional baptismal and resurrection themes of the day but linked them more closely to what they thought was really important: the gospel chronology that placed Jesus' burial between his death and resurrection, and the moral admonition that each individual Christian, in the temporal space between his own baptism and hoped-for resurrection, should apply the Christian message to his own life, so that (in the words of the Easter Even collect) "by continual mortifying our corrupt affections . . . , we may pass to our joyful resurrection." The result could be seen as continuing the medieval shift from action to text. The medieval church lost the action of baptism but retained the vigil with its texts as a daily Mass. The Anglicanism of the Prayer Book dropped the vigil texts altogether and replaced them with different texts. This placed the Prayer Book in a bidirectional dialogue (unless "conflict" is a better word) with the two other approaches of that historical period.

The Roman Catholic approach, conceding as little as possible to the critique of the Protestant Reformers, kept the Paschal Vigil essentially as it was, a baptismal service usually without actual baptisms. On the other hand, the more radical Calvinist reformers, with their emphasis on "Scripture alone," sought to make the textual dimension the controlling one. All traditions that had been handed down in the actional dimension were to be abolished and replaced only by practices that could be justified as explicitly mandated in the Bible itself. Thus for the Puritan John Milton, the Book of Common Prayer was hardly a reform at all but amounted to an unjustified preservation of damnable popish superstitions: "that old Pharisaicall fear . . . , Samaritan trumpery [cf. John 4:22], . . . a *Liturgie* which had no being that wee can know of, but from the corruptest times: . . . the old riffe-raffe of *Sarum,* and other monasticall reliques."[23]

By the twentieth century, therefore, Anglican liturgical historiographers generally saw their mission as an effort to trace a clear line of historical development, from current practice back through history to the New Testament, or as close to New Testament times as possible.[24] This was in response to the ritual criticism of the more Calvinistic English Protestants who denied these practices were biblical, but it was also a kind of rebuke to the Roman Catholics, demonstrating a liturgy rooted in the Bible rather than merely human tradition or ecclesiastical authority.

By the middle of the twentieth century, however, the logic of their liturgical criticism was leading Anglican liturgiologists into making even more ambitious claims. They thought it possible to reconstruct an original, unitary pattern of ceremonies, used throughout the early church, that effectively went back to apostolic times and from which all the Eastern and Western rites of medieval and later times were descended. In the classic description of Gregory Dix, there was a "standard structure or Shape of the Liturgy [which] can be shewn to have had its first formation in the semi-jewish [*sic*] church of the apostolic age. . . . The intricate pattern of local variety overlaid on the unchanging apostolic core of the rite is the product of [subsequent] history."[25] For the initiation ceremonies, this "standard structure" was thought to be revealed most clearly in the writing known as *The Apostolic Tradition* (AT),[26] then assumed to have been authored by Hippolytus of Rome, an approximate contemporary of Clement of Alexandria.[27] AT was very highly valued, therefore: not only was it "the most important source of information we possess on the liturgy of the pre-Nicene church," but it described "the local tradition of Rome, though at an early stage, before developments had become complicated."[28]

In this spirit, Massey Shepherd went even beyond Dix, seeking to demonstrate that the "broad outline" of initiation rites described in AT, read as an early Roman document, could be found in the New Testament itself, specifically the book of Revelation. This project seemed reasonable because AT was "composed about a century later than Revelation" and includes "nothing . . .

Table 3.1. The Roman Paschal Vigil and the Book of Revelation

Roman Paschal Vigil	Book of Revelation	
The Scrutinies	The Seven Letters	Revelation 1–3
The Vigil	The Assembly Before the Throne of God	4–5
(a) The Lessons	The Seals, I–VI	6
The Initiation	The Pause: Sealing of the White-Robed Martyrs	7
The Synaxis	The Seventh Seal	8
(a) The Prayers	The Censing	
(b) The Law (Exodus)	The Trumpets, I–VI = The Woes, I–II	8–9
(c) The Prophets	The Pause: The Little Scroll; the Two Witnesses	10–11
(d) The Gospel	The Seventh Trumpet = The Third Woe:	
	The Struggle of Christ and Antichrist	12–15
	The Vials, I–VII	16–18
(e) The Psalmody	The Hallelujah	19
The Eucharist	The Marriage Supper of the Lamb	19
	The Consummation	20–22

Source: Massey H. Shepherd, *The Paschal Liturgy and the Apocalypse*, Ecumenical Studies in Worship (London: Lutterworth Press, 1960), 83.

that could not have been in use in the first century . . . in churches so well established and developed as those of Asia."[29] Shepherd scrupulously sought to avoid anachronistically reading "a Paschal liturgy of a later age . . . into the Apocalypse" or implying "that the Apocalypse is either a liturgy or a lectionary, or even a liturgical homily." Nevertheless, he found "that the Paschal liturgy has suggested to the Seer [i.e., the author, John] a structural pattern for the presentation of his message," a pattern that looks remarkably like the medieval Roman Paschal Vigil (Table 3.1).[30]

To arrive at such conclusions, however, required a very wishful reading of AT, a reading that Dix made explicit in the subtitles of his translation.[31] For example, AT says that baptismal candidates are to wash on the fifth day of the week, fast on the day before the Sabbath, assemble to be exorcized on the Sabbath, and then attend a vigil and be baptized at cockcrow on a day unnamed (20.5–21.1). Only Dix's subtitles identify these days as "Maundy Thursday," "Friday and Saturday in Holy Week" and "The Paschal Vigil."[32] Although AT mentions a three-year preparatory period for catechumens (17.1),[33] it does not clearly describe Lent, which, Dix was sure, developed as a period of preparation for this nocturnal, paschal baptism.[34] Nor does AT expressly support the Passover and resurrection typology that Dix and Shepherd took for granted, by which the new believer, emerging from the water into the Easter dawn, recalled Israel's passing through the Red Sea, fulfilled by sacramental participation in the death and resurrection of Jesus.[35]

Worse, AT seems not to know of a special baptismal garment. It says only that the newly baptized put their clothes back on after they emerge from the water and are anointed (21.20),[36] as if these were the same ordinary clothes they came in with. Only from the late fourth century do we have unmistakable attestation that special white ritual garments were put on after baptism,[37] and their use has survived, in some liturgical traditions, into modern times.[38] Shepherd's scrupulous restraint and caution would, nonetheless, "legitimately see," in the white garments of Revelation 7:14, a first-century detail of "the initiation ceremony of washing and sealing in the Paschal liturgy," which the author of Revelation would have known from the AT-like celebrations of his own community.[39] By comparison, the white baptismal garments that figure in Dix's imaginary evocation of worship in the earliest house churches seem almost comically anachronistic.[40]

How Anglican all this is will become clear if we consider some of the alternative models that were available in the middle of the twentieth century. A twentieth-century Protestant who read Oscar Cullmann's *Baptism in the New Testament,* for example, would have found even stronger emphasis on "the foundation of baptism in the death and resurrection of Christ" but no mention at all of a nocturnal vigil, a special garment, or AT. Indeed Cullmann's perception of "the oldest baptismal ritual" included an element not found in AT, the Roman rite, or the Book of Common Prayer: "As early as the first century, whenever someone who had come to faith was brought for Baptism, enquiry was made whether any hindrance existed," such as "What is to prevent me from being baptized?" (Acts 8:36) or "Can anyone withhold the water for baptizing these people?" (Acts 10:47, cf. 11:17).[41] If a Protestant who had read Cullmann's book had attempted to forge an early gospel, therefore, it would likely have included such a ritual question, but probably not a night vigil or a linen cloth.

Mid-century Roman Catholic writers on liturgy, like the Anglicans, valued AT as an early Roman source. Moreover, they still celebrated the Paschal Vigil in close to its late medieval form. But since their "two-source theory" of revelation placed Tradition on a par with Scripture,[42] Catholics did not need to trace liturgical practices back to the New Testament. Nor did they need to believe in an "unchanging apostolic core," since they were accustomed to a diversity of ancient Eastern and Western rites, far wider than in any other denomination. Instead, Catholic liturgical practice before the Second Vatican Council aimed at ensuring the fulfillment of the canon law requirements for sacramental validity. The peculiarly Catholic anxiety, therefore, needed reassurance that all seven of the sacraments defined by the Council of Trent[43] had actually been practiced as such in the early church. Therefore, though Louis Duchesne, like Cullmann, found his model of Christian initiation in the book of Acts, he located normativity in different episodes from those that Cullmann selected. For Duchesne, the most telling passages were the ones that supported a clear distinction between baptism and confirmation (Acts 8:12–17, 19:5–6): "The New Testament sets before us, in the earliest times[,] an initiation composed of two acts, by virtue of one of which, viz. baptism with water, the converted person is washed from his sins, while by the other the gift of the Holy Spirit is imparted to the soul of the neophyte."[44] So too, no doubt, would a "secret gospel" — if such a thing had been forged by a twentieth-century Catholic.

STUDIES IN DIVERSITY

But if the Secret Gospel looks very Anglican compared with Cullmann and Duchesne, it looks all the more so when compared with the practices of the early church as we understand them now. Liturgical historians have covered a lot of ground in half a century. What was once a diversity of scholarly positions, which projected our denominational apprehensions onto the remote Christian past, has given way to an ecumenical consensus that the early church was even more variegated than post-Reformation Christianity. This is particularly true of the rites of Christian initiation, which for that early period can only be described as "a study in diversity."[45]

Central to our present understanding of early Christian initiation, moreover, is "the curious fact that the Pauline typology in Romans 6:1ff, depicting the baptized believer's participation in the death and resurrection of Christ, is absent in Christian literature of these earliest centuries."[46] At least two other models seem to have been more popular in the early church. One of them, known in parts of the Latin West, associated baptism with the day of Pentecost (cf. Acts 2:41), emphasizing apostolic preaching and the gift of the Spirit.[47] The other, the original model in Syria, Egypt, and parts of the West, looked to Jesus' own baptism by John, an event commemorated on Epiphany (usually January 6).[48] Instead of death and resurrection motifs, the Epiphany model emphasized themes of blessing the waters and of creation, of rebirth and divine sonship, the seal of priestly and messianic anointing, the heavens opening with light, the descent of the Holy Spirit and of fire.[49] This, indeed, is the kind of imagery we find in Clement's own discussions of baptism[50] and in Egyptian and Ethiopian baptismal liturgies.[51] Over the centuries, however, the Pauline Passover/Easter model gradually spread throughout Christendom to became the dominant one, and the night leading up to Easter became the major occasion for baptisms. In the liturgical traditions that had formerly baptized on Epiphany, therefore, the older practice was commemorated by retaining a portion of the baptismal rite, the blessing of water, on January 6. In these rites for the Great Blessing of the Waters, older themes of Epiphany baptism still survive and Exodus themes remain moderated, though an increased emphasis on exorcism and healing can also be observed.[52]

It is, then, the Epiphany model of water and the Spirit, not the Easter model of death and resurrection, that we should expect to find in any apocryphal gospel that was read at initiation ceremonies in Clement's church. The strongest indication of this is Clement himself. His most developed statement on initiation, *Eclogae Propheticae,* utilizes a wide range of Epiphany-related imagery: from the primeval light of creation and "waters above the sky" (Genesis 1:3–8) to John the Baptist's promise that the one who comes after him "will baptize you in the Holy Spirit and fire" (Matthew 3:11–12, Luke 3:16–17).[53] It is a fine example of a well-developed but non-paschal theology of Christian initiation — yet it could hardly be more unlike the Secret Gospel, underlining the fact that "one place where a preference for paschal baptism certainly appears to have been unknown before the middle of the fourth century is in the patriarchate of Alexandria."[54] If the Secret Gospel, with its resurrection symbolism, actually was read in second-century Alexandria, it would therefore be a remarkable exception to the general trend of sacramental theology there.

Night Vigils

A case could be made that the youth's coming to Jesus in the evening, after six days, was not meant to be a Paschal Vigil but some other sort of nocturnal meeting. Clement is one of many early Christian witnesses to tell us that a lot of worship took place at night.[55] In fact, Clement described a ritual that sounds like the Paschal Vigil but was connected to Epiphany rather than Easter. The Basilidans, he wrote, read a sequence of Bible passages during the night leading up to January 10 or 6 (Tybi 15 or 11 in the Egyptian year), in preparation for baptisms on those days.[56] By the early fifth century the Jerusalem church held such vigils on both Epiphany (January 6) and Easter; later it added Christmas (December 25) as well.[57] From Jerusalem, this type of vigil spread to many other parts of Christendom.[58] But Clement seems not to have celebrated such vigils himself; he described it as a peculiarly Basilidan practice.

As early as the second century there was already more than one way to structure an all-night or predawn service,[59] and in a forthcoming book[60] I expect to show that Clement followed a different, Alexandrian way of structuring the night vigil, which we also find among Philo's Therapeutae: an evening banquet followed by hymn-singing till dawn.[61] The Secret Gospel, once again, suggests nothing of the kind, as if it were written by someone who did not know the worship practices Clement of Alexandria actually used.

Conclusion

In short, it is impossible to argue that the Secret Gospel accurately depicts early Christian worship. Its combination of resurrection symbolism, a period of teaching followed by a night vigil, and the wearing of a white cloth are more suggestive of twentieth-century Anglican theories about early church practices. Clement and the Alexandrian church, in particular, held to a different theology of baptism that was based not on the Easter event of Jesus' resurrection, but on the Epiphany event of Jesus' baptism by John. So far, then, the Secret Gospel looks more like a document of the mid-twentieth century than of the first or second.

The initiation liturgy described in the Mar Saba letter is only one of the five streams of tradition we can identify in that document. But following the stream to its source leads us away from second-century Alexandria into the Anglican ritual criticism of the 1950s. However, another argument has been made, which would take a different approach to placing the Secret Gospel within the early Alexandrian liturgy. It is time to look at it.

Summary

The Secret Gospel presents three elements that appear to be liturgical: (1) resurrection themes, (2) a linen cloth, and (3) a nocturnal initiation following a period of preparation. However, these elements have little to do with second-century Christian worship, particularly at Alexandria, where baptisms were associated with the baptism of Jesus by John, celebrated on Epiphany (January 6). Thus a second-century gospel read at initiations in Clement's church should show Epiphany themes, such as the blessing of waters, Messianic anointing, and the descent of the Holy Spirit. The resurrection and Easter themes implied in the Secret Gospel look more like early Christian worship as it was imagined by Anglican liturgiologists of the 1950s than like second-century worship at Alexandria.

4

The Secret Gospel and the
Alexandrian Lectionaries

*The longer of the passages quoted from the secret Gospel is the one on which
the stylistic conclusions are mostly built. But this passage seems to have been
the central text for one of the most important rituals of Mark's church. If so, it
would have exercised a much greater influence than would ordinary sections
of the Gospel, and the number of parallels to it would of course be greater.
— Morton Smith*

The Bible in Lent

The Secret Gospel cannot be made to fit into the history of nocturnal
worship or Christian initiation at Alexandria. But a case has been made that it
is an important witness to the history of the Alexandrian liturgical lectionary,
the annual cycle of readings from the Bible. Since the Mar Saba letter states
that Mark was read to those who were being instructed, and Secret Mark to
those who were being perfected, it appears to be the earliest Christian writing
to mention the organized reading of a specific New Testament book in coordi-
nation with any kind of liturgical calendar. That in itself would make the Mar
Saba text a source of great value for the history of liturgical scripture-reading
— particularly since, once again, it appears to go against the general trend of
other evidence. The instruction of catechumens seems, usually, to have fo-

cused on Old Testament stories presented as models of virtuous behavior, with the gospels reserved for those who were close to baptism.[1] Such an arrangement is formalized in the fourth- and fifth-century sources of the rite of Jerusalem[2] and in the Roman ceremony of *Apertio aurium,* the "opening of the ears,"[3] posing the question more sharply: Is there any support in the early Christian period for a gospel being read at the early stages of instruction, with a secret expanded recension reserved for the more advanced?

In a very original and important book on the development of the Christian liturgical year, Thomas Talley proposed just such a *Sitz in Gottesdienst* (as he called it, meaning "original liturgical context") for the Secret Gospel.[4] His hypothesis amounts to the best-known and most developed argument that the Secret Gospel was known in ancient times. If he is right, though, the Secret Gospel could not have been very secret: it would have been heard by every adult baptized in Alexandria and would have had a far-reaching impact on the development of Christian liturgy outside Egypt. It would, in fact, explain some curious aspects of the structure of Lent — the most complicated period in the liturgical year, since it emerged, as Talley showed, from the coalescence of a wide range of practices that were synthesized differently in the diverse regions of the ancient Christian world. Attempting to confirm all this will force us to wend our way through a labyrinth of liturgical evidence, but will end in the same sort of result as our exploration of initiation ceremonies and night vigils: foxes have dens and birds their nests (cf. Luke 9:58), but there is no place for the Secret Gospel in the early history of the Christian liturgical lectionaries.

LENT IN CONSTANTINOPLE

What Talley initially sought to explain was the fact that, in some liturgical traditions, baptisms took place not only at Easter, but also a week or more before, while it was still Lent. In the earliest typikon of Constantinople, preserved in manuscripts of the ninth through eleventh centuries, baptisms were celebrated at the all-night vigil from Holy Saturday to Easter Sunday, just as they were at Rome and in Jerusalem. But there was another day for baptism a week before that, on Saturday of the sixth week of Lent (i.e., the day before Palm Sunday). The gospel that day was the story of Jesus raising Lazarus from the dead (John 11:1–45).[5] This might indicate that the Lazarus story was being read as an allegory of Christian initiation, but we do not know how the two came together: the presence of the gospel on that day might have suggested it was an appropriate day for baptisms, or a tradition of baptizing that day might have suggested the gospel. Or gospel and baptisms may have originated independently, their convergence on this particular day being a coincidence. One cannot decide such questions without considering the structure of Constantinopolitan Lent as a whole.

Table 4.1. Hypothetical Course Reading for Alexandrian Lent Compared with Constantinople (After Talley)

	Alexandria (Hypothetical)	Constantinople
	[Epiphany: Mark 1:1–11]	
First week of Lent	Mark 1:12ff	Sabbath: Mark 2:23–3:5
		Sunday: John 1:44–52
Second week of Lent	Continuation of Mark	Sabbath: Mark 1:35–44
		Sunday: Mark 2:1–12
Third week of Lent	Continuation of Mark	Sabbath: Mark 7:31–37
		Sunday: Mark 8:34–9:1
Fourth week of Lent	Continuation of Mark	Sabbath: Mark 8:27–31
		Sunday: Mark 9:17–31
Fifth week of Lent	Continuation of Mark	Sabbath: Mark 2:14–17
		Sunday: Mark 10:32–45
Sixth week of Lent	Friday: Mark 10:32–34, the Secret Gospel, Mark 10:35–45	Sabbath: John 11:1–45
	Sabbath: Mark 10:46–52	
	Sunday: Mark 11:1–11	Sunday: John 12:1–18

Source: Thomas J. Talley, *The Origins of the Liturgical Year,* 2nd emended ed. (Collegeville, Minn.: Liturgical Press, 1991), 211, following (for Constantinople) Juan Mateos, *Le Typicon de la Grande Église: Ms. Saint-Croix n°40, Xe siècle 2: Le Cycle des fêtes mobiles,* Orientalia Christiana Analecta 166 (Rome: Pontificium Institutum Orientalium Studiorum, 1963), 18–23, 28–31, 38–39, 46–47, 54–57, 64–67.

After two preparatory weeks of increasingly rigorous fast, Lent itself lasted six weeks in Constantinople. Each of these six weeks began on a Monday: there were five weekdays of fasting, from Monday to Friday, followed by a Saturday (Sabbath) and a Sunday on which fasting was moderated and the Eucharist was celebrated.[6] On the first five of these weekends there was a course reading of the gospel of Mark — that is, a different excerpt or pericope of Mark's gospel was read each Saturday and Sunday, forming a series that was arranged more or less in canonical order, as if the goal were to read through all the most significant portions of the gospel over the course of the liturgical season (Table 4.1, right column). This kind of arrangement was typical at Constantinople, where the other three gospels were similarly distributed over the Saturdays and Sundays of other seasons in the year: John from Easter until Pentecost, Matthew and then Luke from Pentecost to the following Lent, when Mark was begun again.[7] This tendency to stay with one biblical book for the duration of a season, a practice modern scholars call *lectio continua,* remains a distinctive feature of the Byzantine rite today, which is in part descended from the old rite of Constantinople.[8] In other influential centers, such as Jerusalem[9] and Rome,[10] pericopes were less likely to be read in biblical order because they were selected to illustrate a particular theme derived from the day, the season, and/or the place of celebration.[11]

At Constantinople, the last reading of the Marcan cursus took place on the Sunday following the fifth week of fasting, with Mark 10:32–45, close to the place where the story of Jesus raising the young man was inserted into the Secret Gospel (after 10:34). After five more weekdays of fasting, baptisms were celebrated on the sixth Saturday, and the story of the raising of Lazarus was read (John 11:1–45). The following day, Palm Sunday, featured the next two episodes in John's gospel, the anointing at Bethany and the triumphal entry into Jerusalem (John 12:1–18). Thus Lazarus Saturday and Palm Sunday, with their readings from John, marked a sharp break between the Mark-dominated fast of the forty days and the more austere six-day fast of Great Week, which began on Monday, the day after Palm Sunday, and extended to the day before Easter, the only Saturday that was a fast day at Constantinople. One of the issues we will have to face is this: to what extent was this clear distinction between the forty-day fast and the six-day fast a product of local developments in Constantinople, or a more universal characteristic of Lent that we should expect to find in other places also, such as Alexandria?

LAZARUS IN CONSTANTINOPLE: JERUSALEM VERSUS ALEXANDRIA

Lazarus Saturday at Constantinople has interesting but inexact parallels with the corresponding day at Jerusalem, the Saturday before Palm Sunday.[12] Some would suppose that the church of Constantinople was imitating Jerusalem in this respect, but that would contradict Talley's theory that the Jerusalem liturgical year was originally based on the chronology of Matthew's gospel, which he believed was written at nearby Antioch. To Talley, the Johannine elements in the Jerusalem liturgical year, including Lazarus Saturday and Palm Sunday, appeared to be later intrusions that came to Jerusalem from Constantinople.[13] Thus he thought it more likely that the Lazarus reading at Constantinople imitated not Jerusalem but an Alexandrian practice of reading Secret Mark, including the story of the young man Jesus raised from the dead.

In constructing this theory, Talley relied heavily on an article by René-Georges Coquin on the origins of Epiphany.[14] Coquin began with medieval Coptic writers of the tenth through fourteenth centuries who said that Egyptian Christians originally commemorated Jesus' baptism on January 6, and then followed this with a forty-day period of fasting, which recalled the time Jesus spent in the wilderness after being baptized by John (Mark 1:12–13 and parallels). This forty-day fast would have run, therefore, from January 6, or the day after, to February 15 or 16. It would have had no particular connection to Easter: once the forty days were over, Egyptian Christians would simply have waited until the Jewish Passover was finished, and then celebrated the six-day fast of Passion Week on a Monday through Saturday, followed by Easter Sunday.[15]

Coquin's medieval Coptic sources stated that the forty-day fast was observed after Epiphany up to the reign of patriarch Demetrius of Alexandria (188–230), which happens to have coincided with the time that Clement was in Alexandria.[16] Demetrius was said to have inaugurated the well-known practice by which Alexandrian astronomers — the best in the ancient world — would compute the date of Easter, and the patriarch would announce their findings in an encyclical to the other bishops of Christendom. According to the Melkite (i.e., Greek Orthodox[17]) patriarch Eutychius of Alexandria (died 940), this development led to the forty-day fast being moved, from after Epiphany to before Easter.[18] Coquin thought this dating was mistaken, however. Instead he perceived a more gradual shift in the Festal Letters of Athanasius (patriarch of Alexandria from 328 to 373). The first letter, from 329 CE, mentions only the six-day fast. From 330, though, the letters give the first day of the forty-day fast, which seems to have become increasingly formalized and obligatory through the year 333.[19]

Another tenth-century bishop, the non-Chalcedonian (i.e., Coptic Orthodox) Macarius of Memphis, wrote that baptisms were held on the sixth day of the week (Friday), because Jesus baptized his disciples on that day.[20] Coquin connected this with a medieval Coptic practice of baptizing on Friday in the sixth week of Lent, or at a night vigil from this Friday to the following Saturday morning. He saw this non-Easter baptism as a survival of a time when the forty-day fast had no connection to the six-day fast of Passion Week — thus confirming reports that the forty days once immediately followed Epiphany. But Coquin could not identify the origin of the tradition that Jesus baptized his disciples on that day.[21] It was Talley who proposed that the Secret Gospel, with its story of Jesus raising the young disciple, provided the missing link. This would constitute remarkable proof of the gospel's genuineness, since the Mar Saba fragment was discovered at a time when Coquin's question "hadn't even been asked" yet. As a result, Coquin's entire hypothesis was "dramatically vindicated"[22] — and so was the authenticity of Clement's letter.

Noting that canonical Mark begins with Jesus' baptism, and supposing that Mark's gospel would have been especially valued in Egypt because of traditions connecting Mark to Alexandria, Talley suggested that the first chapter of Mark was read on January 6, with the remainder read, in order, over the subsequent forty days — except, of course, it would not have been canonical

Mark but Secret Mark that was read. Later, when the forty days were relocated to just before the six-day fast, the Marcan cursus would have moved with it, producing a sequence of Marcan pericopes such as we actually find at Constantinople (Table 4.1). Since the Constantinopolitan sequence ended in Chapter 10 of canonical Mark, followed by the raising of Lazarus from John, could it not have been derived from an Alexandrian cursus of Secret Mark that ended with the story of Jesus and the young man? "It was that one item that suggested the later reconstitution in the Byzantine Liturgy of the Alexandrian Markan cursus for the fast," Talley writes. "There, however, the 'secret gospel' has vanished, and its account of the raising from the dead and subsequent initiation of a youth at Bethany, a gospel kept secret at Alexandria, and read only at the conferral of baptism, has been replaced by its only canonical parallel, the raising of Lazarus in the Fourth Gospel on the final Saturday."[23] Thus it was the Secret Gospel story of the young man, originally read at baptisms on the fortieth day after Epiphany, that explained two different phenomena of liturgical history: why Friday in the sixth week of Lent was recalled in Egypt as the day Jesus baptized his disciples, and why the Lazarus story was read on Saturday in the sixth week at Constantinople.[24] What's more, the Egyptian baptism on the sixth day, particularly if this occurred during a night vigil, would seem to echo the Secret Gospel report that Jesus and the young man came together during the night "after six days."[25]

Liturgiologists prize Talley's book for its fresh new interpretations and its willingness to reexamine the evidence and reasoning behind long-standing conventional assumptions about the origins of the Christian feasts and liturgical year. His bold and original proposal that the Secret Gospel of Mark explains the shape of Lent in Constantinople has attracted much favorable attention, therefore, and it looks like a resounding confirmation that the Secret Gospel is a genuine early Christian work, widely known in ancient times. On further examination, however, the theory does not hold up. Neither Coquin nor Talley cited all the evidence that was available when they were writing, and more has become available since. To begin with, Alberto Camplani has come up with a new chronology for the Festal Letters of Athanasius, which "do not permit one to affirm that Lent . . . was introduced gradually. The letters from 329–333 CE do not contain the announcement of the date of the beginning of Lent, even if possibly there is some veiled allusion to it, while from 334 onward the announcement is present in a continuous manner."[26]

Camplani has also taken issue with other aspects of the Coquin-Talley theory, which he sees as improperly built around the testimony of the medieval texts, using the earlier witnesses only for confirmation — even though these earlier witnesses "do not exhibit the ensemble of characteristics of a post-

Epiphany Lent, but only single elements that can be contextualized in another manner."[27] I would point out that, whether or not Alexandrian Lent originally began at Epiphany, there were many traditions in which the beginning of Lent was *calculated from* Epiphany, even though it actually began later in the year. St. Sabbas, for instance, is said to have learned a tradition in which Lent began on January 14, the day after the octave (or "one week later" commemoration) of Epiphany on January 13. But later on he moved the beginning of Lent back a week to January 21, the day after the feast of his mentor St. Euthymius.[28] The Latin evidence is more complicated.[29]

On the other hand, much of Talley's hypothesis could be salvaged by redating the Mar Saba letter. He accepted what he perceived to be the majority view, held virtually in spite of Morton Smith's provocative interpretations, that the Mar Saba letter is a genuine work of Clement of Alexandria. But Talley's argument about the liturgical impact of the Secret Gospel would actually be stronger if the Mar Saba text were written two or three centuries after the time of Clement. In that case, it would still be an ancient writing, but not as early as the second century. What would be more difficult to determine would be the date of the Secret Gospel it quotes from.

A Post-Nicene Pseudo-Clement?

Evidence for stable, annually recurring patterns of liturgical reading generally begins to appear in sermons of the late fourth and early fifth centuries; the earliest extant lectionaries date from the fifth and sixth centuries.[30] Thus "Clement's" linkage of a particular gospel to a specific liturgical occasion seems out of place in the second century. Dating the Mar Saba letter to the fourth, fifth, or even sixth century, on the other hand, would put it at a time when, in many places, traditions of public reading were solidifying into liturgical lectionaries — a time, moreover, when we are more likely to find baptism ceremonies connected with themes of resurrection, celebrated at a vigil after a preparatory period, and involving a white garment. A more plausible form of Talley's theory, then, would explain the Mar Saba letter as pseudonymous — an attempt by some unknown writer to trace the emerging Alexandrian lectionary back to St. Mark on the testimony of St. Clement. A fourth- to sixth-century date would also make it easier to explain other aspects of the letter: the assertion that Mark brought Peter's memoirs to Alexandria from Rome, for instance, could then be derived from Eusebius, the fourth-century "Father of Church History."[31]

Even in this stronger form, however, the proposal cannot ultimately be sustained. The theories of Coquin and Talley involve a series of logical gaps that were bridged by hypotheses but can now be partially filled in with evidence, yielding a very different picture in which the Secret Gospel does not fit after all. On closer inspection, that is, the histories of Epiphany and Lent, traditions about the baptism of the apostles, and the early lectionaries from Egypt do not reveal dependence on, or even awareness of, the Secret Gospel.

EPIPHANY SEASON AT ALEXANDRIA

One obvious issue is the fact that the Secret Gospel makes no mention of water, though water symbolism is abundant in Egyptian theologies of baptism. Coquin's original article, for example, sought to link the origins of Epiphany[32] to pre-Christian imagery connected to the rising and sinking of the Nile, the life-giving annual cycle that provided the only arable soil in the Egyptian desert. On this topic more material is now available than Coquin cited.[33]

Another issue is that, in most Egyptian (and Ethiopian) sources, Epiphany is a celebration of two or three days. The first day (January 6) recalls Jesus' baptism. The second or third day commemorates the wedding at Cana, when Jesus worked his first miracle by turning water into wine (John 2:1–11).[34] The baptismal interpretation of the Cana story has long-standing importance in Christian Egypt;[35] pre-Christian myths about Nile water turning to wine may help explain why Egyptian Christians were particularly interested in the Cana miracle.[36]

One could, of course, speculate that something like the Cana episode was once recounted in the lost portion of the Secret Gospel. A fifth-century Egyptian lectionary fragment in Greek might be used to argue this, for it does seem to point to something like the Coquin-Talley hypothesis (Table 4.2). It now consists of two leaves that are not contiguous: an undetermined amount of missing material once stood between them. The lectionary was originally a list of gospel readings, six of which now partially survive (numbered 1 through 6 in Table 4.2). Each gospel is cited by incipit only, followed by the incipit of a chant text, evidently a remote ancestor of the Coptic and Arabic hymns known as *ṭuruḥāt*.[37] In Table 4.2, each chant incipit is shown indented, after its respective gospel. Two of these musical texts are scriptural, from Ezekiel 47:12 and Psalm 106 [107]:26–30. The other three that survive seem to paraphrase the scriptures rather than quote them directly; they are difficult to decipher because the fragment is a palimpsest (i.e., it was erased so that another text could be written over it), and they cannot be checked against the Bible. It is interesting that one of these texts, which appears to begin "But the Lord says," seems to interrupt the reading of the story of the wedding at Cana (John 2:1–11), coming in the middle rather than at the end.

Table 4.2. Gospels in a Fifth-Century Egyptian Parchment Palimpsest

---

1r
1. Matthew 4:2 (the temptation)
   "And Moses fasted 40 days and 40 nights . . ."
2. Mark 1:9–10 (baptism of Jesus)
   Ezekiel 47:12
1v
3. John 2:1–7 (the wedding at Cana)
   "But the Lord says . . ." [?]
   John 2:8–9 (Cana continued)
[material missing here]
2r
4. Luke 9:39–42 (boy with unclean spirit)
   "The Lord rebuked the Devil . . ." [?]
5. Matthew 8:23 (calming the storm, beginning)
2v
   Matthew 8:24–26 (calming the storm, continued)
   Psalm 106 [107]:26–30 ("They cried to the Lord")
6. Matthew 8:28 (the Gerasene demoniac)

Note: The gospel numbers 1–6 are not in the original manuscript.

Source: British Library Oriental MS 4717 (5) A, as edited in Mario Geymonat, "Un antico lezionario della chiesa di Alessandria," *Laurea Corona: Studies in Honour of Edward Coleiro,* ed. Anthony Bonanno and H. C. R. Vella (Amsterdam: B. R. Grüner, 1987), 186–96, see pp. 188–93.

The sequence of gospels on the first of the two leaves is quite interesting. It begins with the temptation in the desert in Matthew 4, a reading that was often used at the beginning of Lent (see Tables 4.4, 4.5, 4.6, and 4.7 later in this chapter). Its presence here implies we are at the beginning of some forty-day period, particularly as the theme of fasting for forty days is also picked up in the chant text. Then we have the baptism of Jesus as told in the gospel of Mark (1:9–10), followed by the wedding at Cana from John (2:1–9 is extant). Although we are not told what liturgical occasions these readings were meant for, the juxtaposition could represent a day of preparation for a forty-day fast, followed by an Epiphany commemorating the baptism of Jesus, followed (as Egyptian Epiphany usually was) by a commemoration of the wedding at Cana.[38]

We do not know exactly what came immediately after the Cana reading. The second leaf, which did not originally come directly after the first, contains three readings that show Jesus casting out devils and silencing the storm at sea.[39] These readings would be appropriate on days when the catechumens were exorcised in preparation for baptism, and one could imagine the calming of the storm being read on a day when water was blessed. One cannot say for sure, but it is possible that these two leaves preserve part of a sequence of readings for a liturgical season that began with a preparation day for forty days of fasting, an Epiphany that celebrated the baptism of Jesus, another day honoring the first miracle at Cana, and then a series of days devoted to exorcisms and blessings of water. All that would seem to confirm Coquin's theory that Egypt once did have a forty-day fast that began at Epiphany.

As they stand in this manuscript, of course, the readings are from all four gospels. Is it possible that the original practice was to read the Secret Gospel, but that its pericopes were later replaced by "canonical parallels," as Talley thought the young man story was replaced by the Lazarus story? In such a case, the Secret Gospel could have begun with a story of forty days of fasting, followed by the baptism of Jesus, the Cana story, and a series of exorcisms and miracles, leading eventually to the stories of the young man and the three women, as shown in Table 4.3. Is this plausible? The hypothesis might seem to be strengthened by the fact that one of the exorcisms, the boy with the unclean spirit (Mark 9:14–29), also has a parallel in the Marcan lectionary for Lent at Constantinople, on Sunday after the fourth week of Lent (Table 4.1).

There are reasons to hesitate, however. For one thing, all three synoptic gospels, including Mark, say that Jesus fasted in the desert for forty days *after* he was baptized by John (Mark 1:9–13). In the lectionary this order is reversed, evidently to fit the liturgical situation. The boy with the unclean spirit (Mark 9:14–29) is also out of order relative to the calming of the storm (Mark 4:35–41) and the Gerasene demoniac (Mark 5: 1–20). Thus it is safer to conclude that the arrangement we find in the lectionary fragments, incomplete and enigmatic though it is, was shaped by liturgical requirements, not in order to parallel the arrangement of a lost apocryphal gospel. As a general rule it is easier to find examples of biblical pericopes being rearranged to fit a liturgical calendar than cases where a liturgical season was shaped by the contents of a biblical book read by *lectio continua* — though either is possible. With this particular lectionary, had Talley not proposed his theory, we would never suspect that the readings were selected and arranged to follow the order of an older, noncanonical gospel.

Finally, if the fragments do show us the beginning of a Lent that started on Epiphany, they cast doubt on another part of Talley's theory. If the structure of Lent at Constantinople was developed in imitation of Lent at Alexandria, why was the Cana story (not to mention the temptation, the storm and the Gerasene demoniac) omitted when "the Alexandrian Markan cursus" was allegedly "reconstituted" at Constantinople?

Table 4.3. A Partial Hypothetical Plan for the Secret Gospel, Based on Marcan Parallels to British Library Oriental MS 4717 (5) A (see Table 4.2)

---

1. The temptation (Mark 1:12–13?)
2. The baptism (Mark 1:9–11)
3. The wedding at Cana (a lost episode paralleling John 2:1–12)
[gap]
4. The boy with the unclean spirit (Mark 9:14–29)
5. The calming of the storm (Mark 4:35–41)
6. The Gerasene demoniac (Mark 5:1–20)
[gap]
7. The raising of the young man (Secret Gospel story 1)
8. The rejection of three women (Secret Gospel story 2)

THE BAPTISM OF THE APOSTLES

There could be a very simple explanation for the medieval Egyptian belief that Jesus baptized his disciples on the sixth day of the sixth week: it could be after-the-fact speculation, which emerged in the Middle Ages to explain the custom of baptizing on that particular day, long after the true origin of the practice had been forgotten. One finds such things all the time in liturgical history—witness the myriad explanations of why we celebrate the birth of Jesus on December 25 while shepherds watched their flocks by night in the snow.[40] Retrospective explanations are among the most frequent products of the ritual criticism process. There is no reason to assume, as Coquin and Talley apparently did, that there must first have been a tradition about when Jesus baptized, which subsequently dictated the liturgical date. Indeed the opposite is easier to believe: that the tradition was created to explain the practice.

But if a more complex explanation were required, it should be sought in the many patristic discussions of when and how the apostles were baptized, or why they didn't need to be. There was, in fact, a wide range of opinions on this question in early Christian times, but the one ascribed to Clement of Alexandria is particularly unhelpful here: in his lost *Hypotyposeis,* Clement apparently stated that Jesus baptized only Peter. Peter baptized Andrew, Andrew baptized James and John, James and John baptized the others, with slight variations in certain sources.[41] It is not so easy to square this with an annual day commemorating the baptism of all the disciples, and Clement's opinion certainly fails to suggest that he associated the baptism of the apostles with a Lazarus-like story (secret or not) of Jesus raising an unnamed disciple from the dead.

LENT AT ALEXANDRIA

Coquin did not adduce any explicit testimony about the timing of baptisms during the earliest period, when the forty-day fast allegedly still began after Epiphany. Were people baptized on Epiphany itself, the day Jesus' baptism was commemorated (January 6, Coptic Tybi 11)? Or at the Cana commemoration the next day? All through the forty-day period? Or on the fortieth day, February 15 or 16? The only reason Coquin offered for thinking that early Egyptians baptized on the fortieth day after Epiphany was the medieval Coptic practice of baptizing on Friday in the sixth week of Lent.[42] If, therefore, the Secret Gospel reference to "after six days" has anything to do with baptizing on a Friday, then this gospel could not have been written in the second century, when presumably the fortieth day was still fixed on February 15 or 16.

A more fundamental problem is that Egyptian sources document several different ways of structuring Lent, which do not necessarily conform to the Byzantine pattern of a forty-day fast clearly distinguished from a six-day fast. In the Festal Letters of Athanasius, in fact, Lent has only six weeks altogether, with Passion Week (equivalent to Western Holy Week) as the sixth week.[43] We find the same arrangement in the Paschal Homilies of Cyril of Alexandria,[44] to which neither Coquin nor Talley referred. In such a Lent, if baptisms were celebrated at the end of the sixth week (which we don't know), that would have been on Friday or Saturday in Passion Week, one or two days before Easter. Camplani, however, believes that throughout the fourth century there were baptisms on the Saturday night leading to Easter Sunday morning.[45]

After the sixth century, apparently,[46] the six-week Egyptian Lent began to be overtaken by a Lent of eight weeks, with baptisms held at the end of the sixth week, and Palm Sunday on the seventh Sunday. It is possible, then, that the sixth-week baptisms date only from this period, that they are not a vestige of a pre-Athanasian post-Epiphany fast, but of a post-Nicene six-week Lent. On the other hand, a Coptic hagiographical writing says that, during the episcopacy of St. Peter the Martyr (died 310), baptisms took place on Friday in the fourth week of Lent,[47] a timing not accounted for by any of the theories we have seen.

ALEXANDRIAN LECTIONARY TRADITIONS

If the Secret Gospel was ever read in the church of Alexandria, and if it was established enough to help shape the lectionary of Constantinople, then it should have left traces in the most obvious place: the earliest surviving lectionaries from Egypt itself. Neither Coquin nor Talley made use of lectionary evidence, however,[48] and their reluctance is understandable. The early lectionaries of Upper and Lower Egypt, and the presumably related lectionaries of the Coptic and Ethiopic Orthodox Churches, constitute one of the most uncharted wildernesses in all of liturgical studies — a desert that will require a lot more than forty days or even forty years to map out. Many sources that have been published have not been subjected to any comprehensive or comparative study, and so much remains unpublished that it will be a long time before it will be possible to write a comprehensive history of the Egyptian liturgical year and its readings — the annual lectionary (*Katameros*) and the special Passion Week lectionary[49] — utilizing all the extant sources in Greek, Coptic,[50] Ethiopic, Nubian, and Arabic.[51]

In spite of that, I can say that what has been published offers nothing to encourage the hope that traces of the Secret Gospel will eventually be found. The evidence consistently points the other way. First, it does not seem to be true, as Talley supposed, that Egyptian Christians felt a special preference or reverence for the gospel of Mark. Clement himself quoted it less often than any of the other gospels and in general preferred Matthew.[52] John is preserved in more papyri and more dialects of Coptic than any other gospel.[53] Second, Egyptian sources are much less likely to call for course reading of Mark or any other gospel than the lectionary of Constantinople, which specialized in the *lectio continua* approach. Lectionaries from Egypt are more likely to pick and choose, even supplying multiple readings from different gospels on the same day.[54]

Marcan readings are particularly scarce in the baptismal season around the sixth week of Lent. Instead, we tend to find longer or shorter sequences of pericopes from the gospel of John, which often seem to be selected for their baptismal significance. Thus in one sixth-century Greek papyrus, which evidently presumes the eight-week Lent, the Saturday and Sunday gospels are drawn from Matthew (not Mark) up through the fifth Sunday (Table 4.4). On the sixth Saturday we find Jesus' conversation with Nicodemus (John 3, with John 6:47ff given as an alternate), followed the next day (the sixth Sunday) by the story of the paralytic who was healed by washing in the pool at Bethesda (John 5). There the text breaks off, however.[55]

In what may be the oldest intact Coptic lectionary, a parchment codex in the Morgan Library dated between 822 and 914 CE, Epiphany is marked with Matthew's — not Mark's — account of Jesus' baptism, while Lent draws upon all three synoptic gospels until the sixth Sunday — expressly marked as a baptismal day — where once again we find John 3:1–15 (Table 4.5, left column). The raising of Lazarus does not occur at all in this manuscript.[56] It is still the practice to read the Nicodemus pericope on the sixth Sunday of Lent (known as Nicodemus Day) in the Ethiopian Orthodox Church, which often seems to be more conservative in preserving archaic Alexandrian traditions.[57] Egyptian

Table 4.4. Egyptian Lenten Gospels in a Sixth-Century Greek Papyrus

---

Saturday [before Lent]
    Matthew 6:19 ("Do not store up treasures . . .")
Second Sunday [of the pre-Lent season] *when about to begin Lent*
    Matthew 4:1 (the temptation)
Saturday in the first week of Lent
    Matthew 7:7 ("Ask and it will be given . . .")
First Sunday in Lent
    Matthew 13:1 (parable of the sower)
Saturday in the second week of Lent
    Matthew 18:18 ("What you bind on earth . . .")
Second Sunday in Lent
    Matthew 24:3 (the end times)
[gap]
[Saturday in the fifth week of Lent]
    Matthew 24:45 (the faithful steward)
Fifth Sunday in Lent
    Matthew 11:25 (the Father and the Son)
Saturday [in the sixth week of Lent]
    John 3:1 (Nicodemus) or John 6:47 (bread of life)
[Sixth] *Sunday* [in Lent]
    John 5:1 (the paralytic at Bethesda)

Note: Only the incipit of each pericope is given in the papyrus.

Source: British Museum papyrus 455 + 1849, as published in H. J. M. Milne, "Early Psalms and Lections for Lent," *The Journal of Egyptian Archaeology* 10 (1924): 278–82, see pp. 280–82.

lectionaries for the non-Eucharistic weekday offices tend to feature John 3 on Friday morning of the sixth week in Lent, as if in preparation for baptisms that day.[58] Egyptian and Ethiopic lectionary evidence, then, seems to be consistent with other testimony which shows that, in traditions stemming from Alexandria, "The dialogue of Jesus Christ with Nicodemus is the foundation stone of baptismal theology,"[59] not the raising of Lazarus or an unnamed disciple. The only source I know in which Lazarus is assigned to Friday in the sixth week of Lent is the lectionary of the East Syrian rite, which is centered in Iraq.[60] This could be attributable to coincidence, since the East Syrian lectionary otherwise exhibits few relationships with the Byzantine, Latin, or Coptic traditions.

On the other hand, an incomplete paper roll of the tenth century or later,[61] which preserves a tradition similar to the Morgan lectionary, does include the

Table 4.5. Lenten Sunday Gospels in Two Coptic Lectionaries

New York, Morgan Library MS M573	Cairo, Coptic Museum J42572
Sunday of the "Binding In" [of the Lenten Fast] Matthew 4:1–11 (temptation in the desert) *First Sunday* Matthew 5:48–6:6 (almsgiving and prayer) *Second Sunday* Luke 4:1–13 (temptation in the desert) *Third Sunday* Matthew 19:1–12 (divorce)	
Fourth Sunday John 7:14–24 (Jesus teaches in the Temple)	[The fragment begins on a Sunday] John 7:14–
Fifth Sunday Luke 16:19–31 (the rich man and Lazarus)	
Sunday of Baptizing John 3:1–15 (Nicodemus)	[The next Sunday] John 3:1–
Sunday of Zion [= Palm Sunday] John 12:12–19 (entry into Jerusalem)	[Sunday of Zion] John 11:1– (Lazarus) Matthew 26:30– (Peter's denial)
Saturday before the "Release" Matthew 27:57–66 (burial and guard)	*Night of the Sabbath* (= early morning) Matthew 27:62– (guard at tomb)
Sunday of the "Release" [from the fast] John 20:1–18 (Mary comes to tomb)	*Resurrection* John 20:1–

Sources: New York: Morgan Library MS M573: Leo Depuydt, *Catalogue of Coptic Manuscripts in the Pierpont Morgan Library*, Corpus of Illuminated Manuscripts 4, Oriental Series 1 (Leuven: Peeters, 1993), 74–78. Cairo: Coptic Museum J42572: J. Drescher, "A Coptic Lectionary Fragment," *Annales du Service des Antiquités de l'Égypte* 51 (1951): 247–56, and plates I–IV, see pp. 252–55. Only the incipits are given in this source.

Lazarus story on "Zion" Sunday, along with Matthew's story of how Peter denied knowing Jesus. This is the Sunday before Easter, and though the name "Zion" implies the Palm Sunday story (cf. Matthew 21:5), there is no explicit provision for reading the Palm Sunday event in the paper scroll, as there is in the Morgan lectionary (Table 4.5, right column). Since the paper scroll gives only the incipit, it is possible that one read from the beginning of the Lazarus story (John 11:1) all the way through to the end of the Palm Sunday story (12:19), thus incorporating all of the Zion Sunday reading found in the Mor-

Table 4.6. Lenten Gospels for the Eucharistic Liturgy of the Coptic Orthodox Church, from th Lectionary (Katameros)

Preparatory Saturday	(repentance)	*Preparatory Sunday*	(Lord's prayer, fasting)
Luke 13:1–5		Matthew 6:1–18	
First Saturday	(love your neighbor)	*First Sunday*	(trust in providence)
Matthew 5:38–48		Matthew 6:19–33	
Second Saturday	(narrow gate)	*Second Sunday*	(temptation in the desert
Matthew 7:13–21		Matthew 4:1–11	
Third Saturday	(unforgiving servant)	*Third Sunday*	(prodigal son)
Matthew 18:23–35		Luke 15:11–32	
Fourth Saturday	(wicked tenants)	*Fourth Sunday*	(Samaritan woman)
Matthew 21:33–46		John 4:1–42	
Fifth Saturday	(woe to Pharisees)	*Fifth Sunday*	(paralytic at Bethesda)
Matthew 23:13–39		John 5:1–18	
Sixth Saturday	(blind man of Jericho)	*Sixth Sunday*	(man born blind)
Mark 10:46–52		John 9:1–41	
Seventh Saturday	(Lazarus)	*Seventh* [Palm] *Sunday*	(triumphal entry)
John 11:1–45		John 12:12–19;	
		Matthew 21:1–17;	
		Mark 11:1–11;	
		Luke 19:29–48	

Sources: Paul de Lagarde, "Die koptischen handschriften der goettinger bibliothek" [capitalization *sic*] *Abhandlungen der historisch-philosophischen Classe der königlichen Gesellschaft der Wissenschaften z Göttingen* 24 (Göttingen: Dieter, 1879), 39–43, 13–16, 6–7. See also "The Coptic Lectionary" at *http:/ www.bombaxo.com/coptic.html*.

gan lectionary (John 12:12–19). But there is no way to confirm this. It would be hard to argue a baptismal interpretation, in any case, for the Nicodemus story (John 3) is assigned to the preceding Sunday, presumably the sixth Sunday in Lent, marked "Sunday of Baptizing" in the Morgan lectionary.

THE GOSPEL OF JOHN

At some point in the Middle Ages, the second half of Lent in Egypt came to feature a series of readings from the gospel of John that is still in use today (Table 4.6). Not a strict *lectio continua*, it featured episodes that seem particularly pregnant with baptismal significance: the Samaritan woman and the living water (John 4) on the fourth Sunday, the paralytic at the pool of Bethesda (John 5) on the fifth Sunday, the blind man who regained his sight by washing in a pool (John 9) on the sixth. The raising of Lazarus (John 11) occurs on the seventh Saturday (in manuscripts that include Saturday readings), followed by the seventh Sunday, Palm Sunday, with either the Johannine account (John 12) or all four gospels of the triumphal entry.[62] Similar series, with some variations, were used on Lenten Sundays in the early Latin churches, where the gospel

Table 4.7. Lenten Sunday Gospels and Communion Antiphons in the Major Non-Roman Latin Traditions

	Benevento	Milan	Toledo
Sunday before Lent			
Gospel	Matthew 4:1–11	Matthew 4:1–11	Matthew 4:1–11
Communion	Psalm 90:4–5 [91:4] cf. Matthew 4:6		
First Sunday			
Gospel	John 4:5–42	John 4:5–42	John 4:5–42
Communion	John 4:14	John 4:14–15	
Second Sunday			
Gospel	John 8:12–59	John 8:31–59	John 9:1–38
Communion		John 8:31–32	
Third Sunday			
Gospel	John 9:1–38	John 9:1–38	John 7:14–30
Communion	John 9:6, 11, 15, 38	John 9:6, 11, 15, 38	
Fourth Sunday			
Gospel	John 11:1–54	John 11:1–45	John 11:1–52
Communion	John 11:33, 35, 43, 44, 39	John 11:23–24	
Palm Sunday			
Gospel	(Passion according to Matthew)	John 11:55–12:11	John 11:55–12:13
Communion			

Note: At Milan and Toledo, Lent began on a Monday, as it does throughout the Christian East. The preceding day was what is here called "Sunday before Lent," though it was actually called *Dominica in Capite Quadragesimae* at Milan and *In Carnes Tollendas* at Toledo. The Beneventan tradition survives within the context of an adaptation to the Roman rite, in which Lent begins the preceding Wednesday. Thus what is the Sunday just *before* Lent at Milan and Toledo is the first Sunday *in* Lent at Rome and in the Romanized sources we have for the Beneventan tradition. In the sixteenth century, Milan adopted a more Roman-like numbering: even though Lenten fasting continued to begin on Monday, the Sunday just before Lent came to be numbered as the first Sunday *in* Lent. This is the numbering that will be found in sources dating from after the change.

Sources: Benevento: [René Hesbert], "La tradition bénéventaine dans la tradition manuscrite," *Paléographie musicale: Les principaux manuscrits de chant grégorien, ambrosien, mozarabe, gallican, publiés en fac-similés phototypiques*, ed. Joseph Gajard 14 (Tournai: Desclée & Cie, 1931), 60–465, see pp. 220–21, 225–34. *Paléographie musicale* 20: *Le missel de Bénévent VI-33*, ed. Jacques Hourlier and Jacques Froger (Berne and Frankfurt: Peter Lang, 1983) 30r–53v.

Milan: *Missale Ambrosianum Duplex (Proprium de Tempore) Editt. Puteobonellianae et Typicae (1751–1902) cum critico commentario continuo ex manuscriptis schedis Ant. M. Ceriani*, ed. A. Ratti and M. Magistretti (Milan: R. Ghirlanda, 1913), 124–205. Marco Magistretti, ed., *Manuale Ambrosianum ex Codice saec. XI olim in usum Canonicae Vallis Travaliae* 2, Monumenta Veteris Liturgiae Ambrosianae 3 Milan: Hoepli, 1904; repr. Nendeln, Lichtenstein: Kraus Reprint, 1971), 125–61. *Paléographie musicale 6: Antiphonarium Ambrosianum du Musée britannique (XIIe siècle) Codex Additional 34209 transcription*, ed. Charles Mégret,] (Solesmes: Imprimerie Saint-Pierre, 1900), 197–249.

Toledo: Justo Pérez de Urbel and Atilano González y Ruiz-Zorrilla, eds., *Liber Commicus: Edición crítica*, 2 vols., Monumenta Hispaniae Sacra, Serie Liturgica 2–3 (Madrid: Consejo Superior de Investigaciones Científicas, 1950, 1955), 1: 79–319. José Janini, ed., *Liber Misticus de Cuaresma y Pascua (Cod. Toledo, Bibl. Capit. 35.5)*, Serie Liturgica: Fuentes 2 (Toledo: Instituto de Estudios Visigótico-Mozárabes, 1980), 135–38.

Table 4.8. Lenten Gospel-Communion Pairs in the Roman Missal

Day in Lent	Stational Church	Gospel	Communion Antiphon
Sunday 1	John Lateran	Matthew 4:1–11 (temptation in the desert)	Psalm 90:4–5 [91:4] cf. Matthew 4:6
Saturday after Sunday 2	Marcellinus and Peter	Luke 15:12–32 (prodigal son)	Luke 15:32
Friday after Sunday 3	Lawrence in Lucina	John 4:5–42 (Samaritan woman)	John 4:14
Saturday after Sunday 3	Susanna	John 8:1–11 (adulterous woman)	John 8:11
Wednesday after Sunday 4	Paul outside Walls	John 9:1–38 (man born blind)	John 9:6, 11, 15, 38
Friday after Sunday 4	Eusebius	John 11:1–45 (Lazarus)	John 11:33, 35, 43–44, 39

Source: Any manuscript or edition of the *Missale Romanum* through 1962. See also Michel Huglo, *Le tonaires: Inventaire, analyse, comparaison,* Publications de la Société Française de Musicologie, 3rd ser., vol 2 (Paris: Société Française de Musicologie; Heugel et Cie, 1971), 152–54, 171.

pericopes were sometimes paired with communion antiphons (Table 4.7). The Roman form of this series was pushed to weekdays in an early medieval reorganization of the Roman stational calendar (Table 4.8),[63] but some of them (the Samaritan woman, the blind man, and Lazarus) were restored to Sundays in year A of the three-year Roman Catholic lectionary published after Vatican II.[64]

Comparing the early Latin Johannine series with the medieval Egyptian one yields an interesting fact: whereas all the Latin series ended with Lazarus on the Sunday before Palm Sunday, the standard Egyptian series does not include Lazarus on Sunday at all, but only on the Saturday preceding Palm Sunday, where it remains distinct from the baptismal sixth week.[65] This positioning could be attributed to the influence of Jerusalem or Constantinople on Egypt, rather than the other way round. A few Slavonic lectionaries, in fact, include the Samaritan woman and the blind man during Lent,[66] suggesting that there may once have been a Lenten Johannine series at Constantinople too.

LAZARUS AND BAPTISM

Attempting to account for the various positions of John 11 should force us to ask some questions: Was the Lazarus story interpreted as having baptismal significance? When and where did this begin? Not in the gospel itself, according to Raymond Brown: "We can see how Lazarus' return to life might be connected in Christian thought with rebirth by baptism, especially in the light of Paul's theology (Col. 2:12), but the Evangelist, who knew both ideas, makes no attempt to connect them."[67] Oscar Cullmann's book *Early Christian Worship* was structured around a list of Johannine pericopes similar to the Latin and Egyptian series, illustrating Cullmann's opinion that "the Gospel of John regards it as one of its chief concerns to set forth the connexion between the contemporary Christian worship and the historical life of Jesus."[68] Yet Cullmann excluded the Lazarus story from his sequence. A mid-twentieth-century forger who followed Cullmann, therefore, would, willy nilly, have produced a result that looks more like the traditional Egyptian Sunday lectionary than the Secret Gospel does!

Thus it can hardly be taken for granted that, if a Lazarus-like story circulated in a second-century recension of Mark's gospel, it would have been intended or understood to symbolize baptism. Baptismal symbolism is absent even from Chrysostom's fourth-century sermon on Lazarus, even though we would not be surprised to learn that his lectionary placed the reading in its familiar Constantinopolitan position.[69] The apparent connection between the young man of the Secret Gospel and the initiation rites in the letter of "Clement" seems more out of place in the second century the harder we look at it.

ALEXANDRIAN INFLUENCE ON CONSTANTINOPLE?

Finally, there is really no reason (apart from the Secret Gospel) to think that Constantinople derived its Marcan course reading from Alexandria. The history of Lent at Constantinople is in fact very complicated, for it involved the conflation of multiple traditions, not the wholesale importation or imitation of a lectionary from elsewhere. New Testament text critics observed long ago, for instance, that the Saturday readings frequently have different textual affinities from the Sunday readings,[70] suggesting two originally independent series rather than a simple *lectio continua*.

The Byzantine-rite liturgical book for Lent, known as the Triōdion from the kind of three-ode kanon hymns it features, includes an old stratum of hymnody that depended on a course reading of Luke, which seems to have originated in Palestine or Jerusalem.[71] Hymns related to the Marcan series that is standard for Constantinople (Table 4.1, right column) are superimposed on top of the older Lukan layer. A recent study of the Triōdion considers Talley's theory but concludes that "without any reasonable indication that these Markan pericopes were ever used in Alexandria itself, it seems futile to consider them an importation from Alexandria to Constantinople."[72]

Résumé of the Liturgical Evidence

In short, there is no period in the history of the early Christian liturgy where the Secret Gospel could plausibly fit. Its account of a young man coming to faith in Jesus lacks all the themes that are prominent in the earliest Christian baptismal exegesis, particularly in Egypt. The claims in the Mar Saba letter that it was read at initiation services cannot be reconciled with the fact that early Egyptian lectionaries favored John, not Mark, in baptismal contexts, and particularly emphasized the dialogue of Jesus with Nicodemus rather than the raising of Lazarus. Without the Mar Saba letter, one would never suspect that an apocryphal story of Jesus raising a youth from the dead ever had any role in forming early Egyptian baptismal theology or practice, or the structure of Lent at Alexandria. Nor can the Lenten prominence of the Lazarus story in Constantinople, the East Syrian rite, and the Latin West be explained as due to the influence of the Egyptian liturgy. Only in twentieth-century reconstructions of the early liturgy does the Secret Gospel appear to make sense.

What all this means is that, from a liturgical perspective, the Secret Gospel, with its alleged initiation ceremonies, looks like a fish out of water. It doesn't fit in second-century Alexandria. It doesn't fit at any known point in the history of the Egyptian lectionary. It doesn't explain the lectionary system of Constantinople. It doesn't fit anywhere in the early church. The one place where it appears to make sense is as a kind of spin-off from the Book of Common Prayer, in "the early church" as it was imagined by Anglican divines in the middle of the twentieth century. Even if the liturgiology of the Mar Saba document applies only to the fourth of its five streams of tradition, then, it is to relatively modern times that that stream leads us. The time has come to look at some of the other streams.

Summary

In this chapter I take up the claim that the Secret Gospel was once read in secret initiation rites in the church of Alexandria. It has been proposed that Lent in Egypt once began at Epiphany and that the Secret Gospel would have been read throughout the forty days of such a Lent. But it turns out that the Secret Gospel does not fit either the Alexandrian pattern for Epiphany celebrations, nor Egyptian or Ethiopian evidence for the calendar of readings during Lent. The evidence shows, instead, that John's gospel was considered more important in Egypt than Mark's. The conversation between Jesus and Nicodemus in John 3 was the most basic text for Lenten baptismal theology, not the raising of Lazarus or any similar story. Even if we assume that the letter ascribed to Clement was actually written a few centuries after his time, it cannot be made to fit at any point in the history of the Alexandrian liturgy.

5

A Gospel in Fragments

*We often understand texts without knowing their backgrounds. In fact, texts
of which we know the backgrounds are exceptions. How many readers of our
newspapers and journals know the backgrounds of the articles? . . . We can
never fully know the mind of any writer, ancient or modern. Moreover, we
necessarily understand everything we read by relating it to our own experiences and ideas, not to the writer's.* — *Morton Smith*

Scattered Indications

The more enmeshed we get in the complexities of early liturgical history,
the harder it is to believe that we will eventually find traces of the Secret
Gospel. Fortunately, we do not need to — close examination of the Mar Saba
text reveals a simpler explanation of its strange features: it is in fact a cento of
words and phrases from the canonical gospels and other ancient writings,
carefully structured to create the impression that Jesus practiced homosexuality. For the moment we will postpone the question of when this was done
and concentrate instead on exploring how it was done.

Almost as soon as the Secret Gospel was published, some New Testament
scholars began pointing out that it looks as if it had been constructed by
"secondary borrowing" from the canonical gospels. It "seems to represent an
amalgam of Synoptic details," which "has also brought together scattered

memories gleaned from the Fourth Gospel, memories which the author retold in largely Marcan language." "In any hypothesis a remarkable knowledge of individual Gospel style(s) has to be attributed to the author" of the Secret Gospel.[1]

But these "Synoptic details" were not merely patched together at random. The clever amalgamator, whoever he was and whenever he lived, had a specific motive, for he repeatedly made choices that are suggestive of homosexuality. The visit to the youth's house, "for he was rich," recalls another rich young man whom Jesus loved (Mark 10:21; Luke 18:23). The "linen cloth over [his] naked [body]" recalls the young man of Mark 14:51–52 whose covering was torn off him by the crowd that was arresting Jesus, so that he ran away naked. In fact, by slightly shifting the translation of a single word, we can read the entire story as an account of Jesus rejecting a woman in order to help an anguished young man "come out of the closet" for his first (homo)sexual experience.

> And they come into Bethany, and a certain woman, whose brother had died, was there. And, coming, she *bent down to kiss* [*prosekynēse;* italics added] Jesus and says to him, "Son of David, have mercy on me." But the disciples rebuked her. And Jesus, being angered, went off with her into the garden where the tomb was, and straightway a great cry was heard from the tomb. And going near Jesus rolled away the stone from the door of the tomb. And straightway, going in where the youth was, he stretched forth his hand and raised him, seizing his hand. But the youth, looking upon him, loved him and began to beseech him that he might be with him. And going out of the tomb they came into the house of the youth, for he was rich.

The word *prosekynēse* (προσεκύνησε) in Smith's published translation was rendered as "she prostrated herself before" Jesus, as if in an attitude of worship. But in the mid-twentieth century it was thought that the word was related etymologically to the notion of kissing, as one might kiss an idol.[2] Retranslating this one word as "bent down to kiss" has the advantage of making a coherent narrative out of what had been a sequence of perplexing events: why did the disciples rebuke the woman, why and at whom was Jesus angry, and why was there a cry from the tomb before the youth had been restored to life? All these details make sense if they show Jesus rejecting a woman's sexual advance in favor of freeing a young man — in a gospel which (according to Smith) preserves evidence that Jesus practiced a sexual or quasi-sexual initiation rite. The sharpened plotline, in turn, raises the question of whether the unknown author might, in fact, have been someone who learned Greek in the twentieth century, when the word for ritual prostration was thought to be etymologically related to the word for "kiss." In effect, my retranslation proposes that this word be read as a humorous double entendre.

Ehrman has already noted the presence of what he called "interesting, even amusing, aspects" of the Mar Saba text. Once we allow the possibility that there are amusing elements that make sense from the perspective of a twentieth-century reader, we begin to notice more of them. For example, the anger of Jesus and the rebukes of the disciples would be particularly understandable if the Secret Evangelist was an English-speaker who wanted to imply that, while "coming, she bent down to kiss Jesus," the woman was "coming" in the slang English sense — that is, "experiencing sexual orgasm."[3] The quote "And after six days," from canonical Mark 9:2, could suggest a transfiguration of sorts: arriving in the dark of night, minimally clothed, the young man finds out who Jesus really is.

The entire story, in fact, begins to look like another extended double entendre — a popular kind of joke among literate North American males of the twentieth century.[4] But it is in the nature of such jokes that the teller can deny that the sexual elements were really intended: "blaming" the audience for detecting them is part of the humor. The ambiguity is present in this case too. Was the Secret Evangelist a twentieth-century American bent on teasing us? Or am I, a product of mid-twentieth-century American schoolyard culture, misreading an ancient text through prurient eyes? Unfortunately (or not), this question — like Smith's calamitous mood swings — will haunt us for the rest of this book.

HANDS

One indication that the author intended to be suggestive is the suspicious statement that Jesus "stretched forth his hand and raised him, seizing his hand." The pointless duplication of hands is a sure sign that something's afoot. Galatians 2:9 could be cited to propose that clasping hands was a liturgical gesture in early Christian initiation, but there is little if any corroboration for this. AT (21.9) says that "the presbyter grasps each one of those who will receive baptism"[5] but does not specify the hand.

There are inconclusive hints that Gnostic baptismal rites may have involved a liturgical handshake. In the Mandaean sect in Iraq, the only modern group that practices a religion resembling ancient Gnosticism,[6] the priest clasps the hand of the neophyte in a gesture known as *kušta* or "'truth' . . . a demonstration of upright disposition, viz. a symbol of the [neophyte's] union with the world of light."[7] This encouraged Eric Segelberg[8] to see a Gnostic ritual gesture in the Gospel of Truth (30:17–23), where it says: "And the swift Spirit (*pneuma*) followed him up after He (had) caused him to wake up. Having given hand to him who was stretched out on the ground, he set him on his feet, though he had not yet risen up."[9] But the Gospel of Truth could be speaking metaphorically; one commentator would trace the imagery to the creation of Adam rather than to a baptismal rite.[10] To argue that it was describing a ritual gesture, we need further evidence of ritual handclasps in the type of Valentinian Gnosticism that the Gospel of Truth represents. Yet there is no mention of hands in the baptismal texts preserved in the so-called Valentinian Exposition,[11] nor in the possibly Valentinian baptismal rite that seems to be implied in Clement's *Excerpta ex Theodoto*.[12] In the Mandaean kušta rite, the baptizees also kiss their own hands,[13] a detail for which Valentinian parallels are even harder to find. Finally, it is by no means clear what, if any, relationships the Mandaeans may have to ancient Valentinianism, or any other branch of ancient Gnosticism — an essential question if one would appeal to the Mandaean ritual handclasp as evidence for an ancient ritual gesture.[14]

The Manichaean Psalm Book poses a similar problem, for it contains lines like "Jesus my helper, give me thy right hand."[15] This may refer to a liturgical gesture, but to conclude that it must would be like insisting that twentieth-century North American Protestantism had a hand-grasping ritual on the basis of Thomas A. Dorsey's 1938 gospel hymn "Precious Lord, Take My Hand" and Gene MacLellan's 1971 pop hit "Put Your Hand in the Hand" (of the man who stilled the waters).[16] The situation is, therefore, much the same as with the resurrection symbolism and the linen cloth: if the Secret Gospel offered clear evidence of a liturgical handclasp in second-century Christian or Gnostic initiation rites, it would be unique.

Smith, in any case, explained the redundancy differently. Noting that the Marcan Jesus frequently grasped the hands of those he healed and raised from the dead,[17] Smith used this fact to support his view that the story of the young man dates from an early period in the formation of Mark's gospel. Anticipating the objection that the Secret Gospel is a tissue of excerpts from the canonical gospels, as I and others believe it is, Smith retorted that "deliberate compilation from the multiplicity of written texts is implausible. . . . It is hard to believe that any compiler would have produced the awkward repetition"[18] of the word "hand."

But compilers produce awkward results all the time. The explanation that makes the most sense is, once again, that this is yet another element from canonical Mark, repositioned to suggest homosexuality, perhaps humorously. It could do that in at least three ways. First, in ancient times (as today), holding hands could be a sign of love and even of marriage, though it also could signify other kinds of friendship.[19] Second, the word "hand" can also be taken as a euphemism for another, more intimate body part.[20] But there may be a more interesting explanation, for seizing an opponent's hands or wrists was one of the opening positions in ancient Greek wrestling matches, which (as every undergraduate used to know) were done *gymnos gymnō*, "naked [man] with naked [man]."[21] In that case the relationship between Jesus and a young disciple, so hard to place within the history of early Christian liturgy, would seem to evoke the atmosphere of the ancient Greek palaestra or wrestling school, where (as any ancient or modern reader of Plato would know) naked youths were trained by adult men through a unique combination of religious ritual (*Lysis* 204a–207d), unabashed voyeurism (*Theaetetus* 162b), and (of course) profound philosophical conversation (*Theaetetus* 169b–c), leading to the type of erotic mentor/protégé relationship that was known as *paiderastia* or "boy-love." As the aging Socrates once asked his beloved youth Alcibiades, "Now if the Athenians were deliberating with whom they should wrestle closely, and with whom by grasping hands, and how, would you or the boy-trainer (*paido-tribēs*) be a better advisor?" (*Alcibiades I,* 107e).[22] The answer, of course, is that one needs an expert teacher, as Alcibiades needs Socrates' training in philosophy.

It is not inconceivable that an ancient writer might have imagined Jesus as a kind of Socrates, who taught his disciples the true philosophy in the context of intimately loving relationships. It is certainly plausible that a modern forger, seeking for whatever reason to present a homosexual Jesus, would draw on the most obvious and best-known ancient model of homosexuality. In either case, the explanation that best accounts for the singular features of this part of the Secret Gospel is that the unknown author made skillful use of words and phrases from the familiar gospels to paint a very authentic-looking picture of Jesus as a homosexual. When we turn to the other preserved segment of the Secret Gospel we will find much the same thing—only this time the author appears to have drawn on extracanonical material as well.

THE WOMEN IN THE SECRET GOSPEL

Most research on the Secret Gospel has, understandably, focused on the story of Jesus and the young man. Less attention has been paid to the second and shorter excerpt, allegedly interpolated by Mark into his own gospel, after 10:46a: "And after the [words], 'And he comes into Jericho,' [the Secret Gospel] adds only, "And the sister of the youth whom Jesus loved and his mother and Salome were there, and Jesus did not receive them." Of the Carpocratian variants, Clement tells Theodore only that "the many other [things about] which you wrote both seem to be and are falsifications."

A Jesus who refuses to meet with women does not fit well with the Jesus of the canonical gospels, who clearly had female disciples and who was said to have been surprisingly willing to talk to women who were not among the disciples (John 4:27).[23] Nor does a Jesus who avoids women resemble Clement's own policy on initiation: "The Logos is equally the paedagogue of men and of women" because "the woman does not possess one nature and the man exhibit another, but the same."[24]

The significance of the second story, then, seems to lie in its relationship to the first: after Jesus' homoerotic nocturnal encounter with a naked, young, rich man, he refuses to meet some women who want to see him. And who are these women? "His mother," presumably the young man's mother (cf. Luke 7:11–15), and the sister who asked Jesus to raise him, recalling the sisters of Lazarus, whom Jesus loved (John 11:5). The third woman is Salome, who is named, in Mark's gospel only, as a witness to both the crucifixion and the empty tomb (Mark 15:40, 16:1). The name occurs in other ancient writings, though, in which Salome is Jesus' sister, or a midwife who was punished for doubting the virgin birth, or (most interestingly) a disciple: in the Gospel of Thomas, in Clement's citations of the Gospel of the Egyptians, and in Gnostic literature, Salome the disciple has conversations with Jesus on the popular Gnostic theme of transcending or eliminating gender differences.[25] Why, then, would the Jesus of the Secret Gospel refuse to receive her (and two other women)? In the Secret Gospel as we have it, there is no dominical saying to tell us what Jesus' rejection means—as if only Mark's unwritten hierophantic teaching could explain it.[26]

Smith hypothesized that Salome's name had become associated with Gnostic teachings, leading to her eventual exclusion from orthodox writings. He had already pointed out a reference in the polemicist Celsus to "the Harpocratians who follow Salome."[27] "Therefore the story, as it stands, can have been invented and preserved only as polemic against these women or their followers or persons who appealed to their authority."[28] But since the evidence in support of this was limited, "there must have been other early traditions about Salome to explain the later developments."[29]

More recent scholars, however, have refused to support the theory that Jesus is shown rejecting Gnosticism in the person of Salome. Silke Petersen found the whole idea "incomprehensible and problematic," even "implausible."[30] After reviewing the entire dossier of early Christian references to women named Salome, Richard Bauckham concluded:

> Smith assembles most, though not quite all, of the significant references to Salome, but closer study of these references shows his interpretation of the evidence to be seriously deficient. . . . [T]here is no evidence that Salome the disciple of Jesus was "a controversial figure," that orthodox writers denigrated

her or diminished her importance in a deliberate polemic against her role in Gnosticism, or that "there must have been other early traditions about Salome." . . . [T]here are no parallels elsewhere to this kind of denigration of the women disciples of Jesus for reasons of anti-Gnostic polemic. . . . Even the works of church order which refer to the women disciples of Jesus in the context of specifically prohibiting women from teaching (or baptizing) do not deny that Jesus and his male disciples were accompanied by women disciples.[31]

Bauckham's suggestion was to look more carefully into the possibility that the two passages from the Secret Gospel are somehow connected. If the purpose of the first interpolation is to give us additional information about the young man of Mark 14:51–52, the second one "ties the first interpolation more fully into the Gospel by suggesting further identifications between characters," connecting the young man to the three women of 15:40 and 16:1, who include Salome, and to the unnamed women of 14:3–9 and 3:31–35. For this explanation to work, the two passages of the Secret Gospel would have to be regarded as later interpolations to Mark (as Clement's letter says) — not survivals of an earlier, longer text (as Smith advocated[32]). Also, it would have to be the case that "Salome, the only one of the three women who is named, is the key to the redactor's intention."[33] But some questions would still remain unanswered: if the redactor's intention was simply to provide more information about characters in the gospel, why did these interpolations become focal points of controversy with the Carpocratians, and why was Clement so eager to keep the Alexandrian additions secret?

However, Smith hinted at another interpretation of Salome's role. In his Harvard book, he juxtaposed two apocryphal texts that mention her, in a way that suggests a sexual encounter between Salome and Jesus.[34] One of these is a certain Book of the Resurrection of Jesus Christ by Bartholomew the Apostle, in which nine women come to the tomb, including "Salome who tempted him."[35] As Bauckham pointed out, this probably does not refer to sexual temptation but can be explained as a later identification of Salome the witness to the empty tomb with Salome the midwife who tempted God by doubting Mary's postpartum virginity.[36] The other passage, in the Gospel of Thomas (61a), recounts an even more explicit temptation — if, that is, we follow Smith's translation from the Coptic: "Who [are you,] man, as from the one? [*sic*] You get into my bed." In a parenthetical wink, Smith added "The text has, understandably, been corrupted."

But the Thomas passage, too, is susceptible to other interpretations. It now seems clear, for instance, that the furniture in question is not a bed for the night, but a dining couch. Of course, sexual entertainments did take place at ancient banquets, as Xenophon's *Symposium* tells;[37] literary and pictorial evidence show people having many kinds of sex on dining couches.[38] Thus Clement, citing Sirach 9:9, would limit the presence of married women at banquets and forbid unmarried women altogether, particularly when the men are drinking.[39]

In a recent article, therefore, Kathleen Corley suggests once again that sexual concerns may have contributed to textual corruption in this part of the Gospel of Thomas. But her interpretation of the original would not necessarily imply any particular sexual tension between Salome and Jesus. She sees the text as reflecting concerns about the participation of women in a community that valued hospitality to itinerant preachers, and would translate along the lines of "Who are you, mister? You have climbed onto my [dining] couch and have eaten from my table like a stranger" or "a guest."[40] It is possible to imagine this being spoken by a woman who is pulling away, trying to maintain boundaries of propriety — or by one who is simply surprised at an unexpected intrusion with no particularly sexual implications. On this one ambiguous passage, then, rests the entire case for an ancient tradition that Salome sought sexual intimacy with Jesus.

If we entertain Smith's suggestions, however, the two preserved excerpts of the Secret Gospel complement each other in a way that makes sense: in one, Jesus meets at night with a young man who loves him; in the other he refuses to meet with Salome, a woman who wants him. Indeed, he refuses to meet with three women of different generations, as if rejecting womankind in general. The reason for the rejection may be clear enough from the fact that one of the women is "the sister of the youth whom Jesus loved" — this Jesus was the sort who loved (male) youths, not women. In his popular book, Smith strengthened this interpretation by proposing that "the story was going to tell of a conversation between Jesus and Salome," but Clement himself personally excised it to suppress the traditions "that she tempted Jesus (how, is not told)" and "that she inquired about his getting onto her bed."[41]

There is one further item of interest: the woman that Jesus rejected in the first excerpt, the sister of the young man, whose "coming" to Jesus made him angry, is also Salome, according to Smith. The Secret Gospel's narrative of the young man's sister shares wording with Matthew's stories of the Syrophoenician woman (15:22–25) and the mother of the sons of Zebedee (20:20), who came to Jesus with requests of their own. Apparently it was from these stories that the Secret Evangelist copied the details of a woman bending down before Jesus and saying "Son of David, have mercy on me!"

Smith, however, characteristically argued that the dependence went the other way: a whole chain of resemblances "fit together and suggest that Matthew knew the longer text of M[ar]k,"[42] that is, the Secret Gospel. In either case it is interesting, then, that the mother of the sons of Zebedee returns at the end of Matthew's gospel, where she "replaces Salome in M[a]tthew's parallel to M[ar]k's list of the women who witnessed the crucifixion" (Matthew 27:56, Mark 15:40). It is beginning to look as if Bauckham was righter than he realized, and Salome is indeed "the key to the redactor's intention."

RARE WORDS

If the first excerpt from the Secret Gospel demonstrates the Secret Redactor's technique of reassembling tiny excerpts from the other gospels to create a picture of a homosexual Jesus, and if the second excerpt is a mosaic from the gospels and other early Christian traditions portraying a Jesus who rejected women, it is interesting to note that the Mar Saba letter that preserves these gospel fragments seems to have been constructed using a very similar technique of centonization. As A. H. Criddle notes, "the author of the letter, in imitating the style of Clement, sought to use words found in Clement but not in other Patristic writers and to avoid words not found in Clement but present in other Patristic writers. In doing so the writer brought together more rare words and phrases scattered throughout the authentic works of Clement than are compatible with genuine Clementine authorship."[43] The high concentration of rare Clementine words and phrases seems designed to bring out two contrasting themes: the mysterious initiation rites of Clement's church, and the immorality of the Carpocratians. It is almost as if both the Secret Gospel and its cover letter were written by the same highly ingenious person, working in three concentric circles: the story of the young man reuses wording from the canonical gospels, the story of the women combines gospel elements with bits of noncanonical texts, and the letter selects vocabulary peculiar to Clement. But the process doesn't stop there. Smith's controversial interpretation of the Secret Gospel, when analyzed in detail, looks like a fourth circle, a pastiche of elements picked from a wide range of ancient sources that, once again, seems designed to show that Jesus was a homosexual.

More Scattered Indications

In my extensive efforts to locate the Secret Gospel anywhere in the history of early Christian liturgy, I have had little to say about Smith's own hypothesis. That is because his theory about the origins of the Christian initiation ritual is so far-fetched that it hardly intersects at all with the relevant primary sources. Indeed, Smith seems to have read very little of the liturgical scholarship available in his time. Apart from Dix's translation of AT, I have found no citations in Smith's writings of liturgiologists like Dix or Shepherd, though he could hardly have escaped their secondhand influence while he was training and working as an Episcopal priest. Lack of familiarity with liturgical scholarship probably rendered Smith more, not less, susceptible to the conventional attitudes and preconceptions that circulated in his milieu, such as the "common knowledge" that baptism was originally administered during a night vigil, with white garments and Pauline resurrection typology. In the decades since Smith published his fanciful reconstruction of early Christian initiation, liturgical researchers have returned the compliment by ignoring what he had to say. Now is the time to take a serious look at it:

> Through the preceding studies of the relations of Jesus' work to that of [John] the Baptist and of Paul, we have arrived at a definition of "the mystery of the kingdom of God": It was a baptism administered by Jesus to chosen disciples, singly, and by night. In this baptism the disciple was united with Jesus. The union may have been physical (. . . there is no telling how far symbolism went in Jesus' rite), but the essential thing was that the disciple was possessed by Jesus' spirit. One with Jesus, he participated in Jesus' ascent into the heavens; he entered the kingdom of God and was thereby set free from the laws ordained for and in the lower world.[44]

Even without the speculation that the union may have been "physical," this proposal has almost nothing in common with known early Christian initiatory practices or theologies.[45] Possession by Jesus' spirit, for example, is not typical liturgical language. Paul does use expressions like "the Spirit of Christ" (Romans 8:1, 9), "the Spirit of Jesus Christ" (Philippians 1:19), and "the Spirit of his Son" (Galatians 3:14, 4:6), but not with direct reference to baptism. Explicit New Testament references to initiation rites speak of the Holy Spirit, in a Trinitarian context (Matthew 28:19, Ephesians 1:12–14), and this is the kind of language taken up in early liturgical texts.[46]

Again, early Christian writers do not speak of baptism as an ascent to heaven — surprisingly, perhaps, since heavenly ascents were so common in the religions of antiquity as to be practically routine.[47] The notion that baptism sets one free from law sounds Pauline, but once again it is not a theme that occurs in early Christian descriptions of initiation rites. Certainly Paul did not distinguish between lower and higher standards of morality (Romans 6:15). Christian initiation practices in general were not said to derive their authority from initiations that Jesus himself conducted — in some quarters it was even denied that Jesus initiated anyone (cf. John 3:22, 26, 4:1–2).

And, of course, there is nothing at all to suggest one-on-one "physical" unions at any stage in the historical development of Christian initiation rites. The whole hypothesis looks more like Smith testing "how far symbolism" could go, alluding to a common American euphemism for a teenager's first sexual experience.[48] But the importance of this idea for Smith is shown by the fact that he himself took the symbolism significantly farther, in his other book on the Secret Gospel, the one intended for a popular audience. The parallel passage in that book is notably more explicit:

> Thus from the differences between Paul's baptism and that of the Baptist, and from the scattered indications in the canonical Gospels and the secret Gospel of Mark, we can put together a picture of Jesus' baptism, "the mystery of the kingdom of God." It was a water baptism administered by Jesus to chosen disciples, singly and by night. The costume, for the disciple, was a linen cloth worn over the naked body. This cloth was probably removed for the baptism proper, the immersion in water, which was now reduced to a preparatory purification. After that, by unknown ceremonies, the disciple was possessed by Jesus' spirit and so united with Jesus. One with him, he participated by hallucination in Jesus' ascent into the heavens, he entered the kingdom of God, and was thereby set free from the laws ordained for and in the lower world. Freedom from the law may have resulted in completion of the spiritual union by physical union. This certainly occurred in many forms of gnostic Christianity; how early it began there is no telling.[49]

Surely it is going too far to speak as if one knows what "certainly occurred" in Gnostic rituals, particularly when "unknown ceremonies" are being as-cribed to Jesus. All the more so when the "unknown ceremonies" are said to have loomed so large that they reduced the water immersion to a mere "pre-paratory purification"! And what was it that certainly occurred? "Physical union," showing that Smith's notion of "freedom from the law" was really about the suspension of prohibitions against homosexual sex. Smith, more-over, did not really believe that the content of Jesus' initiation ceremonies was unknown, as he said in a footnote: "To judge from the hekalot and Qumran texts, the magical papyri and the Byzantine liturgy, these [unknown cere-monies] will have been mainly the recitation of repetitive, hypnotic prayers and hymns. The magical tradition also prescribes, in some instances, inter-ference with breathing. Manipulation, too, was probably involved; the stories of Jesus' miracles give a very large place to the use of his hands."[50]

This footnote is actually a microcosm of Smith's overall approach, which is well described by the phrase "scattered indications." Smith could have written an extended comparison between the Secret Gospel and Gnostic ritual, dem-onstrating how we know what "certainly occurred" and why the Secret Gos-pel excerpts resemble the Gnostic tradition. Or he could have done the same with the magical papyri, showing why it is reasonable to think that the Secret Evangelist had knowledge of that kind of material. He could have given us a study of Jewish hymnody as revealed in the Hekhalot and Qumran scrolls and argued the relevance of these literatures to the Secret Gospel. Or he could have placed the Secret Gospel in the orthodox Christian mainstream and illustrated its continuity with the initiation rites of the Byzantine liturgy. Instead, he lumped them all together as if they were all the same sort of thing—"mainly the recitation of repetitive, hypnotic prayers and hymns"—supplemented by heavy breathing, manipulation, and . . . we all know where that leads.

In short, Smith could have written an inductive study of the Secret Gospel and its many interesting resemblances to other categories of ancient literature. Instead, he started out with a preconceived theory about how Jesus initiated and made it seem plausible by picking and choosing elements (if indeed they are elements) from wherever he could find them in the religions of the ancient world. Like the Secret Evangelist, that is, Smith started from the premise that Jesus practiced ritualized homosexuality, then picked and chose from the available ancient material to assemble an original and impressive-looking construct that appears to support his claims. The more we look closely at the traditions he appealed to, the clearer it is that this was what he did. Let us take them one by one.

THE MAGICAL PAPYRI

In his books on the Secret Gospel, his later book on Jesus the magician, and some of his articles, Smith made much of the Greek magical papyri, which offer spells for ascending to heaven with a wealth of seemingly relevant details: burial shrouds and white robes,[51] parallels to many of Jesus' miracles, even ways of raising the dead through contact with living naked bodies.[52] But his approach was very selective, for this material also includes many extraneous elements—lying on a roof, self-hypnosis, gazing at the sun, to name a few—that do not fit the early Christian picture and really add nothing to Smith's central thesis.[53]

It is clearer now than it was when Smith was writing, but these magical rites represent a kind of "miniaturization," or domestication for personal use, of what were originally "central elements of the Egyptian temple."[54] Thus we may rightly question whether they were known to or used by Jesus. The idea that Jesus studied magic in Egypt seems to me to be common among modern Orthodox Jews; I understand it comes from Talmudic literature, which seems to confuse Jesus of Nazareth with a certain Jesus ben Ṣṭada, who was condemned for practicing Egyptian magic.[55] Yet Smith, who wrote a dissertation on the Mishnah at Hebrew University, promoted his own image of Jesus as magician without really exploring its Talmudic roots.[56]

Nevertheless, Smith could have made a stronger case than he actually did by studying whole ceremonies in their cultural and historical contexts, instead of excerpting whatever fit his schema and ignoring the rest. For instance, he was particularly interested in the so-called "Mithras Liturgy," which (at least from his perspective) has obvious sexual potential as a levitation rite that begins with heavy breathing — and obvious homosexual potential in its "instructions for 'using a fellow initiate so that he alone may hear with you the things spoken . . . and if you wish to show him (the things seen).' "[57]

Smith neglected to mention that the magician and the initiate were supposed to maintain a state of purity, probably including sexual abstinence, in order to engage in this ritual.[58] But had he been willing to stay within the Egyptian context, Smith might have connected this obscure liturgy with traditions of ancient Hermeticism,[59] linking it to other texts wherein "an embrace between master and pupil, . . . one suspects . . . is no mere outward symbol of inner illumination, but a generative action."[60] Hermetic initiation could even have grounded Smith's antinomianism: "Those who possess reason, whom . . . mind commands, . . . have been freed from vice. . . . [S]ince mind rules all and is the soul of God, mind can do as it wishes."[61] The process of arriving at this exalted state is also described as a changing of garments, leading to graphic descriptions of divine judgment for those who fail to "acquire a good mind."[62]

It is odd that Smith did not make the connection with Hermeticism, for he himself maintained that its ideas were everywhere in the ancient world; its "affiliates spread like crab-grass through Christianity, Egyptian religion, Judaism, gnosticism, and magic."[63] In fact he frequently wrote as if all the religions of antiquity were more or less interchangeable, so that scattered indications from any one of them could be used to bolster statements about any of the others, or about his picture of Jesus. Thus Smith could have written an interesting study of how certain elements of ancient Egyptian religion found their way into an early Egyptian gospel. But it seems that that would not have satisfied him. He wanted to believe that the Secret Gospel preserves very early traditions close to the historical Jesus, and thus he had to bring the scattered indications from magic and the Mithras Liturgy into the Judeo-Christian orbit.

THE QUMRAN AND HEKHALOT HYMNS

One way Smith made the connection was by arguing that the Mithras Liturgy shared a "common ancestor" with the Jewish mystical tract *Hekhaloth Rabbati*.[64] This text presents a kind of individualized spiritualization of the Temple cult that ceased when the Jerusalem Temple was destroyed in 70 CE. Thus it is about the hymns one must sing to have the experience of coming before the thronelike chariot of God, where the seraphim utter his praises forever.[65] What the Mithras and the Hekhalot have in common is that both give instructions for ascending to heaven. As Smith wrote:

> It is impossible to deny the relationship of this ["Mithras"] material to the hekhalot tradition. The contrast between mortal and immortal beings, the ascent from the realm of mortality to that of the immortals, the jealous guards to be mastered by the use of magic names, the entrance of the heavenly realm, when the hostile guards stare at the intruder, the thunder from the heaven above these inferior deities and the opening of the fiery doors and the vision of the world of the gods within and, finally, the fiery god from whose body the stars stream forth — all these characteristics are common to the Jewish and the magical material.[66]

But most of these are commonplaces that occur widely in folklore and imaginative literature. A distinction between mortal and immortal beings who live in different realms? Magic names? Threatening figures that must be placated to secure entrance? Thunder, fire, visions, stars? One can find them all in Grimm's Fairy Tales. The "common ancestor" is Homo sapiens.

The similarity of Mithras and Hekhalot looks much less close if one makes detailed comparisons of the cosmology — the way these imagined universes are actually laid out:

> The Mithras Liturgy, although it acknowledges the seven gods of the world in one invocation, operates within a primarily tripartite cosmos. The magician leaves the realm of the earth and enters into the realm of wandering stars [i.e., the planets] and other astral powers. The boundary of this realm is the doors of the sun, beyond which are the hypercosmic depths that are the realm of the highest god. The magician does not actually enter this realm, but waits at the doors of the sun. . . . [But he must] avoid the face of the moon because the moon is imagined as a malevolent and dangerous mistress.[67]

The imagined heaven of the Hekhalot, however, is not only different in structure (sevenfold rather than tripartite) and described with different terminology — it is ultimately based on a different model: the Temple rather than the Ptolemaic solar system.

> The technical term used for the seven heavens (hekhal, plural hekhalot; lit[erally] "palaces" or "halls") is unique to the Hekhalot literature and refers to the context of the Temple liturgy: It is taken from the architecture of the Temple, in which it is used for the entrance hall to the Holiest of Holies. . . . Hence, the ascent of the Merkavah mystic through the six heavens to the seventh heaven is primarily a liturgical act and has little to do with the exploration of heavenly cosmology. . . .

> Finally, the most striking observation regarding the physical structure of the heavenly world in the Hekhalot literature is that the seventh hekhal, . . . the desired goal of the Merkavah mystic, is not just a single open heaven, but is composed of . . . "rooms," "apartments," or "chambers."[68]

Moreover, the Hekhalot tend to speak of "descending" rather than "ascending," and the mystic eventually arrives at the throne or chariot of the divine glory, rather than waiting at the doors of the sun.[69]

Since Smith mentioned "Qumran texts," that is the Dead Sea scrolls, he could have written an interesting comparison of the Hekhalot with the Songs of the Sabbath Sacrifice.[70] These, being Jewish, potentially have more in common with each other than either would have with the Egyptian-derived magical papyri. But where the Hekhalot look back to a spiritualized version of the destroyed Temple, the Songs of the Sabbath Sacrifice would have been written while the Temple was still standing. That fact is probably related to an essential difference between the two repertories: the Qumran Sabbath songs are "prayers [which] took place in earth; the worshipper does not ascend to heaven to participate in the angels' sacrifice," as in the Hekhalot.[71] There are, nevertheless, those who find the Qumran hymns repetitive and hypnotic.[72] In any case, some three decades later it is still possible to say that there has not yet been "a full-scale study of the relationship of the *Sabbath Songs* to various Merkabah and Hekalot texts."[73]

And yet, just as Smith could have made a stronger case for a magician Jesus by considering the magical and Hermetic traditions more holistically, so he could have argued more convincingly for some kind of Qumran or Temple-mysticism background to the worship of Jesus and his first followers. But to do that he would have had to explore these traditions more fully, with greater respect for their history and integrity and with less certainty about the role of Egyptian magic. One obvious point of comparison with the Secret Gospel would be the frequent ritual immersions practiced at Qumran, which may have provided background to the activities of John the Baptist.[74] Mightn't a very early gospel that shows Jesus bringing a young man to faith have something to do with that? And wouldn't it be interesting if we could show that it did not? But we hear nothing about this from Smith, despite his claim that Jesus "used the Baptist's rite as the first part of his own."[75] He chose to write about hymns and heavenly journeys, even though the Secret Gospel explicitly mentions neither. This is because Smith began with his preconceived notion of what Jesus' initiations were like and sought to persuade us by weaving together whatever scattered indications could be made to support it, ignoring the bulk of his material even when it was arguably more relevant. Smith took what he needed and moved on, as if all the religions of antiquity were fundamentally pretty much the same.

The "scattered indications" approach is methodologically insupportable. Even in situations where there is considerable sharing across religious lines, as there certainly was in late antiquity, it is essential to respect the synchronic wholeness and distinctiveness of each ritual tradition, as well as its diachronic integrity across time. In the twentieth-century United States, for example, the worship of Reformed Jews had some features in common with the worship of Protestant Christians: a central role for the sermon, a sanctuary with pews facing the front (Orthodox synagogues tend to have different seating arrangements), a choir accompanied by pipe organ (which Orthodox Jews reject), even some of the same hymns.[76] These similarities originated historically in eighteenth- and nineteenth-century Jewish anxieties about participation in the wider modern and Western culture. It would, then, be a mistake to infer that the two religions are simply parallel expressions of "late modernity" and therefore probably shared many other things as well: circumcision and skullcaps for the Protestants, baptism and the New Testament for the Jews, Transactional Analysis for everybody (in the twentieth century it spread like crabgrass!). But that is the sort of mistake Smith made, over and over again.

GNOSTICISM

Smith's selective use of scattered indications to uphold his theory, in place of systematic open-ended investigation, is most clearly displayed in his treatment of Gnosticism, and this would be so even if we ignore, as a kind of celestial hallucination, his statement that "physical union . . . certainly occurred in many forms of gnostic Christianity." In recent years there has been much discussion about what the relatively modern term "Gnosticism"[77] ought to mean—a discussion that Smith himself helped inaugurate.[78] The problem is that it is broadly applied to a very wide range of ancient writings and shadowy groups, which would not all have recognized each other as sharing the same beliefs. Thus Michael Allen Williams has proposed an alternative category of "biblical demiurgical" religions: "It would include all sources that made a distinction between the creator(s) and controllers of the material world and the most transcendent divine being, and that in so doing made use of Jewish or Christian scriptural traditions."[79] That is, characters from the Bible are put at the service of beliefs that the material world was created by an evil or inferior spirit (the demiurge), and the task for human beings is to escape from this world, out of our material bodies, back to the upper realm from which our spirits originally came, the location of the high god who is above the creator. The many Gnostic writings that are known today present a wide range of variations on this basic myth, which seems to owe something to the Platonic cosmology wherein the material world is only a shadow of the real world of ideas.

From my own perspective, more focused on cultural history than philosophy or theology, I see it this way: in Gnostic texts, biblical (Jewish and/or Christian) characters inhabit a more or less Platonic universe, with matter at the low end and one all-embracing Mind at the high end. In Christian Platonism, more or less Platonic philosophical notions are used to explain a biblical universe, created by a personal being who makes ethical demands of his creatures. In some ways, then, the two could not be more different. The Carpocratians, at least as Irenaeus described them, would be Gnostic by this categorization because they described Jesus as teaching that the material world was made by angels and that human beings need to escape the cycle of repeated incarnations so that, finally free of their bodies, they can ascend to the God who is above the angels.

Smith was unaware of it, but an interesting case might be made that (some) early Christians differed with (some) ancient Gnostics over whether baptism actually did involve ascents to heaven. April DeConick has argued that the community that read the Gospel of Thomas (which she does not consider Gnostic) practiced a kind of "ascent and vision mysticism" that involved experiences of traveling to heaven to see Jesus.[80] The Gospel according to John seems to criticize their position, with a Jesus who says "where I am you cannot come" (7:34) and a Jesus who tells Doubting Thomas "Blessed are those who have not seen and yet believe" (20:29). For John, Jesus is to be encountered through faith-filled participation in the sacraments of the loving community, which make heavenly visions unnecessary.[81] DeConick says little about how the Thomas people might have practiced or understood baptism, but the apparently Valentinian baptismal rite referred to in Clement's *Excerpta ex Theodoto* includes a series of questions not unlike Gospel of Thomas 50, one of DeConick's core texts.[82] From such resemblances a theory might be constructed of Gnostic baptism as an occasion for experiencing heavenly ascent.

Anyway, the notable thing about the Secret Gospel is that it would work fairly well as a Gnostic scripture. If anyone other than Morton Smith had discovered the Mar Saba letter, he or she might very plausibly have concluded that the Secret Gospel had something to do with emerging Gnosticism.[83] The women Jesus rejects could represent those material, earth-bound aspects of human nature that must be made male, or spiritual (cf. Gospel of Thomas 114).[84] The cry from the tomb could be the young man's soul, yearning to escape from its entombment in a material body. The young man's expression of love could represent some sort of confession of faith used in a Gnostic church—I mean a biblical demiurgical one. The man's love obtains for him the presence of Jesus, at least for a six-day period of uncertain numerological significance, after which the final initiation into the higher mysteries takes place.

Why would a Gnostic gospel show Jesus restoring a young man to earthly life in the material world, before the final heavenly initiation? This could be explained along the lines of Kurt Rudolph's conclusion that "in Christian Gnosis . . . Cross and Resurrection belong closely together, but in such a way that the latter already takes place before or at the same time as the crucifixion; it is the liberation of the spirit and the destruction of the flesh in one."[85] In fact the Gospel of Philip (19, 79) says that believers should follow Christ's example by rising before they die: "If they do not receive resurrection while they are alive, once they have died they will receive nothing."[86] Thus the young man would have been resurrected first, then met with Jesus a week later to experience, naked man with naked man, the Gnostic sacrament of the Bridal Chamber,[87] in anticipation of which (Smith could have assured us) the flesh was at least as willing as the spirit (cf. Mark 14:38).[88] In between, no doubt, they would have enjoyed six days of the kind of long-winded celestial speechifying that often typifies Gnostic scriptures, but which in this case (mercifully, perhaps) has not survived.

Smith could have interpreted the Secret Gospel along these lines, but he did not. If he had, the magical, Qumran, and Hekhalot elements would have receded into the background, and he would have ended up with a Gnostic gospel, something I think he didn't want (I will say why before this chapter is over). How strange Smith's approach really is will become clear if we consider the fact that, with all the evidence he tried to connect to the Secret Gospel, he completely ignored the one ancient text that unmistakably describes a heavenly ascent within the context of a baptismal rite, and incorporates sexual elements to boot. If his aim was to show Jesus initiating disciples by means of a sexual ascent to heaven, Smith could have made the bulk of his case on the basis of this text alone. But he didn't.

I am referring to the work known as *Zostrianos,* part of the Gnostic library discovered at Nag Hammadi.[89] Its protagonist, depressed by the inability of his ancestral gods to answer his questions about the meaning of it all, takes to the desert in suicidal hope of being eaten by animals. (In the twentieth century, it was common for young homosexuals to consider or attempt suicide.[90]) Instead he is upbraided by a messenger of light, at whose invitation he casts off his body (i.e., he disrobes) and ascends through a heaven of numerous levels, each of which he enters through one or more immersions.[91] After being introduced to innumerable deities teaching all sorts of spiritual profundities, and being baptized repeatedly every step of the way, he meets a virgin hermaphrodite (i.e., a being who incorporates all aspects of human sexuality in one body!) who seems to crown him with the seal of the Invisible Spirit — or at least talks about doing so.[92] (In various branches of Eastern Christianity, crowns are used at both baptisms and weddings.)[93] When Zostrianos reaches the point where the gods are asking him the questions, he has learned enough to return to earth, bringing a message that Smith might have put into the mouth of the antinomian, homosexual Jesus who rejected the young man's sister: "seek the immutable ingenerateness. . . . Flee from the madness and the bondage of femaleness, and choose for yourselves the salvation of maleness. You have come not to suffer; rather, you have come to escape your bondage."[94]

So why didn't Smith support his interpretation of the Secret Gospel by comparing it with *Zostrianos*? He could have written an intriguing book, and the Secret Gospel would have entered the scholarly archive as a fascinating fragment of an early Gnostic gospel. Plenty of scholars would have been content to make such a contribution. But for Smith, I believe, it would not have been enough to show that some early gospel fragment imagined a Zostrianic Jesus. He wanted his alleged initiation rite to be the real one, the actual practice of the historical Jesus himself. That could not be demonstrated merely by showing that the gospel he found was influenced by Hermetic magic, Jewish hymnody, or Gnosticism. Thus he proceeded by collecting scattered indications from all of them, from wherever they might be found, rather than by making sustained comparisons between ancient traditions considered in their entirety. In principle Smith had no more interest in understanding Gnostic liturgy on its own terms than he had in the Hermetic or the Hekhalot or the Byzantine. He sought only to line up, like beads on a string, whatever isolated facts could make his allegations about Jesus' initiation rite seem plausible.

And the paradox of *Zostrianos* is that, though it is particularly close to Smith's construction of Jesus' initiation rite, it is also a text that would be particularly difficult to connect to Jesus or early Christianity. According to a recent translator, "we are unable to identify this group on the basis of the reports of Christian heresiologists"; "the author . . . seems to have no specific interest in things Christian." It is easier to identify relationships to "the Neoplatonic school of Plotinus," and indeed "this tractate is . . . mentioned by Porphyry." In short, "*Zostrianos* offers an interesting example of how some Gnostics combined a mythological world view and a philosophical interpretation of it, based on Platonic thought."[95] So the major ancient example of a heavenly journey inside a baptismal rite points to traditions derived from Plato. I find this very interesting, for, as we will see in a later chapter, the real origin of Smith's notion of heavenly ascent will be found in a specific textual community of Plato readers.

LIBERTINISM

Another reason to be surprised that Smith did not show more interest in Gnostic ritual is that he assigned the Gnostics such an important role in his overall theory. He knew perfectly well that the initiation rite he ascribed to Jesus had no support in mainstream witnesses to Christian liturgical history and was irreconcilable with "*orthodox* references to baptism throughout this period."[96] His reply was that the original practice of Jesus represented a kind of "libertinism" that was deliberately and massively suppressed by the ecclesiastical establishment at a very early date. According to Smith, the apostle Paul

> had substantially preserved the teaching of Jesus; and as the potentialities of this teaching became apparent, it also became apparent that Paul had not been safe enough. . . . The Jewish revolts had ruined forever the legalistic interpretation of Christianity, but the libertine interpretation was flourishing and it found in Paul's doctrine everything it needed to justify its inclinations: identification with Jesus, possession by his spirit, ascent to the heavens in his ascension, and consequent liberation from the law. Accordingly, the gnostic teachers, who now emerged from the libertine tradition, made great use of Paul. . . . [Consequently,] Paul's doctrine of freedom was remodeled by the orthodox in the interests of social acceptability. The process can be seen in its simplest form in Acts, where Paul's career is reported, his theology omitted.[97]

Hence the transfiguration story, Smith wrote, was originally "propaganda for a Jewish-Christian libertine group — a group that thought the Law and the Prophets had vanished from 'the freedom in which Christ has set us free,' as Paul put it (Gal[atians] 5:1)."[98] Indeed the real reason for Jewish persecution of Jesus and Paul was "Jesus' teaching of freedom from the Law and the libertine consequences which he and his followers drew from it. . . . Evidently there were elements of libertinism in even the most conservative of early Christian parties, a fact which strengthens our supposition that this side of early Christian thought went back to Jesus himself."[99] According to Smith, Paul and other early Christian figures had actually gone through his proposed Hekhaloth-magical initiation rite, combining water immersion, a linen cloth, naked physical intimacy, paranormal experiences of ascending to heaven with Jesus, possession by his spirit, and freedom from sexual taboos.[100] And as "Paul's doctrine of freedom was remodeled by the orthodox in the interests of social acceptability," it was the Gnostics, and especially "the Carpocratians [who] derived from and continued the primitive libertine Christian tradition" that Jesus himself practiced, so that their sect amounted to "a slightly philosophizing continuation of a sort of Christianity which often developed into or took up gnosticism."[101]

What we need at this point, obviously, is some cogent demonstration of Smith's own statement that "physical union . . . certainly occurred in many forms of gnostic Christianity." Such a proposition would, in fact, be extremely difficult to prove, and Smith never even attempted to prove it. Instead, as if to keep us from noticing, he assembled a collage of scattered indications, taken from anywhere, that could be made to look like evidence that Jesus practiced ritualized "libertinism," that is, homosexuality. To demonstrate that there is no more to Smith's project than this, it is enough to limit ourselves to one crucial element: the claim that the white cloth worn by the young man served as both a baptismal garment and a burial shroud.

The Sindōn

In early Christian writings, imagery of changing clothing frequently appears as a metaphor for the conversion process. By the late fourth century, it was common for newly baptized Christians to put on symbolic white clothing, though we do not know when this practice began. But accepting the authenticity of the Mar Saba letter, especially on Smith's terms, requires us to acknowledge that, as early as the second or third century, new converts wrapped themselves, not in special clothing, but in flat white sheets or linen sindōns, representing both burial with Jesus and new life received in baptism. There are two distinct claims here, both of which need to be proved. One is the liturgical action of clothing oneself in a sheet, the other is the interpretation, in the critical dimension, that the sheet represented a burial shroud as well as a baptismal garment. What is the evidence for either claim? Smith's demonstration is almost a masterpiece — not of perspicacity, but of camouflage.[102]

A key aspect of Smith's approach was his practice of giving long lists of citations to a wide range of obscure texts, without quoting or otherwise indicating what most of the texts actually say. This tactic is easy to justify as keeping the book to a manageable length, but it also ensures that only the most determined reader will look everything up. Everyone else, rather than pick their way through almost three hundred dense pages, will simply give Smith the benefit of the doubt, as in fact many readers have done. If we take the trouble to check everything, on the other hand, we will find that our trust has been completely misplaced: the emperor wears no clothes, so to speak.

Thus, in his commentary on the phrase "wearing a linen cloth over [his] naked [body]," Smith began with a statement that "nudity in baptism is prescribed" by AT "and was required by the Pharisees in proselyte baptism as well as in immersions for purification." As we saw, however, AT prescribes only the nudity; it does not mention a special baptismal garment of any kind. For the statement about the Pharisees, Smith appealed to two Talmudic passages; a reader has to go back to the sources to discover that neither one really supports his claim. One of them (*Bavli Yebamot* 47b) mentions immersion after the circumcision of a convert but says nothing about nakedness specifically. The other (*Mishnah Mikwa'ot* 8 end–9) states that, for a ritual immersion to be valid, water must touch every part of the body. But this need not require nudity: Smith did not tell us that, according to the very next chapter of this tractate (10:3–4), the wearing of loose-fitting clothes or even a linen sheet is not precluded. Such failures to read a text all the way through are typical in Smith's documentation—we have already seen many examples. But in this case it is especially curious because, as we will see, Smith needed all the linen sheets he could get.

Nor did Smith raise any questions here about whether Mishnaic or Talmudic evidence is necessarily attributable to the Pharisees or can be assumed to describe pre-Christian practice.[103] As a result, he created the impression that there is an historical continuity from Jewish ritual nudity to Christian ritual nudity, which Jesus could hardly have avoided or been unaware of.

Next, we are given three citations from New Testament apocrypha, but Smith quoted only the one he considered "particularly close" to the Secret Gospel: Acts of Thomas 121, wherein the apostle, preparing to baptize a woman, told her nurse to anoint her and put a sindōn around her. Smith neglected to mention that after the immersion she put her ordinary clothes back on, suggesting the sindōn may have been more functional than symbolic. The apostle's desire to keep the woman covered may simply reflect the quasi-Encratite disapproval of anything suggesting "filthy intercourse" that pervades this particular work.[104] If this is based on any group's actual practice, it is possible that only the women wore sindōns, not the men; there was such a practice at one time in the East Syrian rite,[105] which could conceivably have a historical relationship to the Syriac Acts of Thomas. One has to be especially careful about the ritual details in these Acts, however, for every recension assumes a different model of the initiation liturgy, reflecting differences of theology and practice between different early Christian and language groups.[106]

The other two apocrypha, which Smith cited but did not quote, could well reflect the baptismal practices of their times but are not early enough to be reliable witnesses to pre-Nicene practice; in any case neither mentions a sindōn. In the Acts of Barnabas 12–13, the apostle exhorts two Greeks to put on "that garment [*endyma*] which is incorruptible forever." But after baptizing them, he and his companion place their own robes (*stolē*) on the two Greeks. In the Martyrdom of Matthew 27, the apostle tells a king he has just baptized to clothe himself in bright or white garments (*himatia lampra, uestes albas*).[107]

Of the six texts adduced so far, therefore, only one, the Acts of Thomas, testifies to the use of a sindōn or flat white sheet in a pre-Nicene initiation rite, though under uncertain conditions. Yet Smith's strategy of piling up unquoted testimonies has produced a kind of "bandwagon effect" with the implication that early Christians, like the Jews before them, were immersed naked but covered themselves with flat linen sindōns. Having created this impression, Smith proceeded to another favorite tactic, building on what has been "established" to present startling new interpretations of New Testament stories, which in this case are actually of doubtful relevance. "In the Johannine footwashing," which was often given baptismal significance in patristic exegesis, "Jesus is naked except for a towel (*lention*, 13.4), which the Syriac versions describe" with the word *sedōnā*, which can mean a shroud; its Hebrew cognate is translated *sindōn* in the Septuagint, the ancient Greek translation of the Old Testament. Thus Smith managed to turn Jesus' towel into a shroud. But even if this is an accurate description of how Jesus was dressed, it ignores the fact that Jesus was not the one being baptized. Earlier on, however, Smith had wrongly asserted that AT directs the clergy to remove their own clothes before entering the baptismal pool with the candidate,[108] so apparently he believed that everyone got naked at Jesus' unknown ceremonies.

The second New Testament story has the advantage of coming from the gospel of Mark, shortly after the place where the second excerpt from the Secret Gospel would have been located. "Is it by chance that the beggar in M[ar]k 10.50 . . . throws away his himation [outer garment] when he comes to Jesus to be cured?" Smith asked. Evidently not. But what about the simpler possibility that removing clothes merely enabled one to run faster or move about unencumbered (cf. Acts 19:16, John 21:7)? Perhaps nothing more than that lies behind the naked flight of the young man of Mark 14:51–52.

Next, Smith presented a florilegium of Christian writings intended to emphasize the earliness of the alleged practice of wearing a sindōn. He began with a proposition: "That naked baptism was already customary in Paul's time is shown by his allegorizing the undressing for it and dressing after it," supported by two quotations and two citations from the epistles.[109] But of course this begs the whole question. Symbolic, metaphorical language may be inspired by preexisting aspects of the ritual, or the ritual may be a response to a text. Ritual language is the cosmic egg, ritual action the mundane chicken, and the riddle for researchers is which came first. Without some confirmation from the performative dimension or the critical dimension, therefore, we cannot infer from the epistles alone what the baptizees in Pauline churches wore or didn't wear.

Next, Smith proposed an argument from independent attestation: "Similar allegorization (not apparently dependent on Paul) appears," he said, in three more texts which, once again, are cited but not quoted. They turn out to be two similar sayings of Jesus, or two recensions of one saying, recorded in the Gospel of Thomas 37 (with Oxyrhynchos papyrus 655) and the Gospel of the Egyptians (as cited by Clement). Asked when the answers to their questions will be revealed, the Jesus of Thomas and papyrus 655 tells the disciples, "When you unclothe yourselves and are not ashamed." The Jesus of Egyptians tells Salome (her again!), "When you have trampled on the garment of shame."[110] Do these two passages refer to an initiation rite? Here Smith ignored an important article, published just as he was writing his Harvard book, which argued that the context is indeed baptismal but that the allegorical theme is one of nakedness as a symbolic return to the childlike innocence of Eden before the fall, not "stripping as death."[111] That would be quite different from the Pauline allegories, which do refer to death (2 Corinthians 5:2), putting on Christ (Galatians 3:27), and even circumcision (Colossians 2:11). What we have, then, are multiple interpretations of the act of disrobing (and in some cases reclothing), some or all of which may relate to an actual, ritual disrobing, but none of which strongly points to what really needs to be proved: the wearing of a flat linen sheet or sindōn. One wonders whether, for Smith, the "garment of shame" is another reminder that all this is really about homosexuality.

And the beat goes on: ten other writings are cited (not quoted) in which "the same general theme recurs." Some of these are clearly allegorical: the Clementine homilies, Justin Martyr on Zechariah 3:4–7, the Sethians according to Hippolytus. Others describe actual initiation rites, but it is up to us to figure out what they have to do with the alleged initiatory wearing of a sindōn by early Christians: Irenaeus on the initiation practices of the Marcosians (Valentinians), *Apostolic Constitutions* on the Hemerobaptists. The three references to Clement's writings[112] are particularly deserving of discussion in a book about Clement of Alexandria, but here they are left unquoted, and even unlisted in the index. Actually checked, they hardly support an affirmative answer to the question: was a sindōn worn in the baptismal rite known to Clement? Yet Smith simply ended this florilegium with the conclusion: "This early dissemination of the theme argues an early origin," as if in ringing endorsement of the "scattered indications" approach.

In spite of all this, so far the only cited text that actually mentions a sindōn is the problematic Acts of Thomas. Yet Smith proceeded anyway to the next stage of the argument, as if the ritual use of the sindōn had been established. "The indicated baptismal practice (nudity and sindōn) lent itself particularly to Pauline exegesis because . . . the initiatory sindōn . . . was also the regular burial garment," he claimed. Three passages from the Palestinian Talmud that mention burial shrouds are cited in support of this, but (of course) a flat sheet or sindōn can be used as a shroud; it is the initiatory or baptismal use that needs to be documented. "Accordingly," Smith continued, "Jesus had been buried in a sindōn (M[ar]k 15.46 and parallels). Paul's interpretation of baptism as death and burial with Jesus suggests that the sindōn over the naked body was the customary costume as early as Paul's time." In fact it has not been shown that there was a "customary costume" for baptisms in Paul's time.

Moving on, Smith sought to show that the sindōn "was not a 'proper' garment," summarizing a story of two Cynic philosophers who shocked people by wearing sindōns in public. That, of course, is the sort of thing Cynic philosophers were always doing. If the story has anything at all to do with Christian baptism, it implies that the wearing of sindōns would have been something unexpected, calling for more comment in early Christian texts than Smith was able to adduce. Yet the Cynic story becomes the basis for the next claim: "Since the costume specified in the longer text [i.e., the Secret Gospel] is unusual and is associated with baptism, it can be used as an indication of baptism" wherever else it occurs: henceforth every white cloth or garment is a symbol both of baptism and of burial.

Now the stage has been set for yet another proof that the Secret Gospel is genuine. The curious fact that the phrase "wearing a linen cloth over [his] naked [body]" occurs both at Mark 14:51 and in the Secret Gospel could, of course, be due to the Secret Evangelist quoting canonical Mark. But according to Smith it "is to be explained as . . . a fixed formula, probably a baptismal rubric" that was in oral circulation through its use in initiation rituals. Since other scholars, such as Cullmann, had identified other patterns of related wording that seemed to be echoes of ritual phraseology, surely this could be a ritual phrase as well, Smith contended.

For apparent confirmation, with another startling reinterpretation of the New Testament, Smith turned to texts that describe the white garments worn by the angelic young men at the tomb of Jesus and by "the saints in the Apocalypse"—even though none of these texts uses the word "sindōn." The bright clothing, of course, symbolizes resurrection and a heavenly state of being, as further Jewish and Christian writings attest. In the process, Smith concluded that he had found the solution, "from an early Markan stratum," to the long-standing puzzle of why a young man wearing a sindōn barely escaped being arrested with Jesus and had to run away naked: "The reader who had read the longer text [i.e., the Secret Gospel] would realize that this youth, too, had come to be baptized." Was there water in Gethsemane? It would matter little if, as Smith thought, the immersion was merely "reduced to a preparatory purification" for the real ritual. In other words, those who came to arrest Jesus interrupted a sexual tryst.[113] All that's missing is some exegesis of Judas' treacherous kiss.

Thus Smith never came close to proving one of the central claims of his thesis: that the earliest Christians were baptized wearing linen sheets, symbolizing both burial with Christ and resurrection. That many of his other claims remain equally vacuous can be confirmed by anyone who bothers to scrupulously check every citation in his more "scholarly" book, slogging through some three hundred pages of scattered indication upon scattered indication, irrelevant citation after misrepresented source. The index of "ancient works and passages discussed" takes up almost sixteen two-column pages by itself, and I've found a number of omissions besides.

WEARING WHITE

When Christians actually began putting on white clothing after baptism is a good question. Whether they were ever buried under white sheets is another. Both kinds of questions, since they relate to the practical dimension of liturgy, tend to receive less scholarly attention than questions about the interpretation of texts. A preliminary exploration, however, offers no particular encouragement to the hope that either the Secret Gospel or Smith's interpretation of it will eventually be validated.

Even if we allow that Smith was doing the best he could for his time, by now we have better collections of early Christian texts on baptism — studies that are simultaneously more thorough and less tendentious. Going by what the texts actually say, it is possible to conclude, with Victor Saxer, that before the fourth century all references to changing clothes are likely to be allegorical or metaphorical, imagistic rather than literal references to ritual practice.[114] On the other hand, since there is no reason to assume that adult converts were baptized fully clothed, most likely they did disrobe before baptism and got dressed again afterwards. The real question, then, is how and when these actions went from being purely utilitarian to partly symbolic, calling for a special kind of clothing. Thus Ante Crnčević takes the more nuanced view that "the ante-Nicene liturgical tradition . . . did not know the rite of conferring the baptismal garment, but the clothing itself cannot be denied and, what is more, the existence of a special dress — white, made of linen — reserved for the baptismal celebration."[115] But it may all be beside the point because what needs to be demonstrated for our purposes is not the nudity or the wearing of special clothes, but specifically the wearing of a sindōn or sheet, with the double significance of birth and death. For that the evidence is very close to zero.

The white garments worn by the newly baptized in the fourth and fifth centuries probably represent a coalescence of several diverse themes, which may originally have been independent. First, imagery of changing clothes is often used to symbolize conversion, as in the Pauline admonition to put on Christ (Romans 13:14, Galatians 3:27), or immortality or "the new man" (1 Corinthians 15:53–54, Ephesians 4:24, Colossians 3:10–12), or allegorical armor (Romans 13:12, Ephesians 6:11, 1 Thessalonians 5:8). This theme appears to have continued in such texts as the Odes of Solomon (21:2–3), the Hymn of the Pearl, and the Acts of Peter and the Twelve Apostles, in which the process of coming to faith is described in metaphors of stripping and changing into new clothes.[116] There is no indication that the clothes were imagined as linen or white, however. Since putting on new or fine clothing was characteristic of weddings, there are also texts in which baptismal clothing is associated with wedding imagery.[117]

In a different metaphor, white could represent purity (Revelation 7:14), and thus more than one ancient religion made use of white clothing.[118] In the Acts of John (38), worshippers of Artemis assemble in white clothes to celebrate the anniversary of her temple in Ephesus, but the apostle shows up wearing black, just asking for trouble, which leads, soon enough, to a miraculous destruction of the temple.[119] Stories like this suggest that some converts to early Christianity may already have been familiar with the wearing of white ritual garb in the religions they came from. The Mithras Liturgy, too, though an esoteric rather than a popular rite, includes heavenly figures dressed in linen.[120]

The dominant symbolism in both Jewish and Christian contexts, however, must surely derive from the linen vestments of the Temple priests (Exodus 28:40–42, 39:27–29), including the High Priest himself on the Day of Atonement, when he put aside his usual golden vestments and dressed more like an ordinary priest (Leviticus 16:4). These were not flat sheets like shrouds, but full suits of linen clothing, including a tunic, breeches, a sash, and a turban.[121] It is only logical, therefore, that in apocalyptic literature such priestly garb is worn by the heavenly host, the priesthood of the heavenly temple. There it is readily connected with themes of shining splendor, passing through water (cf. Genesis 1:7), and priestly anointing.[122] Certainly this, more than any early Christian ceremony, provides the primary background of the white garments in the book of Revelation. The great crowd robed in white, which cannot be numbered (Revelation 7:9–17), is celebrating the feast of Tabernacles before the throne of God. They carry palms and shout "Salvation!" paraphrasing the Hebrew "Hosanna!" (Psalm 117 [118]:25–27). The One who sits on the throne will spread his tent or shelter over them (Revelation 7:15), and the Lamb will lead them to living water (7:17), recalling the special water libations that took place in Jerusalem during this holiday.[123] If there is anything baptismal about this, it is not Pauline burial symbolism, but priestly symbolism: "He loves us and has washed away our sins with his blood, and made us a kingdom of priests to serve his God" (Revelation 1:6, cf. 7:14).[124] Thus it could well be that the first Christians to wear white garments at baptism, whoever and whenever they were, thought they were dressing like heavenly priests, not shrouded like the dead.

It is instructive to note how these themes come together in modern Orthodox Judaism, in practices that Smith could not have failed to observe while he was studying at Hebrew University. Since at least the Middle Ages, religious Jewish men have worn a white garment, called *kitel* in Yiddish, especially on the High Holy Days, where it symbolizes "purity (and hence forgiveness of sins), integrity and piety."[125] As the Yiddish name implies, this is done primarily by Ashkenazic (Eastern European) Jews. However, the Jerusalem Talmud (written about 400 CE) arguably refers to a similar custom when it says that the Israelites (unlike other nations) "wear white, and wrap themselves in white" when facing the divine judgment[126] (though perhaps this refers to the prayer shawl or *tallit*). Nowadays the kitel can also be worn on special religious occasions, for example by the groom at a wedding, by the father at a circumcision, and by the leader of the Passover seder (a fatherlike role). It is not surprising, then, that some Jewish men are buried wearing the kitel. But the kitel is not a flat sheet: the Yiddish word means "smock" or "gown," and the garment typically has a collar, sleeves, and a belt; it is worn over other ordinary clothing, or over the burial shroud, not over the naked body.[127]

Which leads to another question: were people in ancient times buried in, on, or under flat linen sheets? The easiest evidence to find is inconsistent but suggests that grave clothes were often more complicated. Lazarus was bound hand and foot, with a *soudarion* over his face (John 11:44). In the Acts of John (63–86) Drusiana was evidently buried wearing at least two layers of clothing.[128] According to the synoptic gospels Jesus was wrapped in a sindōn (Matthew 27:59, Mark 15:46, Luke 23:53), but according to John he had a soudarion over his head and was wrapped in linen *othonia* (plural), in accordance with what is explicitly described as Jewish custom (John 19:40, 20:5–7). The bodies in the Qumran cemetery "were apparently wrapped in linen shrouds and some were perhaps placed in wooden coffins."[129] However, the complex includes several different types of burials, and the burial clothes are poorly preserved.[130] The textiles in other Jewish graves of the period are similarly deteriorated, though there are also instances of leather shrouds, which would not naturally have been white.[131] The Shroud of Turin is a flat sheet that was evidently placed under and then folded over the body (if it ever was in a grave with a body). That would seem more like the synoptic account of Jesus' burial, though there are those who say it confirms every detail mentioned in all four gospels.[132]

Conclusion

The two excerpts from the Secret Gospel, the letter of Clement, and Morton Smith's two books about them were all constructed by very similar cut-and-paste techniques, as if they were all composed by the same person. Each writing is an assemblage of items excerpted from a variety of sources, carefully arranged to imply that Jesus initiated his disciples through a homo-sexual act. In the story of the young man, the Secret Evangelist appears to have begun with the "good news" that Jesus practiced homosexuality with his disciples and then narrativized this with an expertly crafted mosaic of quotes and near-quotes from the canonical gospels. In the other excerpt, the corre-sponding idea that Jesus avoided women is spelled out in the same way, with the apparent addition of some early extracanonical traditions. In the letter of Clement, the initiation rites surrounding the Secret Gospel are contrasted with the unspeakable Carpocratian teachings in too-Clementine vocabulary. An overconcentration of mystery-rite terminology and reuse of patristic tradi-tions about Mark in Alexandria seem to speak of ancient, secretive initiation rites going back to the earliest gospel.

In telling us what all this really means, Smith seems to have begun with the conviction that Jesus initiated his disciples through homosexual ceremonies — and then spelled this conviction out at imposing scholarly length, once again by reassembling numerous tidbits taken from other contexts. From the Greek magical papyri, derived from ancient Egyptian religion, Smith excerpted expe-riences of ascending to heaven in the company of a disciple. The Qumran hymns and the Hekhalot were said to be describing similar experiences, indi-cating that such practices were known in Jewish environments. From his per-ception of Gnosticism Smith developed the idea that a libertine, ethically un-constrained form of Christianity existed early enough to go back to Jesus, but was later suppressed by the official church, surviving only in ostracized groups like the Carpocratians. And from the epistles of Paul, Smith derived the notion that baptism was originally believed to free the Christian from the constraints of moral law.

Smith's approach is amply illustrated by his attempt to show that early Christians were baptized wearing a flat linen sheet or sindōn, which also symbolized a burial shroud. He presented a vast assemblage of bits and pieces from countless Jewish, Christian, and Greek sources, most of them unquoted, none of which actually support the argument when fully examined on its own.

Yet this procedure is pervasive throughout his scholarly book — a relentless succession of stray facts, held together by quasi-facts, propped up by non-facts, painstakingly built up, like papier-mâché, into something that looks like a deliberate parody of scholarship itself, drumming the glassy-eyed reader into submission like some hypnotic ritual hymn. It is as if we have ascended to a lawless paradise in which all principles of interpretation and reasoning have been suspended, where almost anything can prove almost anything.

Ironically, Smith could have made a much stronger case for his theory by collecting evidence more selectively, then investigating it more deeply, respecting the wholeness and independence of each tradition as well as its chronological development. In that way he could have demonstrated that the Secret Gospel presents us with a magical or Hermetic Jesus, a (pre-)Hekhalot or Qumran Jesus, a Gnostic or Zostrianos-like Jesus. But to do that, Smith would have had to choose which Jesus it would be, and the whole subject would have remained a curiosity for experts, with little likely impact on the popular audience for whom one of his books was expressly written. For Smith, I submit, it wouldn't have been enough to show us that one ancient group or another imagined a homosexual Jesus: it had to be the real Jesus, a homophile messiah who is in all, from all, and for all, despite the best efforts of conventional Christianity to keep him hidden from view. That is why the Secret Gospel had to preserve a very early tradition, as close as one can get to the historical Jesus. It could not just be the gospel of some ancient Hermetic or Jewish or Gnostic sect — it had to be the original and true gospel, confirmed by scattered indications from all over the ancient world, validated by the biggest names in academia at the time.

Smith's peculiar ritual shape — nude baptism, linen covering, physical union, ascent to a heaven above the law — was not deduced from the material, then. On the contrary it was presupposed, and then legitimized by patching together an intimidating phalanx of details, scrounged from wherever in ancient literature they could be found: a cloud of witnesses great enough to fog any lens (cf. Hebrews 12:1). As a result, Jewish, Christian, Gnostic, and magical rites all seem interchangeable, as if each group's esoteric practices were fully shared by all the others, or as if each expressed the same essential spirit in a kind of unitarian liberality.

Smith's propensity for recombining shards into illusory shapes has been observed before. In denying Smith's arguments that the Mar Saba letter was written by Clement of Alexandria, Eric Osborn succinctly described much the same state of affairs: "The question is, . . . 'What degree of probability can be given to a case for Clementine authorship?' Minimal probability is not increased by accumulation of ambiguous evidence. Despite the mass of interesting detail, some of which is germane, the attribution of the document to Clement is a case of nescience fiction."[133]

Why did Smith operate this way? I believe we have to conclude that he had a larger goal than simply authenticating and interpreting an interesting text he had found. In time I think it will be clear that the historic Christian opposition to homosexuality was a subject of great personal importance to Smith, well beyond the investment that any scholar would have in seeing his research findings widely accepted. The shape of Smith's obsession will gradually emerge as we consider what else he had to say on the subject of sex.

Summary

I explore three issues in this chapter. First, I show that the first excerpt from the Secret Gospel, the one with the alleged homosexual encounter, is a kind of mosaic constructed of selections from the canonical Gospels that are arranged to imply that Jesus practiced homosexuality. The passage seems to include a series of humorous double entendres that imply the author understood modern English. The second excerpt, which shows Jesus rejecting a group of women, was constructed similarly but also made use of traditions from early apocryphal scriptures. As Smith interpreted these traditions, they showed that Salome had tempted Jesus sexually, though in fact this interpretation is doubtful. The letter of Clement was constructed by a similar process, using the vocabulary of Clement's genuine writings.

Second, Smith's interpretation of the Secret Gospel was constructed by the same mosaic technique. Elements selected from the Greek magical papyri, the Jewish Hekhalot hymns and the hymns of Qumran, Gnostic writings, and the Byzantine Christian liturgy are reassembled to imply that Jesus initiated his disciples one by one through nocturnal acts of homosexual intercourse, which the disciple experienced as an ascent to heaven to be united with Jesus. Ironically, a more holistic use of any one of these traditions would have produced a more plausible interpretation of the text. But it seems Smith would not have been satisfied to produce a magician Jesus, a Gnostic Jesus, or a Jewish Jesus. He wanted to present a universal Jesus who was a homosexual.

Third, I systematically went through Smith's evidence that early Christians wore a sindōn—a white, flat, linen cloth—which was interpreted as both a burial shroud and a heavenly garment. It turned out that, here too, Smith created a mosaic of "evidence" gathered selectively from widely scattered sources, most of which does not demonstrate the thesis, while at the same time he ignored other evidence that was more relevant or might even have supported his case.

What we have, then, are like layers or concentric circles — the two excerpts of the Secret Gospel, the letter of Clement, and Smith's interpretation — each built up from "scattered indications" to imply that Jesus practiced homosexuality. The similarity in technique suggests that all the layers had the same author.

6

Hypnotic Hymns

Once the group phenomena got under way, they radically changed the character of the sect. Psychological contagion reportedly made converts of thousands at once. . . . No doubt some of Jesus' initiates had learned the technique of ascent and hypnotic suggestion from him and were able to carry on his practice. But his practice took time. A whole night was needed for each initiate. So the secret baptisms of a few individuals, one by one, were soon overshadowed by the mass conversions in the meetings of the churches. The converts . . . had been possessed by Jesus; . . . they were "in" him, so they must be in the kingdom and free from the law. . . . Since Jesus had not foreseen group possession by his spirit, . . . a reference to Jesus was added to the baptismal formula and with this change it was given at once to all the new converts, while the long, secret rite was reserved (as it had been from the beginning) for a chosen few. —Morton Smith

In the last chapter I showed that Smith's construction of Jesus' baptismal rite — "the mystery of the kingdom of God" involving nocturnal union, possession by Jesus' spirit, ascent to heaven, and freedom from law — was presupposed, not deduced from the evidence. Indeed the "evidence" Smith presented consisted of numerous "scattered indications" wrenched from their original contexts (and therefore from their true meaning) and reassembled into a daunting but actually specious pretense at substantiation. Smith could have made a stronger case had he set himself the more limited goal of trying to fit the Secret Gospel into only one of the ancient literary traditions he consulted. That is, he could have argued more plausibly that the Secret Gospel was influenced by the Greek magical papyri, or the Qumran hymns, or the Hekhalot, or the Gnostic writings. By insisting that the Secret Gospel is indebted to all of them, more or less equally, he presented a spurious picture of the ancient world in which all religions were pretty much the same. He also gave his portrait of Jesus a kind of universal quality, as if to say: the Secret Gospel Jesus was not the deity of some obscure ancient sect, but the actual historical figure, witnessed here in the earliest gospel fragment, with exhaustive support from ancient pagan, Jewish, and Gnostic sources.

Christian texts, too, were tossed into the mix, yet there is a conspicuous lack of attention to the kinds of evidence others might deem most relevant: ancient witnesses to and modern scholarship on the early Christian liturgy. That is so, at least, in the book Smith finished first, his "scholarly" Harvard tome. He attempted to correct this imbalance, however, in his second book, the breezier Harper volume, in which he wrote that "the hekalot and Qumran texts, the magical papyri and the Byzantine liturgy" all informed his hypothesis that the "unknown ceremonies" of Jesus "will have been mainly the recitation of repetitive, hypnotic prayers and hymns." By "the Byzantine liturgy," which is never mentioned in the Harvard book, Smith meant the worship of the Greek Orthodox Church, which is also used (in Old Slavonic and other languages) by the other branches of the Eastern Orthodox Church that are in communion with the Patriarch of Constantinople.

There are two reasons why we should be particularly interested in any relationships there may be between the Secret Gospel and the Byzantine liturgy. First, the Hekhalot, the Qumran scrolls, the magical papyri, and the Gnostic texts record long-extinct ritual traditions that must be reconstructed from incomplete data. But the liturgy of the Greek Orthodox Church is a living tradition, with all three dimensions (text, practice, and interpretation) intact and relatively well documented. While there is much uncertainty about ancient Gnostic or Qumran ritual, almost any question that can be asked about the Byzantine liturgy can be answered to some degree. The second reason to focus on the Byzantine liturgy is that it is arguably the central tradition of Christian worship, continuous in some respects with the oldest known practices of Jerusalem, Antioch, and Constantinople, maintained in the original language of the New Testament and Septuagint, preserving many features that are traceable all the way back to early Christian times. How surprising, then, that Smith originally had nothing to say about it while writing the first of his two books on the Secret Gospel. Only after the Harvard book was completed, and Smith began composing his popular memoir about discovering the manuscript at Mar Saba, did he see a way to turn his recollections of the Greek monastic worship he encountered there into further support for his thesis about Jesus' rite of initiation. And what he had to say about his liturgical experiences reveals far more than he intended. Indeed it reveals that Smith's account of his exploits at Mar Saba is not only untrustworthy, but deliberately deceptive.

Indolence at the Time of Psalmody

Smith's first encounter with the Byzantine liturgy was in Jerusalem, where he rented an apartment that happened to be controlled by Archimandrite Kyriakos, who held the high office of Custodian of the Holy Sepulchre. It was Kyriakos who would arrange the first (1941) visit to Mar Saba.

> Thanks to him I saw much of the Holy Sepulchre and fell in love with it and with the Greek Orthodox services. The great cathedral was then undergoing extensive repairs for earthquake damages. . . . Through this fantastic structure passed the long lines of priests and monks in their black robes and glittering vestments, while from above came the clang and thunder of the huge Russian bells. At the beginning of the mass, with the majestic opening of the great doors of the golden altar screen, the unspeakable solemnity of the procedure, I understood what the northern barbarians must have felt when they were permitted to enter Byzantium.
>
> What most of all delighted me was the music. From the Protestant tradition, where church music has a uniform tone of respectable reverence and the organ is regularly used to cover the inadequacy of the performers, I had no idea of what could be done with unaccompanied choirs, nor of the variety and vivacity of the music for the Greek monastic services, which can go from gaiety to grandeur, from passion to awe, with unmatched lightness and power. Father Kyriakos gave me permission to stand in the choir so that I could see the texts as they were sung. (There was little written music; most of the tunes were traditional.) Soon I was memorizing words and tunes, probably to the horror of my neighbors. It may not have been unadulterated altruism that prompted the invitation to go to Mar Saba.[1]

At Mar Saba too, however, Smith was impressed both by the church building and by the hymns:

> I was shown the two libraries, as I was the other sights of the monastery, but at the time I paid them little attention. My main interest was in the services, which gave me a new understanding of worship as a means of disorientation. The six hours in darkness with which the day began[2] were not long—they

were eternal. The service was not moving toward its end, it was simply going on, as it had from eternity and would forever. As one ceased to be in time, one ceased also to be in a definite space. In the enormous church, lit only by the flames of scattered sanctuary lights and candles, there were no visible walls, floor or ceiling. The few small flames far above, like stars, burned again on the polished marble of the nave, as if other stars were an equal distance below. Or were those tiny fires, far down beneath, the earth? [*sic*] The painted walls reflected the dim light as if it came from a remote distance, and in the vast, vaguely luminous space thus created the huge black frescoes of the saints and monks of old stood like solid presences all around, the great figures of the eternal and universal Church, present in this realm among the stars, above space and time, the unchanging kingdom of the heavens, where the eternal service was offered to an eternal God.

The words of this worship, too — the enormous hymns of the Greek monastic offices — were unmistakably hypnotic, interminably ringing the changes of a relatively small number of brilliant, exaggerated metaphors, dazzling the mind and destroying its sense of reality. I knew what was happening, but I relaxed and enjoyed it. Yet at the same time I somehow came to realize that I did not want to stay. For the monks, it was truth, for me it was poetry; their practice was based on faith, mine on a willing suspension of disbelief. When Father Kyriakos came down again, early in Lent, I was ready to return to Jerusalem.[3]

Carefully read, these two descriptions seem contradictory. At the Holy Sepulchre Smith was "delighted" by "the variety and vivacity of the music for the Greek monastic services, which can go from gaiety to grandeur, from passion to awe, with unmatched lightness and power." At Mar Saba, on the other hand, the hymns seem to have been much more repetitive: "The words of this worship, too — the enormous hymns of the Greek monastic offices — were unmistakably hypnotic, interminably ringing the changes of a relatively small number of brilliant, exaggerated metaphors." Is this a discrepancy? If so, it implies the style of performance in the two churches was rather more different than I suspect it was, though no doubt the services in the monastic church would have been wordier and of longer duration than those in the Holy Sepulchre. A literal reading, in fact, indicates that it was the music Smith found varied and vivacious, the words that were hypnotic, interminable, exaggerated. Is that indeed what he meant? Is it possible to be delighted and bored at the same time? Smith's description is hard to believe, and I suspect his recollections have been deliberately but incompletely reshaped to support part of his hypothesis. How he felt about the Greek hymns wouldn't matter much if this were mere travelogue, but it happens to be the whole point: from the "repetitive, hypnotic prayers and hymns," Smith says he gained "a new understanding of worship" that, as we saw in the last chapter, informed his theory about the "unknown ceremonies" Jesus practiced: "To judge from the hekalot and Qumran texts, the magical papyri and the Byzantine liturgy, these will have been mainly the recitation of repetitive, hypnotic prayers and hymns."[4] How he came to believe that is hard to understand at first, for Smith never stated that he attended any Greek baptisms or that Jesus chanted any hymns. To tell the truth, many aspects of Smith's account strain credulity.

To start with, there is at least one obvious falsehood: Smith's explanation of why he didn't stay longer during his first visit to Mar Saba. The Morton Smith of 1973 wrote, "For the monks, it was truth, for me it was poetry; their practice was based on faith, mine on a willing suspension of disbelief." It is improbable that Smith actually felt that way in 1941, when he was officially a student from Harvard Divinity School, preparing for ordination. In fact he was ordained an Episcopalian deacon only four years later (July 1945) and a priest not long after that (March 1946).[5] To believe Smith's 1973 memoir, then, we would have to suppose that he had faith while studying at Harvard, somehow lost it in Jerusalem despite the glorious Byzantine services, then regained it again after he returned to Harvard and was ordained, but had lost it permanently by the time of his second trip to Mar Saba. That is more or less the opposite of what many people would do, which is find faith in Jerusalem and lose it at Harvard.[6] The evidence reviewed in the next chapter suggests Smith lost his faith during the early 1950s.

So Smith's account deceives us about the chronology of his personal religious history. But that is just the beginning. To read Smith's text with the careful thought it demands, considering and remembering all the details, is to proceed from the deceptive to the offensive. During his first visit to Mar Saba, Smith declared, "I was shown the two libraries, as I was the other sights of the monastery, but at the time I paid them little attention. My main interest was in the services, *which gave me a new understanding of worship as a means of disorientation*" (emphasis added). The thesis of Smith's two books, of course, is that the Secret Gospel reveals a new understanding of worship as it was practiced by Jesus. To read his account of Jesus' worship in parallel with his story of the worship at Mar Saba, hypertextually connecting the many indecorous dots, will eliminate any uncertainty about what Smith was really saying: "Thus from the differences between Paul's baptism and that of [John] the Baptist, and from the scattered indications in the canonical Gospels and the secret Gospel of Mark, we can put together a picture of Jesus' baptism, 'the mystery of the kingdom of God.'" At the outset, its most important feature was not immersion in water, but disrobing. "It was a water baptism administered by Jesus to chosen disciples, singly and by night. The costume, for the disciple, was a linen cloth worn over the naked body. This cloth was probably removed for the baptism proper, the immersion in water, which was now reduced to a preparatory purification. After that" came the important part, the "unknown ceremonies," which "to judge from the hekalot and Qumran texts, the magical papyri and the Byzantine liturgy, . . . will have been mainly the recitation of repetitive, hypnotic prayers and hymns. The magical tradition also prescribes . . . interference with breathing. Manipulation, too, was probably involved. . . ." Hypnosis, abnormal breathing, and manipulation are "worship as a means of disorientation" all right. At Mar Saba Smith found that "the enormous hymns of the Greek monastic offices — were unmistakably hypnotic, interminably ringing the changes of a relatively small number of brilliant, exaggerated metaphors, dazzling the mind and destroying its sense of reality." Once the disciple was in such a disoriented, dazzled state, what happened then? "One with [Jesus], he participated by hallucination in Jesus' ascent into the heavens, he entered the kingdom of God, and was thereby set free from the laws ordained for and in the lower world." The Byzantine hymns, too, made Smith feel that "the huge black frescoes of the saints and monks of old stood like solid presences all around, the great figures of the eternal and universal Church, present in this realm among the stars, above space and time, the unchanging kingdom of the heavens, where the eternal service was offered to an eternal God." That might be the most one should expect from a six-hour night vigil service, but for Smith there was a further step: "Freedom from the law may have resulted in completion of the spiritual union by physical union" between Jesus and the disciple. "This certainly occurred in many forms of gnostic Christianity; how early it began there is no telling." However there *is* telling — if one believes with Smith that "the gnostic teachers . . . emerged from the libertine tradition," which "found in Paul's doctrine everything it needed to justify its inclinations," and that "there were elements of libertinism in even the most conservative of early Christian parties, a fact which strengthens our supposition that this side of early Christian thought went back to Jesus himself." Thus, as Smith felt increasingly disoriented by the hypnotic Byzantine hymns at Mar Saba, he could quip, "I knew what was happening, but I relaxed and enjoyed it."[7]

Now the phrase "relax and enjoy it" is the punch line of an obscene joke, well-known in English-speaking countries, which also circulates as "lie back and enjoy it." In the joke, Confucius (or some other Oriental wise man) offers this advice: "If rape is inevitable, relax and enjoy it." Lots of people daydream in church while listening to the music (or even the sermon!), and a superficial reading of Smith's account might suggest nothing more than that. But he himself indicates there was more, by saying "I knew what was happening."

What was happening, by Smith's telling, was that he was gaining "a new understanding of worship as a means of disorientation," a new understanding that he went on to propound in his two books on the Secret Gospel. From the repetitive, hypnotic prayers and hymns of the Greek monastic offices, Smith was discovering what the first disciples experienced in their ritual unions with Jesus: hallucination, possession, ascent, freedom from moral law — which "may have resulted in," well, "completion of the spiritual union. . . ."

We are back to the double entendre problem: could we be reading more into this than Smith intended? Can we be certain that Smith even knew the "relax and enjoy it" joke? In principle, it is usually difficult to determine when a sexual joke originated and by what route it circulated. Because of cultural attitudes in the United States, unlike some other places, obscene jokes "have a tendency to remain in the purely oral tradition, with the consequence that almost all of the urban American folk tales that can be compared with the folk tales of non-literate peoples contain obscenities."[8] Their oral-traditional character makes such jokes particularly fascinating to folklorists, but also exceedingly difficult to research; specialists in the emerging field of "jokelore" regularly complain about "the enormous methodological problems involved" in "the systematic collection of orally communicated jokes."[9] Often it is impossible to trace the provenance, chronology, and tradition history of any single joke, unless it refers to a famous person or event. However, this particular joke has offended so many people over the years that it has generated an unusually long written record, finding its way into print on the average of once per decade: it appears in Georgia court records from 1954, after a deputy sheriff told the joke to an actual rape victim; in 1970, a British-American rock band borrowed the punch line for the title of a record album; in 1976 a New York City newscaster ruined his career by telling it on the air. Since then it has gone on to upset people across the globe.[10] Thus the joke was certainly in wide circulation in the early 1970s while Smith was writing his popular book. Although that fact does not establish by itself that Smith had actually heard the joke, it does rule out more innocuous interpretations of "I knew what was happening, but I relaxed and enjoyed it," given the thesis of the book in which this statement appears — the thesis that Byzantine hymns and other evidence show that Jesus initiated his disciples through disorienting rituals that culminated in "libertine" physical sex.

The appearance of this joke in this context reveals a lot. First of all, it shows that every one of Smith's descriptions of Jesus' alleged initiation rite can and should be read as an extended double entendre. Second, if Smith can tell such a joke in church — in one of the most renowned Christian monasteries! — he can do it anywhere. The hints of sexual humor in the Secret Gospel, therefore, will also have to be taken seriously. Third, it confirms that Smith's memoir was not meant to be truthful. Everyone "edits" his or her recollections to some degree, but Smith's account of his time at Mar Saba was deliberately shaped to persuade us that what he discovered there reveals a remarkable truth about how Jesus initiated his disciples. He had not thought of connecting his argument to the Byzantine liturgy while writing his first book, the one published by Harvard. Only when he began writing the second book, while looking for ways to construct his narrative of visiting Mar Saba, did Smith decide to shape his story so that it served the larger agenda. Smith admitted as much:

> When I began this chapter my conscious intention was merely to explain how I happened to go back to Mar Saba, years later, and find the manuscript. Also I wanted the pleasure of recalling this strange and beautiful experience, and the advantage of beginning my book with this picturesque material. But just now, while writing, I see this story has introduced one of the important themes of the book. For what I really discovered in this first visit to Mar Saba was the inner purpose of the Orthodox liturgy: to make worshipers on earth participants in the perpetual worship of heaven. And this discovery, I now realize, provided one of the key ideas by which I was later enabled to explain the Gospel material in the manuscript. Is this a coincidence? Or has the mystical tradition of Greek monasticism, which shaped the hymns and suggested my experience, preserved and developed the primitive Christian tradition that lay behind the Gospel? Or have I imposed on the Gospel my understanding of the Orthodox rites?[11]

I would say he imposed his understanding of the Secret Gospel on the Orthodox rites. Thus I suspect that "the vivacity of the music" Smith said he heard at the Holy Sepulchre is a more or less straightforward recollection of his experience in 1941, while the "unmistakably hypnotic" words he ascribed to Mar Saba represent a later, more mendacious, Smith, shaping his narrative to support the "important themes" and "key ideas" of his 1973 popular book. One cannot know, of course, what Smith was really thinking about while at the monastery in 1941; it is not uncommon for people to fantasize about being forced into sex.[12] But I think it highly doubtful that the historical Morton Smith of 1941, a seminarian preparing for ordination, actually experienced what the authorial Smith of 1973 described.

Introducing a joke about rape is revealing in a fourth way, by introducing an element of aggression and violence into the story. It makes Jesus' alleged ritual look like the initiation rites used by some college fraternities and sports teams: forms of hazing in which simulated or actual sex acts are used as "celebratory dramas," as "demonstrations of masculine dominance" in which older members ritually "emasculate and degrade," even "infantilize" and "feminize" the younger male recruits[13] This would be a lot of freight to load on a single joke, were it not for the repeated hints of anger and hostility that, as we will see, keep cropping up in Smith's publications on Jesus and early Christian initiation. The more time and labor I invested in reading what he had to say, following his coercive logic and pondering his forcedly suggestive suggestions, the more his entire endeavor came to seem like an attempt at just such an initiation, a felonious textual assault.

Let All Mortal Flesh Keep Silence

Eastern Orthodox Christians would feel outraged at Smith's "understanding" of their worship as "disorientation." Even the historian who does not feel personally affronted should recognize that it typifies Smith's tendency to interpret his "scattered indications" without reference to their contexts, to the meaning they have or had within the communities from which he has filched them. With long-lost Gnostic or magic rituals he might be given the benefit of some doubts. But with the living tradition of Byzantine liturgical hymnody, there is abundant reason to reject Smith's abuse of the "evidence." That double entendres or sexual interpretations have no validity whatever is easy to show. For example, in the most important modern collection of Orthodox spiritual writings, the *Philokalia,* we can read about the desert father Abba Philimon, who would have been one of the early pioneers of monasticism. Philimon did find hymn-singing a heavenly experience. He "spent the whole day . . . chanting and praying unceasingly, and being nourished by the contemplation of heavenly things. His intellect was often lifted up to contemplation, and he did not know if he was still on earth." But Philimon's heaven was hardly a paradise of freedom from law, for he taught that the ideal monk "has illumined himself with the light of divine laws," so that "the saints . . . by keeping the vision of heaven unsullied in themselves . . . made its light shine by observing the divine laws." These laws certainly excluded any possibility of "physical union" with disciples, for Philimon admonished his own followers, "you must above all renounce your own will; you must acquire a heart that is sorrowful[,] . . . weeping over [your sins] day and night; and you must not be emotionally attached to anyone."[14]

The fact that Smith did not know such texts simply nullifies his belief that he "discovered . . . the inner purpose of Orthodox liturgy." For while it is true enough that this purpose is "to make the worshipers on earth participants in the perpetual worship of heaven," Smith has presented a doubly false interpretation of what that statement means. First, the process of becoming a "participant" in heavenly worship is a lifelong pilgrimage of prayer and repentance. While we are still living out our earthly life it would be more accurate to say, with the Byzantine liturgy, that "now the powers of heaven worship with us unseen." In other words, it is the angelic hosts who descend (as it were) to where we are, not we who ascend to where they are (John 3:13). And they come to our level in an invisible way: only after death will we see face to face, knowing as we are known (1 Corinthians 13:12). Second, and more importantly, the Orthodox Christian heaven is nothing like the one Smith envisioned, in which moral laws are suspended to permit homosexual acts on earth. It is, on the contrary, a place where no lawlessness is possible, a state that can therefore be entered only through the merciful redemption of Christ. Thus the Orthodox Christian sings, "I will not give you a kiss like Judas, but like the thief I confess you: remember me, Lord, in your kingdom" (cf. Luke 23:42).[15] Smith's failure to understand this casts doubt even on his statement that, when he first visited Mar Saba, "my main interest was in the services." For the persistent ignorance about Christian worship that permeates all of Smith's publications makes it very difficult to believe that he ever had any real interest in the services.

On the other hand, one aspect of his account is easy to believe, whether or not it actually occurred. Over the course of an all-Greek service lasting from midnight to 6 a.m., it would not be surprising if Smith allowed himself to fall into an absent-minded state of reverie, so that his thoughts began to wander aimlessly. Some people do that even when listening to the more familiar music of their own culture. Once Smith's attention had been set adrift, of course, there is no telling how far it could go. But the Christian tradition is fully aware of this normal human weakness; the literature on prayer and worship is full of admonitions to keep paying attention, and advice on how to do so. "Disorientation" is not the goal to be sought, particularly if it leads to flights of fancy about one's carnal appetites. Distraction from prayer is to be avoided, for it opens the mind to temptations of all kinds. It was precisely against such dangers that the unidentified tenth-century tract Smith found in the Mar Saba library warned: "Remember the eternal fire each evening when you go to sleep and when you get up, and indolence will never overcome you at the time of psalmody." Like most of the texts one will find in monastic libraries, this one reflects a long tradition: it probably refers to the monastic practice of examining one's conscience twice a day. In any case it shows unequivocally that Byzantine liturgy (like all Christian worship) is not about disorientation, but about concentration.

One of the texts most widely read by Greek Orthodox monks today is *The Ladder of Divine Ascent* by St. John Climacus, who was abbot of the community on Mount Sinai in the seventh century. According to St. John, "The beginning of prayer is the expulsion of distractions from the very start . . . ; the middle stage is the concentration on what is being said or thought [in the words of the prayer]; its conclusion is rapture in the Lord."[16] Listening to this degree of attentiveness is not a passivity but an activity. And since monks worship by alternately prostrating and standing up straight, one cannot "relax and enjoy it," even in the ordinary sense. St. Symeon the New Theologian emphasized this in the tenth or eleventh century when he wrote:

> With concentration and diligence [a monk should] go through the whole office, paying particular attention to the beginning of the hymnody, . . . with diligence, without relaxation of the body or putting one foot in front of the other, or leaning on walls and pillars. . . . The mind must not wander off. . . . The eye and the soul must be kept free from distraction and pay attention to nothing else but the psalmody and the reading, and to the meaning of the words of the divine Scripture that are being sung and read, so that no one of these words may pass in vain, but rather that his soul may derive nourishment from all of them and attain to compunction and humility and divine illumination.[17]

Thus, if Smith had really wanted to learn anything about the meaning of monastic hymnody, he should have conferred with one of the monks about what he was experiencing. Had he done so, he would not have been told that worship is a "means of disorientation." He would have been told the opposite: that it is essential to pay attention and to resist temptations to let the mind ramble. This is the kind of advice that another youthful seeker once received from a wise old staretz, or "spiritual elder," on Mount Athos: "When you pray, keep your mind quite free from any imagining, any irrelevant thought, . . . Enclose your mind in the words of your prayer."[18]

In fact, Smith realized that his view of the liturgy differed from what the monks thought. But he believed that he understood it better than they did.

> Another element in my experience at Mar Saba now also seems significant. I became aware of a fundamental difference between my attitude toward the service and that of the monks. For me, at that time, the liturgy was primarily a means for the experience of beauty, and thus a means of revelation, since beauty was of God. For the monks, the liturgy was just what its Greek name said—*leitourgia* means "service"—and this service was primarily a duty. Certain words had to be said, certain actions, to be performed. Whether or not the result was beautiful was, at best, a secondary concern. The mere performance was both essential and effective. This attitude is basically magical. For example, it explains the magical gems of the ancient world, on which spells and figures are often scribbled with no regard at all for their appearance, but with an iron determination to get the necessary words and patterns, somehow or other, onto the stone. During my visit I simply thought the monks' attitude

curious, but I now suppose it helped to shape my understanding of the religious mind and subsequently, without my recalling it, to explain the new Gospel text.[19]

Smith's memory blanks out again: only now, while he is composing his popular book, does it "seem significant" that his attendance at the liturgies "shape[d] my understanding of the religious mind." This understanding enabled him "to explain the new Gospel text" even "without my recalling it" — that is, even without remembering how he learned that "the religious mind" has a "basically magical attitude" that favors "mere performance. . . an iron determination to get [through] the necessary words and patterns, somehow or other." Only after finishing his Harvard book, as he began describing the monastic liturgies in his popular book, did Smith suddenly "remember": it was at Mar Saba itself that he began to realize that early Christian liturgy was "basically magical." In reaching this conclusion, Smith sidestepped a huge scholarly literature on the relationships and differences between religion and magic (and superstition and science).[20] He saw himself as presenting a bold and original insight, but he unwittingly revealed that he had not done even basic reading on what he was writing about. His idea that "the liturgy was primarily a means for the experience of beauty" also has an interesting bibliography, to which we shall return. What is important at the moment is to clarify that, in ascribing his version of a "magical attitude" to the monks, he was utterly mistaken.

No Christian monk, Eastern or Western, would say that the primary aim of worship is the exact and meticulous fulfillment of routines. It would be more accurate to think of the formal liturgy, with its prescribed texts and actions, as a kind of school for personal prayer, a time to practice being attentive to the divine self-revelation to which the texts point, an opportunity for the heart and mind of the individual to learn and practice becoming one's true self, a creature in the right relationship to God. Thus a twentieth-century monk of Mount Athos wrote this about his own spiritual elder:

> The Staretz loved the long church Offices, so rich in spiritual content. Yet with all his affection for the majesty, beauty and music of divine service he would declare that the offices, though instituted by the grace of the Holy Spirit, are but an imperfect form of prayer, given to the faithful as being adapted to the strength of, and beneficial for, all men.
>
> "The Lord gave us church offices with singing because we are helpless children: we do not yet know how to pray aright, whereas singing is good for all men when they sing in humility. But it is a better thing for our hearts to become the church of the Lord and our minds His altar."
>
> And again:

"The Lord is glorified in holy temples, while monks and anchorites [i.e., hermits] praise God in their hearts. The heart of the anchorite is a temple and his mind an altar, for the Lord loves to dwell in the heart and mind of man."

And he would say, too, that when unceasing prayer becomes established in the depths of the heart all the world is transformed into a temple of God.[21]

Like any other kind of learning, striving for this goal is hard work. Indeed it is harder than most, for one begins by working to overcome the passions, the bad habits that are not our true nature, but actually sick, sinful distortions of our natural, God-given impulses and yearnings. As the Mount Athos monk wrote of his teacher:

The whole of Blessed Staretz Silouan's life was prayer. He prayed unceasingly. . . . He had, too, the greater gift of mental prayer, to which he devoted the night hours in the complete silence and darkness propitious to this form of prayer, which consists in guarding the heart from every alien thought, through the exercise of inner recollectedness, so that no foreign influence should disturb communion with God. This discipline may be termed variously sacred silence (hesychia), inner quiet or mental stillness. We have inherited it through the living and written tradition of the holy Fathers: it has come down to us from the first centuries of Christian history. . . .

The ascent to pure prayer begins with the struggle with the passions. As the mind becomes cleansed of passion it grows stronger in the fight against intrusive thoughts, and more steadfast in prayer and meditation; while the heart, in liberating itself from the darkening effects of passion, begins to see spiritual things more clearly and more purely, and finally acquires an intuitive certitude about them. . . .

Unless the heart be cleansed it is impossible to attain real contemplation. Only a heart purified of passion is capable of that peculiar awe and wonder before God which stills the mind into joyful silence.[22]

Thus the "inner purpose of the Orthodox liturgy," as Smith put it, is not "the mere performance" of magical incantations. Nor is it to "dazzle the mind and destroy its sense of reality," setting it loose to meander through random thoughts leading to our passions and temptations. It is more like a kind of athletic training (Philippians 1:27), straining toward the goal of unceasing prayer in the "joyful silence" of the mind in the heart. The primary metaphor for this desired state is not sexual experience, nor even "the experience of beauty" — though Orthodox Christians are hardly unaware of the beauty of their services! — but silence or stillness, as explained by St. Isaac the Syrian: "The movements of the tongue and heart during prayer are keys. What comes afterwards is the entering into the treasury. At this point let every mouth and every tongue become silent. Let the heart which is the treasury of our thoughts, and the intellect which is the ruler of our senses, and the mind, that swift-winged and daring bird, with all their resources and powers and persuasive intercessions — let all these now be still: for the Master of the house has come."[23] The paradox, then: careful, practiced listening to music and text eventually teaches a monk to hear what no music or text can express, a reality for which the only possible language is utter soundlessness. This is expressed in many Byzantine hymns, including one that has become very well known to Western Christians, by way of an English paraphrase that Smith, as an Anglican seminarian, could not possibly have been unaware of:

> Let all mortal flesh keep silence, and with fear and trembling stand;
> Ponder nothing earthly-minded, for with blessing in his hand
> Christ our God to earth descendeth, our full homage to demand.
>
> . . . .
>
> At his feet the six-winged seraph; cherubim with sleepless eye,
> Veil their faces to the Presence, as with ceaseless voice they cry,
> "Alleluia, Alleluia, Alleluia, Lord most high!"[24]

What Smith says about the meaning and "inner purpose" of Byzantine hymnody, then, is a misrepresentation, and at least partly a deliberate misrepresentation. But Smith's deceptions hardly end here. As the next section shows, he asserts much else that could not have happened.

Heavenly Ascents and Bodily Assents

While Smith's claim about "physical union" is largely veiled by jokes and double entendres, it is still only an element within a larger proposal that can and should be taken more seriously — namely, that for at least some early Christians, worship included "disorientation," the experience of altered states of consciousness. Reports of early Christian worship, both in and outside the New Testament, are full of miraculous healings and escapes, dreams and voices and visions, being "filled with the Spirit," speaking in tongues, appearances of the risen Jesus, and other extraordinary phenomena. Why shouldn't these experiences be compared with the paranormal occurrences that have been widely observed in many religions in the modern world, including the charismatic and Pentecostal forms of Christianity? This is a good question, though it is only beginning to receive scholarly attention[25] and had scarcely been broached at all in Smith's time. Smith might be credited for being among the first to call attention to it, with his theory that "the disciple was possessed by Jesus' spirit and so united with Jesus. One with him, he participated by hallucination in Jesus' ascent into the heavens."[26] However, Smith's understanding of these psychological phenomena is so uninformed, even for his time, that his proposals have no real value. Serious investigations into this question will not be constructible on any foundation laid by Smith.

In the 1960s and early 1970s, when many rock stars were experimenting with mind-altering drugs and practices like Transcendental Meditation, it was widely believed that rhythmic, repetitive music could have psychedelic effects, inducing trances or altered states of consciousness,[27] as was dramatized in *Hair*, "The American Tribal Love Rock Musical" produced on Broadway in 1967.[28] Scientists in those days also entertained theories about the psychological effects of drumbeats and other kinds of musical and ritual repetitiveness.[29] Thus Smith saw no real difference between the incantation of angelic names in the magical papyri and the behaviors ascribed to rock music audiences of his own time: "Such jabberwocky is called 'magical words.' These cries (often, as here, including the names of outlandish deities) were used by magicians to work themselves into a state in which they believed they possessed the powers they claimed and enjoyed the experiences they desired. When their experiences resulted in disintegration of the personality they continued to utter similar sounds, involuntarily. Inarticulate utterances play similar roles in many primitive and enthusiastic groups, for instance, the Yippies."[30] Here Smith was using the word "enthusiastic" to refer to religious frenzy, following the ancient Greek meaning of prophetic or creative possession by a deity. The original Yippies were a group of protesters at the 1968 Democratic Party convention in Chicago, whose leaders were later convicted in the infamous "Chicago Seven" trial. Their name, which rhymed with "hippies" and recalled the exultant, carefree yodel of the Old West cowboy, was said to be derived from the acronym for "Youth International Party." However, their protest event had an arguably spiritual dimension: it was originally advertised as an "international festival of youth, music, and theater," and it actually began with "a sunrise service of chants, prayers, and meditation" led by Beat poet Allen Ginsberg.[31] News stories implying that hypnotic rock music could cause bizarre, even criminal, behavior were not uncommon during that period, and more than one spectacular murder was blamed on cults of chanting, drug-crazed hippies.[32] But can such culturally conditioned beliefs be taken seriously as a model for investigating Christian worship two thousand years ago?

The pioneering study of the relationship between music and trance experiences was published in 1980 by Gilbert Rouget,[33] who established some basic facts that are relevant here. First, music by itself cannot cause trancelike experiences. People learn to have them, as part of their inculturation into societies or organizations that value this activity. Thus any kind of music can be associated with trance behaviors, which are themselves instances of a much larger

class of dissociative experiences.[34] It is cultural encoding, not acoustical phys-
ics, that determines which musical characteristics are considered "hypnotic"
and what people do in response to them.[35] No musical characteristics, even
pounding rhythm, monotonous melodies, or repeated phrases, can compel an
unwilling or untrained person to enter a trance or experience a sense of being
possessed: "Music has often been thought of as endowed with the mysterious
power of triggering possession. . . . There is no truth whatever in this assumption. . . . a certain conjunction of emotion and imagination . . . is the source
from which trance springs. Music does nothing more than socialize it."[36] That
is why, when whirling dervishes or other exotic groups perform for Western
audiences, the audience members do not experience comparable trance states
of their own. They have not been enculturated to hear the music in that way;
they have not learned to "whirl." Although they may report that they found
the music "exciting," "spiritual," or whatever, these assessments are made
from within their own cultural worldview, which may even be "informed" by
false stereotypes about dervishes. Unlike drugs, sound waves alone cannot
induce altered states of consciousness in the absence of cultural interpretation
and social learning. This essentially invalidates much of what Smith was trying
to say. Most likely his "disorientation" experiences at Mar Saba were fab-
ricated while he was writing *The Secret Gospel* book for publication in 1973.
But if anything of the sort actually happened back in 1941, it was Smith who
chose to have these experiences and he who determined their characteristics.

Erotic feelings and behaviors definitely occur during some music-related
trance experiences (in cultures that allow this), and it is possible that our very
capacity for ritual behavior is related, at the evolutionary level, to the animal
mating behaviors we also call "rituals."[37] But it is cultural forces, such as
religion, that determine what phenomena are permissible and how they are
interpreted — and they are not typically interpreted in terms analogous to sexual submission. The erotic imagery of Sufi songs may rival the poems of St.
John of the Cross, but neither speaks of a god who forces his will on people.[38]

Even members of a listening audience, whose role could be described as
"passive," do not experience themselves as being overpowered. In one study,
wherein people listening to a storyteller were asked to describe their feelings of
being "enraptured," they tended to describe themselves as choosing a kind of
deliberate passivity, which "liberates the listener from the restrictions of socially imposed ways of thinking . . . and allows the free reign of the imagination."[39] This sense of liberation and "free reign of the imagination" helps to
explain why, in many cultures, ecstatic religious practices are particularly
popular among women and low-status men. As the frequency of Pentecostal
storefront churches in poor American neighborhoods implies, the "downscale

market" for religious ecstasy testifies to the fact that these experiences feel healing and empowering. They offer a much-valued release from the burdensome domestic and employment obligations of daily life, which are more readily compared to being overwhelmed by external forces.[40]

In parts of the Sudan, for instance,

> during possession rites women become men; villagers become Ethiopian, British, Chinese; the powerless and impoverished become powerful and affluent. Essentially irreversible processes — genderization, aging — become reversible; established categories are undermined. Hierarchical orderings are telescoped and undone when Islamic holy men and pagan prostitutes possess the same . . . woman. . . .
>
> The appropriation of meaning is a matter of individual disposition, as villagers' possession histories attest. . . .
>
> And this . . . is the therapeutic import of possession: all the implicit functions and significances . . . seem to work, gradually and cumulatively, toward developing in the possessed a mature, considered perspective of herself and her life situation. A woman's first possession acknowledgement in a sense consummates her transition to adulthood, thence, perhaps, to individuality. . . .
>
> Possession . . . , to use the [possessing spirit's] own parlance, "opens the door" to true adulthood for those who, because they are secluded and treated as jural minors, might otherwise find their desires stymied, their creativity blocked. So if a "rite of protest," possession is more than a contained rebellion against an established social order . . . ; it is also rebellion of the human mind against the fetters of cultural constructs. [Possession rituals,] in obliquely suggesting fresh interpretations for quotidian truths — in their essentially aesthetic task — help to develop adepts' consciousness of themselves, so providing them the possibility of more felicitous outcomes in their encounters with others, whoever those others might be.[41]

But a counterexample shows how profoundly these rituals are shaped by cultural assumptions. Among the Hindu Tamils of south India, when an unhappy wife feels estranged from her husband, this is attributed to her being possessed by an evil spirit. Most often it is the spirit of a man who committed suicide because his family would not let him marry the bride of his choice. The woman is brought to a temple and pressured by the (male) musicians to perform a dance of trance possession, in which the evil spirit is alternately cajoled and threatened into revealing his identity, along with why and when he "caught" the woman he is possessing. It generally transpires that the woman was (as we might say) "asking for trouble" by going to the cinema with other women, or otherwise absenting herself from the domestic sphere. Often she was too attractively dressed at the time. As the male demon speaks through her, she is able to express lascivious feelings that are not normally permissible for women. By a series of symbolic actions the evil spirit is finally driven out and replaced by a goddess, who enables the woman to return and love her husband again — or (the only other acceptable outcome) to become a celibate devotee for the rest of her life in the goddess's temple. From an outsider Western perspective like our own, the whole thing looks like a kind of ritualized aggression, to intimidate the woman into conformity without so much as acknowledging her husband's abusive or problematic behaviors.[42] But if this example shows how trance possession experiences have no inherent meaning as such — they acquire their specific shape and interpretation from the culture in which they are practiced — it also shows how far we have to go to find a ritual that even vaguely resembles Smith's fantasies. For in the Hindu temples of Tamil south India we are a cultural universe away from the monasteries of Greek Orthodox Christianity.

This difference, by the way, points to another Western cultural presupposition in Smith's construction of worship. The idea that his interpretation of what happened at Mar Saba could somehow also explain Jesus' alleged baptism ceremony, constructed as it was from Hermetic, Jewish, and Gnostic potsherds, assumes that all religions are ultimately much the same, at least at the experiential level. This is a common assumption in the modern West (and not only there); it flatters our cherished principles of equality and tolerance. But it is not true — it seems plausible only to those who know very little about the extraordinary diversity of religions in the world.[43]

Thus it is not possible to understand any music or musical behavior without understanding the community of people who do it. To learn any way of responding to music is also to get to know the people who respond to *this* music in *this* way. Ethnomusicologists who seek to gain "experientially based musical knowledge" know full well that their researches should "lead to a more general understanding, not only of music, but of people," even when the researcher personally rejects the religious beliefs of the people whose music he is studying.[44] What is most wrong with Smith's story, therefore, is that he claims to have gained an understanding of the monks' worship and music, while he manifestly failed to gain any understanding of the monks.

This will be easier to see if we compare Smith's report with that of another cross-cultural encounter that happened about the same time, and to a man of about the same age: Colin Turnbull's experience among the Mbuti people of the Congo. In 1951, after studying music at Oxford and in India, Turnbull visited the Mbuti to learn about their music also. He had not yet received any anthropological training, and thus he was no more a professional observer than Smith was when he first visited Mar Saba. Initially "there was no expectation on either side that I ever was or ever would be one of them, or even particularly like them,"[45] Turnbull wrote. Yet as Turnbull learned to sing and dance along with the Mbuti, somewhat as Smith sang along with the Byzantine hymns, Turnbull did begin to have transcendent experiences, briefly including a sense of oneness with his hosts. Even then, however, he knew he was not really having the same experience the Mbuti were having:

> On the third occasion, no longer afraid that I was going to miss anything, and no longer looking for any explanation, just intent on enjoying myself, I closed my eyes . . . ; I felt free to let my own body move as though, not being able to see myself[,] nobody else would be able to see me. And by the same illogic I felt free to join in the singing. And in an instant it all came together: there was no longer any lack of congruence, and it seemed as though the song was being sung by a single singer, the dance danced by a single dancer. Then I made the mistake of opening my eyes and saw that while all the others had their eyes open too, their gaze was vacant . . . there were so many bodies sitting around, singing away, but I was the only person there, the only individual consciousness; all the other bodies were empty. Something had been added to the importance of sound, another mode of perception that, while it in no way negated the aural or visual modes of observation, none the less went far beyond them.[46]

Turnbull went back to his music studies at Oxford, but three years later he paid another visit to the Mbuti, this time with camera and recording equipment. On this visit he discovered that his status within the group was similar to that of an uninitiated youth, who knew something of the culture but wasn't fully a member.[47] By the end of his stay, however, his presence was being taken more seriously:

> When the time came for me to leave, all the filming and recording being finished in both village and forest, the Mbuti did not want me to leave. They said I *could* not leave, I had heard too much. This was not said as a threat, merely as a statement of fact. They were puzzled that I should even think of leaving. Was it to do with the fact that I was not married? They cut the marks of eligibility into my forehead. It was done very seriously, and I felt nothing but mild discomfort. But when I returned to the camp and the women saw the marks and burst into laughter, ridiculing me, I felt something very strongly . . . not so much embarrassment as the touch of power . . . an awareness that something had happened to me, and that departure was now that much more difficult. Yet I could not or would not give up my plans to return to the world I thought I still belonged to.[48]

At that point the Mbuti invented some humorous, spontaneous rituals that made it possible for him to leave. When Turnbull returned the third time in

1957, he was a graduate student in anthropology intending to write a dissertation. That was when things really got complicated, as his Oxford-trained ethic for objectivity clashed with his growing sense of belonging within the Mbuti community. But that is a story I don't need to tell here.[49]

Now if Smith had told us that, as he listened to the Byzantine hymns, he had felt drawn toward becoming an Eastern Orthodox Christian, or a monk, we could readily believe that he was acquiring some understanding of how the Mar Saba monks experience their hymnody, much as Turnbull came to feel a sense of belonging with the Mbuti. Even if Smith knew he could never share the monk's faith, he should at least have acquired some real understanding of what it means to live as an Orthodox monk and developed some personal sympathy for the individuals who, after all, had welcomed him into their monastic home. Ethnomusicologist Jeff Todd Titon has attempted to describe this process:

> Burt Feintuch . . . writes beautifully of his experiences in growing into the community of Northumbrian pipers. The old-fashioned folklorist in him who traffics in and arbitrates authenticity worries a little about this: how can he enter this community without a birthright? How can he act and "sound like a Northumbrian without being one?" Adoption is the answer: they have adopted him. The adopted child seeks reassurance: . . . "I have no way of demonstrating that my experience resembles that of the local musicians," he writes. . . . This is not a problem unique to adopted outsiders in musical communities. Whenever we have a transcendent experience — falling in love, for example — we feel compelled to express this experience, however difficult it is, and we do: we embody it and we enact community. Two lovers bridge that language gap, through empathy, and come to understand, and trust, that one's experience resembles the other's — that the inner experience corresponds to and complements the outer.
>
> That this is also the case among certain religious groups, such as the Old Regular Baptists, is plain to me. Here the urge is to demonstrate experiences with God, and the church provides forms for this: conversion narratives, for example. . . . But of course, full participation is not possible in every community. I did not become an Old Regular Baptist. Were my musical experiences, then, the same as theirs? Not exactly. The wife of a professor at Berea College once asked me, "How can you sing with them when you don't believe as they do?" "But I think I believe in music as they do," I said. What I meant was that I felt I had shared, with them, in a musical experience that was, indeed, spiritual but that transcended the particularities of any denomination or doctrine. And I think they agreed.[50]

Adoption, empathy, trust, sharing, community — none of these terms come to mind when reading Smith's account of the singing at Mar Saba. Smith was writing only about himself and described what he heard solely in terms of his own cultural and religious conceptual world, full of 1970s American mythology about what repetitive, hypnotic hymns can do to people. His observations and experiences, then, even if honestly reported, would have no value for understanding early Christian or modern Orthodox worship, or anything else except twentieth-century American notions about the psychological effects of music.

But Smith's experiences are not reported honestly. What can be inferred about his likely religious opinions in 1941 differs greatly from his self-report of 1973. As a seminary student approaching ordination, he most likely regarded himself as a Christian and would therefore have been interested in how the Greek monastic liturgy compared with the liturgy he would soon be authorized to celebrate. If so, it is a bit curious to see him describe himself as "from the Protestant tradition, where church music has a uniform tone of respectable reverence and the organ is regularly used to cover the inadequacy of the performers." His experience was actually quite atypical for a Protestant: dozens of Middle East travelogues were published in the nineteenth and twentieth centuries by English-speaking Protestants, and virtually every one of them states how shocked and appalled its author felt when encountering Greek Orthodox worship for the first time in the places where Jesus walked. Harry Emerson Fosdick (1878–1969), who was thrown out of the Presbyterian church for advocating religious tolerance and inclusion,[51] found nothing tolerable in Eastern Orthodoxy. To him it was "a decrepit Christianity. . . . It was not Christ that Islam crushed but a Christianity which had become an organized denial of Christ. . . . Never was a religion's founder more tragically misrepresented than Jesus has been in his home country." His loathing extended to Mar Saba hymnody — even in the very Westernized form in which he knew it: "One hymn which is still in our hymn books came from this monastery:

> Art thou weary, art thou languid?
> Art thou sore distressed?

Having been there, I have no desire to sing it again."[52] And he felt this way about a hymn that a near-contemporary described as "one of the great hymns of all time," a hymn that moreover exhibited "little of the original Greek in it."[53]

Why was Smith's reaction more positive than Fosdick's? One reason, I think, was that Smith had a good knowledge of Greek and could understand what was being sung — at least while he was permitted to stand in the choir and read the texts. But another reason, I believe, is that Smith's outlook was actually not very Protestant. As the next chapter will show, he seems to have

identified with the "high church" or "Anglo-Catholic" wing of Episcopalian-
ism, and he subscribed to (an extreme form of) the "branch theory" of the
Christian church. This ecclesiology identifies the Anglican Communion, the
Roman Communion, and Eastern Orthodoxy as the three branches of the
ancient, undivided Catholic Church, but regards Protestant groups as eccle-
siologically deficient.[54] Thus I would wager that in 1941 Smith regarded the
monks as no more nor less Catholic than himself (a view they would not have
reciprocated). That might help explain why he felt qualified to draw his own
conclusions about the meaning of the monks' worship — and why, even years
later after losing his faith, it never occurred to him that he would be unable to
understand the Greek liturgy without reference to the monks' own beliefs and
experiences.[55] We will never know for sure, however, because Smith's account
is a palimpsest: the true story of the 1941 Morton Smith has been overwritten
by the Morton Smith of 1973.

Shamanism and Schizophrenia

It is unfair, of course, to blame Smith for being uninformed about the
study of musical trance experiences. Rouget's 1980 book hadn't been published when Smith was writing in the 1960s and 1970s. But it is painfully clear
that Smith had not even read publications that were well-known and highly
regarded in his time. In particular, Smith's attempts to depict Jesus as a magician sometimes invoke the concept of shamanism — an academic construct
introduced in Mircea Eliade's influential 1951 book *Shamanism*, translated
into English in 1964.[56] Eliade's model proved highly congenial and has been
widely (I would say too widely) invoked by scholars seeking to explain all
kinds of religious experiences and unusual phenomena.[57] According to Smith:

> What really proves Jesus practiced magic is the essential content of most of
> the major stories in the Gospels. In Mark Jesus appears as one possessed by a
> spirit and thereby made the son of a god; so do magicians in the magical
> papyri. Other stories say he was fathered by a god; the same was said of other
> magicians. Like them, he was driven by the spirit into the wilderness and there
> met repulsed evil spirits; this is a typical pattern of shamanic initiation. And
> like the shamans he is sometimes represented as possessing a spirit, sometimes
> as himself possessed.
>
> The claim to have ascended into the heavens was often made by magicians,
> especially shamans, and therefore fits Jesus' character and career. We should,
> in fact, be surprised had he not made it.[58]

Smith does not cite Eliade's book, and shows no evidence of having read it.[59]
He seems, instead, to have picked up the term "shamanism" from somewhere

in the academic environment (such as informal conversations with colleagues) but without really knowing what it meant — for Eliade's opening chapter makes clear that "shaman" is not a mere synonym for "magician," as Smith seems to believe:

> Magic and magicians are to be found more or less all over the world, whereas shamanism exhibits a particular magical specialty, . . . not every magician can properly be termed a shaman . . . every medicine man is a healer, but the shaman employs a method that is his and his alone. As for the shamanic techniques of ecstasy, they do not exhaust all the varieties of ecstatic experience. . . . Hence any ecstatic cannot be considered a shaman; the shaman specializes in a trance during which his soul is believed to leave his body and ascend to the sky or descend to the underworld.[60]

Eliade, in other words, is careful to make distinctions; Smith seems willing to toss in anything that might connect Jesus to magic. Eliade has carefully drawn up an explicit definition of what he is talking about; Smith presents a hodgepodge that repeatedly contradicts Eliade's definition. Eliade's shamans are not fathered by gods, they are human beings. They are not typically understood to be possessed by spirits, but rather are able to control them. Shamans do ascend to heaven, but this is something that *distinguishes* them from magicians in general:

> A similar distinction is also necessary to define the shaman's relation to "spirits." All through the primitive and modern worlds we find individuals who profess to maintain relations with "spirits," whether they are "possessed" by them or control them. . . . But the study of shamanism does not require going into all this; we need only define the shaman's relation to his helping spirits. It will easily be seen wherein a shaman differs from a "possessed" person, for example; the shaman controls his "spirits," in the sense that he, a human being, is able to communicate with the dead, "demons," and "nature spirits" without thereby becoming their instrument. To be sure, shamans are sometimes found to be "possessed," but these are exceptional cases for which there is a particular explanation.[61]

Finally, Eliade has an entire chapter on shamanic initiation, which little resembles Jesus' experience in the wilderness.[62] For example, the shaman's teacher plays a very important role in the initiation process, whereas Jesus went into the desert alone; not even John the Baptist is presented in the gospels as Jesus' teacher. In other words, Smith was not applying a current scholarly paradigm to new material. "Shamanism" for him was just another scattered indication.

As Smith moved from Jesus to the early church, he switched from the vocabulary of magic and shamanism to a metaphor of psychiatric disease:

With Acts 2 we reach the story of the coming of the spirit as a group phenomenon. This looks like a late reflection of reports about the "speaking with
tongues" in Paul's churches — reports the author [of Acts] did not correctly
understand, since he turned the incomprehensible sounds uttered by the possessed into a super-language thought by all its hearers to be their native
tongue. So what really has to be explained is not the imagined miracle of Acts
2, but the appearance of hysterical symptoms as group phenomena in the
early churches. Critical scholarship generally has been quite unable to explain
this "coming of the spirit." . . .

The reasons now can be guessed, especially if Acts is right in reporting that
the phenomena began with the first group in Jerusalem.[63] That was a congregation of which many members had been prepared for group possession by
their experience of individual possession in Jesus' baptism. Jesus seems to
have had a peculiar attraction for and power over schizophrenics. Hence his
"exorcisms." . . . Hence, too, his following of "women who had been cured of
evil spirits" (L[u]k[e] 8.2).

The stories of his disciples' sudden, total abandonment of their ordinary
lives to follow him (M[ar]k 1.16ff; 2.14; J[oh]n 1.43) probably reflect the
same power and indicate an instability in the disciples' characters that explains why they yielded to possession by Jesus in baptisms. Their baptismal
experiences will in turn explain the possession of whole groups of them by his
spirit after his death. Such group hysteria usually begins with individuals in
the group; their visions and other symptoms are contagious — cf. the history
of the witchcraft trials. Mass conversions followed. Both converts and the
original followers, when they went abroad, communicated the psychological
infection to the circles they formed in other provinces. Paul presumably
caught it in Jerusalem: his first serious attack occurred while on the way to
Damascus; he later spread the symptoms through Asia Minor and Greece.[64]

At the time of his death, Smith was expanding this picture in a book called
Paul the Possessed, "whose thesis was to have been that Paul is a primary
example of 'spiritual possession.' "[65] In the passage just quoted from *The
Secret Gospel,* Smith was writing in his usual knowledgeable-sounding tone,
but he presented no factual information. He simply strung together the names
of several scary-sounding mental conditions — hysterical symptoms, possession, schizophrenia, instability of character — without even asking if they all
refer to the same thing. Then he described this amalgam as a "contagious . . .
psychological infection." But even back in 1973, people knew that schizophrenia isn't an infection you can "catch," like the influenza virus.[66] And as
Eliade emphasized, shamans are not insane: "the mentally ill patient proves to
be an unsuccessful mystic or, better, the caricature of a mystic."[67] If Smith had
actually done any research on "group possession," he should have found the

much better-informed history of this phenomenon by Ronald Knox, a Catholic priest who disapproved of this kind of religion but tried hard to be open-minded about the meaning of such experiences, and respectful of the people who have them: "What right have we to assume that the man who lays credit to heavenly illumination must be either a saint or a fraud? . . . (if we are wise) we shall not therefore put down the whole of his message to diabolic possession, or to hysteria. George Fox [the founder of the Quakers] may yet have something to tell us about religious toleration."[68] Compared with that, Smith seems positively abusive, like an angry person willing to utter any insult that might stick, no matter how far-fetched. In the coming chapters we will, for better or worse, have occasion to learn more about Smith's anger at Christ, and about Jesus' anger at women in the Secret Gospel.

Summary

Smith claimed in 1973 that he acquired a new understanding of worship from listening to the Byzantine hymns in the monastery at Mar Saba. He found the hymns were repetitive and hypnotic, tending to produce a psychological state of "disorientation." Smith believed that the initiation rites Jesus used, as shown in the Secret Gospel, were designed to produce a similar effect, in which the disciple felt himself rising to heaven in union with Jesus. However, Smith's interpretation of the Orthodox liturgy cannot be reconciled with the traditional understanding that is handed down in the Orthodox Church, which he seems to have been completely unaware of. While scholarly observers need not subscribe to the religion of the people whose rites they are studying, they cannot responsibly promulgate interpretations that are uninformed by the experience of the community that actually creates and uses these rituals.

Moreover, Smith's account of his experiences at Mar Saba can be shown to be disingenuous. First, he never mentioned the Byzantine hymns in his earlier scholarly book, but only in his popular book, which was written second. It is as if he had not thought of this angle until he began recounting his experiences at Mar Saba in a popular vein. Smith's experience of Byzantine worship played no part in the original formulation of his theory; he only claimed that it did after the fact, and shaped his account of his Mar Saba visit accordingly. Second, Smith wrote that he had had no religious faith during his first visit in 1941, when in fact he was preparing at the time for ordination that took place in 1945. Third, Smith inserted an obscene joke into his description of his own "disorientation," consistent with his earlier insinuations that Jesus' secret initiations were sexual encounters.

While it is possible that some early Christians made use of practices related to trance possession and the cultivation of altered states of consciousness, Smith's understanding of these phenomena is uninformed even for his time, and without scholarly merit today. The study of trance experiences in connection with music, as it has developed since Smith's era, shows his representations to be absurd. Contrast with other research shows that the experience of learning to understand the music of a foreign culture necessarily entails an improved understanding of and empathy for the people of the culture, but this did not happen in Smith's case. Finally, Smith's comparisons of early Christian worship to "shamanism," "enthusiasm," and mental illness show that he had not even read the bibliography on these topics that was available and respected at the time.

7

The Happiness of the Dead:
Morton Smith on Christian Morality

I would be very interested to learn how this parish priest of the 1940s came so to oppose the religion in which he was ordained, because the words that ran through my mind constantly while reading Jesus the Magician *were those of Schweitzer about Reimarus: "Seldom has there been a hate so eloquent, so lofty a scorn."* — O. C. Edwards, Jr.

To quote a distinguished Roman administrator, "What I have written, I have written." — Morton Smith

Who Was Morton Smith?

Morton Smith briefly served as a priest of the Protestant Episcopal Church (the U.S. branch of the Anglican Communion), but never resigned. Thus for some forty years, even after his death on July 11, 1991, he was listed in the two serial directories of Episcopalian clergy,[1] as if he were a priest in good standing — even though (as his writings show) he no longer subscribed to Christian faith. This was no mere oversight, for he took the trouble to keep his listing current, updating it as he changed jobs, issued new publications, and received new fellowships. As a result, it is relatively easy to establish the chronology of his career, adding further information from his obituary and other honorary and memorial publications.[2]

Robert Morton Smith was born in Philadelphia on May 28, 1915. He attended the Academy of the New Church, a local preparatory school with a good reputation for getting its alumni into elite colleges. The school was affiliated with the General Church of the New Jerusalem, a Swedenborgian denomination, so it must have been there that he first heard about journeys to heaven, though I have not detected any Swedenborgian influences in his writings. As a Harvard undergraduate, Smith majored in English, graduating with an A.B. magna cum laude in 1936. In 1940 he received a Bachelor of Sacred Theology degree cum laude from Harvard Divinity School and evidently meant to continue on for a Th.D. (Doctor of Theology) degree. In 1940–42 he held a Sheldon Fellowship for study in Jerusalem but became stranded there when the United States entered the Second World War. It was then that he first visited Mar Saba. He subsequently was Thayer Fellow at the American School of Oriental Research in Jerusalem (1942–43), but he also enrolled at Hebrew University (1940–44), from which he received a Ph.D. in classical philology (1948) with a dissertation on the Mishnah (the core text of the Talmudic literary corpus). His Harvard Th.D. was finally awarded in 1957, with a dissertation on "Judaism in Palestine" up to the time of the Maccabees (second century BCE).[3]

Smith was ordained a deacon for the Episcopal Diocese of Maryland in July 1945 and a priest in March 1946. He held several short-lived parish jobs in Philadelphia (1945–46), Baltimore (1946–48), and Boston (1949–50), the last while continuing his studies at Harvard. From 1950 on he held only university teaching jobs: in the Department of Biblical Literature at Brown University (1950–55), in a visiting position at Drew University (1956–57), and finally in the History Department at Columbia University, from 1957 until his retirement in 1985. Although Smith had not worked in a church since 1950, it is only from 1956 that he is listed as "non-parochial," meaning that he had his bishop's approval to hold nonecclesiastical employment.[4] In order to maintain this nonparochial status, Smith had to file a written report every year with the bishop of Maryland. Had he stopped doing so, canon law dictated that one of three things should happen: (1) he could have declared his intention to leave the priesthood and gone through the church's "Renunciation of Ministry" process; (2) he could have formally left the Episcopal Church by way of the "Abandonment of the Communion" process; or (3) had he simply stopped communicating with the bishop, after two years there would have been an ecclesiastical trial for "Abandoning the Work of the Ministry."[5] Evidently none of these occurred, and he kept his listings up-to-date. This implies he was ambivalent—no longer having the faith to continue as a priest, but unwilling to make a definitive break with the ministry or the church. To my knowledge there is no published information about why, when, or how Smith lost his faith, though this seems to have coincided with his switch to an academic career in the early 1950s. However, a 1949 article by the Rev. Morton Smith of Harvard Divinity School, one of his earliest publications, does give us a glimpse into what his clerical career was like, hints at significant personal struggles that may well explain his departure, and sheds not a little light on the Mar Saba portrayal of Clement as a churchman who advocated swearing false oaths for the sake of "the true truth."

Pastoral Cares

The *Journal of Pastoral Care* was founded shortly after the Second World War, evidently to foster a newly emerging interest in enriching traditional Christian spiritual direction with insights from the developing science of psychiatry. Published at Harvard Divinity School, its early issues are full of optimistic articles about exciting new possibilities for caring and empathic pastoral counseling. But where they spoke peace, Smith was ready for war (cf. Psalm 119[120]:7). His article "Psychiatric Practice and Christian Dogma" is chaotic and disorganized, querulous and vociferous, more like an emotional outburst than a considered reflection on its topic.[6] It presents, and seems to endorse, a terrifying picture of Christianity as representing a kind of tyranny of the mob, a living death made inescapable by the ruthless enforcement of majority opinions that Smith does not question, yet seems to hold at a mental arm's length — as if he himself did not really believe them, and doubted that Jesus did either. As the following excerpts show, a naive reader with no prior knowledge of Christianity would never suspect that things like compassion, forgiveness, or even conscience play any role whatever in Christian morality, or that repentance is supposed to occur within an ongoing spiritual journey of faith and hope, prayer, and grace.[7]

> The end or function of psychiatry is . . . to make people happy [by] persuading the patient that what he supposed a sufficient cause for unhappiness is not, after all, so important as he thought it [p. 12]. . . . [I]t is obvious that the end of Christianity is quite different. . . . That of psychiatry, we saw, was to make people happy, that of Christianity to make them Christians, to unite them with Christ in his body, the Church. It is doubtless a teaching of Christianity that only by such union can man attain true and eternal happiness. . . . But such "true and eternal" happiness is sharply distinguished from what this world calls happiness, which is declared false and transitory; and while the greater saints may occasionally enjoy glimpses of the bliss to come — and while most Christians manage to live reasonably contented lives — it is the

consistent teaching of Christianity . . . that we have not yet attained . . . , that while alive we are given over to death[8] . . . , that now we see through a glass darkly. . . . Meanwhile, the wicked flourish like the green bay tree (Ps[alm] 37.35) . . . this, too, has been the consistent teaching of Christianity. Indeed it has been possible for Christians to remain orthodox while teaching that this world is wholly given over to the power of evil and that the only satisfactory form of adjustment to it is hostility [p. 14].

[Christianity] has consistently maintained that the good life is not any life which leads to happiness in this world, but only that life in which union with Christ is achieved and progressively realized. It has taught that the realization of this union requires the observation of a moral code. And it has universally taught that those who refuse to observe this code, though they may here live and die happy, will, after death, be dreadfully undeceived, will eventually be reunited with their bodies and will bodily go into Hell, which has generally been described as eternal torment [p. 15].

The psychiatrist will be content if he can turn out the patient reasonably happy and adjusted to society in some way which society finds acceptable; the pastor, on the other hand, must frequently use every effort to prevent the parishioner from resorting to some agreeable and socially acceptable adjustment which is, unfortunately, sinful, and must sometimes do all he can to secure a course of action which will probably lead to a long period — if not an entire life — of unhappiness [p. 16].

The fact that Hell is unpopular does not justify us in allowing others to be ignorant of the universal Christian doctrine stating its existence and wide range of usefulness. . . . [A]ll men are dying, only some do it faster than others. . . . Such a reply may not contribute much to the happiness of the dying, but the happiness of the dying is the concern of the psychiatrist, whereas the concern of the pastor is the happiness of the dead.

    In a word, Christianity always has been, is by nature, and therefore . . . always will be an authoritarian religion. . . . [T]he constant growth, through the past nineteen centuries, of the authority and power of the Church, and especially of the Roman Catholic Church, is an indication that men have accepted its authority willingly, from a realization of their own instability, and that its authoritarian attitude is no less wise psychologically than it is dogmatically helpful to many believers [p. 18].

Anyone, therefore, who departs from the interpretation set by that general consensus, and relies on his own interpretation of individual texts, is departing from normative Christianity to devise a more-or-less novel religion of his own. Whether the religion he devises be better or worse than Christianity is not here in question, the point here is that, anyhow, it must be different [p. 14].

Yet Smith did not locate this unchallengeable authority in any of the usual places, such as the Bible, the teaching of Jesus, or even Tradition as generally understood. By his account, the truth of this nearly Manichean dualism is guaranteed solely by centuries of majority despotism—a "general consensus" so almighty that it can even ventriloquize Jesus, putting words into his mouth that some might regard as comforting, but that Smith knows are really calls to arms:

> At the heart of Christianity there is, indeed, peace, but a supernatural peace which is at war with the fallen nature of humanity, and with the corrupt society which is the expression of that fallen nature. So St. John makes Jesus say '. . . In the world you have tribulation, but take courage, I have overcome the world' (J[oh]n 16.33). The same doctrine is elaborated at length by St. Paul in Romans 7 and 8, and has been taught by all branches of the Church ever since. A contemporary illustration is provided by an anecdote . . . [in which a] liberal said magnanimously [to a monk], 'Well, I trust you have at least found peace in your religion.' 'No.' said the Christian, 'War' [p. 20].

At the least, Smith's statements are carelessly worded. At the theological level, they veer toward the doctrinally dubious, and at the pastoral level, they would have been positively harmful. While there is certainly a concept of spiritual warfare in the Christian tradition, particularly in monastic spirituality, the war is against evil spirits, not "the fallen nature of humanity": "For our struggle is not against enemies of blood and flesh, but . . . against the cosmic powers of this present darkness" (Ephesians 6:12).[9] And if Smith was telling people that the war against sinful humanity was to be fought in the name of a "universally taught moral code," rooted in nothing more than what the disciples "made Jesus say," he was close to preaching a kind of idolatry that places the church higher than God.

That this distorted his pastoral counseling is clear from one of his own examples, for his article presents three case studies of the kinds of people who must be given this depressing advice, evidently based on actual penitents who came to him for confession.[10] All three, as it happens, are people involved in forbidden sexual practices they are unable to give up. One of them is a divorced woman in a sexual relationship with another man she wants to marry. Since Jesus taught that marriage cannot be dissolved except by death (Mark 10:11–12, Romans 7:2–3, 1 Corinthians 7:39), in both Anglican and Catholic traditions her marriage was regarded as still in effect, despite the civil divorce. She could not remarry in the church while her husband was living, nor should she be in any other kind of sexual relationship. But according to Smith, "She must therefore be told that remarriage would add to the sin of adultery the even greater sin of open defiance of the laws of the Church." This amounts to misinformation because traditional Christian morality does not recognize a category of "sins against the Church."[11] Moreover, it is hardly self-evident that "defiance of the laws of the Church" should be counted as worse than adultery. Nor did Smith mention that, under the laws of the Episcopal Church at the time, the final decision as to whether she could remarry belonged to the bishop, not the local priest.[12] If this case is representative of Smith's counseling approach, the members of his flock could be forgiven for thinking they had a hell of a pastor. His work with parishioners should have been better supervised.

A HOMOSEXUAL YOUNG MAN

More relevant for our purposes is the second case in Smith's article:

> A young man has been attracted to the parish, evidently by the music and ritual of the services. Gradually he becomes a regular attendant, makes himself helpful in parish activities, shows, even, some interest in doctrine and devotional literature. Then, one day, he brings the conversation around to homosexuality. He doesn't see that if two adult males enjoy each other sexually, any harm is done to anybody. As for adult-adolescent relationships, one of his closest friends (i.e., he himself) is homosexual and he says the friendships he formed during adolescence are among those he has found most helpful. He doesn't seem to be unstable, keeps his job, gets on well in society, has lots of normal friends, and seems generally happy. And, after all, homosexuality has been characteristic of some of the greatest men — Plato and Shakespeare, etc. He must be told that homosexuality is a sin far more serious than fornication, and that unwillingness or inability to repent of it automatically debars the sinner from the sacraments. Whether or not psychological or social arguments against homosexuality are used, it must be made clear that the sinfulness of a sin is not a matter for dispute nor for private judgment, but is established by the Christian tradition which individuals can only accept or reject. Finally, for the good of the congregation no less than for his own good, he must sooner or later be made to choose between his new attachment to the Church and his previous sexual adjustment, even though there be great probability that he will find no other adjustment so satisfactory [pp. 16–17].

There was ultimately no middle ground, therefore: a homosexual must "sooner or later be made to choose" between the church and "his previous sexual adjustment," no matter how personally costly this choice may be, even though it may mean "an entire life of unhappiness." From our historical position, having witnessed the sexual revolution and the gay liberation movement, it is easy to suppose that Smith was (as he himself insisted) simply reaffirming the age-old Christian viewpoint on homosexuality.[13] But comparison with other writings in circulation at the time shows that he was not even stating the contemporary consensus of his own denomination. After consulting many of the books that were used to educate Anglican priests of Smith's generation, I have yet to find a single one that echoes his aggressively negative tone, affirms that psychology and Christianity are irreconcilable, or maintains that all homosexuals must be "automatically debarred" from the sacraments. Although none of these books questions the traditional belief that homosexual acts are always serious sins, the pastoral approach they recommend differs from Smith's on three important issues: the seriousness of the sin, access to the sacraments, and the role of psychology.

"A SIN FAR MORE SERIOUS THAN FORNICATION"

The sources I am about to discuss take for granted that morality is about choice, and therefore only exists where choice is possible. Thus in the Christian ethical tradition, homosexual acts or thoughts count as sins if they are deliberately chosen. Impulses and feelings, if they are not accepted or acted upon, are temptations rather than sins. In a traditional Christian context, therefore, any discussion of sexual morality is about deliberate thoughts and acts, not about unchosen mental states or psychological phenomena like "sexual orientation."[14] A natural proclivity toward homosexual behavior, whether inborn or caused by environmental factors, would not in itself be a sin if the person has not chosen it. Such a tendency may weaken a person's capacity to choose freely, but it does not change the ethical requirement that in all circumstances he or she should always choose to refrain from deliberate homosexual thoughts or acts.[15] Thus I emphasize that the writings I discuss are about homosexual *behavior*, not about the condition of being homosexual. I also emphasize that I am trying to recapture the perspectives of 1949, ignoring (for historical reasons) any new insights, changes of emphasis, or doctrinal developments that may have taken place since then in some denominations. The orthodox position at the time Smith was writing is summed up in a 1952 book called *Psychiatry and Catholicism:*

> With regard to a homosexual's moral responsibility, the basic rule is that voluntary actions and desires of a homosexual nature are objectively a grievous sin against the natural law. Granted, for the sake of argument, that some forms of homosexuality have a biological organic cause, one cannot claim that the homosexual therefore has a right to give in to his urges. A heterosexual may be said to be biologically urged to normal sexual activities, but that does not give him the right to sexual satisfaction outside marriage. Neither can one claim that, again granted a biological disposition to homosexuality, the indi-

vidual's will is necessarily determined in such a manner that he cannot act differently. However, there are cases in which homosexuality is like a compulsion that blindly drives the individual to give in to his passion, and even to seek the occasion to do so. In such cases, the action may be said to be willed, but it is no longer freely willed; hence, complete guilt may be questioned. But, as in all other similar conditions, reduced responsibility does not give the penitent a *carte blanche* to continue his practices; in other words, the most important question in deciding the subjective guilt of the homosexual is whether he sincerely strives to control himself. Now, it has been seen that the honesty of the willingness to do so may, sometimes, be seriously called into question. This is a point that the confessor [i.e., the priest] should keep in mind. The homosexual may sincerely repent his past sins in the confessional, but the purpose of amendment is sometimes rather weak. The reason is, as we pointed out, his conviction that he cannot get rid of his habit anyway — a conviction that frequently is strengthened by the reading of propagandistic literature. In such a case, words of encouragement are needed to lift up the penitent's morale and to prepare the proper disposition for receiving absolution.[16]

Smith's idea that homosexual acts are "more serious than fornication" goes back to medieval theology as codified by St. Thomas Aquinas (1224–74). In his usual Aristotelian way, Aquinas attempted to classify the sins of lust (*luxuria*) according to six categories, which he ranked according to "grievousness" (*gravitas*). The first four were less serious because at least they "presupposed natural principles," whereas the last two were judged "most grave and shameful" because they "act against things as determined by nature." Thus the "least grave" sin was (1) "simple fornication" (heterosexual sex between people not married to each other) because "it is committed without injustice" to a third party, except for any resulting children. Next came (2) the seduction of a virgin, because it also involves injustice toward her father or guardian. However, (3) adultery was worse, because it includes injustice toward the husband, who (unlike a father or guardian) has "authority as regards the act of generation." Any of these three sins would become still worse if it were also (4) a rape, because then it would be "aggravated by the use of violence." Seduction or rape of a nun or consecrated virgin was worse yet because it also involved sacrilege; however sacrilege is not a subcategory of lust. The two unnatural sins of lust were (5) incest, "which . . . is contrary to the natural respect which we owe persons related to us," and (6) the "vice against nature" (*vitium contra naturam*) "since . . . man transgresses that which has been determined by nature with regard to the use of venereal actions."[17] The vice against nature, however, could itself be divided into four different categories, which Aquinas did not attempt to rank in order of severity. In the order he mentioned them, they were (1) masturbation ("procuring pollution, without any copulation, for the sake of venereal pleasure"), which was also known as impurity (*immunditia*) or effeminacy (*mollitia*); (2) bestiality ("copulation with a thing of undue species"); (3) homosexuality between men or women, which Aquinas called the "vice of sodomy"; and (4) "not observing the natural manner of copulation, either as to undue means, or as to other monstrous and bestial manners of copulation," evidently a roundabout way of describing such things as oral or anal sex, fetishism, and whatever else could be deemed unnatural.[18]

St. Thomas was accorded paramount authority in the Roman Catholic Church between 1879 and the Second Vatican Council (1963–66).[19] But he could not have had that degree of importance in the Anglican Communion to which Smith belonged because Anglicans differed with Aquinas on transubstantiation and other issues. In principle, therefore, an Anglican priest like Smith had access to alternative viewpoints on the classification of sexual sins. For instance, the Anglican bishop Jeremy Taylor (1613–67) published two books on Christian morality, *Holy Living* and *Holy Dying,* which have been in print continually down to modern times. Yet Taylor mentioned homosexuality, or rather sodomy, only once, and without implying that it is worse than any other violation of the commandment "Thou shalt not commit Adultery": "They sin against this commandment 1. Who are adulterous, incestuous, sodomitical, or commit fornication. 2. They that commit folly alone [i.e., masturbate], dishonouring their own bodies with softness and wantonness. 3. They that immoderately let loose the reins of their bolder appetite, though within the protection of marriage."[20]

Thus Smith was misrepresenting the Anglican tradition if he insisted, as he apparently did, that the Thomist classification (with homosexuality worse than fornication) was the only possible one. And he was doing his parishioners a disservice if he gave them the impression that this lower ranking of homosexuality was "not a matter for dispute nor for private judgment, but is established by the Christian tradition which individuals can only accept or reject." But Smith's attitude here seems to reflect a pattern we will see more of: a preference for Roman Catholic writers and theological positions. As we read earlier, he believed that "the constant growth, through the past nineteen centuries, of the authority and power of the Church, and especially of the Roman Catholic Church, is an indication that men have accepted its authority willingly." It is almost as if Smith actually thought he was a Catholic. That probably means he subscribed to the "branch theory" ecclesiology, which was favored by the "high church" or "Anglo-Catholic" minority within the Anglican spectrum. As one writer defines it: "The branch theory of the Church, as it has been called, is essential to the Anglo-Catholic position. It rests on a view of

Christianity which is wider than that held by Papal or Eastern Catholicism, since it holds that every part of Christendom which has maintained continuity with the past by a true succession of Apostolic Orders and teaching is part of the visible organization of the Body of Christ on earth."[21] Thus the Anglican Communion, the Roman Catholic Church ("Papal Catholicism"), and the Eastern Orthodox Church ("Eastern Catholicism") are the three branches of the ancient Catholic Church, even though neither "Papal" nor "Eastern Catholicism" endorses this "branch theory." Each branch has maintained continuity with the original church through apostolic succession, meaning that its bishops were ordained by bishops who stand in a direct lineage of ordination going back to the apostles.

Smith, however, seems to have held an idiosyncratic form of the branch theory. In the view of most Anglo-Catholics, the Protestant denominations lack the continuity of apostolic succession due to a defective theology of Holy Orders and other problems. Therefore, Protestant churches are not "part of the visible organization of the Body of Christ on earth," even though individual Protestants, if they are saved by the grace of God, hold invisible membership in the one Catholic Church. Yet Smith's article of 1949 seems to endorse an extreme or extended form of the theory that would also include Protestant groups. He speaks of what "has been taught by all branches of the Church," and even states more explicitly: "Historically speaking the term 'Christianity' refers *a posteriori* to the Orthodox Church and the various national Churches which have broken away from it in the East, to the Roman Catholic Church and to the major denominations which broke away from it or from each other."[22] Thus he seems to have held the illogical opinion that Roman Catholic positions (such as Aquinas' classification of sins) are the correct ones because they are Catholic, and they are therefore recognized as correct by all Christian denominations because all are branches of the Catholic Church. This is obviously untrue, for the denominations disagree on a great number of issues, as almost any Catholic or Protestant could have told him. I suspect one of Smith's reasons for leaving the active ministry, therefore, was that he could not realistically maintain this unsupportable ecclesiology.

SINNERS AND SACRAMENTS

"He must be told that homosexuality is a sin far more serious than fornication," wrote Smith, "and that unwillingness or inability to repent of it automatically debars the sinner from the sacraments." Assuming that by "homosexuality" Smith meant homosexual acts, not homosexual orientation, he was attempting to describe a practice that both the Roman and Anglican communions had inherited from the medieval church. He has, however, somewhat oversimplified it. The issue was primarily admission to Holy Communion, not to all the sacraments. A sinner would not be denied Confession or Extreme Unction in principle, though (if unrepentant) he could be denied absolution. In the Roman church, mere repentance was not enough; sacramental confession was also mandatory before the sinner could receive communion: "The Council of Trent has defined that no one conscious of mortal sin and having an opportunity of going to confession, however contrite he may deem himself, is to approach the Holy Eucharist until he has been purified by sacramental confession."[23]

However, the medieval church recognized a second principle with regard to this issue: the need to avoid scandal. Onlooking parishioners should not be given occasion to wonder why an individual is being denied communion, nor should they see communion being administered to someone widely known to be a serious sinner. Thus if the priest was aware of "occult" or private sins, he was supposed to tell the sinner privately, not publicly, to refrain from coming up for communion. But if the sinner came anyway, the priest should give him or her the host to avoid scandal.[24] In the twentieth century, both the Roman and Anglican churches continued to recognize this principle in different ways: the Episcopal Church in Smith's time even had a law permitting the person "who has been repelled from the Holy Communion" to appeal to the bishop.[25] Thus the Book of Common Prayer that Smith used (the 1928 American edition) mentioned only the publicly known sinner: "If among those who come to be partakers of the Holy Communion, the Minister shall know any to be an open and notorious evil liver, or to have done any wrong to his neighbors by word or deed, so that the Congregation be thereby offended; he shall advertise him, that he presume not to come to the Lord's Table, until he have openly declared himself to have truly repented, and amended his former evil life, that the Congregation may thereby be satisfied."[26] Therefore, if Smith's parishioner had actually committed homosexual acts and had not repented, Smith would have acted correctly in telling him not to receive communion. But if the homosexual came up for communion anyway, Smith should have done whatever avoided scandal: denied communion if the person was known in the parish to be "an open and notorious evil liver" — or given it, if withholding communion would call attention to sins the community was unaware of.

There was room for more than one opinion, however, on how to balance the two issues of the sinner's moral state and the potential for scandal. Smith's pastoral approach seems harsh, even inadequate, when compared with that of Kenneth E. Kirk (1886–1954), a professor of moral and pastoral theology who became bishop of Oxford and was one of the most learned and respected Anglican ethicists of his era. Kirk's position on avoiding scandal, informed by more than a dozen pre- and post-Reformation sources going all the way back to St. Augustine, was that the priest's authority to withhold communion was limited, to such an extent "that communion may not be refused by a priest even to a penitent to whom he has personally refused absolution."[27] Since a priest would refuse absolution if he thought the person in the confessional had not truly repented, this seems to mean that an unrepentant homosexual could not be denied communion as long as he kept his sins out of public view.

As Kirk saw it, though, there was a more important issue, which seems to have eluded Smith altogether. The pastor's chief concern was not to protect the Holy Eucharist from being profaned by sinners, but to guide the parishioner toward a fuller spiritual and sacramental life that draws the maximum spiritual benefit from the Eucharist. Kirk seems to have thought, in fact, that it would rarely be necessary to deny communion because a person struggling with serious sin would be likely to avoid it of his own accord:

> A conscientious man harassed by mortal sin has usually a not unnatural reluctance towards receiving the Holy Communion, even though at the same time he is struggling hard against his sin. This is especially the case with young men in the grip of youthful passions. A growing irregularity of attendance at the Eucharist may therefore be not merely a symptom of serious sin, but also a sign of an awakened conscience. Yet such reluctance to receive the sacrament, though natural and laudable, is wholly misdirected. So long as the struggle against temptation continues, so long the Eucharist will be the greatest force the Christian can have upon his side. If it be neglected, the danger of ultimate submission to sin is increased tenfold. "I who always sin, should always seek this medicine." [citing St. Ambrose, *De Sacramentis,* iv.6]
>
> The maintenance at all cost of the full spiritual life, restored to grace by confession and absolution, and sustained by the Eucharist as by all other means of religious progress, must be the first step in countering deadly sin.[28]

The contrast is stark. Compared with Smith's approach, Kirk's seems more humane, more charitable, indeed more Christian. Where Smith perceived in the homosexual only an absurd refusal to conform to nineteen centuries of Christian ethical unanimity, Kirk was able to see both sides of the struggling person: both the "serious sin" and the "awakened conscience." Smith would have "sooner or later" given the homosexual parishioner an ultimatum: a lifetime of unhappiness as the price of Holy Communion and eventual salvation, or the certainty of "eternal torment" as the price of "socially acceptable adjustment" in this life. Kirk's goal was less dramatic, but more realistic and beneficial: the "maintenance of the full spiritual life" of the individual Christian. Indeed, Kirk would probably have considered Smith's approach ("he must be made to choose") to be dangerous. Although uncompromising as to the sin, Kirk was deeply concerned about the spiritual health of the sinner, which included his emotional health. Thus it was very important to avoid "heroic resolutions" that would only lead to failure, discouragement, and worse:

> In cases of mortal sin the habit must be broken once for all. It is scarcely necessary to emphasize the extraordinary difficulty often met with in such an attempt. Only a supreme effort of will on the part of the sinner is competent to effect it. Hence in advising the step — and it often has to be advised — the priest must take certain precautions. An attempt to break a sinful habit which ends in failure is a disaster to be avoided at all costs. It may lead to despair, abandonment of the struggle, and callousness. It may be the mother of hypocrisy, leading the sinner either to dissimulate his real condition from the priest whose help he has sought, or to run from one adviser or confessor to another so that none may guess the urgency of his case.
>
> To minimise this danger, therefore, anything in the form of heroic resolutions must be discouraged.[29]

Far from advising lifelong misery as the ticket to postmortem joy, Kirk was determined not to harm a penitent's capacity for growth in virtue and empathy: "it must be noticed that it is just in the giving up of occasions of sin that there occurs most frequently the mutilation of personality of which we have previously spoken. . . . For occasions of sin are occasions also of virtue; and to cut them off is to remove the soul from opportunities of realising its full possibilities and developing its strength. They are also occasions of experience; and experience, particularly experience of temptation, is the most powerful factor in making for sympathy."[30] That "heroic resolutions" which deny the reality of a person's feelings are counterproductive to the growth of virtue and humanity was evident, to Kirk, from the Christian tradition itself:

> It is clear that any such violent inhibition of feeling is unnatural, and must involve danger to the soul. The emotion which has been expelled from consciousness will gain added strength and vehemence in the subconscious region, and may either break out in overwhelming force, or be the parent of some other excess of character, or even finally overthrow reason itself. The undue mortifications to which ascetics have sometimes been addicted have almost always issued in one of these three results. Either they have led to disastrous and irretrievable relapses, or to some abnormal morbidity of character very far from the true Christian ideal, or to a condition bordering on lunacy itself. Anything more than a limited and temporary inhibition of feeling has always been condemned by responsible theologians. Thus St. Thomas urges that self-mortification should only be employed "within the measure of reason." "Tame the emotions but do not extinguish nature: remember the words of the Apostle, 'Present your bodies as a living sacrifice'; to which he adds immediately 'which is your *reasonable* service.' "[31]

It seems to me, therefore, that Smith was seriously shortchanged in his training for the priesthood. In the writings of Kenneth Kirk he would have found a different and more attractive (not to say accurate) picture of the Christian ethical and pastoral tradition at its best, as something that advocates realistic steps toward growth in virtue, spirituality, and compassion, rather than a heartless and ruthless demand for unquestioning conformity at any price. Smith also would have seen that Christian ethics is not diametrically opposed to psychology. As the last quotation shows, Kirk understood the relatively new concept of "the subconscious region" and the danger, even moral danger, of repressed emotions. Smith's attitude toward psychiatry, like many other aspects of his writings, raises serious questions about how well he recognized and understood his own repressed emotions and motivations, and how much he might have benefited from the help of a pastoral counselor trained by Kirk.

One wonders what training Smith did receive in matters of ethics, church law, and pastoral practice (wasn't he attending Harvard at the time?). He certainly seems to have missed out on the entire twentieth-century dialogue between psychology and Christian spirituality that the *Journal of Pastoral Care* was founded to foster. As a result he did not understand, as plenty of his Christian contemporaries did, that psychotherapy need not aim to "make people happy . . . and adjusted to society." By creating "a situation in which a person can be completely honest with himself and with a fellow human being" it can enable the person to become a responsible moral agent.[32]

Books that were written for Anglican priests of those days seem to show that, whether the issue was the role of psychology, the authority of Christian tradition, or the moral status of homosexuality, the mainstream was much closer to Kirk than to Smith. I have not found a single author from that time who was open to the possibility that homosexual acts might not be sinful. But neither have I found any author who would agree with Smith that Christianity boils down to a choice between happiness now or happiness after death.

PSYCHOLOGY AND HOMOSEXUALITY

As far as I can tell, Kirk wrote nothing about homosexuality specifically. The advice of his that I quoted above applied to any serious sin, though his reference to "young men in the grip of youthful passions" may be a veiled allusion to homosexual behavior. From our perspective it may seem unfortunate that he never addressed the issue directly, for few moral theologians in the twentieth century were as well qualified as he to state, especially from an Anglican perspective, what the entire Christian ethical tradition had had to say. However, Kirk's silence implies that he saw no reason to question the traditional view that homosexuality is a serious sin, whereas he did feel compelled to weigh in on the morality of contraception and divorce, which were becoming controversial in his day, as twentieth-century developments were raising new questions about long-standing prohibitions.[33]

It is actually rather difficult to find much thoughtful comment on homosexuality by Anglican or other Christian writers before the twentieth century. To some extent this is due to terminological differences, for the term "homosexuality" originated within psychology late in the nineteenth century. Christian writers traditionally called it "sodomy," with the understanding that this was the sin for which Sodom was destroyed,[34] or else they used some kind of circumlocution, like Kirk's "grip of youthful passions." In any case it seems that homosexuality (by any name) was rarely singled out for specific discussion. As in Jeremy Taylor's writings, it was simply one of many varieties of extramarital, non-procreative, and therefore sinful, sex, regarded in much the same way as masturbation or adultery.

But in the twentieth century, as psychological terms and concepts worked their way into popular thinking, the Christian clergy came under increasing pressure to deal with homosexuality as a discrete issue, not simply another item in the list of sexual sins. The idea was spreading that, rather than a wrong ethical choice or a bad habit, homosexuality might be a medical or psychiatric condition, such that one could reasonably wonder about its causes, and about the individual's culpability and capacity for change. It would seem that these new questions caught many priests as unprepared as was T. W. Pym, who was chaplain of Balliol College in 1935:

> A young man, aged twenty-five or a bit more, wrote and asked whether he could come and see me. We had never met, but in approaching me he had followed the advice of some friend of his known to me. I was given to understand that the subject upon which he needed help was that of homosexuality. Now the first thing to note is that most clergy would feel rather awkward and not know what to say. Some would even require a translation of the word before they could understand it. Understanding it, many would regard it as a very peculiar and rather disgraceful thing; so peculiar indeed as not to fall within the clerical scope at all. This is just not true. Homosexual tendencies in bisexual people, both men and women, are common enough to fall within the scope of the shepherd of souls. Habitual adult inverts or perverts [i.e., exclusively homosexual people] are common enough to require that a shepherd of souls should know enough of the subject to be able at least to start dealing with them. Yet it is unlikely that many, if any, theological colleges so much as mention the subject. It is hard to imagine a course of lectures for clergy on moral theology that would contain any reference to the subject at all.

But for the purposes of our illustration we will suppose that the clergyman approached by the young man is one of the minority which has some knowledge of the subject and thus some equipment for trying to help the victim. But his professional propensity for talk may still lead him into serious error. After a few minutes he gives his visitor an excellent talk upon homosexuality, but it is not wanted, certainly at that stage. I am not reluctant to explain what I did; for in trying to show that in acting differently I acted right, I do not pose as one with a very good talk on homosexuality to produce. The whole point is that I did not talk at all. I got him talking and I kept him talking for about forty minutes all about his life and his difficulties in life. At the end of that time it was abundantly clear that his fundamental trouble was not homosexuality at all! It was quite obvious that that particular trouble was actually caused by something else. It was about the something else, which was not even sexual, that he needed help, which I then tried to give. The main point I would make from this story is that he who would help another soul must first be a good listener. A secondary point is that sex is not necessarily an explanation of every moral difficulty, even of those which at first sight seem to be wholly sexual.[35]

Even more surprising than Pym's naiveté is the fact that he had the nerve to market his bewilderment in the form of a how-to book for his fellow clergymen. (Of course the importance of being a good listener is always worth reiterating.) But the important observation for our purposes is this: not only had the Rev. Pym never been told about the nineteen centuries of consensus dictating that homosexuals must be denied communion and urged to accept lives of misery — he didn't know any other priest who had heard this either. The clerical culture he inhabited, not much more than a decade before Smith's 1949 article, was not one in which homosexuality was mercilessly condemned or ruthlessly suppressed, but one in which its very existence barely registered.

Try to imagine what a parson-to-parson conversation between Smith and Pym would have been like! At the least, Pym would have disagreed with Smith's assessment of psychiatry as incompatible with Christianity. As early as 1921, when Smith was only five years old, Pym was marveling at their uncanny similarity:

The advice of the religious teacher and of the physician strangely agree; the former besides urging the need for true repentance and forgiveness . . . says: "To cure impurity of heart cultivate thoughts that are positively good; occupy the mind positively; pray for the positive virtues and believe in God's power to make you clean. To cure fornication find other and creative channels for surplus physical energy. Consider your duty to the community; you must not degrade yourself and others. Other people are involved in your sin." The psycho-therapist . . . says: "Interest yourself in people unselfishly; get out of yourself; find new occupations for spare time and energy. Apply your creative instinct in some other direction positively. Take plenty of exercise, have a cold bath, etc." It is surely unnecessary to fit these two counsels together; if only all religious teachers would learn from the new psychology how sexual vice works in the human personality, and if all psycho-therapists believed in the power of God and not merely in the power of instincts, both penitent and patient alike would receive even better advice.[36]

COUNSELS OF HOPE

Among Pym's contemporaries, some did "learn from the new psychology" and felt competent to deal with homosexuals, or "inverts" as they were often called. Among the best-informed Anglicans of the time may have been Lindsay Dewar and Cyril E. Hudson, who were, respectively, a canon of York and an honorary chaplain to the bishop of St. Albans.[37] Some people today might regard their advice as ludicrously quaint or positively harmful, but it has three aspects that were meant to be relatively constructive, and are utterly absent from Smith's tirade. Without endorsing the commission of homosexual acts, Dewar and Hudson strove hard to (1) foster a positive self-image on the part of the homosexual, protecting him from social ostracism and prejudice. They also tried to (2) identify special traits or talents in the homosexual condition, which could enable a person to make unique contributions to society. And they (3) advocated listening to the experiences of other homosexuals who were striving to live a Christian life. Thus much of what they say is adapted, paraphrased, or quoted from a book published by a homosexual Roman Catholic layman under the touching pseudonym "Anomaly."[38]

Like Pym and many other authors of the period, Dewar and Hudson began by asserting that most people are not irreversibly homosexual but rather bisexual; they thus can be helped to make a heterosexual adjustment. The following advice, then, was intended only for cases of "true inversion" where such change is not possible:

> Here it is useless to recommend a person to seek association with the opposite sex; still more so, to urge him to get married. The first requirement in the priest is that he should show the invert that he understands his case. At all costs he should not manifest any kind of horror or repulsion towards an invert. Such an attitude is both un-Christian and un-scientific. The invert is no more responsible for his condition than if he had been born with a club foot. The horror which is popularly felt and even expressed against inverts is largely responsible for making them (what, as such, they are not) pathological, and sometimes leads them to run amok, on the principle that one might as well be hanged for a sheep as a lamb. The priest, therefore, will do his utmost to prevent the invert

from thinking himself a moral degenerate or a "lonely victim of some obscure disorder."

What he needs most is sympathy. It should be carefully pointed out to him that there is nothing in his condition of which he need be ashamed, and, in fact, that, until and unless God wills him to be changed, it is his vocation to be an invert. He should be shown how his peculiar temperament affords him various opportunities of service which are denied to his more normal brethren. Inverts, it has been well said, occupy a position "in the middle of the road." This gives them a special advantage as advisers, and it is perhaps the secret of their undoubted gift of friendship which leads others naturally to turn to them for help. If the invert be a man, he should be shown that his position is not essentially different from that of many normally constituted women. For his real privation and trial is that he must cut the possibility of marriage out of his life; and this is the case with many normal, heterosexual women.[39]

Although Anomaly offered quite a lot of advice on many topics, Dewar and Hudson reprinted two lists of admonitions that Anomaly specifically recommended to the "clergyman, physician, or layman who is faced with the immediate task of helping and directing the invert." These admonitions were "not offered because there is anything inherently objectionable in many of the points noted, but is dictated by the need of discretion," that is, to avoid detection and ridicule.[40]

In setting down the kind of advice which should be given by the priest to the invert, we cannot do better than quote again the experience of one who is himself an invert, and who has, by the grace of God, evidently found his vocation therein. Let us begin with his negative advice:

"Don't commit to writing any admissions as to your inclinations; don't masquerade, on any occasion whatsoever, in women's clothes, take female parts in theatrical performances, or use make-up; don't be too meticulous in the matter of your own clothes, or effect extremes in colour or cut; don't wear conspicuous rings, watches, cuff-links or other jewellery; don't allow your voice or intonation to display feminine inflection — cultivate a masculine tone and method of expression; don't stand with your hand on your hip, or walk mincingly; don't become identified with the groups of inverts which form in every city; don't let it be noticed that you are bored by female society; don't persuade yourself into believing that love is the same thing as friendship; don't become involved in marked intimacies with men who are not of your own age or set; don't let your enthusiasm for particular male friends make you conspicuous in their eyes, or in the eyes of society; don't occupy yourself with work or pastimes which are distinctly feminine; don't, under any circumstances, compromise yourself by word or action with strangers."

His positive advice is as follows:

> "Hold frank conversations with suitable persons, thereby avoiding mental repression; encourage every symptom of sexual normalization; cultivate self-esteem; become deeply engrossed in a congenial occupation or hobby; observe discretion and practise self-restraint."[41]

Whatever one may think of this advice today, Anomaly was nevertheless a remarkable individual, who evidently came to terms with his homosexual identity as a Catholic layman committed to a life of celibacy.[42] His book went through two editions and was highly regarded by priests who were involved in counseling homosexuals.[43] Yet it completely escaped Morton Smith, evidently, despite his preference for Roman Catholic authors. Had Smith ever read it, he would have found his main contentions contradicted. To start with, Anomaly found the Christian religion more considerate of the homosexual's plight than society at large, the opposite of Smith's view:

> At the present time the position [in society generally] is that inverts are penalized on all the major counts of life. They are outlaws of Nature. . . . They are pariahs of society, and are branded as degenerates, perverts and moral derelicts. They are dangerous people in the eyes of the law, and when they break it are almost the only class of "criminals" for whom the ancient rigour of penalties has not been abated.
>
> Only religion, though severe in condemnation, is merciful in treatment.[44]

Indeed it was Anomaly's experience that understanding priests could be found if one made the effort to look for them.

> It would seem that the sacrament of Holy Orders conveys no concomitant quickening of intelligence nor illumination of the mind. This being the case, one must expect to find priests who do not understand problems which in practice they may not often meet. The invert who seeks charity and wisdom as well as the sacramental benefit of absolution, or who, quite naturally, shrinks from the ordeal of much explanation in a confession which must always be difficult, will therefore be well advised to exercise his lawful discretion in the choice of a confessor or director. The difficulties which confront the Catholic invert will not be lessened if his spiritual advisor has a horror of inversion because he believes it to be a cultivated perversity. It is therefore helpful to the peace of mind and conscience that the penitent should find a confessor who understands his difficulties and realizes that there is a state of *inversion* which is at least "quasi-innate," as well as a state of *perversion* induced by deliberate libidinous actions, or resulting from pathological disorder.
>
> While instructed Catholics will understand me, it is possible that non-Catholics may misinterpret this advice. I wish, therefore, to make it perfectly

clear that I do not suggest that Catholics should or could find confessors who would abate one jot or tittle of the prescriptions of moral theology. I know, however, that a priest who is instructed in the matter of inversion will not misunderstand his penitent, treat him with excessive severity, or recommend remedies, such, for instance, as marriage, which may be futile or even disastrous.[45]

Or, to put it in the language we use today, one should find a priest who recognizes the difference between an unchosen homosexual orientation and (always immoral) homosexual acts. The distinction was not between differing theological positions on sexual ethics, but between realistic familiarity with the experiences of homosexual people and the lack of such familiarity. Knowledgeable priests might be in the minority, but their more compassionate attitude could make all the difference: "A priest who in confessing an invert lad pictures in detail the sins and punishments of the Cities of the Plain may drive his penitent out of the Church, or even out of his mind; while a fair and honest facing of the peculiar difficulties of mind, body and conscience which envelop him may turn a potential sinner and criminal into a happy and useful member of society."[46] The Rev. Smith clearly was apparently of the former variety, who conjured up images of sin and punishment, who would "drive his penitent out of the Church, or even out of his mind," rather than help him with "a fair and honest facing of [his] peculiar difficulties." But even priests of this sort would not usually have espoused a Smithian ecclesiology of a church that puts words in Jesus' mouth and judges sins against itself more harshly than sex outside of marriage.

In another contradiction of Smith, Anomaly did not see the homosexual as forced to choose between suffering in this life or suffering in eternity. He presents a much more understanding and affecting picture of the problem (which even many psychiatrists did not understand) — but also a more optimistic solution.

> Thus inversion is involuntary, not voluntary; it is constant, not inconstant; and it is instead of, not in addition to, the normal [i.e. heterosexual] impulse.
>
> Another point of great importance, and one that is ignored, not only by the public, but by many psychiatrists, is that an invert is an invert not only physically, but psychically. I have said that he may or may not be lustful, but he cannot help being human, and to be human implies at least some small measure of need of human relationships, and responsiveness to the personalities of others. "It's love that makes the world go round," and for the invert, love of whatever kind, passionate, romantic, or platonic, can hardly mean anything but love for one of his own sex. . . . Physically, emotionally, romantically and spiritually he is vulnerable to men and invulnerable to women. . . .
>
> Thus his problem is not the mere suppression of lust, but the far more

difficult problem of suppression, diversion, or control of his whole emotional nature.[47]

Since the natural tendency of "his whole emotional nature" could never be permitted to take its course, the "invert" was condemned to a life of tragic secrecy.

> Here and elsewhere, then, when I speak of the tragedies of inversion, I do not only mean those with which the world is only too familiar — tragedies of a criminal nature — but those which are pent up in a man's bosom and unknown often to his family and nearest friends. If anyone is inclined to feel that because he personally has never to his knowledge encountered these so-called "tragedies," let him consider that, of its very nature, inversion involves secrecy, caution and concealment, and then, knowing how many of life's normal conflicts must, perforce, be borne concealed beneath an unrevealing exterior, let him be reminded that probably in the hearts of some of those with whom he fancies himself to be on terms of greatest intimacy there are desperate secrets. It is to the courageous bearers of these concealed burdens that I should particularly like to bring some comfort.[48]

Trapped in such desperate isolation, the invert struggled alone, to avoid the twin pitfalls of utterly demoralizing guilt and the complete dereliction of moral responsibility.

> One of the frequently noticed reactions of youthful inverts to the discovery of their peculiar sex symptoms is a veritable nightmare of desolation. Each one believes himself to be a lone example of a terrifying mental and physical confusion, for which it is useless to seek relief, and against which he must struggle in grim and isolated silence. He has perhaps heard of secret sins and solitary vices; there have been half-veiled references to one of the sins which "cry to heaven for vengeance"; the very namelessness of the "nameless crimes" which the press wrap in incomplete mystery has not been lost on him. If he is not quite alone in this miasma of morbid emotions, he fears that his sole companions of the mist are fantastic sinners, shut out of heaven and denied the ordinary compensations of the World, the Flesh and the Devil. Is it any wonder that many a youthful invert arrives at a state of nervous collapse and spiritual dereliction, on the road to self-knowledge?
>
> Succeeding the period of lonely desolation, and immediately following the acquisition of a superficial knowledge of inversion, the youth may take a firm hold of the pendulum and swing to the other extreme. During his reaction from loneliness and exaggerated alarms, he will probably persuade himself, or be persuaded by some ignorant confidant, that inversion is the most ordinary thing in the world, that more than half of mankind is — consciously or unconsciously — inverted, and that the other half would be if it could. He may also

feel that the subject is insufficiently aired, and appoint himself explainer-in-chief to the uninitiated.

If left without direction, such a young man may become a subject for police surveillance, or a member of one of those furtive groups which haunt cheap eating-places, the lobbies of expensive hotels, or the incense-reeking boudoirs of the decadent—the choice of setting depending on his purse, intellect and education.[49]

With proper direction, on the other hand, a fulfilling and happy life of celibacy could be obtained.

One might as well ask a man to tear out his heart as suggest that he completely stifle his romantic emotions. What then is the invert to do? I recommend, in all seriousness, that he first cultivate a sense of humour, then practise temperance, continence and social discretion; and finally attempt the sublimation of his affections. If he allows humour—however grim—to come to his aid, he will appreciate how ridiculous he is to the normal mind. This realization will save him many bitter experiences.

Now, my lad, buck up. You have heard the worst, you have seen the ugly, you have felt the thorns. Having deplored the dark clouds, let us look for the silver lining, that when it is uncovered we may part with a smile.

It is a thousand pities that I cannot write as specifically as I should talk did I know you personally, and were we sitting over our coffee and cigarettes, or — and better still — paddling our canoe into the sunset of some piney northern lake. But, although I cannot be specific, not knowing the special features of your individual case, I can write frankly on the general aspects of your condition.[50]

It was important that advice should be tailored empathically to each individual case, but in general the "silver lining" had half a dozen components. First, "there are many who have risen above, or upon, the obstacle of their inversion," because "when a man with a good mind and a healthy body is denied the usual distractions and responsibilities of life, he devotes his energies and talents to the attainment of distinction in his work." Thus it is no wonder that history presents such a long roster of high-achieving homosexuals, particularly since "there is little doubt that frequently . . . he has a very special talent for the arts, or for some branch of social service which involves dealing with the young, the sick, the criminal, or the infirm—in fact with the 'under-dogs.' "[51]

Second, "you probably possess certain definite and valuable assets which go far to counterbalance your social handicaps. You find it easy and pleasant to establish friendly contact with an unusually wide range of men and women. . . . At all events, count as one of your compensations an unusual gift for friendship." Inverts tend to have "qualities of sympathy and understanding, but also a neutral-mindedness which is of great practical value," so that they are often sought out as "confidants" and "skilful and kindly advisers," not only to "under-dogs," but even to "over-dogs" — to such a degree that "normal men" will sometimes be found "indignantly and sincerely defending invert friends against innuendoes which are perhaps deserved."[52]

Third, inverts are especially sensitive: "There may be colours in a sunset and contours in a hill which you see better than most men, fragrance in forest or garden which reaches you only, and motifs in the symphony of spring the sense of whose harmony is denied to all but you. And when your heart leaps at some appeal to which others are unresponsive, you may often bless rather than curse the fates which made you not quite as other men. . . . this fact no doubt accounts, in some measure, for the facility in the arts possessed by many inverts."[53]

Fourth, "It is perhaps because we inverts are an incongruity of nature that we are, often, happily endowed with more than the average sense of humour." Fifth, inverts miraculously tend to be "unusually youthful in appearance" and to "possess a definite *élan* of youthfulness" which they retain to a marked degree far beyond middle life, an advantage that the rest of "mankind — or, to be more accurate, womankind" must find "in face creams and mechanical appliances."[54] Finally, Anomaly was optimistic about the future:

> So surprisingly charitable has been the attitude of every person whose help I have sought — and I include those whom I approached with the greatest diffidence — that I am almost tempted to revise or soften some of my comments on public opinion and the need for discretion. But, all told, I think at the present moment they must stand. Better be safe than sorry. On the other hand, I predict that the next decade will witness a better understanding of the facts of inversion by all educated people, and better understanding will relieve inverts from much of the present necessity for dissimulation.
>
> In the meantime I pray that inverts may have Faith, that advisers may give counsel of Hope, and that society may learn to treat the problem with Charity.[55]

My point, of course, is not that Anomaly was right and Smith wrong, but that Smith's approach was out of step even for its time. Even if only a minority of priests in those days were "instructed in the matter of inversion," as Anomaly put it, a priest of Smith's intelligence and resourcefulness could have obtained such instruction. If, after fulfilling whatever educational requirements were expected of him, Smith was having trouble counseling people with sexual difficulties, he should have sought out experienced pastoral counselors at Harvard for help with the problems his parishioners were bringing him. Had he done so, no doubt he would have been directed to appropriate training opportunities, and would eventually have learned about Anomaly's book. Reading what Anomaly had to say, Smith would have found his own views challenged on at least three points. Where Smith thought that a pastor "must frequently use every effort to prevent the parishioner from resorting to some agreeable and socially acceptable adjustment which is, unfortunately, sinful," Anomaly had found that homosexuals "are pariahs of society . . . penalized on all the major counts of life. . . . Only religion, though severe in condemnation, is merciful in treatment." While Smith insisted that "the fact that Hell is unpopular does not justify us in allowing others to be ignorant of the universal Christian doctrine," since "the concern of the pastor is the happiness of the dead," Anomaly knew that such an authoritarian stance would more likely "drive his penitent out of the Church, or even out of his mind; while a fair and honest facing of the peculiar difficulties of mind, body and conscience . . . may turn a potential sinner and criminal into a happy and useful member of society." Finally, while Smith would "do all he can to secure a course of action which will probably lead to a long period — if not an entire life — of unhappiness," Anomaly could adduce five or six reasons why a homosexual could find happiness in a life of celibacy.

The tragedy of Smith's brief clerical career, insofar as it can be judged from this one article, is that he preferred to blast the experts for failing to recognize that the church (as he bewilderingly conceived of it) had nothing to learn from listening to people's pain. He never made the effort to learn, and his school did not succeed in teaching him, that empathic and positive approaches that did not compromise the traditional Christian proscriptions against homosexual acts were available to Anglican and Catholic priests in those days. Indeed the full Christian tradition, even from centuries before the twentieth-century encounter with psychology, may have had quite a bit more to offer than Smith or most of his contemporaries suspected. For example, the twelfth-century Cistercian abbot St. Aelred of Rievaulx (ca. 1110–67), worked out a theology of chaste, Christ-centered "spiritual friendship" that has attracted much interest in recent decades, since Aelred himself appears to have been wrestling with a homosexual orientation.[56]

"INSTABILITY AT THE ROOTS"

For all his expertise in biblical studies, then, Smith was seriously underinformed about the Christian ethical tradition he claimed to be championing, and about the pastoral care of homosexuals (and other people) as it was carried out in his time. His one article of 1949 reveals an ignorance so ramified that it can be characterized in at least four ways. First, he had nothing like Kirk's knowledge of the Christian ethical tradition, and probably didn't even know about Kirk. What he did know was interpreted through the lens of a preposterous ecclesiology that made his positions almost unrecognizable as Christian. Second, he did not know how his more competent fellow priests were actually counseling homosexuals, or the book by Anomaly that was their main source of information on the Christian homosexual experience. Third, he knew nothing about psychology or psychiatry and did not even realize how little he knew. On the one hand he blamed psychiatrists for trying to make people "reasonably happy and adjusted to society." On the other hand he also blamed them for enforcing arbitrary social conventions of what is acceptable: "[I]t is primarily the demand of society which has made the [psychiatric] profession so critical of the socially unacceptable forms of self-satisfaction (mania and some forms of schizophrenia) and has led it to expose the instability which lies at their roots. The instability which lies at the roots of highly successful careers is noted only when such careers end up in the psychopathic ward. Otherwise the 'individual,' if happy in his success, has 'made an unusually adequate adjustment.' "[57] This from a man who was only a year away from abandoning his own clerical career! Smith's characterization of mania and schizophrenia as "socially unacceptable forms of self-satisfaction" is every bit as perverse and irresponsible as the comments in his 1973 popular book on the Secret Gospel (quoted in the last chapter) about early Christianity being a manifestation of schizophrenia, "instability," and "psychological infection."[58] And he seems not to have noticed the contradiction: if schizophrenia is simply a "socially unacceptable form of self-satisfaction," and if Christianity began as a highly contagious form of schizophrenia, then why should we side with "society" to ridicule Christianity?

Fourth, Smith was at least equally deficient in the area for which his parishioners had a right to expect that he had been professionally trained. He seems to have had no concept that people who came to him for confession or counseling were looking for help to feel closer to God, and no idea how to help them. In contrast, Reginald Ward, one of the most respected Anglican spiritual directors of the generation before Smith, would have emphasized the importance of developing loving human relationships with other people as a way to develop a more grateful appreciation of the love of God. Ward's advice to a priest who hears the confession of a "homosexual" (the penitent in this example is what we would call a "pedophile" or child molester) includes the following (among other things):

> The sex instinct is one of the most powerful and useful of all instincts, it is a driving force for creative work and the most powerful instrument for bringing us into contact with our fellow beings. Those who are attracted to their own sex provide some of the best trainers and teachers, because this attraction gives them a special understanding and sympathy. In both classes [i.e., bisex-

uals and exclusive homosexuals] the possibility of a sinful use of this sex endowment is due to a selfish misuse of one kind of self-expression, a use which puts the procuring of sex-sensation before the good of others and which twists bodily functions into a channel for which they were not intended. Dwell on the value of this sex endowment and the way in which it could have been used in this man to help many others. . . . He is spoiling and wasting his gift and injuring others. Try to stir him to the ambition to use the gift. But this is not the most important part of his misuse of God's gift of sex. By misusing it he has eclipsed with a thick cloud of selfishness his sight of God's love and beauty which was once so dear to him, and which he has so often proved could help him. It is an awful thing to throw away the greatest beauty and love that a man can find. Tell him to turn away for a moment from thinking about himself and try to think of the tenderness of God's love trying to reach him and being rebuffed. Such ingratitude is really foreign to what in his inmost being he knows and believes.[59]

People today may disagree on what *should* be said, but this example shows some of the things Smith *could* have said. Smith's article betrays no sense whatever of sexuality as a divine gift, or of the spiritual rewards of helping and loving other people as a way of opening to the experience of God's love. It is as if Smith himself really had no experience with such things. One wonders how his article even got published in a journal devoted to counseling and spirituality. Did the editors see it as an alternative point of view, an example of what pastors integrating psychology with spirituality were "up against"? Did they see it as illustrating how badly pastoral counseling was needed in the life of the church? Were the editors short on material? Or was it simply that they just couldn't turn a fellow Harvard man down? They could not have known, as we do know, that only a year later Smith would leave the active ministry. Read with the hindsight that he would eventually reject Christianity altogether, Smith's screed reveals itself as the heart-rending cry of a man in great pain. But it also throws some very unexpected light on one of the strangest features of Clement's letter to Theodore in the Mar Saba document.

"O Truth, How Many Lies Are Told in Thy Name!"

For all its fire-and-brimstone dogmatism and its appeals to age-old Christian tradition, Smith's 1949 outburst is essentially undocumented; the footnotes are all devoted to impugning the orthodoxy of other articles in the same periodical. Only twice does Smith refer to books he read: in each case the book is cited incorrectly, its content is misrepresented, and there is no footnote. But (as always) the errors are revealing. Smith's memory slips are the kind that anyone might make, but the author of a professional-level publication is supposed to correct such mistakes by checking his recollections against the actual book and citing the source correctly so others can find it. As it is, the informational gaps are like portals into the highly emotional private world of Morton Smith—though this time we are seeing, not the light-hearted obliviousness of the man who can't remember how he discovered a homosexual Jesus, but the angry sense of unjust rejection, of not being listened to or taken seriously enough.

At one point, the Smith of 1949 praises an unnamed article in "the recent Roman Catholic symposium, *Making Converts*,"[60] revealing again his preference for Catholic writers. But the book I think he means is actually called *Winning Converts*, and I cannot tell which article he is referring to; none of them is about counseling troubled people, all are about how to get potential converts into religious education classes and keep them there as long as it takes.[61] Smith's praise of the book seems to confirm other indications that he did not understand the counseling process, but saw his job as one of browbeating people into miserable submission to nineteen centuries of "authoritarian religion." Converts were to be made rather than won.

The other book Smith mentions is the classic autobiography of John Henry Newman (1801–90), an Anglican priest who became a Roman Catholic cardinal, the most famous English-speaking convert of the nineteenth century:

> Christianity is a group of organizations, claiming supernatural origin and authority, and undertaking to save men from a future existence of eternal torment by uniting them with the incarnation of God. Such union these organizations with remarkable unanimity declare and have always declared to require willing submission to a rather ascetic moral code, and they are all agreed that the observance of this code is more important for the individual than his happiness or his health or his very life. As Newman said at the end of his *Apologia* (he was defending Roman Catholicism against charges of laxity brought by an Anglican), the Catholic Church believes it preferable that everyone in the world should perish in torment rather than that one soul should commit one venial sin. Hence it follows that ... particular conflicts should arise whenever the psychiatrist's concern for the patient's immediate happiness runs counter to the pastor's concern for the parishioner's eternal salvation.[62]

Once again, Smith endorses the Catholic position—or at least what he thinks is the Catholic position—against the Anglican one. And once again, he ascribes this position to the whole of Christendom ("a group of organizations ... [which] with remarkable unanimity declare and have always declared")—even though Newman was in fact "defending Roman Catholicism against charges . . . brought by an Anglican"! But once again Smith's memory has misled him. The statement in question, which he quoted inaccurately, does not really come at the end of Newman's book, during the discussion about "laxity" and the morality of lying. It is found rather earlier, in a section on the infallibility of the Catholic Church. This is of no small interest to us, for both the ethics of lying and the truth of church teaching are major themes in the Mar Saba letter, as so many scholars have noticed. But to understand what Newman was saying will require a fair amount of explanation, and to understand how Smith misunderstood it will require even more.

After a dozen years as a leader of the Oxford Movement, Newman was received into the Roman Catholic Church in 1845. He continued to write profusely on behalf of his new faith. In 1864, a controversy broke out that resulted in Newman's writing his most famous book, *Apologia pro Vita Sua*,[63] the story of his own spiritual journey. The controversy began when Charles Kingsley, a layman of the Church of England who has been regarded as a "liberal Protestant" but considered himself conservative,[64] wrote a book review in which he charged:

> The Roman [Catholic] religion had, for some time past, been making men not better men, but worse. We must face, we must conceive honestly for ourselves, the deep demoralization which had been brought on in Europe by the dogma that the Pope of Rome had the power of creating right and wrong; that not only truth and falsehood, but morality and immorality, depended on his setting his seal to a bit of parchment. . . .
>
> So, again, of the virtue of truth. Truth, for its own sake, had never been a virtue with the Roman clergy. Father Newman informs us that it need not, and on the whole ought not to be; that cunning is the weapon which Heaven has given to the saints wherewith to withstand the brute male force of the wicked world which marries and is given in marriage. Whether his notion be doctrinally correct or not, it is at least historically so.[65]

Newman felt slandered, denied he had ever written such a thing, and wrote a letter of protest to the editor of *Macmillan's Magazine,* which had published Kingsley's review. Kingsley replied in a letter identifying the source, a sermon Newman had published in 1844, when he was still an Anglican.[66] In fact, however, Newman had preached the opposite of what Kingsley accused him of saying. Newman had said that the Church's weapons of prayer, holiness, and innocence were so incomprehensible to a sinful world that what the Church called "wisdom" and "harmlessness" must have seemed to unbelievers to be "craft" and "hypocrisy."[67]

A flurry of letters followed, involving the two men, their many allies, and *Macmillan's Magazine.* In one of them Newman even grew unusually lyrical: "O Truth, how many lies are told in thy name!"[68] Meanwhile, Kingsley made a thorough search of Newman's writings and published every incriminating quote he'd been able to find in a pamphlet titled "What, Then, Does Dr. Newman Mean?" One of them was the statement to which Smith referred in his 1949 article, which Kingsley quoted as follows: "The Catholic Church 'holds it better for sun and moon to drop from heaven, for the earth to fail, and for all the many millions on it to die of starvation in extremest agony, as far as temporal affliction goes, than that one soul, I will not say should be lost, but should commit one single venial sin, should tell one wilful untruth, or should steal one poor farthing without excuse.' "[69] For Kingsley, this statement was an instance of Newman's hypocrisy: how could Newman have written this, when, a few pages later, he describes "consent . . . to a single unchaste wish as indefinitely more heinous than any lie that can possibly be fancied?" Kingsley had no doubt that lying was worse than unchaste wishing, and the net effect of all the Newman quotations he collected was to demonstrate that "this man has no real care for truth. Truth for its own sake is no virtue in his eyes, and he teaches that it need not be. . . . Dr. Newman, for the sake of exalting the magical powers of his Church, has committed himself unconsciously to a statement which strikes at the root of all morality. If he answer, that such is the doctrine of his Church . . . I can only answer, So much the worse for his Church. The sooner it is civilized off the face of the earth, if this be its teaching, the better for mankind."[70] Kingsley's accusation then, was not merely that Newman was lenient about lying, but that Newman, like all Catholics, effectively justified lying when it was done to advance the purposes of the Catholic Church.

In support of this, Kingsley also cited an 1843 sermon of Newman's on "the development of doctrine." This idea, which Newman elaborated further in subsequent publications, has proved to be his most important intellectual contribution, making it possible for twentieth-century theologians, both Catholic and Protestant, to acknowledge that Christian doctrines have unfolded over time, "in such a way that the sameness of faith in the course of history was not to be conceived as a static immutability but as a dynamic continuity."[71] Before Newman, the role of historical developmental processes was not widely recognized. It was not uncommon for Christians to write as if the faith had been delivered fully formed and fully understood to the twelve apostles and that subsequent controversies were caused by a weak or sinful inability to accept what the apostles had plainly taught. Words like "innovation" and "novelty" were used as synonyms for "heresy."[72]

In trying to explain the unfamiliar idea that doctrines have developed over the course of history, Newman attempted an analogy to the familiar pastoral practice of shaping the message to the audience: "And so, again, as regards savages, or the ignorant, or weak, or narrow-minded, our representations must take a certain form, if we are to gain admission into their minds at all, and to reach them."[73] For example, statements in the Bible that the sun moves around the earth were shaped to the understanding people had at the time these texts were written; they did not preclude or contradict subsequent discoveries that the earth moves around the sun.

In this context Newman had added, in a footnote, "Hence, it is not more than an hyperbole to say that, in certain cases, a lie is the nearest approach to truth. This seems the meaning, for instance, of St. Clement, when he says, 'He (the Christian) both thinks and speaks the truth, unless when, at any time, in the way of treatment, as a physician toward his patients, so for the welfare of the sick he will be false, or will tell a falsehood, as the sophists speak.' "[74] "If St. Clement said that," Kingsley sniffed, "so much the worse for him. He was a great and good man. But he might have learned from his Bible that no lie was the truth, and that it is ill stealing the devil's tools to do God's work withal."[75] Newman's original footnote on Clement, however, was not a random patristic citation. Clement's statement was a *crux interpretum* in the nineteenth-century argument between those who considered the Roman Church the one infallible teacher of the truth and those who thought it a sinister cabal that absolved its henchmen in the confessional for lying in its name.[76] Thus the author of the Mar Saba letter could have been a nineteenth-century partisan in this controversy. Or he could have been, like Morton Smith and many other Anglo-Catholics of his generation, a twentieth-century reader of Kingsley's pamphlet against Newman, in which Clement is depicted as an advocate not only of lying, but of lying on behalf of the Church.

Newman replied with two more pamphlets and then wrote the autobiographical *Apologia,* in which each chapter chronicled the "History of my Religious Opinions" for a certain period of his life.[77] The *Apologia* concludes with the topic that had initially exercised Kingsley, a discussion of whether "under certain extraordinary conditions it is allowable to tell a lie."[78] But there is no more there about Clement; Newman's remarks in that section are based on Catholic and Protestant authors who lived after the Reformation.

TEMPORAL AFFLICTION

What, then, did Dr. Newman mean when he wrote that the Church "holds it better for . . . millions . . . to die"? When he originally made the statement in 1850, he was responding to a charge that the Catholic countries of Europe were less technologically and socially advanced than the Protestant countries, suggesting that the Catholic Church itself was a backward-looking, retrogressive institution that did not care about the physical and material welfare of its people. Newman's reply was that the Church had higher priorities: the spiritual welfare of the faithful was infinitely more important. His remarks are easier to understand in context:

> This, then, is the point I insist upon, in answer to the objection which you have today urged against me. The Church aims, not at making a show, but at doing a work. She regards this world, and all that is in it, as a mere shadow, as dust and ashes, compared with the value of one single soul. She holds that, unless she can, in her own way, do good to souls, it is no use her doing anything; she holds that it were better for sun and moon to drop from heaven, for the earth to fail, and for all the many millions who are upon it to die of starvation in extremest agony, so far as temporal affliction goes, than that one soul, I will not say, should be lost, but should commit one single venial sin, should tell one wilful untruth, though it harmed no one, or steal one poor farthing without excuse. She considers the action of this world and the action of the soul simply incommensurate, viewed in their respective spheres; she would rather save the soul of one single wild bandit of Calabria, or whining beggar of Palermo, than draw a hundred lines of railroad through the length and breadth of Italy, or carry out a sanitary reform, in its fullest details, in every city of Sicily, except so far as these great national works tended to some spiritual good beyond them.[79]

Even in its original context, the passage may seem rhetorically excessive, but the point is clear — that no amount of "temporal affliction" can outweigh the spiritual imperative for salvation.

Nowadays, of course, many Christians recognize that widespread hunger, starvation, and other "temporal afflictions" are indeed moral and spiritual issues, even if the proximate cause is a natural disaster such as the sun and moon "dropping" or the earth "failing." Neither the incompetence or venality of local governments that neglect the needs of their people nor the complacency or selfishness of people in wealthy, historically Christian countries can be excused on the ground that spiritual values are more important. The modern recognition that sin is not a purely individual matter, but can also be found in social structures and public policies, owes much to the social encyclicals of the popes, beginning with *Rerum novarum* in 1891.[80] But Newman, who worked out the modern theological understanding of the development of doctrine, was writing in 1850.

Since the quote had resurfaced when Kingsley cited it in his controversy with Newman, however, it was convenient for Newman to reutilize it in his *Apologia,* where he made it the basis of a different argument. Newman conceded nothing to those who had meanwhile found his remarks objectionable, and admitted no rhetorical excess: "I have nothing to withdraw." Instead, he made it the preamble of his argument on the infallibility of the Church.[81] Since there is so much evil in the world, with the human race so estranged from the Creator by the rebellion of sin, is it not reasonable that a loving God would have placed an infallible religion among us, which people could absolutely rely upon to teach the truth? As Newman wrote, "It is because of the intensity of the evil which has possession of mankind, that a suitable antagonist has been provided against it."[82]

In the turbulent memory of the 1949 Morton Smith, however, both Newman's wording and his meaning began to shift. The passage itself moved, in Smith's recollection, from the argument about infallibility in the middle of Newman's book to the argument about lying at the end. Newman's words "die of starvation in extremest agony" transmogrified into Smith's "perish in torment" (suggesting the eternal fire of Hell), and the entire statement became a defense against "charges of laxity brought by an Anglican." "Laxity," in the Catholic theology of those days, was a technical theological term for what we now call "permissiveness" or "moral relativism," defined as the belief that one can safely choose a course of action that has a low probability of being the most ethical one.[83] But to Smith's state of mind back in 1949, it had all come to mean that some Anglican had attacked the Catholic Church for being too lenient on issues such as lying, and that Newman had replied, with the moral absolutism that was the only position possible, that the Church would rather consign everyone to eternal fire than overlook even one venial sin. Now that's rigorism to be reckoned with, and among its harsh demands is the question: Which church did Smith think he belonged to, anyway? Smith had written, "As Newman said at the end of his *Apologia* (he was defending Roman Catholicism against charges of laxity brought by an Anglican), the Catholic Church believes it preferable that everyone in the world should perish in torment rather than that one soul should commit one venial sin."[84] If the Rev. Smith believed that, it is not surprising that he soon found its implications unbearable and took for himself the step he had recommended to everyone else who disagreed with his version of Christianity: "ecclesiastics who do not believe the teachings of their Church should have the decency to leave it."[85]

"A MORE-OR-LESS NOVEL RELIGION"

In the shadows behind the Secret Gospel story, then, we begin to see the outlines of a poignant tale. An idealistic young priest, struggling with the burden of counseling people caught in patterns of sexual sin, lashes out at the competition, the newly popular psychiatry, which seems to offer an easy way out—to falsely promise earthly happiness at the expense of eternal happiness. The priest insists that Christianity amounts to centuries of obdurate consensus, issuing ethical mandates against which there is no appeal, and cites a half-remembered book he had taken to say that the church prefers any amount of suffering over even the smallest infringement. Behind that book lies a more fundamental debate over whether this same church is the ensign of truth or a fomenter of lies, a debate in which all sides repeatedly quote St. Clement of Alexandria.

A year later, the priest has given up and begins to establish a career as a professor. He returns to a monastery he had loved as a young student, and there, in a neglected tower library, discovers a fragmentary text: a long-lost letter from the same Clement of Alexandria, attacking heretics for teaching sexual sins but also advocating that loyal Christians must lie to protect the Church's truth.

Remarkably, the letter also quotes from certain unknown gospels that say (or do they?) that Jesus himself initiated his disciples through acts of homosexual sex. From this the ex-priest concludes that Jesus taught a "libertine" religion that was soon deliberately concealed by discomfited church leaders, who created an irrefutable majority consensus that became the mainstream, orthodox church, willing to condone any lie to suppress the memory that Jesus himself had promised freedom from moral laws.

To support this interpretation, the former priest constructs an elaborate collage of ancient evidence and pseudo-evidence that betrays a notable resemblance to the way the new gospel, and the letter containing it, were also built up from ancient excerpts. In the process he himself becomes the kind of person he had once inveighed against, the sort who prefers "his own interpretation of individual texts . . . departing from normative Christianity to devise a more-or-less novel religion of his own." But it no longer matters, for (he is now convinced) Christianity itself is nothing more than a hysterical stampede of madmen and schizophrenics, of people who had caught some bug and, as a result, were desperately in need of psychiatry.

This outline may seem far-fetched, but there is more. Smith's conception of Christian morality as a tyrannical conspiracy reappears in an article of 1972. Published in close chronological proximity to the two books on the Secret Gospel, it seems intended to prepare the ground for the shock to come. The canonical gospel of Mark, Smith argued, "reflects the practice of a church which made a sharp distinction between the more and the less advanced," resembling, it would seem, Clement's distinction between the "perfected" and the merely "instructed." Anticipating the still-unpublished Mar Saba text, with its secret oral teaching and Carpocratian distortions, Smith asserted that even in the familiar Marcan gospel "the contrast between the more and the less advanced serves also an apologetic purpose against other Christian groups.

Here, it says, is the true teaching which was privately revealed to the closest followers; accept no substitutes."[86]

Yet in Smith's view this "true," private teaching actually involved the suppression, not the preservation, of Jesus' original message:

> [T]he Jesus who taught his moral regulations and explanations of difficult texts (in secret, to the closed circle of the church) could well have been the projection backward of the Christian teacher of a later generation, in this instance not the wandering preacher but the incipient bishop. . . . Of all the things [Jesus] said, the church represented by Mark wants only those which provide assurance for its hopes, authorization for its doctrines or practices, and answers to the questions which are in dispute among its members. . . . Therefore the bulk — if any — of Jesus' teaching would seem to have been either unknown to Mark, alien to the concerns of the church for which he wrote, or deliberately withheld by him from presentation in his Gospel. Why?[87]

Why indeed? Given Smith's picture in his books on the Mar Saba fragment of an "orthodox" majority suppressing Jesus' original "libertine" teaching in the name of "social acceptability," there is little doubt that he thought Jesus' teaching was not "unknown to Mark," but rather "deliberately withheld" as "alien to the concerns of the church for which he wrote."

The complaint that institutionalized Christianity has betrayed the original message of its founder has been heard throughout history, of course. But in Smith's earlier and later writings we can witness a startling reversal of ecclesiologies — or rather the same ecclesiology viewed from two different sides. In 1949, Smith forcefully argued that all the Christian denominations, "with remarkable unanimity," "require the observation of a moral code" that demanded rigorous, unquestioning obedience from every believer, even to the point of suffering "an entire life of unhappiness" for the sake of "union with Christ" — a Christ whose words had actually been put in his mouth by the disciples. Even though this moral code was not from Jesus, it was "preferable that everyone in the world should perish in torment rather than that one soul should commit" even a minor infraction against it. By 1972, Smith was arguing that the gospel of Mark deliberately omits most of Jesus' actual teaching, in order to serve the institutional interests of the church to which Mark belonged. Paramount among these interests was the refutation and suppression of other groups claiming to be Christian and the maintenance of a two-tier membership structure in which the most important teachings were known only to the more privileged inner circle. A year later, Smith would announce that parts of the secret, inner-circle version of Mark's gospel had been rediscovered, preserved in a letter in which, indeed, the leaders of the institutional church could be seen conspiring against a group with a different tradition of ethical teaching.

The Mar Saba document fits awfully well between the two mirror images of 1949 and 1972. Some may consider this proof enough that Smith himself created the document. But I say we should not jump to that conclusion, or not yet. Although Smith's montage of excerpts from ancient sources markedly resembles the centonate construction of the Secret Gospel and the Mar Saba letter, and strikingly inverts his own youthful ecclesiology, these resemblances only amount to circumstantial evidence. We cannot, at this point, exclude the possibility that Smith really did discover a text he did not compose. Many unanswered questions remain.

In particular, we must ask about the sexologies of the Mar Saba document. At first glance they seem rather different from Smith's. In the Secret Gospel, homosexuality seems to be an initiatory rite sought by a disciple from a master who angrily rejects all relationships with women. If Smith is correct, it aimed at a joint experience of heavenly ascent, though this is not explicitly stated in the gospel itself. On the other hand the author of the letter, identified as Clement of Alexandria, seems to deny or not recognize that the Secret Gospel depicts a homosexual liaison, even while he condemns in the harshest terms the immorality of the Carpocratians, whose gospel does seem to make the homosexuality explicit.

Smith's 1949 article gives us a glimpse of his own sexology, which is difficult to square with the Mar Saba fragment. His parishioner is a young man who views relationships with adult men as "most helpful" but who is also supportive of relationships between adults. He seems to be an aesthetically sensitive soul: initially drawn to the church by its music and ritual, he admires famous men like Plato and Shakespeare who were reputedly homosexual themselves. Such elements are not clearly present in the Mar Saba text, unless the intent is to add Jesus to the roster of history's famous homosexuals. Could the two young men (in the Secret Gospel and in Smith's article) be products of the same mind or the same era? Or do their differences point to different historical periods? The time has come to face squarely the issue that has repeatedly inserted itself into our investigations, only to be deferred: to what historical date and milieu does the homosexuality described in the Mar Saba fragment really belong?

Summary

In this chapter I examine Smith's brief career as an Anglican priest. An early article of his shows that he held extremely rigid ethical views and an illogical theology of the Church. His counseling of homosexuals and people facing other sexual difficulties was uninformed and incompatible with the best practices in use at the time. His notions of mental illness and the role of psychotherapy indicate a complete lack of training and experience. One can infer that Smith was going through some kind of psychological crisis of his own relating to his abandonment of the priesthood the following year.

Unexpectedly, the early article reveals two other things that seem to shed light on the Mar Saba text. Smith depicted the history of Christian morality as a universal, ironclad consensus, suppressing all dissenters down through the ages, closely resembling Clement's persecution of the Carpocratians. A 1972 article on the canonical gospel of Mark interestingly inverts Smith's 1949 ecclesiology, arguing that leaders of the early church conspired to suppress the original teaching of Jesus. Smith's early article also referenced a nineteenth-century debate between Catholics and Protestants over whether Clement believed that lying was justified if it was done on behalf of the church. The Clement of the Mar Saba letter insists that it is.

8

Hellenistic Homosexualities

When he sent a couple of disciples to make preparations for the Passover meal, he did not tell them the address, but told them to look for a man carrying a pitcher of water. (Carrying water was women's work, so this was like saying, "Look for a man wearing lipstick.") — Morton Smith

Ancient Greece

The study of ancient Greek (male) homosexuality, like the study of early Christian liturgy, has developed considerably since the Mar Saba text came to light. The landmark book of K. J. Dover, with its thorough synthesis of textual and pictorial evidence, did much to clarify ancient Greek behaviors and attitudes associated with sex between males, and it has provoked much further research.[1] I believe it can be shown that, just as the Mar Saba document reflects a mid-twentieth-century Anglican conception of early Christian liturgy, so it also assumes a conception of ancient homosexuality that was common in academic circles before Dover's publication, but is no longer tenable now.

Two controversies that emerged in the wake of Dover's book are relevant here. Some have objected that Dover did not pay enough attention to evidence that paederasty originated in ancient religious rituals of initiation, going back perhaps to the Indo-Europeans.[2] Others have felt that the phenomena Dover described should not even be called "homosexuality" — "if by that is meant a strong individual drive directed toward the attainment of sexual satisfaction, because boy-love was a social institution for which everyone in general potentially assumed responsibility, because it was restricted to boyhood and youth, and aimed at the development of these young people toward the group's adult ideal."[3] At the intersection of these complex problems lie the two issues — individual identity and community expectation — that define many of the cultural and historical differences between one construction of homosexuality and another.

SELF, SEX, AND SOCIETY

In the modern industrialized world, people place a very high value on personal autonomy and self-expression. The basic unit of society, in many respects, is the individual, and ethical issues tend to be formulated in terms of personal rights. Unconventional sexual drives may be deemed too important to ignore or suppress if the anticipated self-fulfillment seems more important than the negative effects of social disapproval. In very traditional societies, on the other hand, the needs of the group tend to be given much greater weight. The basic social unit may be something larger than the individual, such as the family (however configured), and ethical issues tend to be formulated in terms of the individual's responsibility to the whole. The community's interest in reproduction, kinship, lineage, and inheritance may make the need to regulate sexual behavior so compelling that it cannot be flouted merely for the sake of an individual's personal inclinations.[4] A reputation for sexual misbehavior besmirches the entire group (cf. Sirach 42:9–14). When even the decision of whom and when to marry is made by the family leadership, not the individual, the condition of "being in love" may be insufficient justification for either heterosexual or homosexual activity. As one historian of marriage customs put it:

> The idea that marriage is based on the personal feelings or inclination of those marrying may strike us as self-evident. Yet the majority of societies would take the view that marriage is far too important a matter to be left to the individuals concerned and that "feeling," "emotion," "love," between the prospective partners are largely irrelevant. This is not to say that "love" or deep affection between members of the opposite sex are unknown. There is plenty of evidence for these emotions in simple societies, and to a certain extent in tribal societies "love matches" are recognized as a basis for marriage. It is therefore wise . . . to eschew an absolute dichotomy between societies which base their marriages on personal attraction and those which arrange them. Nevertheless, particularly in peasant societies, marriage is largely based

on arrangement by kin or other wider interests, and the personal feelings of an often very young couple are not of concern. In order to show how unusual the individualistic "love-based" marriage system [is] . . . , we may cite a number of comparative sociologists and anthropologists.[5]

To date and place any document that focuses on love or sex, therefore, we have to find the right balance of psychological factors (like "romance" or "sexual orientation") and social factors (like status and function).

In the West, of course, there has been a general trend toward greater individual freedom in recent centuries. Thus an influential historian of European marriage customs has observed a steady increase in "affective individualism" in the seventeenth and eighteenth centuries, as personal preference took on a greater role in marital choice.[6] It would not be surprising if economic change played a role in this, and indeed a very recent study concludes: "In agricultural societies, fertility is all-important because of high infant and child mortality. Anything that interferes with childbearing — such as divorce, homosexuality, abortion, and jobs for women outside the home — is therefore strongly discouraged. With industrialization, infant and child mortality decline markedly. . . . In postindustrial societies women have a substantial share of management and professional jobs. Fertility falls, late marriage becomes more acceptable, and the traditional two-parent nuclear family erodes."[7]

The ancient Greek-speaking world, of course, was not a single monolithic culture,[8] but its most literate communities, the ones we know best, certainly struck a different balance than we do between individual and social constraints. Thus Werner Jaeger saw in the emergence of the Greek polis a "new cult of individuality," reflected in poets such as Archilochus, for whom

> individuality is not expressed in the modern manner, as the experience of an individual wrapped up in himself . . . , as the utterance of purely private feelings. The conscious solipsism of modern poetry may be no more than a reversion to the primitive. . . . Although the Greek poet, in exploring the new world of individuality, expresses ideas and emotions which are truly personal, he is still somehow bound by universal standards, and recognizes the law which rules his fellow-men. . . . The Greeks always thought of personality as actively related to the world (in fact, to two worlds, the world of nature and the world of human society) and not as isolated from it.[9]

In poetry and the other arts of our time, of course, "conscious solipsism" is so prevalent that there would seem to be little agreement on what might constitute binding "universal standards" — or even whether such things exist. Yet even within modern Western culture, there are broad agreements that tend to be taken for granted as more or less universal in principle. For example, it is very hard for us to understand how people can spend their lives in arranged marriages, putting societal concerns above their own power to choose. But it is even harder for us to accept that, in some societies, even homosexual sex can be shaped by social conventions that overrule personal inclination.

For example, adults in our culture who seek sex with young people often believe that their attentions have "educational value" for the victim — an idea that Smith's young parishioner also seems to endorse. Most other adults today (and I would agree) disapprove of this belief as a mere rationalization or self-serving excuse.[10] We think sex should be reserved for grown-ups because we consider it psychologically harmful for children, who are also individuals with rights. Other ancient and modern cultures, however, condone or even ritualize the idea that "transgenerational" or "age-structured" forms of homosexuality[11] are not harmful but educational, part of the inculturation process by which children mature into social and sexual adulthood.[12]

In the Spartan *agōgē* ("training"), for example, young males training as warriors were divided into three age groups, marked by religious ceremonies, graded sports, and increasing levels of participation in the men's dining clubs. The young men in the oldest group, between the ages of twenty and thirty, inaugurated sexual partnerships with the males between fourteen and twenty, while the younger boys were off-limits. The older men (over thirty) oversaw the entire process.[13] In Crete there was a differently structured agōgē with a different sequence of age groups and some of the familiar characteristics of a rite of passage.[14] Following highly regulated procedures, the boy was ritually abducted by an older man, held in isolation for up to two months, and then reintegrated into society through a ceremony in which he received gifts of military equipment, a drinking cup since he would now dine in the men's club, and an ox with which to offer his first adult sacrifice.[15] If we were to discover an ancient Greek epistle that made sense in the context of Spartan or Cretan customs, therefore, we would naturally want to place it in a Spartan or Cretan milieu of appropriate date. We ask no more of the Mar Saba letter and the Secret Gospel than that they, too, be assigned to the historical time and place that their assumptions about sexuality imply.

THE LAW OF PAEDERASTY AND THE LAW OF PHILOSOPHY

The best-known ancient paradigm, of course, is the Athenian model of "boy-love." Strictly speaking it belonged to the fifth and fourth centuries BCE, but to readers of Plato and other writers it remained a familiar benchmark all through late antiquity and down to modern times. Like the other "age-structured" Greek patterns, Athenian paederasty assumed a sharp division of roles between the adult lover (*erastēs*) and the young beloved (*erōmenos*).[16] "The fundamental opposition between different types of sexual behavior was not the heterosexual/homosexual contrast, but the active/passive contrast, the former category — activity — being characteristic of the adult male, while the latter — passivity — was reserved for women and boys" and other low-status people such as slaves, foreigners, and prostitutes (male and female).[17] The behavioral expectations for each party, "active" and "passive," were quite different, but two important issues stand out: one is that most of the rules had to do with defining or preserving distinctions of status; indeed the terminology for boys of different ages and for the types of men who were permitted access to them could get very complicated.[18] The other was a kind of cultural fiction that boy-love was not really about sex, but about imparting higher social and spiritual ideals.

Thus Athenian boy-love began with a lengthy process of courtship (today we might call it "stalking"), as a mature man pursued a youth who, at the oldest, was showing only the first signs of puberty. Pausanias's speech in Plato's *Symposium* describes the erastēs begging on his knees, swearing oaths he cannot keep, spending all night on the boy's doorstep, "willing to do slavish acts of a sort not even a slave would do."[19] The boy, however, was not supposed to give in, even when threatened with violence or offered gifts or money or political influence. It was appropriate for him to acquiesce only when he perceived that the relationship had initiatory value — that is, that the man had the ability and motivation to train him in the mores of the culture. Thus the pursuit was a test of character for both man and boy, as Pausanias put it: "The aim of our practice is to test [adult] lovers thoroughly and in the right way, to ensure that boys gratify one type but keep away from the other. That is why, at the same time, we encourage lovers to chase boys and encourage boys to run away from lovers. It's a kind of competition to test which type the lover belongs to and which type the boy belongs to. This explains why it's considered wrong to be caught quickly."[20] If the pursuit developed into a relationship, each partner followed a different set of rules. The adult lover was subject to what Pausanias calls "the law of paederasty" or the love of boys, the young beloved to "the law of philosophy," or "the love of wisdom and other virtue" (*Symposium* 184d).

> These conditions are realized when lover and boyfriend come together, each observing the appropriate rule: that the lover is justified in any service he performs for the boyfriend who gratifies him, and that the boyfriend is justified in any favour he does for someone who is making him wise and good. Also the lover must be able to develop the boyfriend's understanding and virtue in general, and the boyfriend must want to acquire education and wisdom in general. When all these conditions are met, then and then alone it is right for a boyfriend to gratify his lover, but not otherwise.[21]

In such a culture, it makes sense for Socrates and Phaedrus to discuss the rhetorical technique of a written speech whose author, Lysias, was trying to seduce a boy by arguing: "I don't think I should lose the chance to get what I am asking for, merely because I don't happen to be in love with you. . . . A lover will admit that he's more sick than sound in the head. He's well aware that he's not thinking straight; but he'll say he can't get himself under control . . . [Y]ou can expect to become a better person if you are won over by me, rather than by a lover."[22] What does not make sense in this culture is the Secret Gospel. Jesus does not pursue an unwilling young man (who in fact is dead!). Instead, he seems to be answering a call from the youth, who is the first to express love. Is this imaginable in ancient times?

COULD A YOUTH EXPRESS LOVE FIRST?

We can readily believe that many boys in ancient times did not want to be involved in sex with men; a few texts describe impassivity, pain and tears,[23] even suicide[24]—no wonder fathers attempted to protect their sons (*Symposium* 183c–d)! If we try to look for counterexamples, for boys who sought out or desired such relationships, we come up against a troubling fact: no ancient texts or artifacts directly communicate a boy's perspective—a clear indication of how inferior the boys' status was. It is probably because there are no texts authored by boys that the modern discussion has tended to focus on the artistic representations, which are commonly found on ancient Greek vases and drinking vessels. According to Dover, these hardly ever show the boy in a state of sexual arousal. When a boy is shown responding positively, he touches the man's face or head with his hands, making tender gestures of *philia* more than *erōs*.[25] The relatively rare pictures of sexually aggressive boys were perhaps intended to be humorous.[26] At times, men and boys are shown grasping each other's hands or wrists as if wrestling; some would interpret this as the boy attempting resistance, but others as his "responsive eros."[27]

A reminder is called for here that artistic representations, like texts, music, architecture and everything else, cannot be interpreted in disregard of their intended function, and it is difficult to think of a function for these images that would permit them to represent anything but the man's viewpoint. For example, if the Greek vases and cups held wine or oil that was given to boys as courting gifts, the imagery would likely have represented a kind of message from the adult to the boy, picturing the result the adult hoped for. If, on the other hand, the vessels were intended for use at dinners or symposia, where the boys acted as waiters to the adults, the men may have felt entitled to interpret such artwork as a message from the boy. In that case too, it would have been the man's fantasy that was being depicted. The men's dining room had an important social function: like the wrestling school, it combined worship and philosophy with the training of boys into manhood.[28] Thus it would be naive to treat these pictures as if they are candid "snapshots" of "what really happened." If we imagine a future historian trying to reconstruct twenty-first-century sexual practices from the pictures some men look at today, we can see how skeptical one has to be.[29]

"THE POLITICS OF REPUTATION"

It is hard to see, then, what basis there could have been for respecting the feelings or choice of any boy who did make the initial approach to a man. The compelling issue in classical Athens was not personal fulfillment, but an extremely potent "politics of reputation, whose normative poles are honor and shame."[30] Athenian law criminalized prostitution and sexual assault (*hubris*), and to those ends it also regulated the operation of schools.[31] But beyond that there was an extensive sphere of legally unregulated private life in which "the fundamental antinomy that underlies all of the most important accounts of homoerotic courtship is that of honorable vs. shameful eros."[32] Thus a heavy responsibility was placed on the boy to keep suitors at bay, and to decide wisely when to submit, based on nonsexual criteria. If he failed, he could incur severe social stigma: "Whatever a boy might do in bed, it was crucial that he not seem to be motivated by passionate sexual desire for his lover," or "he risked identifying himself as a *kinaidos*, a pathic, a catamite: no modern English word can convey the full force of the ancient stigma attached to this now-defunct entity"[33] (cf. Plato, *Gorgias* 494e). Similarly, if a free Athenian adult male were to take the demeaning "passive" or receptive sexual role with another man or youth, he would be subjected to severe opprobrium.[34] Issues of status and reputation were so important that both erastēs and erōmenos risked curtailment of their citizenship rights in the polis if they failed to comply with accepted norms.

Thus Aiskhines, in 346 BCE, defended himself against treasonous capital charges by arguing, not his own innocence, but his accuser's ineligibility to bring the charges. The accuser, Timarkhos, could not exercise the rights of an Athenian citizen, Aiskhines claimed, because years earlier, as an adolescent, Timarkhos had been the erōmenos of several men, living in their houses and conspicuously possessing too much money, indicating he had accepted gifts from them. The money and the multiple relationships meant that Timarkhos had violated laws against prostitution, which in Athens was forbidden to free Athenians, though permitted to everyone else. To make his argument, Aiskhines had to distort the actual text of the law and rely heavily on rumor for the "facts" of what Timarkhos had done. Aiskhines also had to point out that his own more recent escapades were not really relevant because as an adult he had taken only the erastēs role and faithfully stayed within its expectations. The jury of citizens was persuaded; Aiskhines prevailed and Timarkhos was disenfranchised.[35]

The ancient Athenian ideal, then, could be summed up this way:

> In classical Athens, . . . sex did not express inward dispositions or inclinations so much as it served to position social actors in the places assigned to them, by virtue of their political standing, in the hierarchical structure of the Athenian polity. . . . a relatively small group made up of the adult male citizens held a virtual monopoly of social power and constituted a clearly defined élite within the political and social life of the city-state. The predominant feature of the social landscape . . . was the great divide in status between this superordinate group, composed of citizens, and a subordinate group, composed of women, children, foreigners, and slaves — all of whom lacked full civil rights (though they were not all equally subordinate). Sexual relations not only respected that divide but were strictly polarized in conformity with it.[36]

Moreover, "society tolerated deviance from the ideal norms so long as the forbidden acts remained secret and the rules were obeyed."[37]

From this perspective, clearly, the young man's behavior in the Secret Gospel cannot be justified. He seems too interested in the relationship, which in ancient times would be taken to imply that he was a person of poor character, probably more motivated by sexual interest than by a genuine desire to be trained in virtue. It is as if the Secret Gospel were written by a modern person who assumed that ancient homosexuality would have followed Plato's model of an older teacher with a young disciple, but who did not really understand the distinction of roles between erastēs and erōmenos with their particular expectations. One could object, of course, that a Christian, quasi-Christian, or Carpocratian gospel, written in the first or second century of our era should not be expected to conform fully to social standards that prevailed in classical Athens four or more centuries earlier. But if the standards or customs were different, we have virtually no information about what they were, and as we shall see, every ancient Hellenistic model of homosexuality existed in some sort of dialogue with Plato's writings. The inevitable result is that, the more fully we engage Plato's writings, the more difficult it is to maintain that the Secret Gospel was written in any ancient Greek-speaking environment.

The Spiritual Meaning of Homosexuality

If the issue for the erōmenos was to identify the best mentor, while avoiding at least the appearance of sexual interest, the erastēs, too, had to make a choice between better and worse kinds of love. And for the man, as for the boy, the better kind sought to transcend the physical and aspire to something higher than sexual pleasure. In the *Symposium*, Pausanias gropes toward this recognition when he distinguishes two gods of love. In the merely "common" love of Pandemic Aphrodite, "inferior people . . . are attracted to women as much as boys, and to bodies rather than minds . . . partners with the least possible intelligence, because their sole aim is to get what they want." But the love of the "heavenly" or Uranian Aphrodite, "who has nothing of the female in her but only maleness," attracts a man only to boys, "who are naturally more vigorous and intelligent." Indeed it is only to boys of the right age, "when they start to have developed intelligence, and this happens around the time that they begin to grow a beard."[38]

But when Socrates speaks, he describes the matter more profoundly, reporting what he had been taught by the wise Mantinean priestess Diotima: ideally, the erastēs should rise above his erotic attraction toward a beautiful boy and ascend to a direct experience of Beauty itself. Although this famous passage is often dubbed "the ladder of love,"[39] the ladder or stairway metaphor is actually the second of two. The first and more pervasive metaphor is that of an initiation rite, as the priestess describes the lover's progress from the Lesser Mysteries, or *erōtika*, to the ultimate vision, the Greater Mysteries, the Eleusinian *epoptika*.[40] Diotima, like the Clement of the Mar Saba letter, speaks in the vocabulary of mystery religion, though it seems to me that modern translations and commentaries have not fully engaged the cultic or ritual features of this text.

Diotima's scheme of initiation goes through seven stages, as the lover's attention moves from physical attraction to the body of one boy, to the beautiful conversations he has with that boy, to a more generalized appreciation of the beauty of all bodies, to recognizing that the beauty of minds is more valuable than the beauty of bodies, to seeing the common beauty that underlies the laws and cultural practices that the lover teaches to the virtuous youth, to contemplating the "great sea of beauty" that permeates all knowledge and sciences, to the ultimate vision of *that* beauty — Beauty itself (*Symposium* 210a–210e). It is her second description that speaks of a ladder, with five steps or rungs: from one body to two, from two to all beautiful bodies, and on to beautiful practices, then to beautiful learning, finally to the knowledge of *that* Beauty (211c).

The journey is not easy, for as the man progresses he "will relax his intense passion for just one body, despising this passion and regarding it as petty."[41] Diotima is doubtful, therefore, whether Socrates can leave passion behind to make the full ascent (209e–210a). But the Socrates of the *Phaedrus* is able to explain the difference. Standing on the banks of the Illisos River, near the sanctuary where the Lesser Mysteries were celebrated, he says that the philosophers are capable of a higher form of madness than other lovers, certainly higher than the kind that Lysias disparages (244a–245c). Before they were born into earthly bodies, the philosophers followed Zeus, experiencing the highest level of initiation and the most perfect vision of Beauty itself. It is because they remember this vision that they became philosophers in this earthly life, unlike those who followed other gods, whose experiences before birth were less profound and memorable, amounting to lower levels of initiation (249c–252b). Since "everyone spends his life honoring the god in whose chorus he danced" before birth,[42] the philosopher, who danced for Zeus, will be able to practice restraint and inspire the same in his boy (252c–257a): "Now if the victory goes to the better elements in both their minds, which lead them to follow the assigned regimen of philosophy, their life here below is one of bliss and shared understanding. They are modest and fully in control of themselves now that they have enslaved the part that brought trouble into the soul and set free the part that gave it virtue."[43] In this way the boy, too, can be led to a kind of reciprocal eros, the medium for which is not physical sex but beautiful philosophical conversation.[44]

Thus there is a certain resemblance between the loftiest ideal of Athenian homosexuality and Smith's eccentric theory of early Christian initiation. Both Smith and Diotima begin with erotic attraction between males. Diotima invites Socrates to ascend by steps that include recognizing the beauty and order of the virtuous practices the man taught to the boy, then transcending all this to arrive at the vision of Beauty itself. Smith imagines the younger party ascending to heaven with Jesus.

But there is also an important difference: for Socrates and Diotima, the ascent involves transcending physical sex: "It is characteristic of a ladder that one leaves the lower rungs behind as one climbs."[45] It may be no coincidence that the Hierophant, the high priest of the Eleusinian Mysteries, was required to abstain from sex during the days of the festival.[46] For Smith, on the other hand, it seems that the physical union with Jesus *is* the initiation. Diotima's *erastēs* would rise above "the right kind of love for a boy"[47] in order to proceed, through a series of relinquishings, to the vision of Beauty itself. The disciples of Smith's Jesus leave nothing behind: their first homosexual experience begins an ascent to a paradise where they are "set free from the laws ordained for and in the lower world"—free, that is, to engage in homosexuality for all eternity.

Where the Secret Gospel seems to ignore ancient Greek distinctions of status, Smith's concept of heavenly ascent seems to ignore ancient Greek concerns about transcending merely physical sex. Both the supposed ancient gospel, that is, and its discoverer's interpretation, lack precisely those aspects of ancient sexuality that are most foreign to our thinking today, the very things that a modern forger would be most likely to overlook and a modern reader least likely to notice the absence of. What could be more out of step with our culture than the idea that sexual restraint can be spiritually positive or benefi- cial? Nowadays, even popular books aimed at conservative Christian buyers are rife with upbeat reassurances that "the more godly a person is, the better performer he or she will be in the bedroom."[48]

AN EXCEPTION THAT PROVES THE RULE

Obviously, to speak of sociocultural expectations is to speak in gener- alities. Real-life people in ancient times did not always do what they knew was expected of them, just as some people defy cultural norms today. Anything *could* have happened back then, and probably did. But our issue is not whether the events recounted in the Secret Gospel actually happened, or could have hap- pened, but how there came to be a gospel fragment that says they happened. It is in order to figure out who the Secret Evangelist was, or at least when and where he lived, that we ask what his stories reveal about his concept of sexuality.

Thus we cannot ignore the fact that in ancient Athens there was one histor- ical individual, Alcibiades, who (according to Plato) violated all cultural sanc- tions by demanding to become Socrates' erōmenos. Could not some ancient evangelist have imagined a young man like Alcibiades making a similar de- mand of Jesus? Here it is essential to understand that Plato's Alcibiades repre- sents a humorous reversal of contemporary cultural conventions, a joke with a serious purpose that reemphasizes Athenian norms—and especially Plato's philosophical interpretation of them—by his failure to conform to expecta- tions. It is probably the most hilarious story in all the extant literature of ancient philosophy.

At the beginning of Plato's *Symposium,* Socrates enters the banquet room in Agathon's house. Agathon, who has just won the prize for his first tragedy, is alone on the host's couch and invites Socrates to recline with him so that he may share some of Socrates' wisdom, as if by physical contact. Socrates agrees that it would be wonderful if wisdom flowed like water from a fuller vessel to an emptier one, but in that case it is he who hopes to acquire wisdom from Agathon. "You outrageous mocker [*hubristēs*], Socrates!" Agathon replied. "You and I can argue these claims about wisdom a little later, when we'll use Dionysus as the judge."[49] Dionysus, of course, was the patron both of sym- posia and of the contest Agathon has just won.

Smith appealed to this passage (the only direct citation of the *Symposium* in his scholarly book) to support his theory of baptism: an ancient practice (Smith alleged) of bringing a corpse to life by lying down on it *gymnos gymnō* provided "the underlying idea" behind Plato's image of wisdom transferred, like flowing water, between Socrates and Agathon lying down together on a dining couch.[50] That there actually was such a practice Smith ascertained from the Old Testament miracles of Elijah and Elisha (1 Kings 17:21 and 2 Kings 4:34) — but he uncharacteristically failed to cite Acts 20:10, where the young man who fell out a window at Troas was revived when Paul "threw himself on him and hugged him" (Revised English Bible). Thus Smith, in neglecting to add this scattered indication to the dossier supporting his theory, unaccountably missed a twenty-four-karat opportunity to catch the author of Romans 1:18–32 in flagrante delicto.

When it is Agathon's turn to speak, he delivers a textbook encomium to Love, utilizing all the rhetorical skills that helped him win the prize, and describing Eros as a beautiful young poet much like himself (*Symposium* 194e–197e). Socrates, in his usual questioning way, gets him to admit that love has to be love of something, implying that Agathon has little love for anyone but himself. In fact love is the desire for the Beautiful, which is also the Good. Agathon admits to having lost the argument (201b–c), and Socrates recounts his conversation with Diotima, ending with the Ladder of Love. But the judgment of Dionysus shows up at the end, in the person of Alcibiades: very drunk, held up by the aulos-girl, garlanded and crowned with flowers in the Dionysiac manner, and awarding his own crown to Agathon in honor of his victory two days earlier. Self-indulgence belatedly declares self-love the winner.

Climbing onto the couch with Agathon and Socrates, Alcibiades delivers a eulogy not to love, like the others, but to Socrates. Yet it is simultaneously a complaint about his long-standing inability to become Socrates' erōmenos,[51] filled with Dionysiac inversions. He had invited Socrates to dinner, "just as though I were the lover and he the boy I had designs on."[52] He had kept Socrates talking far into the night so that it would be too late for him to walk home. He had given Socrates a bed and made his intentions very explicit, in the accepted vocabulary of social initiation: "Nothing is more important to me than becoming as good a person as possible, and I don't think anyone can help me more effectively than you can."[53] He had lain in the same bed with his arms around Socrates the whole night, but with no success; by morning he was thinking ruefully that even offering money wouldn't work (219e). Unable to recognize that Socrates actually was trying to help him become a good person, modeling a philosopher's continence and restraint by withdrawing from physical pleasure for the sake of that higher love of Beauty, Alcibiades makes his own disappointment out to be Socrates' fault: "I'm not the only one he's done this to; there's also Charmides . . . and many others. He deceives them into thinking he's their lover and then turns out to be the loved one instead."[54]

But in fact Alcibiades was nothing like Charmides, who possessed, not only physical beauty, but the *sōphrosynē* or self-control to appreciate the advice of the Delphic oracle: "Know thyself" (*Charmides* 164e). While Charmides was the perfect candidate for training in virtue, Alcibiades' capacity for self-knowledge was so limited that he could not even see how unsuited he was for the pursuit of philosophy. This is what all ancient writers say about him. To Plato's contemporary Xenophon, for instance:

> Alcibiades . . . [was] the most dissolute and arrogant of all the democrats. . . . [one of] the most ambitious persons in all Athens, determined to have personal control over all State affairs and to be famous above all others. . . . [He] courted Socrates' society [not] because [he] desired his way of life and the self-discipline which he had, or because [he] thought that by associating with him [he] would acquire the highest efficiency in speech and action. . . . As soon as [he] felt superior to the rest of the company, [he] broke away from Socrates and took up politics, the object for which [he] had courted [Socrates'] society.[55]

The more we compare the *Symposium* with the biography of the historical Alcibiades, in fact, the more ingeniously clever Plato's depiction turns out to be. One of the early predicaments in Alcibiades' incredibly swashbuckling life was the time he was sentenced to death in absentia for staging a mocking parody of the Eleusinian Mysteries, which ended up with a band of drunken hooligans breaking the phalluses off all the Hermes statues guarding the homes of Athens. He got out of that one by defecting to Sparta, betraying his new allies to the Athenian fleet and then returning home to Athens in triumph. There he used his troops to protect the worshippers at Eleusis and restore the mystery rites to their original glory, "bearing in mind how it would enhance not only his piety in the eyes of the gods, but also his reputation among men," as Plutarch put it. The lower classes began to demand that he take over the city as a tyrant, which naturally put him at odds with the patricians who ran the Athenian democracy. "He could change more abruptly than a chameleon," wrote Plutarch. "Alcibiades seems to be a clear case of someone destroyed by his own reputation." Ancient accounts differ as to which of his many enemies was responsible for setting his house on fire and shooting him down as he fled.[56] But the long story need not detain us here — it is enough to observe that Plato's Alcibiades makes a mockery of the truth Diotima had taught Socrates, just as the real-life Alcibiades ridiculed the Eleusinian mystery rites that structured Diotima's teaching, and demonstrated an utter lack of idealism and fidelity to principle throughout his life.

Thus the deutero-Platonic dialogue known as *Alcibiades I* reports a conversation, some years after the *Symposium*,[57] in which Socrates tries to persuade

Alcibiades to learn philosophy in order to rule well. Explaining that he loves Alcibiades' soul rather than his body (*Alcibiades I* 104e–105a, 131c), Socrates is still trying to teach him to "Know thyself" (124b). But the Alcibiades of the *Symposium*, like the historical one, is impervious to instruction. He had missed all the other speeches, including Socrates' account of Diotima's teaching. He compares Socrates to a satyr, but his speech is itself compared by Socrates to the satyrs' play that, according to Athenian custom, was staged after every three tragedies to provide comic relief (222d).[58] With no idea what Socrates had been talking about, unable to understand Socrates' encouragement to transcend merely physical love, Alcibiades provides the comic dessert to this banquet of serious speeches: drunk, clumsy, self-serving where Agathon is lyrical and self-aggrandizing; physical and debauched where Socrates is spiritual and self-disciplined. Alcibiades, then, reaffirms Athenian and Platonic assumptions about sexual roles and ideals by his inability to conform to them, hilariously inverting with his salacious demands an ancient Greek ideal that a man should lead a boy to transcend mere sexuality for the sake of more spiritual goals.

Is the Mar Saba document also a satyrs' play? It too has aspects that are "hard not to find amusing,"[59] despite being full of vocabulary derived from the Eleusinian Mysteries. Eventually it will become clear that the Mar Saba text, too, is wickedly funny when viewed from the perspective of its true author—and certain other perspectives besides. But it is not ancient Athenian homosexuality that is being satirized. Jesus is no Socrates, and the young man no Alcibiades. The butt of the joke lies elsewhere, as it were. On the way to finding it, we must first look at Jesus' angry rejection of women—a theme so important that it occurs in both of the extant excerpts from the Secret Gospel.

Ancient Male Homosexuals on Women

If the sister of the young man greeted Jesus by kissing him and "coming," she would appear, if anything, even more brash than her brother. It is hard to believe that a respectable woman of those times would be so bold in expressing sexual interest in a man to whom she was not married, and "tempting" him in the presence of other men (in the sister's case) or other women (as Salome seems to be doing in the second excerpt). By contrast, Hipparchia of Maroneia, who insisted on marrying Crates the Theban Cynic over her parents' and even Crates' objections, was clearly motivated by her desire to learn philosophy, not by mere heterosexual attraction.[60]

But even if social conditions (or Salome's reputation) were such that it would not have been considered "something new on earth" when "a woman courts a man" (Jeremiah 31:22, Jewish Publication Society, 2nd ed.), by most ancient standards there was no social or ethical reason for the man to turn her down. Jesus' angry rejection cannot be attributed to conventional ancient restrictions about a prior homosexual commitment, for there were none. Being the elder partner in a paederastic pairing was no obstacle, for an erastēs would often have a wife and mistresses also. A free adult man could have sex with whomever he wanted, as long as he didn't violate the rights or reputation of another free adult man.[61] Indeed many ancient Greek men in the erastēs role may not have had the freedom to refrain from marrying a woman, for adult males were socially expected to marry and father children.[62] "To be 'homosexual' (in the modern sense of the term, which rules out relations with women) cannot have been easy in Greece."[63] Unapologetic bisexuality seems to have been the norm rather than exclusive homosexuality. Sophocles, whose frolics with boys were almost as famous as those of Socrates, had both a legitimate son with his wife and an illegitimate one with a foreign woman.[64]

Nor does it make sense to argue that Jesus was constrained by Jewish or early Christian prohibitions against sex outside of marriage, if he also engaged in sex with male disciples.[65] The Jesus of the Secret Gospel could only be acting from sheer personal inclination: he doesn't want Salome. He is not interested in women at all. It is the young man he loves. This sounds rather like the modern concept of "sexual orientation": could an ancient author have imagined such an exclusive attraction to males?

Nowadays one often encounters (in one form or another) the notion that the ancient world had no concept of sexual orientation, that it recognized only categories of behavior, not of personal psychology. This opinion is often ascribed to Michel Foucault, whose views were actually more complicated.[66] In any case, it is increasingly being criticized.[67] Ancient astrological texts, for example, clearly state that celestial configurations at the time of birth will determine a person's sexual personality, including the gender he or she will be attracted to.[68]

If any ancient writers lacked a concept of sexual orientation, in my opinion it would be the Jews, like Paul,[69] Philo, and Josephus,[70] who wrote as if everyone is potentially capable of choosing to commit a homosexual act, but no one may ever do so lawfully. No doubt they were relying on statements in the Holiness Code of the Torah, that "lying with males" is one of those abominable, idolatrous acts that had caused the Canaanites to be expelled from the Promised Land (Leviticus 18). As with child sacrifice, insulting one's parents, incest, adultery, or bestiality, it was therefore punished by death—for both parties, with no distinction made between insertive and receptive roles (Leviticus 20).[71] Since the historical Jesus presumably had even less exposure to

Hellenic culture than Philo, Josephus, and Paul, it is hard to think of a *historical* reason why he would have been more accepting of homosexuality than they. The absence of preserved sayings from Jesus on this issue may be a sign that, in his environment, the whole subject was uncontroversial — unlike, say, the grounds for divorce or the payment of Roman taxes.[72] This, in turn, makes it very difficult to argue that the Secret Gospel depicts a non-Greek or Semitic model of homosexuality that was present in some putative Aramaic *Vorlage*.

In ancient Greek literature, on the other hand, there are male characters who seem to advocate and practice homosexuality exclusively and by preference, as if motivated by an individual psychological makeup or orientation. Some may be in liaisons that were originally paederastic but did not end when the younger party matured; others belong to warrior couples, aspiring to heroic comradeship in battle,[73] which of course is not what we find in the Secret Gospel. It is possible, however, that many of these men actually did have wives who, given the low valuation of women in those times, were deemed too unimportant to mention. We know Socrates had a wife (and children!), for example, only because his male companions were embarrassed by her "just like a woman" expressions of grief at his impending execution.[74] Otherwise, we could plausibly but wrongly conclude that Socrates was exclusively paederastic. Are there ancient instances, then, of men facing a situation like the one Jesus is presented with in the Secret Gospel, and making a deliberate decision to forgo women completely and love only men?

One well-known example from Greek mythology is the case of Orpheus, who (according to Ovid and others), after emerging from the underworld without Euridice, swore never to love another woman but thenceforth only males; his unfortunate death, torn to pieces by either Thracian women or Maenads, was interpreted in this tradition as the revenge of the fair sex.[75] This is certainly not a case of innate predisposition or sexual orientation, but of a reaction or overreaction to the loss of the great heterosexual love of his life. An apologetic theme in some early Christian art and literature, notably Clement's,[76] would make Jesus a more profound or pacific singer than Orpheus, but does not take up Orpheus' second career as a homosexual or the circumstances of his death.[77] In any case, there is no trace of Orpheus symbolism in the Secret Gospel.

There are four ancient debates, all fictional, on whether man-boy love is superior to man-woman love. All date from late antiquity, closer to Clement's time than Plato's. As it happens, two of them depict the dilemma of an erōmenos faced with the possibility of marrying a woman. The other two deal with the erastēs's problem of whether to practice sexual restraint in order to rise to a higher knowledge. None of them reproduces the exact dilemma of the Secret

Gospel Jesus — that of an erastēs approached by a woman — suggesting that such an occurrence was either inconceivable or not a problem. No debate frames the issue in terms of personal identity (such as, "Am I constitutionally homosexual?"), nor even in terms such as Aristotle's distinction between those who desire sex with males "by nature" and those who do so "by habit."[78] Instead, all four debates are conducted in terms that demonstrate the continuing validity of Plato's Athenian construction of homosexuality.

THE ERŌMENOS'S DILEMMA

In a subplot in the novel *Leucippe and Clitophon* by Achilles Tatius (second century CE), Clinias, who has been "initiated into the cult of Eros,"[79] competes with other men for the affection of the boy Charicles; he wins by buying Charicles the gift of a horse. Crisis erupts when Charicles' father arranges for him to marry an unattractive but wealthy woman. It is clear that Charicles feels no heterosexual attraction to this particular woman; his dilemma is strictly about social and family responsibility. In the ensuing discussion, Clinias tries to persuade Charicles not to marry, using two arguments. One is the treacherousness and faithlessness of women, illustrated with a long list of female characters from literature and mythology who killed or otherwise inconvenienced their men. The other argument is that the youthful male body is more beautiful than the female body, and it would be a shame for Charicles to waste his as long as he is young enough to have one. What he might do once he has aged a bit remains unspecified. Charicles never states his own feelings or opinions; he can only say that he remains unsure what to do. That issue becomes moot, however, when, taking the horse out for its first ride, he falls off and is killed, leaving Clinias feeling shocked and guilty.[80]

A much longer and more subtle exploration of the same problem is Plutarch's dialogue *Eroticus*, written at the end of the first century CE. It narrates a debate that takes place in the temple of the Muses during the Thespian quadrennial festival of Eros, prompted by the dilemma of Bacchon, a beautiful youth with many male lovers who is now being pursued by the very desirable widow Ismenodora. Young, beautiful, wealthy, of high aristocratic rank and ethical reputation, she is everything a man could want, and has no shortage of suitors. But she wants to marry Bacchon so badly that she has arranged to have him abducted and forcibly clothed in the bridegroom's traditional garb. Bacchon himself is never brought onstage to express his own opinion about all this.[81]

What gets the debate underway is the debaters' own anxiety about the social status issues his predicament raises. For example, although Ismenodora is young, she is older than Bacchon: "We would be marrying an immature lad to a woman older than he is by as much as the bridegroom should be older than the bride," objects one disputant.[82] Even Bacchon's mother is said to be concerned about Ismenodora's higher aristocratic status.[83] Pisias, "the most serious-minded of [Bacchon's male] lovers," opposes the marriage on the ground that, since Ismenodora is wealthy and accustomed to having her way, she would be the dominant figure in the relationship, when everyone knows that the man should be dominant.[84] His ally Protogenes opines that heterosexual desires are merely natural impulses, like the appetite for food, but cannot be considered love. "True love has nothing whatever to do with the women's quarters," full of perfume and jewels and "softened by pleasures that have no manliness in them."[85] It cannot rise to the heights of friendship, philosophy, and love of virtue that men find in the gymnasia and the wrestling schools. Relationships with women cannot be about anything but sex: one might as well "love" a slave.[86]

But Pisias is accused of hypocrisy by Bacchon's older cousin Anthemion, who favors the marriage. "For all his moral principles . . . [Pisias] was doing as bad lovers do, seeking to deprive his friend of family, marriage, and great prosperity, in order to keep him fresh and unsullied, to strip for him in the wrestling-school as long as possible."[87] No one points out that Anthemion could also be accused of a self-serving agenda: as a member of Bacchon's family, he has a stake in its "great prosperity."

Some of the interlocutors speculate that Bacchon permitted himself to be kidnapped because he actually wants the marriage. But even if he did, that in itself would hardly settle the matter, for issues of social status were more important. In the course of twenty pages no one ever says, as a modern advice columnist would, that Bacchon should decide for himself who he is and what he wants. It is not so much that the disputants have no concept of sexual orientation—it is as if they think it wouldn't make any difference. Thus Protogenes reminds the group of "Aristippus' remark, when he answered the man who complained that [the boy] Lais did not like him by saying that he didn't think his wine or his fish liked him, though he enjoyed both."[88] So much for the youth in the Secret Gospel!

The bulk of the dialogue consists of a long speech by Plutarch himself, demonstrating that Eros, the most powerful of the gods, ennobles women as well as men, bringing out their best qualities. Mere appetite for boys or women, paedomania or gynaecomania, should not be confused with love; the lifelong union of marital fidelity that Eros makes possible is superior to the short-lived relationships of boy-love and the various forms of unmarried heterosexuality. It is not heterosexuality as such that is superior, it seems, but marriage, which (everyone seems to agree) can only occur between a man and a woman.[89] In the end, Pisias accepts an invitation to attend the wedding of Bacchon and Ismenadora; he even leads the procession through the agora to the temple.[90]

These two debates do not seem directly relevant to the Secret Gospel. Although Ismenodora's behavior makes Salome's forwardness seem positively demure, it is Jesus that Salome and the other women approach, not the youth who is in the position of Charicles and Bacchon. The misogynistic arguments voiced by Clinias and Protogenes can be paralleled in many other ancient and not-so-ancient texts, but not in the Secret Gospel, which does not mention anything wrong with women as such. There is no roll call of infamous biblical women, like Jezebel, who could be invoked as exemplifying the dangers of heterosexual involvement. We can almost imagine Jesus putting the women off with the modern relationship-killing cliché, "It's not about you, it's about me." Indeed it is Jesus who is angered by the whole thing, not Clinias or Protogenes.

THE ERASTĒS'S DILEMMA

Another debate in the novel *Leucippe and Clitophon* takes place from the perspective of the erastēs. Clitophon, the male heterosexual protagonist, while traveling with Clinias, the bereaved erastēs of Charicles, falls in with the Egyptian Menelaus, an erastēs who still mourns for the erōmenos he had accidentally killed while they were hunting together. The boy's parents had sued him in court, and the grief-stricken Menelaus had asked for the death penalty. But the jury, moved by pity, had given him only a three-year exile. As Menelaus and Clinias commiserate on the loss of their beloved boys, Clitophon tries to stop the weeping by distracting them with a debate on the merits of boy-love versus woman-love. The fact that boys are attractive for only a short time seems a disadvantage, Clitophon proposes. But Menelaus replies that the delight in something that must be snatched quickly only increases longing, and he puts his argument in quasi-Platonic terms. The heavenly Aphrodite "is distressed at being chained to mortal beauty," as one would be in a heterosexual marriage, "and seeks to fly swiftly heavenwards,"[91] just as (according to Homer) Zeus brought Ganymede to heaven to make him wine steward at the table of the gods. Clitophon replies that Zeus has also brought female lovers up to heaven with him, then switches to a different argument: sex with women is more pleasurable. Menelaus predictably disagrees. Women's beauty is artificial, due to cosmetics, perfume, and hair dye, and women's bodies are too soft. It cannot be compared to the freshness of an inexperienced, hard-bodied boy. This discussion, like the earlier one about Charicles, ends with no clear winner.

Menelaus, though, seems like a straightforward example of a man of ancient times with a true homosexual orientation: he simply likes boys but not
women. He evidently has no wife or household since he is traveling on his own
in exile. His understanding of the heavenly Aphrodite does not include a
concept of renouncing physical pleasure, for Zeus brought Ganymede up to
heaven with him. Menelaus is no Socrates — he must have danced for a lesser
god before birth. He does not even rise to the level of Plato's Pausanias by
recognizing the man's responsibility for the boy's training in virtue. Yet he also
does not harbor the anger at women that Jesus displays in the Secret Gospel;
Menelaus simply doesn't care for them.

A more thoughtful and complex discussion of the same issues occurs in the
dialogue *Amores,* dubiously ascribed to Lucian of Samosata (third century,
but more likely dating from the fourth).[92] In the temple of Heracles, Theomnestus, who loves both women and boys, asks his friend Lycinus which love is
better. In response, Lycinus recounts an earlier dialogue he had heard, which
began in the temple of Aphrodite at Cnidus, between Charicles of Corinth
(who loved women) and Callicratidas of Athens (who loved boys). This Charicles had argued that homosexuality was unnatural, unknown to the animal
world, and had emerged relatively recently in human history. It was hypocritical to identify homosexuality with philosophy, for there is no correlation
between physical beauty and the possession of wisdom. Women are more
beautiful than boys, and for a much longer portion of their lives. Heterosexual
intercourse is enjoyable for both partners — indeed women offer two receptive
orifices while boys have only one. Finally, if sex between men could be justified, then lesbian sex would be justifiable as well — an evident impossibility to
Charicles.

Callicratidas retorted that the eros of males "is the only activity combining
both pleasure and virtue."[93] True, sex with women was essential in the early
days to ensure the expansion of the human race, but with the growth of
civilization — including agriculture, architecture, clothes-making — we should
"assess as superior the later additions invented by human life when it had
leisure for thought."[94] Callicratidas does show some real anger at women: he
wishes their gold serpentine bracelets would turn into live, biting snakes.[95] But
women remain necessary for procreation, unfortunately — would that we
could just go to a temple and buy an heir for gold or silver! Since we cannot,
relationships with women will have to continue. But their beauty is artificial;
without paint and hairstyling, clothing and jewelry, they would look like mon-
keys. A boy, on the other hand, gets up in the morning, washes his face with
pure water, goes to school to train his intellect with philosophy and music, and
then goes to the gym to "perfect his body with noble exercises."[96] The relation-

ships of Orestes and Pylades, Socrates and Alcibiades, show that "those who love thus, having nothing disgraceful on their conscience, find their lifetime sweetest and after their death their glorious report goes out to all men."[97]

Lycinus now offered to Theomnestus the same verdict he had rendered to Charicles and Callicratidas: "Marriage is a boon and a blessing to men when it meets with good fortune, while the love of boys, that pays court to the hallowed dues of friendship, I consider to be the privilege only of philosophy. Therefore all men should marry, but let only the wise be permitted to love boys, for perfect virtue grows least of all among women."[98] Theomnestus concurs, but with one proviso: he will not accept the philosophers' view that the erastēs should forgo physical pleasure for the sake of something higher. In an obviously humorous parody of Diotima's teaching, he says that the love of boys should proceed by steps, like a ladder, from looking to touching to kissing to pleasure. He cannot imagine that even the greatest philosophers acted any differently. Does anyone really believe that nothing happened when Alcibiades lay in bed with Socrates all night, or between Achilles and Patroclus? "No, pleasure was the mediator even of *their* friendship."[99] By reconfiguring Diotima's ladder, Theomnestus confirms that, in the ancient understanding, pleasurable sex with boys was not the means of ascent to a higher level, but something that had to be left behind, a trade-off Theomnestus, for his part, was unwilling to make. He is the sort of person that the Socrates of the *Phaedrus* would describe as unsuited for the Greater Mysteries, the sort who followed lesser gods before birth, and never had the perfect vision of *that* Beauty which motivates philosophers to control their bodily impulses for the sake of something better.

The characters in this dialogue, then, concur that "all men should marry." Probably few men in ancient times were so committed to boy-love that they would forgo marriage and the chance to beget legitimate heirs. The Jesus of the Secret Gospel, on the other hand, has no use for women at all; he is angrier and more rejecting than Callicratidas. In a strange way he seems more like the mellower Menelaus: completely unaware of the philosophical advantages that can be achieved through the practice of sexual restraint. This would make Jesus even more benighted than Theomnestus, who at least has heard such claims, even if he doesn't believe them. Why would anyone write a gospel about someone like this—a man so annoyed by women that he will beget no heirs, so unaware of philosophy that he aspires to nothing higher than physical pleasure, seemingly teaching his disciples that sex with males is heaven enough?

There are two reasons that I can think of why someone might write such a gospel. One is that a modern author, who really did not understand ancient homosexuality, might unintentionally ascribe to Jesus a more modern kind of eroticism, just as he might misrepresent early Christian liturgy as having the characteristics of more recent worship. The other possible reason is that the Secret Gospel was meant to be satirical, to ridicule Jesus as a mere pedophile and Christianity as his misbegotten offspring. I think there is truth in both of these possibilities, but the second one forces us to look one more time at the conflict between Clement and the Carpocratians. Do their dueling gospels express an ancient conflict or a modern one?

A Carpocratian Gospel?

It is possible that the Carpocratian notion of freedom from law was not a freedom from sexual constraints, but actually a freedom from the commandment to increase and multiply (Genesis 1:28), which would only imprison more souls in material bodies through "the inherently defiling act of intercourse."[100] But the Carpocratians are presented as libertines in ancient reports, which derive their information from the same few sources — the heresy catalogues written from the perspective of orthodox Christianity. However, Carpocratian teachings evidently did exhibit a certain "color Platonicus," and they are said to have displayed icons of Jesus along with Plato and other Greek philosophers.[101] Could they have practiced a form of homosexuality that they identified with Plato's writings, but which differed in some respects from the conventions Plato knew? Although this seems perfectly possible, it is not easily argued from the sources we have. The one sexual vice that was specifically attributed to the Carpocratians was the communal sharing of wives, which Clement believed they had derived from Plato's *Republic* (457d, 543a).[102]

In a recent book, Kathy L. Gaca retraces an actual debate about sexual morality between Clement of Alexandria and Epiphanes, who was the son of Carpocrates.[103] We do not have what Epiphanes wrote, except to the extent that it was quoted by Clement. But as Gaca interprets from what we do have, Epiphanes (whose position she much prefers over Clement's) was a Christian Platonist who, in agreement with Plato and the Stoic philosophers, saw private property as a major obstacle to a just society. Monogamous marriage was a big part of the problem because it fostered the idea that the man "owned" his wife and because the resulting family would strive to control as much wealth as it could, at the expense of other families. Thus Epiphanes was "an ardent communalist in his sexual and social principles." Since "human beings must liberate themselves from the private ownership of persons and goods in order to curtail the incorrigible appetites and the myriad vicious desires that spawn from the appetites . . . , [s]exual communalism is thus paramount to attain an equitable Christian society. . . . His egalitarian sexual principles thus have a genuinely Christian motivation, even though they have been wildly misrepresented since antiquity as the prurient fantasies of a libidinous heretic."[104]

In Gaca's opinion, "Clement's procreationist position derives ultimately from Pythagoreanism," even though the Carpocratian belief in reincarnation offers a more obvious connection to the traditions descended from Pythagoras.[105] Gaca identifies the Pythagorean ideal as dictating "that men and women who engage in sexual intercourse should do so only in marriage and for the express purpose of reproduction, and that excitement during intercourse should be kept as sedate as possible." Clement read this ideal into Philo's and Paul's interpretations of the Greek Bible, so that his own ethic surpassed the usual Christian position that marriage and celibacy are the only two ethical options. Sexual desire was inherently idolatrous: the Greek word for it was the name of the goddess Aphrodite, recalling the Old Testament prophets who often used adultery as a metaphor for idolatry. Thus the enjoyment of sex was forbidden even to married Christians, who could justify sexual intercourse at all only when it was engaged in for the purpose of reproduction. Fortunately, a special grace "allows the married couples strictly to reproduce in Christ the Lord without any desire whatsoever."[106]

Epiphanes, on the other hand,

> is also a strong enough Platonist to see why it is impossible and undesirable to eliminate sexual desire from human experience, which Christian Platonists such as Clement believe is mandatory for salvation. He [Epiphanes] tries to counter this belief by declaring it manifestly absurd to deny the sexual impulse with which all human beings are born. Epiphanes thus is "libidinous" only in the sense that he respects Plato's position that human beings have a libido and should act on it moderately and in the interest of social justice.
>
> Clement's polemic against Epiphanes' fornicating justice is grounded in the conviction that "the Law, the Prophets, and the Gospel" alone authorize permissible sexual conduct. Since, on Clement's view, holy scripture demands either perpetual virginity or monogamous Christian procreationism conjoined with no sexual desire, Christians would flagrantly fornicate against their husband the Lord if they followed Epiphanes' proposals and even wanted to enjoy moderate sexual pleasure, let alone if they actually did so, especially on the magnitude of a communally sexual social order. Clement accordingly escorts Epiphanes from his church of bridal chastity as "not one of us."[107]

I have outlined Gaca's interpretation at length, not to endorse it, but to show how differently from Smith one can construe the conflict between Clement and the Carpocratians. It is possible to see Epiphanes' view as a reasoned philosophical position based on important ancient thinkers; it does not have to be categorized as "unbridled madness," as Irenaeus put it. In any case what

Epiphanes advocated was not homosexuality, but an alternative model of heterosexuality. If Irenaeus is correct that the Carpocratians believed each soul had to have "every experience in life," there is no explicit testimony in the texts we have that this included homosexual experiences. Nor is it quite the same as believing, in Smith's words, that "sin was a means of salvation."

The Mar Saba letter ascribed to Clement reveals no awareness that communal sharing of wives was a Carpocratian practice that Clement contested. In fact it takes the incompatible position that one should have no relations with women at all. Thus the "profile" of the fifth stream of tradition — the Carpocratian gospel and teaching — seems incompatible with the known historical facts. It seems doubtful that the Mar Saba text provides accurate information about the ancient Carpocratians, or about ancient Christian perceptions or misperceptions of them.

But let us try to read the letter as an ancient person of Hellenistic education might have — someone like Clement's unknown addressee Theodore, who presumably was familiar with late antique constructions of homosexuality. Jesus, angered by a woman's request, follows her anyway to a tomb. A voice cries out, and Jesus opens the tomb and raises the young man by the hand. The youth looks at him, loves him, and begs to be with him. So Jesus moves into the young man's house for six days where they evidently enjoy his great wealth. After that, following instructions, the young man comes to Jesus at night (but where?), wearing only a linen sheet. Jesus teaches him, naked man to naked man, then moves on, leaving the young man behind. Subsequently, he refuses to meet with the sister and some other women. Thus the Carpocratian form of the gospel.

Problems emerge, however, when we try to move from the gospel to the letter that contains it. Clement's execration of the Carpocratian text would be easy to understand if he took the suggestions of homosexual activity literally and responded with the usual Judeo-Christian disdain for same-sex relations, regardless of pretext. But then it becomes difficult to explain why Clement's form of the gospel — treated with special honor and secretly reserved for the most important ritual occasions — is so similar. It too contains the rejection of the women, the grasping of hands, the youth's expression of love, the cloth over the naked body — every element we know of except the phrase "naked man with naked man." Since these elements cannot be explained in terms of the Alexandrian liturgy, what are we to make of them? Smith believed that the similarity of gospels was actually an embarrassment from which Clement sought to divert attention, with his hypocritical moralizing fulminations and his demand for absolute secrecy.[108] What did he have to hide, unless it was the embarrassing "truth" that the Carpocratians had preserved the real religion of Jesus?

Or, taking another approach, let us suppose (however implausibly) that Clement was the truer Platonist, who understood the "law of paederasty" and blamed the Carpocratians, in effect, for being satisfied to remain at the carnal level, refusing to climb Diotima's ladder. Their Jesus lies *gymnos gymnō* with the youth, unconcerned about anything more than physical pleasure. The youth, too, is so brazenly unprincipled that he demands to become Jesus' *erōmenos*, and Jesus is so depraved as to comply: the *kinaidos* and the unphilosophical Jesus deserve each other. In this reading, Clement is the philosopher who knows enough to practice restraint in order to mount up to that vision of the highest Good. His position is that the love between master and disciple should be "merely Platonic." Unfortunately for this interpretation, the youth behaves just as badly in Clement's gospel as he does in the Carpocratian one. And of course it would not be the disciple but Jesus, the *erastēs*, who ascends to the vision of Beauty if anyone does. That would be no problem for the Carpocratians, perhaps, because they evidently believed that Jesus was "begotten by Joseph and . . . made like men" but had received a "power" from God that enabled him to ascend to God the Father.[109] But it would make no sense to Clement if he believed that Jesus had always been divine. Moreover, a true Platonist would not write in the condemnatory tones of the Mar Saba Clement. For Plato, eros motivated by pleasure was not so much immoral as "petty." This reading, then, is even less plausible than the previous one: even if we can accept that the Carpocratians were as unprincipled as the Mar Saba Clement says they were, we cannot make this Clement intelligible as a Platonic paederast.

No matter how we look at it, then, we end up with nonsensical results — but only for Clement's side of the story. It is the Carpocratian gospel and interpretation that can be made consistent and understandable, even if historically unverifiable: they practiced a form of homosexuality that they imbued with a religious meaning. It is the Alexandrian tradition that seems incomprehensible, for (despite our best efforts to explain it) Clement's Christianity seems to amount to nothing more than a Carpocratianism without the homosexuality — or a Christianity in denial of its own homosexual tendencies.

And that, I think, is the point. Up to now we have been reading the Mar Saba document backwards, assuming that Clement represents more-or-less familiar Christianity, and the Carpocratians the barely known marginal group. That is why we have had so much trouble figuring out what the text means. It all begins to make sense if we assume that the letter was actually written by a Carpocratian, or by an author who intended the Carpocratians to represent his true sympathies. Perhaps an author who, like Morton Smith, believed that it was the Carpocratians who preserved the original libertine character of Christianity, while the orthodox church, led by people like Clement of Alexandria, knowingly suppressed it. Reading the Mar Saba letter correctly, then, involves a reversal even more unexpected than finding a twentieth-century Anglican liturgy in second-century Egypt. It is Clement who is being portrayed as the false teacher, whose position makes no sense — who in fact is shown dishonestly trying to suppress the evidence that the oldest and most honored traditions of his own church have, disconcertingly, too much in common with the Carpocratians.

Reading the document through such "Carpocratian" eyes, we quickly learn two other things. First, the five streams of tradition that the Mar Saba letter describes are not really different from each other. At least three of them — the Secret Gospel, the Carpocratian gospel, and the Alexandrian initiation rite — all converge on the same message as Clement's letter as a whole, that Jesus practiced ritual homosexuality, as if they had all been written by the same person. The canonical gospel of Mark is presented as not containing this message, intended for the lower-level initiates who aren't yet ready for it. Only the hierophantic teaching that Mark did not write down is still unaccounted for, though in time we will get to that too.

The second thing we learn is that the Mar Saba letter, a unitary document expressing only one perspective, is actually a kind of riddle: that its author was really a "Carpocratian" is only the first clue. We will encounter many other inversions as we unravel this topsy-turvy text, wherein nothing is what it seems to be. The entire picture is only visible when seen from the correct angle — but from that vantage point everything falls into place, like the punch line of a complicated joke. If we begin by seeing the Carpocratians as the "good guys," we will end by seeing that, as usual, Socrates was right after all: the same man has written both comedy and tragedy (*Symposium* 223d).

But it is tragicomedy of a modern and personal kind, a sort of "disaffective individualism." For the Secret Evangelist was one angry man, and although he wrote in the ancient genre of satire, there is too much in it of himself. Who better than "Sigmund of Vienna" (as Smith mockingly called him)[110] could explain this mystery?

> Our hostile impulses towards our fellows — ever since our childhood as individuals as well as the childhood of human culture — have been subject to the same restrictions, the same progressive repressions, as our sexual urges. . . . Violent hostility, forbidden by law, has given way to verbal invective. . . . Ever since we have had to give up expressing hostility by our actions . . . we have developed a new technique of insult, just as we did in the case of sexual aggression, which aims to draw [a] third person into becoming an ally against our enemy. By making our enemy small, mean, contemptible, comical, we take a roundabout route to getting for ourselves the enjoyment of vanquishing him, which the third person — who has gone to no effort — endorses with his laughter.

> We are now prepared for the part played in hostile aggression by the joke. The joke will allow us to turn to good account those ridiculous features in our enemy that the presence of opposing obstacles would not let us utter aloud or consciously; again, that is, it will *get around restrictions and open up sources of pleasure that have become inaccessible*. It will, further, bribe the listener with his own gain in pleasure into taking our side without probing very far.[111]

This last sentence may not apply here, though. Instead, I suspect the Delphic Oracle may be taken as a broad hint that, before we are through, more loud cries will be heard from other tombs.

There are, in sum, three reasons why the Mar Saba text cannot be an ancient document: it presents the wrong kind of liturgy, the wrong kind of homosexuality, and even the wrong kind of humor. To place it in its proper historical setting, then, we need to identify an environment with all of the following characteristics: it would have to be a situation in which it was possible to obtain an expert knowledge of ancient Greek, to produce a man with the Secret Evangelist's masterful ability to imitate the style and vocabulary of Mark and Clement. It should also be a context in which homosexuality was imagined to be much the same as the homosexuality described by Plato, but was actually rather different — less concerned about ancient Athenian issues of social role and status, and angrily excluding all relationships with women. We should look for a community that placed high value on the Platonic idea that same-sex attraction could be the basis for an ascent to heaven or to the highest beauty, so that a homosexual act could serve as a kind of ersatz religious ritual, expressed in the language of the Mysteries. And we need a milieu in which the early history of the Christian liturgy was perceived from an Anglican perspective, but where there was also a tendency to identify with ancient heretical sects, like the Carpocratians, as preferable to orthodox Christianity. There actually was such a time and place, and not too long ago nor far away.

Summary

Ancient Greek homosexuality, which involved the pursuit of boys by older men, was different in many respects from what we think of as homosexuality today. Because of cultural issues regarding status and reputation, it is inconceivable that a young man at the time of Jesus would initiate a relationship, as the young man in the Secret Gospel seems to. Plato's *Symposium*, one of the most influential writings on this subject, clearly teaches that the man was ideally supposed to rise above physical desire and give up sex, in order to take the relationship to a higher spiritual plane, and experience a vision of the ultimate heavenly Beauty. Men in ancient times who were involved with boys were usually married to women also, if only to beget heirs. The result is that ancient Greek homosexuality was less misogynistic than the Jesus of the Secret Gospel, who rejects women altogether.

These differences between ancient and modern homosexuality cannot be explained by supposing that the Mar Saba document represents a Carpocration sexology that differed in some respects from Plato. But if the letter of Clement is read as if its modern-seeming homosexuality was "Carpocratian," then Clement's position as the defender of traditional Christian morality becomes nonsensical. Thus the point seems to be that homosexuality is the true Christianity. It is clear that the apparent five streams of tradition are not really different; they converge in an angry joke that ridicules Christianity's opposition to homosexuality as a denial of the truth.

Uranian Venus: A Homoerotic Subculture in English Universities

*A good way to attack any historical problem is to locate it in time and space.
The main outlines of occidental history are pretty well known; so are the main
characteristics of the occidental countries and cultures. Therefore, if you can
place your problem in a given country at a given time, the history and characteristics of that country and time will both suggest the likely answers and give
you a set of limits within which any possible answer must fall.*
— Morton Smith

It is not uncommon for culturally censured behavior to be defined as
foreign or alien, typical of people less civilized than ourselves. Thus the Latin
vocabulary for homosexuality presents it as a Greek phenomenon, while Philo
of Alexandria, a Greek, considered it Italian.[1] The Holiness Code regards
homosexuality as something only non-Israelites do. In the 1980s, as the AIDS
virus began to spread, some national governments blithely assumed that "the
Gay Plague" could never become a problem in their country.[2] In the English-
speaking world, from at least the eighteenth century, there has been a long
history of identifying homosexuality as ancient Greek or Persian behavior, not
native to the English. Recent research has shown that the composer George
Frideric Handel (1685–1759), whose personal life had always seemed unduly
sparse in female love interests,[3] worked in a London subculture in which

Orpheus, Nero, Xerxes, and other figures from classical literature served as
secret ciphers for homosexuality.[4]

With the revival of Plato studies in the nineteenth century, a subculture
developed in English-speaking universities that encoded contemporary homosexuality in the vocabulary of Platonic boy-love. The Platonic model brought
much-needed definition in a Victorian context where both the desire for and
the reality of sex between men was so submerged in shame that, as we will see,
there were not even legal or medical terms for it. In fact it was within this
culture that some of the first attempts were made to develop a scientific terminology. Oxford classicist John Addington Symonds, who wrote the first scholarly study in English of ancient Greek homosexuality,[5] also contributed much
information to one of the very first medical books on the subject, *Sexual
Inversion* by Havelock Ellis.[6] Ellis pioneered the terms "invert" (for the person) and "inversion" (for the condition), as if the poor fellow had merely
gotten it all backwards. But this was less emotionally loaded than the more
traditional word "Sodomite" and a step toward the scientific terminologies
used today. Academics in the humanities, however, tended to prefer a phrase
adapted from Pausanias's speech in the *Symposium:* Uranian Venus.[7]

As a somewhat hidden element within the Anglophone academic world, the
subculture of Uranian Venus has only recently begun to attract ethnogra-
phers.[8] But there are numerous studies of the many learned and creative individuals who inhabited it. Not a few of these highly literate "Uranians"[9] left
behind written records that, knowingly read, enable us to recover a sense of
what it was like to live in that alien culture. One of the most straightforward
examples is E. M. Forster's novel, *Maurice,* which he wrote in 1913–14 but
never published; it first appeared after his death in 1970. At one point in the
story

> the reader learns that the finest classical scholar among the students in the
> Dean's translation class has been drawn to the study of the classics because he
> considers that the ancient Greeks gave temperate and exquisite expression to
> homoerotic feelings identical to his own. Study of the Greeks, especially Plato,
> has enabled this young man gradually to accept himself and his desires as he
> had never been able to do in the course of his religious upbringing; the Greeks
> provided an ideological weapon against the condemnatory reflexes of his own
> Christian conscience, offering him, in its place, "a new guide for life." . . . as
> Forster wrote, somewhat guardedly, in a 1934 biography of his mentor at
> Cambridge, Goldsworthy Lowes Dickinson, "The Greeks — and Plato partic-
> ularly — understand our political and social confusion, but they are not part
> of it, and so they can help us."[10]

Thus ancient Greek literature provided a kind of imaginary refuge for
thoughts and feelings that had no socially acceptable outlet for expression — if,

of course, one assumed that the Greek writers were expressing "feelings identical to his own." Given the social mores of the time, however, where no type of homosexuality was ever condoned, there was no socially meaningful distinction to be made between the same-sex acts of consenting adults and those between males of unequal age. The status and social concerns of ancient Athens had no relevance to the "political and social confusion" of the day.

"A Strange Idolatry"

Symonds had been very careful to emphasize the importance of sexual restraint for Plato, comparing it to the love of Dante for Beatrice, and the poetry of medieval chivalry in which the knight's adoration of his idealized lady was rarely consummated.[11] He tried to depict Greek homosexuality as profoundly moral — even though uninformed by the Bible — by connecting it to the idealized naked bodies of ancient Greek art: "The Greeks were essentially a nation of artists. . . . Guided by no supernatural revelation, with no Mosaic law for conduct, they trusted their αἴσθησις [*aisthēsis*, i.e., their aesthetic sense], delicately trained and preserved in a condition of utmost purity. . . . If their morality was aesthetic and not theocratic, it was nonetheless on that account humane and real."[12] Symonds's reticence may have reassured non-homosexual readers, but within a subculture filled with talented and creative people, there was much less interest in Plato's advocacy of self-restraint than in his depiction of homosexual love as a ladder leading to the experience of ultimate Beauty. The feeling began to grow that homosexuality virtually endowed a man with a superior artistic sensibility, and the creative person's perennial demand for artistic freedom came to represent the homosexual's desire for affectional freedom, like those ancient Greeks whose morality was aesthetic, not theocratic, unhampered by divine revelation or Mosaic law.

Symonds contributed to this perception in other research. For example his biography of Michelangelo, the first to utilize the newly available archives of the Buonarotti family, recovered the originally homoerotic texts of the sculptor's poems, which had circulated for centuries in bowdlerized form. There we can observe one of history's greatest artists struggling with unlawful desires and imagining an ascent to a purified love in heaven:

> Sense is not love, but lawlessness accurst:
> This kills the soul; while our love lifts on high
> Our friends on earth — higher in heaven through death.[13]

We can observe the continuation of this trend in the work of Oxford's pioneering art critic Walter Pater, who has been described as "a philosopher who had gone to Italy by mistake instead of to Germany."[14] His view of Plato, as summed up in the careful wording of a younger contemporary, offered a model of the aesthete whose refined artistic sensitivity, and capacity for intense relationships with male friends, obviates the need for explicit moral strictures:

> [Pater] can hardly be said to have had any philosophical system, just as he himself believed Plato to have had none. Plato's writings represented to Pater an atmosphere, not a defined creed. . . . He shows that Plato was in no sense a doctrinaire, but held that ideas and notions are not the consequence of reason but the cause of it. . . . He shows that Plato was by constitution an emphatically sensuous nature, deeply sensible to impressions of beauty, and to emotional relations with others; but that he regarded the appeal to the senses as a species of moral education; that the philosophical learner passed from the particular to the general, from the love of precise and personal beauty to the love of the central and inner beauty.
>
>   And thus Plato is not so much a teacher as a noble and inspiring comrade; those who love Plato do not sit at his feet and absorb his wisdom, but take service with him in his adventurous band, journeying from the familiar scene and the beloved home to the remote and distant mountains that close the horizon, but from which there may be a prospect of hidden lands.[15]

Thus the humanism of the Renaissance, with its revival of Greek learning and a return to the naked bodies of classical art, represented a welcome opportunity for Pater to express himself more directly, as he did in his book *The Renaissance:*

> One of the strongest characteristics of that outbreak of the reason and the imagination, of that assertion of the liberty of the heart . . . which I have termed a medieval Renaissance, was its antinomianism, its spirit of rebellion and revolt against the moral and religious ideas of its time. In their search after the pleasures of the senses and the imagination, in their care for beauty, in their worship of the body, people were impelled beyond the bounds of the Christian ideal; and their love became sometimes a strange idolatry, a strange rival religion. It was the return of that ancient Venus, not dead, but only hidden for a time in the caves of the Venusberg, of those old pagan gods still going to and fro on the earth, under all sorts of disguises.[16]

Even Botticelli's madonnas, apparently, yearned to join the revolt:

> [S]he too, though she holds in her hands the "Desire of all nations," is one of those who are neither for Jehovah nor for His enemies; and her choice is on her face. . . . Her trouble is in the very caress of the mysterious child, whose gaze is always far from her, and who has already that sweet look of devotion which men have never been able altogether to love. . . . Once, indeed, he guides her hand to transcribe in a book the words of her exaltation, the *Ave,* and the *Magnificat,* and the *Gaude Maria,* and the young angels, glad to rouse

her for the moment from her dejection, are eager to hold the inkhorn and to support the book. But the pen almost drops from her hand, and the high cold words have no meaning for her. . . . He paints Madonnas, but they shrink from the pressure of the divine child, and plead in unmistakable undertones for a warmer, lower humanity.[17]

Certainly there were people who objected to these characterizations. Yet the passage that caused the most uproar, as likely to lead young men astray, seems innocuous today: an aesthete's call to treasure the moment, which climaxed with the line "To burn always with this hard, gem-like flame, to maintain this ecstasy, is success in life."[18] Contemporary readers evidently perceived that aesthetic experience was standing in for homosexuality, and this section was removed from the second edition of Pater's book, though it was restored in the third.[19]

Pater's angry mistreatment of women, meanwhile, makes the Jesus of the Secret Gospel look almost chivalrous. Once, while Pater was attending "a brilliant affair" at "a Ladies' College," "almost every Oxfordian of note being present," "the lady head of the house" playfully dropped a white kid glove in his path. But Pater, "instead of gallantly picking it up, walked on and trod on it." To the whispered shock of a nearby male friend, Pater pointed out that Queen Elizabeth had ultimately had Sir Walter Raleigh beheaded: "Believe me, my dear sir, it was an insinuation of the devil that caused this woman to drop her glove."[20] It is no surprise that such attitudes appear in Pater's art criticism as well. Pater was sure that Michelangelo, for example, shared his aversion for women: "What passionate weeping in that mysterious figure which, in the [Sistine Chapel] *Creation of Adam,* crouches below the image of the Almighty, as he comes with the forms of things to be, woman and her progeny, in the fold of his garment! What a sense of wrong in those two captive youths [Cain and Abel], who feel the chains like scalding water on their proud and delicate flesh!"[21]

Michelangelo's poems, according to Pater, reveal a Platonist struggling to conform to heterosexual Christian ideals, but ultimately accepting his inability to do so:

> Beneath the Platonic calm of the sonnets there is latent a deep delight in carnal form and colour. There, and still more in the madrigals, he often falls into the language of less tranquil affections; while some of them have the colour of penitence, as from a wanderer returning home. He who spoke so decisively of the supremacy in the imaginative world of the unveiled human form had not been always, we may think, a mere Platonic lover. Vague and wayward his loves may have been; but they partook of the strength of his nature. . . .
>
> But his genius is in harmony with itself. . . . The interest of Michelangelo's

poems is that they make us spectators of this struggle; . . . the struggle of a deso-
lating passion, which yearns to be resigned and sweet and pensive, as Dante's
was. . . . Dante's belief in the resurrection of the body, through which, even in
heaven, Beatrice loses for him no tinge of flesh-colour, or fold of raiment even;
and the Platonic dream of the passage of the soul through one form of life after
another, with its passionate haste to escape from the burden of bodily form
altogether; are, for all effects of art or poetry, principles diametrically opposite.
Now it is the Platonic tradition rather than Dante's that has moulded Michelangelo's verse. In many ways no sentiment could have been less like Dante's
love for Beatrice than Michelangelo's for Vittoria Colonna.[22]

Pater's description of the *Mona Lisa,* meanwhile, is positively bloodcurd-
ling:

> Leonardo's masterpiece . . . is expressive of what in the ways of a thousand
> years men had come to desire. . . . It is a beauty wrought out from within upon
> the flesh, the deposit, little cell by cell, of strange thoughts and fantastic
> reveries and exquisite passions. Set it for a moment beside one of those white
> Greek goddesses or beautiful women of antiquity, and how would they be
> troubled by this beauty, into which the soul with all its maladies has passed!
> All the thoughts and experience of the world have etched and moulded there,
> . . . the animalism of Greece, the lust of Rome, the mysticism of the middle age
> with its spiritual ambition and imaginative loves, the return of the Pagan
> world, the sins of the Borgias. She is older than the rocks among which she
> sits; like the vampire, she has been dead many times, and learned the secrets of
> the grave.[23]

In Pater's writings, then, we have most of the elements we are looking for,
though some of it is obliquely expressed: a homosexuality that angrily ex-
cludes even polite conversations with women, an artistic sensibility that looks
back to presumed ancient Greek sexuality, a rejection of Christian orthodoxy,
in Pater's case by a rebellious cult of aestheticism.

By the twentieth century, however, "those old pagan gods" were out in full
force; there was no longer any need to beat around the bush. Thus the most
succinct description ever written of ancient Greek homosexuals as artistic
revolutionaries was penned by . . . Morton Smith:

> It was individualism and pride in their bodies that led the Dorians first to
> exercise naked. It was love of beauty that persuaded the rest of the Greeks to
> follow their example, gave the gymnasium its name (from *gymnos,* "naked"),
> made it the afternoon club of the well-to-do, the center of leisurely discussion,
> and consequently an instrument for intellectual as well as physical education
> of the boys and young men who were brought into conversation with their
> elders. Among these elders were the artists; the gymnasium contributed
> greatly to the Greek's development of a new art, above all a new plastic art

formed by a new hope — to communicate the four-dimensional reality of the body, to present it not as a flat picture, but as a solid and moving object. This hope, although occasionally obscured, remained the most pervasive element in western plastic art until World War II. Even now, it lives on; the human body has some strange appeal for human beings.

The Greeks who frequented the gymnasia were not insensitive to this appeal; the conversations begun there rapidly developed into homosexual love affairs of which Greek cities were remarkably tolerant. . . . The cities' tolerance made possible a new freedom in expression of the diverse forms of human sexual life, and many Greeks came to believe that both men and women have two sides to their characters, passive and dominant, and that both of these may properly prevail in turn — a boy if loved by a man may properly return his love, as would a girl; a woman may properly make love to, and be loved by a girl, as might a man. This notion reflected the hopes of millions of persons throughout antiquity, as it does today, but the Greek expressions of it were socially unique and became classical. In consequence of them, intimate friendship with a man became a recognized part of a Greek boy's education, and with the new acceptance of this extension of sexual activity the hopes of individuals changed accordingly, each interpreting the newly possible relationship according to his own temperament, some as an opportunity for sensual pleasure, others, for ambition or affection or instruction or influence, Plato, as an image of man's desire for disembodied beauty.[24]

What is particularly interesting about this description is its unawareness of Athenian anxieties about differential status roles. Surely nothing could be more foreign to ancient Hellenistic sexology than the notion that every individual, male and female, has a two-sided personality, both passive and dominant.[25] The natural habitat for that idea would be, rather, a modern "artsy" environment where unconventional sexual behavior counts as creative self-expression; as Smith elsewhere quipped, "the main interest of the *avant-garde* is the *derrière*."[26] How he ever divined that this rarefied, elitist ideal "reflected the hopes of millions" is beyond me. But in an imagined context where "intimate friendship with a man became a recognized part of a boy's education," it is possible to conceive of a young man like Smith's homosexual parishioner, who believes that the "adult-adolescent relationships . . . he formed during adolescence are among those he has found most helpful." Or even, perhaps, one like the youth in the Secret Gospel, asking for Jesus' love.

"A Rival Religion"

Pater was not exaggerating when he called his aesthetic antinomianism "a strange rival religion." As highly educated homosexuals discovered their own feelings in ancient philosophical texts, they naturally started to look with new eyes upon that other ancient Greek corpus, the one written by Christians. And as Pater reinterpreted Botticelli's madonnas, others began applying their own creativity to constructing alternative Christianities, often in humorous or ironic form. Forster, for instance, belonged to a Cambridge group called the Apostles, "an elite . . . debating society" with "its own distinctive and unashamed homoerotic ethos,"[27] which has achieved a regular place in the historiography of homosexuality.[28] It included a great many learned and creative people (not all of them homosexual) who would become prominent in English society.[29] In one of Forster's short stories, "The Life to Come," a Christian missionary named Paul struggles to suppress the memory of a homosexual relationship he has had with an African who has taken the Christian name of Barnabas (cf. Acts 13–14). However, Barnabas will not forget, for he cannot separate his notion of homosexual love from his notion of heaven. The published recension ends with Barnabas killing Paul and himself, but in an early draft there was a subsequent scene in which God tells the dead Paul, "if he had died first you would have taken him to your heaven, but he has taken you to his instead. I am very sorry, oh good and faithful servant, but I cannot do anything."[30]

Walter Pater's contribution along the same lines was his wordy and meandering novel *Marius the Epicurean*, set in the time of the emperor Marcus Aurelius (161–180 CE). Marius, a sensitive and inquisitive orphan, is educated by the poet Flavian, three years older than he, to whom he is deeply attached. As Flavian lies dying of plague, desperately trying to finish "a kind of nuptial hymn, which . . . celebrated the preliminary pairing, and mating together, of all fresh things, in the hot and genial spring-time," Marius climbs into Flavian's bed to keep him warm.[31] After the poet's death, Marius, now eighteen, wanders around the Roman Empire, listening to philosophers of all persuasions and observing the rituals of every religious cult. Arriving in Rome, Marius befriends a legionary named Cornelius, who somehow does not share his curiosity about temples and arcane rites. One day Cornelius reveals that he belongs to the secretive sect of Christians and takes Marius to Vespers in a house church on the Appian Way, adjoining a catacomb full of early Christian art and inscriptions. A few days later, looking for Cornelius, Marius stumbles into a Eucharist—or rather, the Pontifical High Mass of Christmas morning, celebrated in Latin by the bishop of Rome himself—which Marius finds an otherworldly aesthetic experience. Although he never assents to Christian faith, Marius dies during a persecution anyway, after bribing a guard to take Cornelius's place in prison so that his friend can marry a Christian woman. In the final dramatic moments of a short and inquisitive life, the dying Marius is surrounded by the brethren, crosses are drawn in oil on his hands and feet, the viaticum is lovingly placed in his mouth, and he is buried in a martyr's tomb, to be venerated ever after as a saint. Greater love hath no man, as it were . . . (John 15:13).

Today, the Mass that Marius witnessed seems laughably out of place in the second century[32] — an earnest concatenation of the fourth-century travelogue of Egeria with the eighth-century *Ordo Romanus I*,[33] Pliny's second-century letter on the Christians with the sixth-century Gallican rite,[34] the Vulgate psalms and antiphons,[35] and portions of the medieval Roman Mass.[36] Besides, there is almost no evidence for Latin being used by Christians in Rome before the fourth century; surviving texts are in Greek. The liturgy in *Marius the Epicurean* was actually based on the antics at St. Austin's Priory, Walworth, a suburban London hotbed of solemn high Ritualism where Pater was immensely impressed by the pastor's efforts to revive early Christian worship in all its presumed artistic glory.[37] Thus Pater combined his antinomian quest for beauty with an anachronistic conception of liturgical history. Like Marius the Epicurean, and like the homosexual parishioner in Smith's 1949 article, he felt profoundly attracted to the aesthetics of Christian liturgy, while remaining unenthusiastic about Christian beliefs. Like Morton Smith, he evidently felt that "liturgy was primarily a means for the experience of beauty." And like the Secret Evangelist, Pater envisioned the worship of the early church through the lens of more recent Anglican practices.

In fact the Uranian subculture of the English universities was densely populated with such massively learned, relentlessly witty men, who endlessly amused each other by satirizing Christian scriptures and traditions. Oscar Wilde, who won the gold medal in Greek at Oxford (a pawn ticket for it was found among his meager possessions after his death), enlivened many a pub table by tossing off scintillating impromptu apocrypha. A chreia recorded by André Gide, for example, seems to show Lazarus suffering from Gnostic tendencies: once, when Jesus found him crying and asked why, Lazarus replied, "Lord, I was dead and you raised me up. What else should I do but weep?" On another occasion Wilde told William Butler Yeats: "I have been inventing a new Christian heresy. It seemed that Christ recovered after the Crucifixion, and escaping from the tomb lived on for many years, the one man on earth who knew the falsehood of Christianity. Once St. Paul visited his town and he alone in the carpenters' quarter did not go to hear him preach. Henceforth the other carpenters noticed that, for some unknown reason, he kept his hands covered."[38] If someone had "discovered" this heresy written up in ancient Greek (a translation Wilde would have been capable of), it could have sparked decades of debate on whether first-century towns actually had a "carpenters' quarter" and whether any of the ancient heresy catalogues ever mentioned the

Gospel of the Carpenters (under another name, perhaps?) or the people whose scripture it was.

Wilfred Owen, the homosexual soldier-poet who was killed a week before the armistice that ended the First World War, attended less famous schools and did not know Greek well, but his letters are full of amusing passages written in King James English. One extended parable that he wrote from the war zone to his younger brother is a lot like the Secret Gospel, in that it is essentially a cento of biblical excerpts; here are parts of it:

> And it came to pass that a woman besought him saying "Give me, I pray thee, a little water to drink." Instead of water he gave her the milk. And the same woman was bent double for eighteen years. And went out sorrowful, and wept by the river of Babylon. And all fish that were in the river died.
>
> And he knowing that the time of harvest was near at hand, and of the creeping things that creep upon the earth, went down into that water and washed seven times.
>
> And he was covered with boils from head to foot.
>
> And they put him on his own ass and took him to an inn.
>
> And in the process of time, he saithe unto him that kept the inn "I will drink a little wine for my stomach's sake. Fill me seven barrels full."
>
> And they filled them unto the brim.
>
> And there was silence for the space of half an hour. . . .
>
> But he, stooping down, began to tie the latchet of his shoe. Now because of the new wine and the old leather, it came to pass that the same was rent in twain. And he stood up and cursed them.
>
> And hell followed after.
>
> Then cometh he that kept the inn, grievously tormented seeking goodly pearls.
>
> But he turned and saithe unto him: Go to! and when I come again I will pay thee.
>
> And he answered and saithe: "Peradventure thou wilt not return. I will follow thee withersoever thou goest."
>
> And he led him up to a pinnacle of the temple; and let him down vehemently through the roof: so that even the stones cried out.[39]

This particular patchwork seems not to have had a serious point, but Owen wrote to his mother with pride that he had composed it all from his own memory "without any reference to the Book, of course; and without any more detraction from reverence, than, say, is the case when a bishop uses modern slang to relate a biblical story. I simply employed seventeenth century English, and was carried away with it." He also confessed to her that he was feeling increasingly estranged from the Church of England over its support of the war:

Incidentally, I think the big number of texts which jogged up in my mind in half-an-hour bears witness to a goodly store of them in my being. It is indeed so; and I am more and more a Christian as I walk the unchristian ways of Christendom. Already I have comprehended a light which never will filter into the dogma of any national church: namely that one of Christ's essential commands was: Passivity at any price! Suffer dishonor and disgrace; but never resort to arms. Be bullied, be outraged, be killed; but do not kill. It may be a chimerical and an ignominious principle, but there it is. It can only be ignored: and I think pulpit professionals are ignoring it very skilfully and successfully indeed.[40]

Thus Owen's humorous biblical centos tended to confirm his feeling of being a better Christian than the hypocritical institutional church. It is not hard to imagine him identifying with one of the heretical groups of ancient times, had he known of one with pacifist leanings. Nor was he the only English homosexual of those times who saw himself as "more a Christian" than Christendom.

"Unchristian Ways"

Probably many such efforts at "Christianity retold" circulated as oral folklore, or in ephemeral media like personal letters, and were soon forgotten. Doubtless many of them were far less worthy of preservation than Oscar Wilde's. One misbegotten attempt to rewrite dogma in doggerel, now of purely historical interest, was written by the understandably forgotten nineteenth-century priest, E. E. Bradford:

> Our yearning tenderness for boys like these
> Has more in it of Christ than Socrates . . .[41]

One wonders what the Morton Smith of 1949 would have said to that.

More relevant to our quest is an exegesis that seems to have been widely disseminated, according to which the young man of Mark 14:51, the one whose garment was torn off him as he ran away, was actually a *kinaidos* or male prostitute — why else would he have been so scantily clad? As early as 1817, Jeremy Bentham proposed that this young man was a "rival" who sought to displace the Beloved Disciple as Jesus' partner.[42] Since Bentham was attempting to promote greater tolerance for homosexuals, arguing that Jesus did not share Paul's opposition to homosexuality, there is no telling how far the symbolism could go. The notion that the Beloved Disciple had a sexual relationship with Jesus was centuries old even then. It can be traced all the way back to the sixteenth century, when Christopher Marlowe was accused of advocating it, along with other sentiments that would later be considered "high church": an unseemly preference for popish liturgical ceremonies, an opinion that Christ should have "instituted the sacrament with more ceremoniall reverence," and the concomitant opinion "that all protestantes are Hypocriticall asses."[43] Since Marlowe was a playwright, we should not be surprised if he was particularly attuned to the practical dimension of action and ceremonial, as much as or more than the verbal dimension.

Thus I would wager that the Secret Gospel has at least this much in common with its ancient counterparts: it is based on oral traditions that circulated in the evangelist's community, to which we no longer have direct access apart from written texts. But since conventional Christian culture did not recognize distinctions between different roles or kinds of homosexuality, there was no reason to be scrupulous about "the many respects in which Greek sexual practices *differ* from 'our own.'"[44] The young man who ran away simply became a cipher for homosexuality in general, without a trace of cultural proscriptions against youths seeking out older men. The Secret Evangelist, expert Hellenist though he was, simply took the story as he found it, already tailored to the cultural situation he was actually in—thereby leaving us a substantial but unintentional clue that he himself was no ancient Greek.

We can easily imagine, then, some inhabitant of that lost world, torn between his feelings and a strong Christian upbringing, privately longing for a different kind of Christianity where Jesus practiced "Greek love," where sex with other males was not a sin but a sacrament—even the basis for a Platonic mystical ascent to the highest heavenly beauty, finally freed of moral constraints. And we can imagine, if less easily, that someone who spent too much time thinking such thoughts, investing them with a lot of pent-up emotion that had no other outlet, might conceive a desire to persuade people that such a Christianity had once actually existed, that traces of it could still be found in those tedious patristic catalogues of ancient heresies. The "discovery" of an unknown gospel would be just the thing to accomplish this, and it could be skillfully manufactured by someone who knew the Greek Christian literature as well as Wilfred Owen knew the King James Version. Nothing stood in the way, once the would-be evangelist persuaded himself that something of the sort must actually have existed at one time, that he wasn't really creating anything new but only undoing the age-old repression of the ecclesiastical authorities who had "lost" the original. Like the pseudonymous authors of so much of the New Testament, he might tell himself, he would only be bringing new clarity to the true teaching that had always been there . . .

This, then, is the world of the Secret Gospel: a hidden world of homosexuals who, finding solace in the belief that "the Greeks understand our confusion and can help us," felt that their homosexuality made them uniquely qualified to appreciate the highest beauty. A community that revered a pantheon of famous men whose homosexuality enabled them to reach high levels of artistic achievement. An incipient renaissance of artistic freedom from moral strictures that would universally impose a philistine heterosexuality. A yearning for a heaven of homosexual love that could be reached more easily by ancient Greeks or African natives who had had the good fortune to be raised outside of Judeo-Christian traditions. An alternative church of scriptures reassembled, heretics reaffirmed, and Christianity remade, practicing a morality deemed higher than that of more conventional Christians. Fantasy liturgies that identified aesthetic with spiritual experience, projecting modern liturgical practices back into early Christian times.[45]

With the Mar Saba fragment, however, we can go beyond circumstantial evidence and imaginative reconstruction. We can demonstrate dependence on a specific literary work: one of the most famous retellings of a biblical story in the English language, and one of the most popular texts that circulated within that academic Uranian ("heavenly") culture.

Summary

In this chapter I explore a culture into which the Mar Saba text fits much better than in second-century Alexandria: the "Uranian" homosexual subculture of nineteenth-century English universities. These men practiced a kind of homosexuality that they identified with the ancient Greek kind, even though it was more misogynistic and less concerned with the status issues of boyhood and manhood. The ancient Greeks were seen as artistic rebels who practiced a higher kind of morality than the kind taught by the church. Groups that were defined as heretical by the institutional church were seen relatively positively. Some people in this subculture were particularly drawn to "high-church" Anglican liturgy that purportedly revived practices from the early church. Many of them were given to constructing satirical gospels or heresies that somewhat resemble the Secret Gospel and the Mar Saba Carpocratians.

The Wisdom of Salome

Salome, in early Christian literature, was a very shady lady. This one should not be confused with the Herodian princess celebrated by Oscar Wilde. The name was common.   — *Morton Smith*

Morton Smith warned us that "there must have been other early traditions about Salome," and indeed there were, in a way. The Secret Evangelist has intentionally conflated the Salome of canonical Mark with another New Testament character, whom later tradition has identified as an archetypal temptress and named Salome. If we recognize this character in the Salome of the Secret Gospel, we can locate a stream of twentieth-century thought in which the text fits perfectly. All its perplexing details that have given us so much trouble cohere into an intelligible message, all its characters have meaningful roles to play, every mystery is ultimately revealed.

Salome Who?

According to the first-century Jewish historian Josephus,[1] Salome was the name of a daughter of Herodias; since the Middle Ages she has been identified with the unnamed daughter whose dance so beguiled Herod that he consented to give her the head of John the Baptist on a platter (Mark 6:22–

29). John was brought to this fate, according to Mark, for criticizing Herod's marriage to Herodias, which by biblical reckoning was both adulterous and incestuous.[2] In the nineteenth century, many people found Herodias's daughter a more interesting character than the little-known Salomes who were Jesus' sister, midwife, and disciple. Thus the tale of Salome and Herodias, dripping with the perennially fascinating mixture of illicit sex and violent death, was a popular theme in the art and literature of the time. In literary retellings, such as Heinrich Heine's *Atta Troll*, Gustave Flaubert's *Hérodias* (set as an opera by Jules Massenet), and Stephane Mallarmé's unfinished *Hérodiade,* a motif developed of sexual attraction between John the Baptist and Salome or Herodias, and mother and daughter began to exchange traits or even merge into a single character.[3] As a result "the Salome/Herodias figure was almost as popular among nineteenth-century artists as the Virgin Mary was among medieval artists."[4] She was represented in literary, visual, and musical creations by "a wide array of nineteenth- and twentieth-century artists ranging from Heinrich Heine to Evan John, from Henri Regnault to Pablo Picasso, and from Jules Massenet to Paul Hindemith"[5] — the most influential being a series of paintings by Gustave Moreau (1826–98).[6]

The themes of seduction, adultery, and murder came together most effectively in Oscar Wilde's eponymous play *Salomé.* The title character, a virginal teenager, lusts for Jokanaan (John the Baptist), also a virgin and the only man who doesn't feel compelled to gaze at her great beauty. She woos him in language recalling the Song of Songs[7] but is rebuffed three times. After making sure that Herod has committed himself to granting whatever she requests, Salomé dances her captivating "dance of the seven veils," then vengefully demands John's head on a silver charger. Herodias supports this of course, but it is Salomé's idea. Herod regrets his vow and tries to appease her instead with a sequence of increasingly valuable gifts: half the kingdom, the world's largest emerald, his entire flock of prize peacocks, magic jewels that no woman has seen, the High Priest's mantle, and finally the veil of the Holy of Holies. But she will have none of it. In a ghastly scene of "extraordinary, sick tenderness,"[8] Salomé kisses the severed head and professes her love for it — until Herod, remorseful and disgusted, orders that she be killed too.

Many of these elements were not original to Wilde: in fact his indebtedness to his predecessors was so obvious that he was accused, at times, of unoriginality, prompting his response: "Of course I plagiarize. It is the privilege of the appreciative man."[9] Yet it was Wilde's that became the most influential telling of the Salome story, inspiring drawings by Aubrey Beardsley, Richard Strauss's opera *Salome,*[10] plays by W. B. Yeats,[11] and a number of films.[12]

The dance of the seven veils, however, was one element that Wilde himself invented. In his play it is simply a stage direction, with no description of what the actress should actually do: "Salomé dances the dance of the seven veils." In the century since, not surprisingly, many people have gazed into this void and seen an intriguing panoply of meaningful color, gesture, and movement. Some, following Moreau, have perceived the Mysterious East, an icon of the exotic that mirrors back to us our intersecting Orientalist and anti-Semitic prejudices.[13] Among these was the composer Richard Strauss, whose opera *Salome* is based directly on Wilde's text. The music for the dance was the last part of the opera to be composed, and he was still thinking about the choreography twenty years later. The effect he strove for was that of "a pure oriental dance, . . . as if on a prayer mat," by "a chaste virgin and an oriental princess," so that her death at the end of the opera will "excite . . . sympathy" instead of "disgust and terror."[14] As each veil comes off, therefore, musical elements that Europeans would mark as "oriental" or "exotic" become more prominent.

Others see in Salome the popular nineteenth-century figure of the femme fatale — an alluring yet frightening vision of the struggle between men and women to control the sexual sphere. Thus Salome is a "personification of Eros and Thanatos, lust and lethal cruelty."[15] Seasoned cultural critics, of course, are quick to unveil deeper meanings. "Salome is everyone's favourite *fin-de-siècle* dragon lady," writes Lawrence Kramer, who would prefer to "treat Salome not as a monstrous sexual icon but as a focal point for the representation of a bundle of instabilities produced by the *fin-de-siècle* gender system."[16] Unraveling the bundle, Carolyn Abbate even finds "masculinity in the subjunctive."[17]

Wilde himself avidly studied the many visual and literary depictions of Salome that circulated in his time and was clearly fascinated by the character. While writing the play he tried and discarded so many ideas that (it might be said) his conception of Salome was as changeable and indeterminate as a multiply veiled dancer[18] — an anarchy of conflicting moral oppositions, which somehow combined "the goddess of immortal Hysteria" with "the desire of vice for virtue, pagan for Christian," and even "the extremity of renunciation."[19]

The Mystery of the Seven Veils

For the Mar Saba writer, as for Wilde, Salome is an ethical mayhem, who confounds the principles of everyone around her. Thus Clement, the spokesman for orthodox Christian ethics, thunders self-righteously about "silencing the unspeakable teachings of the Carpocratians . . . who wander from the narrow road of the commandments into a boundless abyss of the carnal and bodily sins," brandishing a gospel that says "naked [man] with naked [man]," and other things left unquoted. Against them Clement upholds his own "more spiritual gospel," written by Mark himself, to "lead the hearers into the innermost sanctuary of that truth hidden by seven [veils]."[20] The authentic works of Clement do not refer to seven veils in this way,[21] but in the Mar Saba letter the veils hide a truth that is diametrically opposed to what the carnal Carpocratians are about: what healthy heterosexual wouldn't want to see what is behind those seven veils? Gazing on that hidden mystery, Clement falls all over himself in an ecstasy of moral hypocrisy: "Even if they should say something true, one who loves the truth should not, even so, agree with them. For not all true [things] are the truth, nor should that truth which [merely] seems true according to human opinions be preferred to the true truth. . . . To them, as I said above, one must never give way; nor, when they put forward their falsifications, should one concede that the secret Gospel is by Mark, but should even deny it on oath." It gets weirder, as Clement cites an even higher moral authority — or is it? "For this [reason] the Wisdom of God, through Solomon, advises, 'answer the fool from his folly,' teaching that the light of the truth should be hidden from those who are mentally blind."

The figure of Sophia or Wisdom turns out to be Salome once again, if we accept Smith's claim that "in the Manichaean Psalm Book . . . , Salome appears as the equivalent of the O[ld] T[estament] 'Wisdom' who builds her house, the Church [cf. Proverbs 9:1]."[22] Like the image of Salome tempting Jesus, however, this identification is something of an overinterpretation: the Manichaean psalm in question does show Salome building a tower, the parts of which have allegorical significations. But the psalm does not use the word Sophia or wisdom, nor the word church, nor does it make any direct allusion to Proverbs 9:1 ("Wisdom has built her house . . ."). Moreover, Smith's commentary shows that the authentic works of Clement use the expression "the divine Wisdom" but not "the Wisdom of God." As with the seven veils of the innermost sanctuary, the phrase is actually a para-Clementism; its true source is Luke 11:49, where Jesus seems to be quoting from an unknown book.[23]

Going deeper, the Wisdom that Clement invokes is the wisdom that came "through Solomon." But the name Solomon, of course, is the masculine equivalent of Salome. The pun is even more delightful in Hebrew, naturally, since Shlomo and Shulamit[24] are the paradigmatically heterosexual couple in the Song of Songs — the same Song of Songs that Wilde's Salomé redirected toward John the Baptist. And while we're erecting allegorical towers, for those willing to be seduced into a state of moral confusion, here is Wisdom: "I am a wall, and my breasts are like towers; so in his eyes I am as one who brings Shalom[e]" (Song 8:10).

Having achieved this mystical climax, Clement descends quickly, in a flurry of biblical quotes ending, "All things are pure to the pure" (Titus 1:15) — a line his Carpocratian opponents might well have applied to themselves to justify their licentious ways. The satire is razor sharp, as Clement comes off looking like Salome's "straight man" in a perverse comedy duo. In the process, we are also given an explanation of why we had never heard of the Secret Gospel before: the guardians of revealed truth deliberately lied about its existence. And they had good reason to do so, from their perspective, because it was embarrassingly close to the gospel the Carpocratians had.

Thus the Mar Saba document presents us with a remarkable cast of characters: a Jesus who rejects the company and attentions of women, but who spends the night teaching "the mystery of the Kingdom of God" to a rich young man who loves him. A church father, Clement, who speaks in Gnostic fashion of truths so secret he cannot admit they exist, of a gospel "read only to those who are being initiated into the great mysteries," which evidently are not so great as the mystery into which Jesus initiates. A mystagogical evangelist, Mark, who wrote "a more spiritual Gospel for the use of those who were being perfected," intended to "lead the hearers into the innermost sanctuary of that truth hidden by the seven veils." And what is inside this innermost sanctuary, hidden by the seven veils? A selfish, vengeful teenager who could have possessed the veil of the Holy of Holies, but chose necrophilia. A bloodthirsty temptress, even more terrifying than Walter Pater's vampire Mona Lisa. A homicidal virgin, child of an incestuous adulteress, wantonly cooing to the Baptist's head, "I know that thou wouldst have loved me, and the mystery of love is greater than the mystery of death" (cf. Song of Songs 8:6). Only Jesus is pure, for he has not defiled himself with women (cf. Revelation 14:4). Refusing to have anything to do with Salome and all her sex, he loves a man in the dark of night—something that only the initiated will understand. To find our way into the innermost sanctuary, past the seven veils, is to find conventional heterosexual morality turned inside out: a sanctimonious Christian condemns the carnality of the Carpocratians, invoking an ideal of male-female attraction that, once unveiled, turns out to be nothing but violence and revolting depravity.

And that's not all. To those who know the secret of the seven veils, there is yet a further level of meaning, for Wilde's play is itself a drama within a drama. He wrote it in French in Paris in 1891, while associating with poets of the French Symbolist movement. It was translated into English by Lord Alfred Bruce Douglas, who was simultaneously the dedicatee, Wilde's sexual partner, and the son of a powerful English aristocrat. The translation's 1893 publication caused a predictable stir in Victorian England, but it could not be performed there because of an Elizabethan-era law forbidding theatrical representations of biblical characters, which had been a popular practice before the Reformation.[25] In fact Wilde was never to see his work staged: he missed the 1896 premiere in Paris because he was doing hard labor in Reading Gaol, convicted of "gross indecency" for hiring "rent boys" for sex, a proclivity that came to light only after he filed a libel suit against Douglas's disapproving father, who had called Wilde a "posing Somdomite [*sic*]."[26] To penetrate the sanctuary hidden by seven veils, then, is to gain a kind of mystical binocular vision: behind the Mar Saba text lies yet another narrative, with another martyr, another example of heterosexual morality revealed as profoundly immoral — even another writer accused of having his way with other people's texts.

Another Martyr?

"Gay people honor him as a martyr" states the *Encyclopedia of Homosexuality* matter-of-factly of Oscar Wilde.[27] With the passing of time, though, Wilde's story became a nexus for a variety of resentments, as if he had been sentenced "for daring to pursue an intimate relationship with the son of a peer of the realm, when he was a mere Irishman and a commoner."[28] Gradually Wilde's reputation expanded (as the odor of sanctity will do) to fill the available space, and he became a "martyr to the cause of freedom of choice"[29] — even "a hero of modernism," ironically invested with the trappings of Christian sainthood.[30] If this seems extreme, three facts may help make it understandable.

First, Wilde's celebrity was perceived as cultlike even in his own lifetime, when he was one of the models for the poet Bunthorne in Gilbert and Sullivan's 1881 operetta *Patience, or Bunthorne's Bride*. Bunthorne is constantly surrounded by adoring aesthetes who happen to be female, officially known as the Rapturous Maidens. But he confesses early on to "a sentimental passion of a vegetable fashion . . . An attachment *à la* Plato for a blushing young potato."[31] It is also interesting to note that Gilbert had trouble making up his mind whether he was satirizing the aesthetic movement in contemporary literature or high-church Anglicanism.[32]

Second, the representation of Wilde as a salvific figure is arguably rooted in his own prison writings. Denied most reading materials other than the Bible, he produced extended meditations on the meaning of Jesus' life and suffering that perhaps foreshadowed his deathbed conversion to Roman Catholicism.[33] Less than a decade afterward, England's best-known Christian apologist, G. K. Chesterton, astonishingly could write:

> His was a complete life, in that awful sense in which your life and mine are not complete; since we have not yet paid for our sins. In that sense one might call it a perfect life, as one speaks of a perfect equation; it cancels out. On the one

hand we have the healthy horror of the evil; on the other the healthy horror of the punishment. We have it all the more because both sin and punishment were highly civilized; that is, nameless and secret. Some have said that Wilde was sacrificed; let it be enough for us to insist on the literal meaning of the word. Any ox that is really sacrificed is made sacred.[34]

Third, as so often happens, the emerging cult got at least as much help from its enemies as it did from its friends. Editorialists of the day who approved of Wilde's conviction exhibited a peculiar tendency to lapse into metaphors of occult ritual:

He was one of the high priests of a school which attacks all the wholesome, manly, simple ideals of English life, and sets up false gods of decadent culture and intellectual debauchery. The man himself was a perfect type of his class, a gross sensualist veneered with the affection of artistic feeling too delicate for the appreciation of common clay. To him and such as him we owe the spread of moral degeneration amongst young men with abilities sufficient to make them a credit to their country. At the feet of Wilde they have learned to gain notoriety by blatant conceit, by despising the emotions of healthy humanity and the achievements of wholesome talent.

Such people find their fitting environment in the artificial light and the incense-laden air of secret chambers curtained from the light of day. . . . Wilde's fate will teach them that brilliant talent does not justify disdain of all moral restraints.[35]

But that was nothing compared with what would be said after Wilde's death.

PURITY IN PUBLIC LIFE

When *Salomé* finally had its first commercial performance in England,[36] twenty-five years after it was written, it immediately became embroiled in the wartime paranoia of 1918. Noel Pemberton Billing, a member of Parliament, cousin by marriage to Albert Schweitzer and self-proclaimed mouthpiece of the "Purity in Public Life" movement, seized on the play as proof of allegations he had been printing in his nationalist newspaper, which had recently changed its name from *Imperialist* to *Vigilante*. If Scotland Yard would only bother to investigate those who had bought tickets, he asserted, it would discover he had been correct all along in claiming that forty-seven thousand morally compromised Britons, constituting a veritable "Cult of the Clitoris," were being induced to betray the Empire by blackmail threats from German agents. The fact that the assistant editor who provided much of this "information," an American named Harold Spencer, had been discharged from the British army (in wartime!) for psychiatric problems seems to have provoked no skepticism among *Vigilante* readers.[37] Maud Allan, the Canadian-born, American-raised bisexual who played Salomé, filed her own libel suit, which was heard in the same court building as Wilde's had been. Other British political figures secretly assisted her case, in hope of sending to prison an obstreperous and tiresome critic of England's insufficiently bellicose government and its German-surnamed king.

But Billing managed to obfuscate the whole question of who or what exactly was on trial. Taking refuge in the position that an obscure medical term most people would not understand could not possibly meet the legal definition of obscenity (though the charge was actually libel), he spent much of the trial conjuring up a presumption of guilty cult membership for anyone who admitted knowing the meaning of that unsayable word (though the defendant was actually himself). The other side, needless to say, had its own creative approach to litigation. When the office of Prime Minister Lloyd George secretly hired a woman to lure the defendant into "a male brothel" where a photographer lay in wait, Billing (a handsome devil) simply recruited her into his stable of mistresses, and the band played on. Soon she too was in court, testifying that the judge hearing the case was one of the forty-seven thousand reprobates named in that infamous German list.[38] When anonymous death threats failed to change her story, His Majesty's Government petulantly filed bigamy charges based on long-forgotten flings. She tried appeasement, swearing out a statement that Harold Spencer, like the Mar Saba Clement, had lied under oath; but this strategy did not save her from prison.[39] Spencer himself seems never to have been prosecuted for perjury, though he was later imprisoned for anti-Semitic libels against an artist who wasn't Jewish. After being released he was convicted again and fined, this time for unspecified "disgusting behaviour."[40]

In spite of everything, it was Billing who won over the jury, with an impassioned speech that sounds more like the Mar Saba "Clement" than anything else we've seen:

> Are you going to send me to gaol for this? . . . this social leper, Oscar Wilde, had founded a cult of sodomy in this country, and travelled from end to end of it perverting youth wherever he could. He was not satisfied even that his evil influence should die with him; he left behind his works, so that his crimes may be perpetuated even after he was dead. And I tried to stop that . . . Have I convinced you that this is a beastly play? . . . the evidence showed it was a common thing for perverts (reliable medical evidence was called to support it) to commit these crimes in actuality, and for others to do them in pantomime.[41]

There is not only a Clement-like rhetoric of abuse — there is even a claim about a spiritual leader bequeathing writings to his followers to ensure that his teachings were passed on. As for Billing's beloved Empire — it was rather like the church of Alexandria, unjustly deflowered of its profound spiritual knowledge by a horrifying ritual use of the carnal variety: "In lesbian ecstasy the most sacred secrets of the state were betrayed."[42]

It cannot be shown that the author of the Mar Saba document had Noel Pemberton Billing specifically in mind. Although the British news media of the time dubbed the proceedings "the trial of the century," a very long book could be written about all the tribunals that earned that sobriquet between 1900 and 2000 CE. The fact is that Billing's sentiments were widely shared — Allan lost her suit, after all, as Wilde had lost his. No doubt the "Clement" figure in the Mar Saba letter represents a type rather than an individual — a type of "holier-than-thou" moralist that the Secret Evangelist and his audience found all too familiar, particularly wherever slogans like "Purity in Public Life" were unfurled.

Indeed the Billing trial, not surprisingly, exacerbated animosities and provoked new conflicts in every direction. Shortly afterward, with the Great War still raging, the British government banned a novel about a homosexual artist-pacifist. Its self-fulfilling Christological title, *Despised and Rejected* (Isaiah 53:3, King James Version), would have reminded any English churchgoer of a famous aria from Handel's *Messiah*.[43] Traditional British propriety reasserted itself, however, when a still-blustering Billing, his wife's Prussian parentage now exposed by the Secret Service, was physically carried from the House of Commons by a sword-wearing serjeant-at-arms and four officers smartly attired in gold chains and immaculate evening dress. Backbenchers cheered as he was dumped at the kerb, and disjointed narrative elements from the Trial of the Century were soon taking on a life of their own in the "playground folklore" of British schoolchildren[44] — whence there is no telling how far they may have traveled.

Tales from the Twentieth Century

It was in this sort of environment that the Mar Saba text was written: a period when an established Christian polemic against homosexuality was confronted by a culture of opposition that revered Oscar Wilde in almost-serious religious terms. The author (whoever he was) sought to depict this anti-homosexual Christianity as morally bankrupt, and the heterosexuality it advocates as inferior to the love that occurs between men who reject the love of women. He did this by slyly building on a (misinterpreted) ancient hint that Salome tempted Jesus, in order to transform her into Wilde's Salomé, rejected by Jesus — a conscientious objector in the battle of the sexes that destroyed his cousin John. This Salome's confrontation with a paederastic Jesus was packaged as a long-suppressed excerpt from the earliest gospel, together with a story of a young man seeking Jesus' love and finding "the Kingdom of God." The package, in turn, was a "lost" ancient letter by a stereotypically bigoted heterosexual churchman, a hypocrite who advocates lying in the name of the church, who is shown trying unsuccessfully to hide and distort the embarrassing "truth" that homosexuality was the religion of Jesus himself.

Thus the Mar Saba "discovery" tells a very twentieth-century tale, and that in more ways than one. Three decades after it was published, we can now see more easily that it does not fit well into the history of early Christian liturgy, nor does it present Hellenistic constructions of homosexuality accurately. Like strokes of paint that seemed to match perfectly when they were applied but have since aged to a different color from the surrounding original paint, the Mar Saba letter and the Secret Gospel are now easily recognized as the work of a later retoucher, bent on altering our view of the early Christian landscape. But his vision of an originally homosexual church is out of focus: in fact it exhibits the four characteristics that have been identified as typifying the "gay" sexuality that is common in the industrialized world today:[45] (1) The relationship between Jesus and the disciple is "egalitarian": the partners do not have distinct roles of pursuer and pursued, with the older one wooing the younger one until he finally submits; in fact the younger one is the first to express love. (2) All possibility of heterosexual sex is excluded, as shown in Jesus' refusal to receive the three women. (3) There is "a consciousness of group distinctiveness," an us/them divide between the "gays" (Jesus and the young man, but also the Carpocratians) and the "straights" (Salome, Clement, and Clement's correspondent Theodore). This naturally leads to the establishment of (4) "separate institutions and culture (de-assimilation)" such as we find expressed in the sharp dividing line between the Carpocratian church and the church of Alexandria, each with its own distinct scriptures and initiation practices, which, however, mirror each other closely. The third and fourth categories are as significant as the first two, for in some ways Clement is an even more modern character than Salome or the gay Jesus. With his elevated language of mystagogy, the innermost sanctuary, the truth hidden by seven veils, Clement sounds like some members of the clergy today, who speak in lofty terms of "the mystery of human sexuality" but know nothing of the excruciating entanglements some people can't find their way out of, nor the crushing loneliness of those for whom love remains a mystery unattained. Clement's excoriation of Carpocratian practices, too, echoes the preaching of not a few modern pastors, whose idealistic vocabulary and feigned compassion belie their angry intolerance, even hate. In the Clement character, such people are savagely ridiculed: his high heterosexual ethic turns out to be an orgy of incomprehensibly murderous violence, his hold on moral superiority so feeble that he even advocates lying under oath for the sake of "the true truth."

We historians do not judge texts by whether we personally approve of their ethical character; we have to assign them to the historical context they fit best. This text exhibits many startling and confusing features, but the interpretation that accounts for all of them compels us to conclude that the Mar Saba oddity is not a writing of the early Christian period. Nor did its two unknown expansions of the gospel of Mark ever exist except in the mind of the modern author. Historians of the future, then, will see this latter-day pseudo-Clement as a fascinating artifact of a unique period of historical change: a last gasp of the academic subculture of Uranian Venus, yet somehow also a harbinger of the new, more aggressively self-affirming sexualities that would soon bring humanities departments everywhere back from the dead. Written "at the dawn of the Sexual Revolution,"[46] it anticipates numerous other writings of the later twentieth century that depict heterosexual Christian moralists as liars and violent hypocrites but homosexuals as innocent, unjustly punished for the sole offense of loving honestly, as archetypally represented by the "martyrdom" of Oscar Wilde. But I will leave it to future historians to explain all this in their own inimitable way.

Why the Dog Didn't Bark

However we choose to view it, then — political manifesto, uproarious send-up, bizarre perversion, "nice ironic gay joke,"[47] "gimcrack false-antiquity"[48] — the letter about the Secret Gospel of Mark differs from other "modern apocrypha"[49] only in that it is so expertly crafted: the most outrageously successful "inside job" ever perpetrated in the modern field of early Christian studies — at least that we know of. Whom do we have to thank or blame for this unparalleled feat? I will let others argue, if they wish, that there are more likely candidates than Morton Smith. For their sake I refrain from suggesting that, in the story of the Alexandrian presbyter enslaved by the deceitful arts of Carpocrates into revealing the Secret Gospel, we may see a tauntingly sarcastic, even a prescient self-portrait of the former priest who went on to write *Jesus the Magician.* I never met Smith myself, after all, and have access only to his textual avatars. He must have enjoyed Wilde and other "Uranian" writers as an English major at Harvard, but so have millions of other people around the world. He was, in any case, hardly the only person in the twentieth century who boldly imagined Jesus and the disciples as homosexuals — nor was he the first.[50]

Yet the list of plausible suspects could not be very long, even if we discount

the fact that the document seems to build on Smith's questionable identifications of Salome as temptress and Sophia, or his view that it was the Carpocratians who preserved the real religion of Jesus. To "out" this pseudo-Clement,
whoever he was, we need to identify someone who had the skill and ingenuity
to hide his creation behind seven veils, as it were. First, he had the linguistic
know-how to create a document that "is *more* like Clement than Clement ever
was," enfolding within it another work that "is too Marcan to be Mark."[51]
Second, he was resourceful enough to plant the letter in a library that seems
actually to have possessed letters of Clement in the eighth century, when they
were quoted in a work ascribed to John of Damascus.[52] Third, he had the wit
to inscribe the work — in believable eighteenth-century script — into an early
modern edition of patristic texts, facing a last page that reads, "This impudent
rascal can fill many pages with these trifles. . . . Farewell, future reader, whoever you may be, and if any things have escaped the hurried [editor], forgive
[them]."[53] A forged ancient papyrus, he well knew, would be too easily discredited. Fourth, he knew how to create just the sort of text that would fasci-
nate his fellow scholars: what could be more seductive than a fragment of a
lost work by a major church father, which speaks of unique textual variants
and lost early gospels, with bits of theological controversy, hints of liturgical
practice, and an obscure ancient sect thrown in for good measure? Entire if
modest careers have been built on far less. Fifth, he surely knew enough to
appreciate that publishing this "discovery" with Harvard University Press,
under a mountain of minute and erudite commentary that quotes personal
missives from all the most eminent scholars of the day, would engender a
weighty atmosphere of seriousness tantamount to credibility — while launch-
ing into the popular media a claim that new evidence shows Jesus was homosexual would guarantee enough controversy to keep a secret gospel in orbit
indefinitely. Smith's simultaneous publication of a scholarly and a popular
treatment certainly had both effects. Sixth, the author had the literary imagination to build on some adventurous interpretations, turning one Salome into
another, knowing that her performance at the climax of the original play
would, like a seventh veil, hide within it another climactic performance:

"The True Explanation and That Which Accords with the True Philosophy . . ."

Chesterton's statement that Wilde's sin had been "nameless and secret"
would have been understood instantly by his readers; it refers to English common law, wherein the crime of sodomy was delicately called in Latin *peccatum
illud horribile, inter Christianos non nominandum* — that horrible sin that

among Christians is not to be named.[54] This comes directly from the New Testament: "But fornication and impurity of any kind, or greed, must not even be named among you, as is proper among saints. Entirely out of place is obscene, silly, and vulgar talk; but instead, let there be thanksgiving. Be sure of this, that no fornicator or impure person, or one who is greedy (that is, an idolater), has any inheritance in the kingdom of Christ and of God. Let no one deceive you with empty words, for because of these things the wrath of God comes on those who are disobedient. Therefore do not be associated with them" (Ephesians 5:3–7, New Revised Standard Version modified).

The interpretation that homosexuality is the "impurity" that "must not even be named" goes back to a medieval exegesis that identified "the wrath of God" with the destruction of Sodom, inspiring generations of Christians to go forth and do likewise.[55] If I am right that this is primarily a Latin interpretation that began with Pelagius,[56] then it is one more element that does not fit in Clement's Alexandria.[57] Yet the Clement of the Mar Saba letter speaks from within this tradition; his ultimate hypocrisy is that, though he castigates "the unspeakable teachings of the Carpocratians," the most treasured teaching of his own church consists of "things not to be uttered" that were received from the same source, the evangelist Mark. Thus he exemplifies the belief of many modern homosexuals that the most ferocious "homophobes" are driven by a terrified denial of their own homoerotic impulses.

Now that we have all been initiated into the church of the Mar Saba text, our eyes can be opened to recognize the biggest secret of all: the third of the five streams of tradition, "the things not to be uttered . . . , the hierophantic teaching of the Lord" which Mark did not write down but which provide the interpretation for everything else in the Secret Gospel and the strange letter that contains it. The Greek word that Smith rendered as "things not to be uttered" (ἀπόρρητα; *aporrhēta*), a term from ancient mystery religion that the historical Clement did use, can also refer to words that should not be spoken because they constitute "obscene, silly, and vulgar talk."[58] Smith could have translated that Mark "did not divulge the ineffable secrets" or "forbidden things." By Englishing it as "things not to be uttered," Smith was accessing a long-standing trope in English literature, marking the unspeakable as interpretive key to the unheard of.[59] Indeed he was referencing a particular constellation of texts that spell out the core story in the hagiography of Oscar Wilde.

Lord Douglas revealed it most memorably in his best-known poem, *Two Loves* (1894): the two loves are represented by two young men who argue about what to call each other, until one resigns himself to being "the love that dare not speak its name."[60] When Wilde was on trial, according to the published transcripts,[61] the prosecutor read from this poem in open court and demanded of Wilde, "What is 'the love that dare not speak its name'?" Knowing that he risked being convicted, Wilde replied with an impromptu speech, trying to inspire sympathy by connecting such love to both a distinguished history and an aesthetic spirituality, and invoking the names of Plato and other great men. The cheers and hisses it elicited from the courtroom have been reiterated many times since.

> "The love that dare not speak its name" in this century is such a great affection of an elder for a younger man as there was between David and Jonathan, such as Plato made the very basis of his philosophy, and such as you find in the sonnets of Michelangelo and Shakespeare. It is that deep, spiritual affection that is as pure as it is perfect. It dictates and pervades great works of art. . . . It is beautiful, it is fine, it is the noblest form of affection. There is nothing unnatural about it.[62]

David and Jonathan, Plato, Michelangelo, Shakespeare, but not Jesus. Spiritual, artistic, and beautiful, but not in the Holy Ghost. The Mar Saba document with its Secret Gospel was written after Wilde's speech, and with the same ultimate purpose: to provide for homosexuality a respectable history, and a literary and spiritual tradition. It was no mere professorial prank, nor was it — like so many forgeries — a cynical attempt to gain money or notoriety. The "letter of Clement" discovered at Mar Saba is rightly seen as a highly original work of twentieth-century literature, an astoundingly daring act of creative rebellion that aimed, against all odds, to prepare a place for the second love in the mystery of the kingdom of God, and give it at last a Christian name.

Summary

Here I show that the Secret Gospel is actually based on one of the most famous literary works to emerge from the Uranian culture: Oscar Wilde's *Salomé*. The letter of Clement also reflects other cultural themes that have circulated among modern homosexuals who regard Wilde as a martyr and cult figure, notably the perception of Christian moralists as hypocrites. Seen in this light, the Mar Saba text ridicules the Christian ideal of monogamous heterosexuality and attempts to show that Jesus practiced a purer, homosexual love that "dare not speak its name."

The One Who Knows

Perhaps, a gifted paleographer could write an eighteenth century Greek hand that would fool the experts in Athens and Western Europe. Perhaps, with Stahlin's [sic] index to Clement and recent stylistic studies, he could also compose three pages in Clement's style. Perhaps, if he had worked on Clement for years (I have never published an article on Clement), he might even catch Clement's habits of thought and forms of exposition. But can we believe he could do so without any verbal imitation or quotation (except for clichés that Clement himself repeatedly repeats)? And can we also believe that this imaginary genius, when he had to forge a gospel text, would produce an amateurish imitation of M[ar]k full of phrases found in the gospels? The faith that could believe in such a man could move mountains. It would have mountains to move. — Morton Smith

Imagine that the Dead Sea Scrolls had been discovered, not by a Bedouin lad, but by an American scholar making a private retreat in the desert. He photographs some of them and then walks out of the desert, leaving the scrolls where they were. He spends ten years analyzing his photographs and after fifteen years publishes a long analysis of the grammar, vocabulary, and handwriting of the scrolls. He concludes a book with a statement that he is not sure how the scrolls came to be where he found them, for strange accidents are always occurring in the desert, but at least "as far as I know, they are still where I left

them." If that were the story of the Dead Sea scrolls, would the Morton Smith whose high critical standards gave us the classic "Comments on Taylor's Commentary on Mark" . . . not himself be raising questions about their authenticity?
— Quentin Quesnell

I had great difficulty organizing this book; in some ways it was the most difficult thing I have ever tried to write. Almost every section of the book as it now stands was somewhere else in an earlier draft. Eventually I came to the conclusion that, since my subject was an act of deception, it was bound to keep collapsing in on itself. A "real" subject, I think, would have a certain inherent structure, so that one could write a coherent narrative simply by describing that structure.

Looking back now, however, I can see other ways that one might organize a book about the Mar Saba document. For example, if I am right that the text "is rightly seen as a highly original work of twentieth-century literature," then a book could be built around its characters — most of whom, as I showed, have a long prehistory in folklore that was certainly familiar to Morton Smith. Most obvious are the two characters from the nineteenth century: Clement the liar emerged in a Catholic-Protestant polemic of great relevance to Smith's high-church ecclesiology, a polemic Smith knew from his reading of Cardinal Newman (Chapter 7). Salomé the temptress, one of Oscar Wilde's best-known characters, may have captivated Smith when he was a callow undergraduate English major.[1] He certainly knew of her by 1973, when he felt the need for a Clement-like denial that she had anything to do with the Salome of the Secret Gospel (see the epigraph to Chapter 10). A longer history, going back at least to 1817, attaches to the anonymous, nearly naked young man who sought Jesus' love. However, his alleged rival for Jesus' affections, the Beloved Disciple, has been spotted as far back as the sixteenth century — no doubt his story could fill an entire book by itself. Their supposed inamorato, the homosexual Jesus, would presumably also have a history at least as long. Hence from a literary perspective the Mar Saba document, an ingenious reshuffling of traditional characters from unrelated stories, could perhaps be assigned to the genre known as "fakelore": the faux folktales, peopled by the likes of Paul Bunyan and John Henry, that are passed around in literate cultures as if they were actual remnants of old-time oral heritage.[2]

Meanwhile, the unnamed Alexandrian presbyter who defected to the dark side, bewitched by mysterious arts into revealing secret traditions, looks like nothing so much as a cameo role for the mastermind himself, like one of the minor characters Alfred Hitchcock would play in the opening scenes of his own movies. We need not look much farther to find Theodore, the recipient of

Clement's letter. He shares half a name with Luke's correspondent Theophilus (Luke 1:3, Acts 1:1) — but in fact he is ourselves, the true addressees of the letter's true author.

Harder to identify is the dedicatee of Smith's popular book, *The Secret Gospel;* it was inscribed "For the One Who Knows." Quentin Quesnell, who was one of the first to question the authenticity of the Mar Saba fragment in a comprehensive manner, did his best to leave open the possibility that the forger was someone other than Smith. Yet Quesnell had to ask, "Who is 'the one who knows'? What does he know?"[3] Quesnell wondered whether the knower might be Arthur Darby Nock, Smith's Harvard teacher and the dedicatee of Smith's "scholarly" book. According to Smith, Nock never accepted the Mar Saba text as genuine. Was that because he knew?

There are other ways to read the dedication, however: maybe it is directed to an imagined "Carpocratian" reader — "one who knows" would, after all, be a Gnostic. Perhaps Smith anticipated that some readers, clandestine Wilde cultists who knew all about Salomé and had heard the secret stories about Jesus and a young man, would appreciate fully what Smith himself was really up to. Which leads to an obvious question: What exactly *was* Smith really up to?

One of the slippery things about the whole Mar Saba venture — both the "original" document and Smith's various publications on it — is that there seem to be three messages, which shift in and out of focus depending on how one looks at it, and which tend to undermine each other. First of all, Smith clearly wanted us to believe he had discovered major new evidence that Jesus approved of homosexuality — even engaged in it, even imbued it with religious significance. Accordingly, the Secret Gospel would be the earliest and most trustworthy of all ancient gospels. But how could we take Smith's proposal seriously when, on closer scrutiny, it keeps dissolving into dirty jokes? Or perhaps into only one long-winded, tortuous joke, wending through the fragment, the two books, and several articles — the most elaborately extended double entendre ever heard of. But then, just as we are about to dismiss the whole thing as a prank — lewd, crude, and facetious — the humor fades into hostility. All the experts and eminences whose endorsements Smith claimed to have obtained, and all the other scholars who became convinced that he had discovered a genuine ancient writing, will have good reason to feel abused, more than amused, by the whole sordid mess — arguably the most grandiose and reticulated "Fuck You" ever perpetrated in the long and vituperative history of scholarship. Were all three messages equally intended? Did Smith fully realize what he was doing? To paraphrase Quesnell: who was Morton Smith and what did he know?

While writing this book I stoutly resisted every temptation to delve into

Smith's biography and psychological history, or even to read all of his writings. Investigating Smith's inner life has been rendered more difficult by the destruction of his papers, but many of his former colleagues and students are still around and would have a big head start over anything I could do. My original footnote on the Secret Gospel has gotten way out of hand, and I am overdue back at my day job as a musicologist.

But there is no denying that, of all the singular characters in this outlandish fiction, Morton Smith is the murkiest, the hardest to pin down or explain. I suspect his spiritual journey was rather more complicated than the kind of straightforward "homosexual priest versus homophobic church" morality play that some might want to make of it, or the "one sin leads to another" lesson that others will propose (cf. Matthew 12:44–45). I have already pointed out that, even when Smith was working as a priest, his ecclesiology and pastoral approach were so unconventional as to raise questions about his training. My impression is that Morton Smith was a man in great personal pain, even if (which I don't know) he was usually able to hide this fact from the people who knew him. But since he regularly disparaged psychiatry and denied the reality of mental illness (except when it came in handy to explain the spread of Christianity), I suspect that he actually had very little insight into his own motivations and feelings; unpublished anecdotes I have heard about him tend to support this impression. The irony is that an author with so little self-understanding would have chosen a Gnostic sect to represent his own point of view, teasing his readers in a warped game of "I know something you don't know." As I struggled to forge this dross into a book, I sometimes wondered whether Smith's unnamed dedicatee was actually himself, congratulating his own creative brilliance in a narcissistic mental mirror, trumpeting through the fog: Behold the One Who Knows!

Except that he didn't know, or at least he forgot: the knowledge the Gnostics taught was anything but carnal—it was about how to escape the carnal. Thus in a sense—in several senses—one could say that Smith did not know what he was doing. I conjecture that the letter of "Clement" may have begun as a purposeful, even a wistful, attempt to set the historical record "straight" (or rather "gay")—but that it quickly fell afoul of Smith's nasty sense of humor, which in turn became the transparent mask of his considerable rage— I suspect without his fully realizing or understanding what was happening. The anger is no less real for being unacknowledged, just as the forged document is no more real for having been published by Smith in such agonizing detail. But I don't think Smith could perceive clearly what he was actually communicating.

Neither, of course, could most of his readers, given the head-scratching fact that his fabrications were taken so seriously by so many for so long. Only two years after Smith's books were published, Quesnell was already asking some of the obvious questions: "Why is there such a high percentage of inaccuracies in such a serious study?" "Can any scholarly reason be assigned for most of the documentation the book includes?"[4] Yet few of these red flags were ever followed up by anyone. One of the reasons was foreseen by Quesnell himself:

> When useless or irrelevant information is richly and painstakingly documented, the cause of scholarship can be actually impeded rather than advanced.
>
> It is not only that the non-specialist may be too easily dazzled by the mere sight of heavily annotated pages and foreign scripts. But also, unless the author has taken great care to distinguish the important from the trivial, the central from the incidental, even the specialist can be oppressed by the excessive labor it would take to come to grips with the author's thought; not being able to check everything, he may see little point in checking anything; having work of his own to do before he dies, he may feel constrained to settle for a temporary appraisal of "very scholarly," laying the work aside for a leisurely thorough analysis in some vague future.[5]

However, it was not just that scholars couldn't afford the "excessive labor." As it turned out, the average reader of Smith's books was actually more interested in how the Secret Gospel might illuminate "work of his own" than in Smith's crackpot theories about what his "discovery" proved. What could we learn from this of the early traditions about Jesus, or the origins of the written gospels? — that was what most people wanted to know. This may help explain why no one challenged Smith on his misuse of terms like "shamanism" and "schizophrenia," or his disgraceful characterization of Greek Orthodox hymnody, or his habit of treating all ancient religions (indeed all religions!) as if they were pretty much the same. He would never have gotten away with such things for so long had he had a wider range of readers, interested in more aspects of his material. The nearly exclusive focus on Smith's "evidence" for the textual history of the New Testament may also explain why so few seem to have noticed the jokes, or the oddball reference to seven veils in a text about Salome. All this raises deeper questions about ourselves as Smith's audience: Who are we? What do we know?

It seems to me that the saga of the Secret Gospel raises two methodological issues. One has to do with the study of ancient rituals. Historical research on Christian ritual, in particular, has been dominated by practitioners of "liturgiology," which is a branch of Christian historical theology. It began during the Reformation and Counter-Reformation; its earliest practitioners were seeking evidence that could be used to justify, reform, or abolish the practices of their own time. Liturgiology received a further boost during the liturgical movement of the nineteenth and twentieth centuries, led by theologians and "liturgists" who were . . . , well, seeking evidence that could be used to justify, reform, or abolish the practices of their own time. Thus most of the research interest focused on the historical origins of modern practices. Only very recently has much attention been paid to practices and rituals that did not survive, such as the early Alexandrian construction of baptism, rooted in interpretations of Jesus' own baptism by John at Epiphany, rather than in his burial and resurrection at Easter. And because liturgiology is essentially polemical, it has tended to focus too narrowly on the interpretation of texts, marginalizing and largely ignoring the nonverbal data that are less amenable to theological interpretation, the kinds of things that could be uncovered by archaeology, anthropology, or the history of the arts and other cultural phenomena. Thus even fairly simple questions like "When, where, and why did Christians begin to wear white garments at baptism?" or "How were Christian bodies prepared for burial?" remain unanswered and underexplored.

It happened to be the Anglican brand of liturgiology—the attempt to read the Prayer Book back into the New Testament—that Smith was exposed to and then abused for his own purposes. But the familiarity of the liturgiological approach in all denominations meant that no one questioned the white sheet, the resurrection symbolism, the Lazarus echoes in the Secret Gospel's apparent outline of a very early Christian initiation ceremony. What Smith really demonstrated, then, is how far-fetched and unreal the historical investigation of ancient rituals can get when it is based solely on textual interpretations, uncontrolled by social science research on how individuals and communities actually worship, or nontextual evidence on how early Christian groups actually did worship. Anyone seeking to investigate ancient Christian, Gnostic, or other religious rites must understand, as Jewish liturgiologists are beginning to, that the central focus of attention cannot be on texts, but on (what were once) living communities, with their own self-images and worldviews, ideals and stories, organizational structures and factions, unexamined assumptions and unexplained customs. One does not have to be a member of a community to understand it, but one does have to understand the insiders' point of view if one's own theories and speculations are to be anchored in reality. As Rabbi Lawrence Hoffman has put it, in cases where the known historical evidence consists mostly of texts, the aim must be

> to take the liturgical text as a necessary starting point, but then to go beyond it, using a holistic view of the process by which that text is actually prayed to reconstruct the identity of the people who pray it. . . . At issue is not any particular claim, so much as the entire enterprise, a commitment to discover the identity of a praying community—its world view (the way things are), its

ethos ("the tone, character and quality of its life, its moral and aesthetic style and mood"), and the place it occupies in both—and to do so through an analysis of its praying, rather than going the other way around, that is, assuming that we know enough (relatively speaking) about the community's self-perception and need most now, on the basis of that knowledge, to reproduce the recension history of its prayers.[6]

This is more or less what I have done in this book: begin with the document, and go in search of the praying community behind it. Initially it looked as if five streams of tradition would have to be connected to five historical communities, or five historical stages of one community. What I found instead was not exactly a community, and was hardly praying: it was more like one unhappy man who had constructed a religion of his own, borrowing from the underground quasi-cult of Oscar Wilde and dressing it all up with snippets of writing from all over late antiquity. In fifteen and more years of work, he never even suspected that worship cannot be studied in isolation from the people who do it. No ritual—baptism, magic, shamanism, hymnody, or anything else—can be understood apart from the human community that creates it and gives it meaning. But Smith always imagined he knew better than the worshippers themselves.

There was, however, one community he did understand. Because he made the most of his expert insider knowledge of the rituals of scholarship, he was able to use them against the scholarly community itself, so deftly that hardly anyone realized his published "offerings" were full of carelessly gathered but craftily muddled data. By speaking the tongues of textual criticism he proclaimed spellbinding creation myths about the earliest gospels, so theatrically that no one noticed the puppeteer for more than thirty years. Because he cloaked anger as atheism and atheism in the vestments of objectivity, the sermon he preached was not recognized for what it actually was, the hurtful commination of a hurting man. He got away with it all, because he pretended to be playing the same misguided game as everyone else—assuming that early Christianity was relatively known, Carpocratianism relatively unknown, and thus trying to fit the new "evidence" into generally accepted thinking about the formation of the gospels, the ritual imagery of baptism, Alexandrian traditions about Mark, and the writings of Clement. Because so much seemed so familiar, even those who noticed that the Mar Saba text didn't fit in well still couldn't see how bad the fit really was. No one ever guessed what would happen if we read the text Rabbi Hoffman's way: putting all presuppositions aside, assuming nothing about the original authors, we would eventually read our way into a "Carpocratian" community, viewing Clement's letter through the looking-glass of The One Who Knows.

The other methodological issue raised by the Mar Saba misadventure could be applied to any suspected forgery. Forgers always have a vested interest in distracting our attention from what they are really doing, like the prestidigitator who waves a handkerchief with one hand while rearranging the cards with the other. Those who saw Smith's work as a contribution to the early history of the gospels basically fell for the trick. Morton Smith might have been caught out sooner if his readers had been less focused on their own issues and more willing to ask the cui bono question about Smith's issues: who benefits? What difference would it make if Smith were right, if there really were very early testimony that Jesus had ritualized sex with his disciples? Taking his proposals seriously, scholars might have noticed that Smith was asking them to suspend the usual criteria of historical judgment. To begin with, we were supposed to accept that these two fragments of the Secret Gospel, preserved only in an (allegedly) eighteenth-century copy, represented a text as early as, or even earlier than, any canonical New Testament writing. Next we were to assume that, given its early date, the Secret Gospel should be regarded as an unusually trustworthy and factual account of Jesus, whereas every text critic knows that the earliest witness need not be the most accurate. Entertaining these two claims might have led to the question, "*Why* are we to assume that the Secret Gospel is so early and so factual?" The true answer would be: "For the sake of the theory that was spun out of it, that Jesus employed an initiation ritual suggestive of homosexual acts with his disciples." The search for alternative explanations to avoid this conclusion might have focused more attention on the fact that the Carpocratian Gnostics were being presented as the heroes of the story, the ones who preserved Jesus' original practice. This in turn might have underlined how little we really know about the Carpocratians. The utter lack of evidence that they practiced homosexuality might have forced us to ask questions about what we should mean by "homosexuality" in ancient times, and thus come to see that Smith had imported a modern construction of homosexuality into the first century, replete with a Pater-like liturgy and characters derived from Wilde and Newman.

The reality might then have become inescapable: that Smith was asking us to engage in acts of anticriticism or fundamentalism, asserting that historical change is impossible when a timeless truth is at stake. The "truth" in this case would have been a kind of fundamentalist sexology: Homosexuality, or all human sexuality, has always and everywhere been the same. Immune to the forces of historical change, it is therefore in some sense timeless, and thus can be treated as a kind of moral universal or absolute. Indeed, for Smith, its demands are so absolute as to justify a rewriting of history. With that act, of course, Smith became what he opposed: a hypocritical Clement who condoned lying for the sake of the (presumed) truth. The denial of historical difference where we should expect it produced anachronisms in the text that ultimately proved the document unhistorical.

For a while, ironically, the forces of historical change worked in Smith's favor. Even as his books were being published in 1973, the impact of the 1969 Stonewall riots was already transforming the cultures of American homosexuality, so that with time, fewer and fewer people were "in the know" enough to recognize the commonplaces of his post-Uranian construction of sexuality. Since then, of course, history has moved on, in directions the Secret Evangelist could hardly have foreseen. The United States and some other countries wrestle with the legality of "gay marriage" and other forms of "same-sex unions," while Smith's own Anglican Communion is struggling to keep from breaking up over the question of ordaining active homosexuals. The emergence of AIDS has raised the stakes on many fronts. "Homoeroticism in the Early Church" has, I discovered while writing this, become an academic subfield, unimaginable a mere half-century ago.

The underlying philosophical question is also being asked more pointedly: Is it human nature that is fundamentally immutable, while moral principles change with the times? Or are there enduring values that remain constant in all historical circumstances, while human nature changes? In academia nowadays, probably no truism is heard more often than the one that gender and sex roles are culturally and historically constructed (and therefore open to being reconstructed, preferably as soon as possible). Yet scientists are increasingly finding evidence of biological bases for a wide range of human behaviors, and the hunt is on for a "gay gene," which, if discovered, might have a greater impact on the abortion rate than on cultural attitudes toward homosexuality. The morality of Morton Smith's major "contribution," too, will be evaluated differently by different people, both today and in the future.

The alleged mutability or immutability of human nature, and of ethical standards, is probably something that requires more serious thought today, given the claims invoked both by those who seek change and those who resist it. Thus opponents of "gay marriage" have been known to assert that the "one man, one woman" model of marriage has always been a universal cultural and historical norm, though anyone who reads the Old Testament will find its heroes engaging in polygamy, concubinage, and even surrogate parenthood (e.g., Genesis 16:2, 30:1–13). On the other hand, the mere fact of cultural or historical relativity, in itself, offers little if any basis for ethical decision-making. One could hardly justify things like human sacrifice, slavery, genital mutilation, widow immolation, ear-splitting music, or pedophilia merely by pointing out that there are or have been cultures that accepted and even rewarded such behavior. Appeals to cultural difference may be compassionate attempts to promote tolerance, liberty, and human dignity — or cynical attempts to repress them.[7] Obviously, knowledge and sensitivity to cultural and historical difference need to be balanced by ethical principles that are based on something less transitory than culture or history. Hence the Second Vatican Council called for modern Christians to "constantly further the values of marriage and family . . . distinguishing between eternal verities and their changeable expressions."[8]

There have been times, of course, when history was studied as a repository of ethical examples, of great men and women who faced the trials of their times armed with the unchanging virtues of courage or integrity. But I would say that, in many societies, the most important medium for confronting the permanent and the impermanent is neither history nor ethics, but ritual. This is certainly true in the Christian tradition, where it is preeminently in liturgy and prayer that what is time-bound and corruptible encounters what is infinite and immortal. The finite human person, who is always a mystery to himself or herself, stands facing the ultimate Mystery in Whose image we were created, from Whom we have received all that we are, and with Whom we communicate both through words and beyond words. Morton Smith had the right to disbelieve this, of course: the trouble is that he seems to have been completely unaware of it, whatever his experiences in the caves at Mar Saba, as an ordained priest, or while praying in his own secret closet (Matthew 6:6). Smith's concept of worship contrasts starkly with that of another author who struggled with great personal contradictions, apparently including a suppressed homosexual identity.

Nikolai Gogol (1809–52) was regarded in his lifetime as a novelist deeply imbued with the spirit of Ukrainian folklore, though he actually wrote in Russian. It is now clear that his sensibility was largely Western, owing more to German opera than the folktales of his native Ukraine.[9] Gogol also read widely and wrote on religious topics but often wavered closer to Protestant or Catholic forms of Christianity, away from his native Eastern Orthodoxy. Twentieth-century critics, less shy about such things than people used to be, have noticed that Gogol's life seems to have been full of longing for intimate relationships with men, even while his fiction was full of anxiety and guilt about intimate relationships with women.[10] There is still much uncertainty about the circumstances of his untimely death; the details may have been deliberately obscured by his friends. It appears, though, that Gogol fasted to death under the tutelage of an ascetical extremist, ignoring the admonitions of the more mainstream Russian Orthodox clergy.

Yet there is wide agreement that at least Gogol got the liturgy right. His commentary on the Byzantine-rite Eucharist, uncharacteristically based on authoritative Orthodox sources, has been read appreciatively for more than a century by both Eastern and Western Christians. It closes with a summary that renders Smith's assertions about worship completely unrecognizable:

> The significance of the Divine Liturgy is great; it is celebrated visibly and openly in the sight of all, and yet it is full of mystery.
>
> If the worshipper but follow each act reverently and attentively, his soul will be uplifted; it becomes possible for him to fulfil the Commandments of Christ, the yoke of Christ will be easy and His burden light. On leaving the church where he has been present at the divine Feast of love he sees in all men his brethren. . . .
>
> And all who have attentively followed the Divine Liturgy go forth gentler, kindlier in dealing with others, friendlier, quieter in their behaviour. . . . It insensibly builds up and forms a man, and if society still hold together, if people do not breathe inveterate hatred against one another, the secret cause is the Divine Liturgy reminding man of holy, heavenly love towards his brother.[11]

Thus the liturgy is not magic, or the routine repetition of incantations. The worshipper's role is not to slip into "disorientation," as Smith would have it, but to "follow each act reverently and attentively." The fully involved worshipper will not find the liturgy "dazzling the mind and destroying its sense of reality" — on the contrary his "soul will be uplifted" to a high state of attunement or attentiveness. In that state the liturgical words and actions have a silent, insensible effect, enabling the Christian to fulfill, without quite knowing how, the supreme commandments to love God and neighbor (Mark 12:28–34). Because this creative action of divine grace cannot be directly perceived, except through its effects, it is called a "mystery" — utterly unlike the sexual "mystery of the kingdom of God" taught by the Secret Gospel.

Smith would have had the same right as everyone else to argue that Gogol's faith was false, that his understanding of the liturgy was inaccurate or untrue, or that it doesn't seem to have "worked" even in Gogol's case. The problem is not that Smith disagreed with the Christian understanding of liturgy, but that for all his learning he seems never even to have heard of it. As a priest in 1949, struggling with the counseling of parishioners' sexual problems, he shows no knowledge of the claim that attentive participation in worship can help make burdens light. If he had learned from the Mar Saba monks that reverent attention to the liturgy can make keeping the commandments possible, he might never have gone back there to plant an obscene gospel in their library. If "the divine Feast of love" had helped him see all people as his brothers and sisters, and become "gentler, kindlier in dealing with others, friendlier, quieter," he might not have carried out a plan to embarrass so many of his professional colleagues, or treated those who questioned his discovery so uncharitably. And if he had understood the Christian liturgy better, he might have been more reluctant to publish such absurd claims about its origins.

Even after becoming an atheist professor, if Smith had known what Christian worship means to those who make use of it, he could (if he had wanted to) have written a thoughtful and learned critique, even a devastating refutation of all of Christian belief and practice. But in fact he did not understand that rituals are enacted by communities, and he did not know, despite his own former membership, what the community he was attacking actually believed about its rituals. Had he known, he could still have chosen to spin unheard-of theories about Jesus, but he could not have written hundreds of slovenly pages filled with ignorance, foolishness, and angry jokes about the meaning of early Christian baptism. The tragic paradox of the man who thought he exchanged Christianity for a latter-day Carpocratian Gnosticism is not that he wasn't a good Christian, but that he wasn't even a very good Gnostic. Despite all his priestly experience, his visits to monasteries, his two doctorates, his enviable skill with ancient languages, his prestigious research grants and access to world-famous libraries, he wrote what he did not know.

Appendix: Morton Smith's Translation of the Mar Saba Letter of Clement

From Morton Smith, *The Secret Gospel: The Discovery and Interpretation of the Secret Gospel According to Mark* (New York: Harper & Row, 1973), 14–17. Biblical and other citations are added in parentheses.

From the letters of the most holy Clement, author of the *Stromateis*. To Theodore:

You did well in silencing the unspeakable teachings of the Carpocratians. For these are the "wandering stars" (Jude 13) referred to in the prophecy, who wander from the narrow road of the commandments into a boundless abyss of the carnal and bodily sins. For, priding themselves in knowledge, as they say, "of the deep [things] of Satan" (Revelation 2:24), they do not know that they are casting themselves away into "the nether world of the darkness" (Jude 13) of falsity, and, boasting that they are free, they have become slaves of servile desires. Such [men] are to be opposed in all ways and altogether. For, even if they should say something true, one who loves the truth should not, even so, agree with them. For not all true [things] are the truth, nor should that truth which [merely] seems true according to human opinions be preferred to the true truth, that according to the faith.

Now of the [things] they keep saying about the divinely inspired Gospel according to Mark, some are altogether falsifications, and others, even if they do contain some true [elements], nevertheless are not reported truly. For the true [things], being mixed with inventions, are falsified, so that, as the saying [goes], even the salt loses its savor (Luke 14:34).

253

[As for] Mark, then, during Peter's stay in Rome he wrote [an account of] the Lord's doings, not, however, declaring all [of them], nor yet hinting at the secret [ones], but selecting those he thought most useful for increasing the faith of those who were being instructed. But when Peter died as a martyr, Mark came over to Alexandria, bringing both his own notes and those of Peter, from which he transferred to his former book the things suitable to whatever makes for progress toward knowledge [*gnosis*]. [Thus] he composed a more spiritual Gospel for the use of those who were being perfected. Nevertheless, he yet did not divulge the things not to be uttered, nor did he write down the hierophantic teaching of the Lord, but to the stories already written he added yet others and, moreover, brought in certain sayings of which he knew the interpretation would, as a mystagogue, lead the hearers into the innermost sanctuary of that truth hidden by seven [veils]. Thus, in sum, he prearranged matters, neither grudgingly nor incautiously, in my opinion, and, dying, he left his composition to the church in Alexandria, where it even yet is most carefully guarded, being read only to those who are being initiated into the great mysteries.

But since the foul demons are always devising destruction for the race of men, Carpocrates, instructed by them and using deceitful arts, so enslaved a certain presbyter of the church in Alexandria that he got from him a copy of the secret Gospel, which he both interpreted according to his blasphemous and carnal doctrine and, moreover, polluted, mixing with the spotless and holy words utterly shameless lies. From this mixture is drawn off the teaching of the Carpocratians.

To them, therefore, as I said above, one must never give way, nor, when they put forward their falsifications, should one concede that the secret Gospel is by Mark, but should even deny it on oath. For, "Not all true [things] are to be said to all men" (Philo). For this [reason] the Wisdom of God, through Solomon, advises, "Answer the fool from his folly" (Proverbs 26:5), teaching that the light of the truth should be hidden from those who are mentally blind. Again it says, "From him who has not shall be taken away" (Matthew 25:29), and, "Let the fool walk in darkness" (Ecclesiastes 2:14). But we are "children of light" (1 Thessalonians 5:5), having been illuminated by "the dayspring" of the Spirit of the Lord "from on high" (Luke 1:78), and "Where the Spirit of the Lord is," it says, "there is liberty" (2 Corinthians 3:17), for "All things are pure to the pure" (Titus 1:15).

To you, therefore, I shall not hesitate to answer the [questions] you have asked, refuting the falsifications by the very words of the Gospel. For example, after "And they were in the road going up to Jerusalem" (Mark 10:32), and what follows, until "After three days he shall arise" (Mark 10:34), [the secret Gospel] brings the following [material] word for word:

"And they come into Bethany, and a certain woman, whose brother had died, was there. And, coming, she prostrated herself before Jesus and says to him, 'Son of David, have mercy on me.' But the disciples rebuked her. And Jesus, being angered, went off with her into the garden where the tomb was, and straightway a great cry was heard from the tomb. And going near Jesus rolled away the stone from the door of the tomb. And straightway, going in where the youth was, he stretched forth his hand and raised him, seizing his hand. But the youth, looking upon him, loved him and began to beseech him that he might be with him. And going out of the tomb they came into the house of the youth, for he was rich. And after six days Jesus told him what to do and in the evening the youth comes to him, wearing a linen cloth over [his] naked [body]. And he remained with him that night, for Jesus taught him the mystery of the kingdom of God. And thence, arising, he returned to the other side of the Jordan."

After these [words] follows the text, "And James and John come to him" (Mark 10:35), and all that section. But "naked [man] with naked [man]" and the other things about which you wrote are not found.

And after the [words], "And he comes into Jericho" (Mark 10:46), [the secret Gospel] adds only, "And the sister of the youth whom Jesus loved and his mother and Salome were there, and Jesus did not receive them." But the many other [things about] which you wrote both seem to be and are falsifications.

Now the true explanation and that which accords with the true philosophy . . .

Notes

Book epigraph. *The Complete Letters of Oscar Wilde,* ed. Merlin Holland and Rupert Hart-Davis (New York: Henry Holt, 2000), 995.

Chapter 1. "A Discovery of Extraordinary Importance"

Epigraph. Morton Smith, *The Secret Gospel: The Discovery and Interpretation of the Secret Gospel According to Mark* (New York: Harper & Row, 1973), ix, or p. xii in the reprint ed. (Clear Lake, Calif.: Dawn Horse Press, 1982).

1. "Mar" means "Saint." In Greek the name is often spelled "Sabbas," but in Semitic languages like Aramaic and Arabic, which are less likely to double consonants or end masculine names with *s,* it is usually "Saba." Thus both spellings occur in English and other Western languages.

2. Joseph Patrich, *Sabas, Leader of Palestinian Monasticism: A Comparative Study in Eastern Monasticism, Fourth to Seventh Centuries,* Dumbarton Oaks Studies 32 (Washington, D.C.: Dumbarton Oaks Research Library and Collection, 1995), especially pp. 61–107, map following pp. 286, 323–30. Yizhar Hirschfeld, *The Judean Desert Monasteries in the Byzantine Period* (New Haven, Conn.: Yale University Press, 1992), 24–26.

3. Cyril of Scythopolis, *Lives of the Monks of Palestine,* trans. R. M. Price (Kalamazoo, Mich.: Cistercian Publications, 1991), 93–219. Patrich, *Sabas,* 37–48.

4. Albert Ehrhard, "Das griechische Kloster Mar-Saba in Palaestina: seine Geschichte und seine literarischen Denkmäler," *Römische Quartalschrift* 7 (1893): 32–79, plates I–II.

5. Andrew Louth, "John of Damascus and the Making of the Byzantine Theological

Synthesis," *The Sabaite Heritage in the Orthodox Church from the Fifth Century to the Present,* ed. Joseph Patrich, Orientalia Lovaniensia Analecta 98 (Leuven: Uitgeverij Peeters en Departement Oosterse Studies, 2001), 301–4. St. John of Damascus, *Three Treatises on the Divine Images,* trans. Andrew Louth, Popular Patristics Series (Crestwood, N.Y.: St. Valdimir's Seminary Press, 2003). Jaroslav Pelikan, *The Christian Tradition: A History of the Development of Doctrine 2: The Spirit of Eastern Christendom (600–1700)* (Chicago: University of Chicago Press, 1974), 117–33, 136–37, 234–35. St. John's cell and cenotaph are preserved at the monastery as a reverential space; a photograph can be seen in Pia Compagnoni, *Deserto di Giuda,* 2nd ed. (Jerusalem: Franciscan Printing Press, 1978), plate LIV following p. 63; see also the bibliography on Mar Saba, p. 76.

6. Cyril, *Lives,* 220–44, see pp. 227, 228, 241. Pietro Bertocchi, "Giovanni il Silenziario," *Bibliotheca Sanctorum* 6 (Rome: Istituto Giovanni XXIII, 1965): 904–5. J. Patrich, "The Hermitage of St. John the Hesychast in the Great Laura of Sabas," *Liber Annuus: Annual of the Studium Biblicum Franciscanum, Jerusalem* 43 (1993): 315–37, plates 17–18. Otto Meinardus, "Notes on the Laurae and Monasteries of the Wilderness of Judaea: 2," *Liber Annuus* 15 (1964–65): 328–56, see pp. 348–49.

7. Tamila Mgaloblishvili, "The Georgian Sabaite (Sabatsminduri) Literary School and the Sabatsmindian Version of the Georgian *Mravaltavi* (Polykephalon)," *The Sabaite Heritage,* 229–33. Sebastian Brock, "Syriac into Greek at Mar Saba: The Translation of St. Isaac the Syrian," *The Sabaite Heritage,* 201–8.

8. J. A. Devenny, "Theōdūrus Abū Qurra," *New Catholic Encyclopedia* (New York: McGraw-Hill, 1967), 14: 28–29.

9. Francesco Antonio Angarano, "Teodoro di Edessa," *Bibliotheca Sanctorum* 12 (1969): 250.

10. J. Patrich, "The Sabaite Laura of Jeremias in the Judean Desert," *Liber Annuus* 40 (1990): 295–311, plates 35–40. J. Patrich, "The Sabaite Monastery of the Cave (Spelaion) in the Judean Desert," *Liber Annuus* 41 (1991): 429–48, plates 47–52. Otto Meinardus, "Notes on the Laurae and Monasteries of the Wilderness of Judaea," *Liber Annuus* 15 (1964–65): 220–50.

11. John Thomas, "The Imprint of Sabaitic Monasticism on Byzantine Monastic *Typika*"; Vassilios Tzaferis, "Early Christian Monasticism in the Holy Land and Archeology"; Yizhar Hirschfeld, "The Physical Structure of the New Laura as an Expression of Controversy over the Monastic Lifestyle," *The Sabaite Heritage,* 73–83, 317–21, 323–45.

12. Svetlana Popvić, "Sabaite Influences on the Church of Medieval Serbia"; Axinia Džurova, "Les manuscrits grecs enluminés du monastère de Saint-Sabas et leur influence sur la tradition slave: Sabas 248 de la Bibliothèque du Patriarcat grec de Jérusalem," *The Sabaite Heritage,* 385–407, 409–29. Nicholai Velimirovich, *The Life of St Sava* (Crestwood, N.Y.: Saint Vladimir's Seminary Press, 1989), 113.

13. M. delle Rose, "Cellae Novae, Monasterium," *Lexicon Topographicum Urbis Romae* 1 (Rome: Edizioni Quasar, 1993), 257–59 and Fig. 147.

14. Nicolas Egender, "La formation et l'influence du *Typikon* liturgique de Saint-Sabas," *The Sabaite Heritage,* 209–16. Joseph J. Patrich, *Nezirut Midbar Yehudah batekufah ha-Bizantinit: Mif'alam shel Sabas ve-talmidav* [The Judean Desert Monasticism

in the Byzantine Period: The Institutions of Sabas and His Disciples; in Hebrew] (Jerusalem: Yad Izhak Ben-Zvi; Israel Exploration Society, 1995), 185–204. Robert F. Taft, *The Byzantine Rite: A Short History,* American Essays in Liturgy (Collegeville, Minn.: Liturgical Press, 1992).

15. Peter Jeffery, "The Earliest Christian Chant Repertory Recovered: The Georgian Witnesses to Jerusalem Chant," *Journal of the American Musicological Society* 47 (1994): 1–39, especially pp. 23–33. Jeffery, "The Earliest Oktōēchoi: The Role of Jerusalem and Palestine in the Beginnings of Modal Ordering," *The Study of Medieval Chant, Paths and Bridges, East and West: In Honor of Kenneth Levy,* ed. Peter Jeffery (Woodbridge/Cambridge, U.K.: Boydell Press, 2000), 144–206, especially pp. 194–200. Jeffery, "A Window on the Formation of the Medieval Chant Repertories: The Greek Palimpsest Fragments in Princeton University MS Garrett 24," *The Past in the Present: Papers Read at the IMS Intercongressional Symposium and the 10th Meeting of the Cantus Planus, Budapest & Visegrád, 2000* (Budapest: Liszt Ferenc Academy of Music, 2003), 2: 1–21.

16. Peter Jeffery, "Jerusalem and Rome (and Constantinople): The Heritage of Two Great Cities in the Formation of the Medieval Chant Traditions," *Cantus Planus: Papers Read at the Fourth Meeting, Pécs, Hungary 3–8 September 1990* (Budapest: Hungarian Academy of Sciences, Institute for Musicology, 1992), 163–74. Jeffery, "Rome and Jerusalem: From Oral Tradition to Written Repertory in Two Ancient Liturgical Centers," *Essays on Medieval Music in Honor of David Hughes,* ed. Graeme M. Boone, Isham Library Papers 4 (Cambridge, Mass.: Harvard University Department of Music, 1995), 207–47.

17. Joseph-Marie Sauget, "Stefano Sabaita, il Taumaturgo," *Bibliotheca Sanctorum* 12 (1969): 14–15.

18. Christian Hannick, "Hymnographie et hymnographes sabaïtes," *The Sabaite Heritage,* 217–28.

19. Cf. Benedictine Rule 53:16, as translated in *RB 1980: The Rule of St. Benedict in Latin and English with Notes,* ed. Timothy Fry et al. (Collegeville, Minn.: Liturgical Press, 1981), 259.

20. Smith, *Secret Gospel,* 1–6, quotations from pp. 4, 1, 6.

21. Ibid., 5.

22. Ibid.

23. Ibid., 8, 9. However, Smith, in *Clement of Alexandria and a Secret Gospel of Mark* (Cambridge, Mass.: Harvard University Press, 1973), says that he spent "a fortnight" at Mar Saba (p. ix). Taken literally, this would indicate a period of two weeks.

24. Morton Smith, "Hellēnika Cheirographa ek tē Monē tou Hagiou Sabba [Greek Manuscripts of the Monastery of St. Sabbas; in Greek]," trans. Konstantinos Michaelidēs, *Nea Siōn* 55 [year 52] (1960): 110–25, 245–56. MS 15 is in "the little library adjoining the Church" (p. 115), while MSS 16, 17, 19, and 40 were "shown to me by Father Sabbas [the librarian?] and will not be found in the Tower" (pp. 115–16, 125).

25. Smith, *Secret Gospel,* 10–11.

26. See the horarium described in ibid., 4.

27. Euthyme Mercenier, a monk who gives a well-informed account of the daily schedule and round of services about 1946, says the meal was "vers dix heures"; see "Le monastère de Mar Saba," *Irénikon* 20 (1947): 283–97, especially p. 293. Seton Dearden's

Introduction to Robert Curzon, *Visits to Monasteries in the Levant* (London: Arthur Barker, 1955), p. 14, states that in 1952 there were services from 1 to 5 a.m., and the only meal of the day was at 10:30 a.m.

28. Smith, *Secret Gospel,* 10.

29. Mercenier, "Monastère," 287–91. For explanations of the different services of the Byzantine daily cursus, see Robert Taft, *The Liturgy of the Hours in East and West: The Origins of the Divine Office and Its Meaning for Today,* 2nd rev. ed. (Collegeville, Minn.: Liturgical Press), 273–91. Mother Mary [Sonia Hambourg Bessarab] and Kallistos Ware, trans. and eds., *The Festal Menaion Translated from the Original Greek* (London: Faber and Faber, 1977), 38–41, 67–97.

30. The numbers run from 1 to 76, but numbers 3–5 and 7–8 are left undescribed because they are in Russian and Romanian.

31. According to Jean-Marie Olivier, *Répertoire des bibliothèques et des catalogues de manuscrits grecs de Marcel Richard,* 3rd ed., Corpus Christianorum (Turnhout: Brepols, 1995), p. 398, no. 1296, a manuscript described in a turn-of-the-century catalogue (pp. 393–94, no. 1286) "does not seem to figure" in Smith's catalogue.

32. Smith, "Hellēnika," 111, 256.

33. Ibid., 256.

34. Morton Smith, "Monasteries and Their Manuscripts," *Archaeology: A Magazine Dealing with the Antiquity of the World* 13 (1960): 172–77, quotes from pp. 175, 177.

35. Smith, *Secret Gospel,* 11.

36. Smith, *Clement,* ix, referring to Smith, "Hellēnika," which he describes in *Secret Gospel,* 11 n. 1 as "the complete list of my findings, translated and edited by Archimandrite Constantine Michaelides." The article is listed without Michaelides' name in the bibliography of Smith's writings in Morton Smith, *Studies in the Cult of Yahweh* 2: *New Testament, Early Christianity, and Magic,* ed. Shaye J. D. Cohen, Religions in the Graeco-Roman World 180 (Leiden: Brill, 1996), 261, though both names are given in Smith, *Clement,* 431.

37. If I may offer my own youthful catalogue by way of contrast, even though I wrote it as a work for hire and not a personal research project, it was not conceived merely as a list of individual manuscript descriptions: every opportunity was taken to present evidence bearing on the history of the library as a whole: Donald Yates and Peter Jeffery, *Descriptive Inventories of Manuscripts Microfilmed for the Hill Monastic Manuscript Library,* series 1: *Austrian Libraries,* vol. 2: *St. Georgenberg-Fiecht* (Collegeville, Minn.: Hill Monastic Manuscript Library, 1985). Yates began the catalogue (including most of the archival manuscripts) and then left to take another job. I catalogued the rest (including most of the library manuscripts), compiled a list of manuscripts that had moved to other locations (pp. 328–48), edited two early book lists (pp. 349–50), prepared lists of dated manuscripts and concordances of all the historic numbering systems (pp. 395–400), and wrote a preface outlining the library's origins and history, utilizing notes Yates had made for that purpose (pp. xi–xv).

38. The date is variously given as May 13 and 23, 1834, in Monk Neophytos of Cyprus, *Annals of Palestine, 1821–1841: Manuscript* (Jerusalem: S. N. Spyridon, 1938), 76, 120, wherein the social chaos and physical destruction are described in detail. Some information on the rebuilding is given in Paolo Acquistapace et al., *Guida biblica e*

turistica della Terra Santa (Milan: Istituto Propaganda Libraria, 1992), 388–90, see p. 389. Jerome Murphy-O'Connor, *The Holy Land: An Oxford Archaeological Guide from the Earliest Times to 1700,* 4th rev. ed. (Oxford: Oxford University Press, 1998), 332–35, see p. 333. Earlier that very year, 1834, the intrepid Lord Curzon saw three collections of manuscripts at Mar Saba: the prime collection of about one thousand manuscripts was housed in a small room above the pre-earthquake church, reachable only by a ladder. Another collection of about a hundred liturgical manuscripts, which he was told were in active use, was kept on a shelf in the apse of the church. The tower library contained "about a hundred MSS., but all imperfect." Characteristically, he did not describe any collections of printed books. Robert Curzon, *Visits to Monasteries in the Levant* (London: John Murray, 1849; repr. Lewiston, N.Y.: Edwin Mellen Press, 1995), 203–4, 206. Curzon, *Visits* (1955), 187–88; this edition, based on Curzon's last (1865), contains an informative introduction by Seton Dearden and an appendix of recent photographs of Mar Saba. Other nineteenth-century visitors are listed in Ehrhard, "Das griechische Kloster," 61–62. Smith, *Clement,* 288, cites another part of Curzon's book but not the section that describes what he observed at Mar Saba!

39. Smith, "Hellēnika," 256.

40. Aristarchos Peristeris, "Literary and Scribal Activities at the Monastery of St. Sabas," *The Sabaite Heritage,* 171–77, see p. 175. Reviel Netz, "Archimedes in Mar Saba: A Preliminary Notice," *The Sabaite Heritage,* 195–99. Ehrhard was able to list twenty-one former Saba manuscripts in "Das griechische Kloster," 63–65.

41. Smith, "Hellēnika," 256. In *Clement,* ix, Smith wrote laconically, "there were some twenty distinct manuscripts and two large folders full of scraps which I did not have time to study."

42. Smith, *Secret Gospel,* 12, 37; the latter is evidently a photograph of MS 22, see Smith, "Hellēnika," 119–21.

43. Found in MSS 22 and 75 in Smith, "Hellēnika," 121 n. 1 (see photo in Smith, *Secret Gospel,* 37), 254.

44. MS 18, in Smith, "Hellēnika," 116. *Patrologia Graeca* 62: 759.

45. Morton Smith, "Symmeikta: Notes on Collections of Manuscripts in Greece," *Epetēris Hetaireias Vyzantinōn Spoudōn* 26 (1956): 380–93, see pp. 380, 392. Smith, "Monasteries," 177. The abstract of Morton Smith, "Minor Collections of Manuscripts in Greece," *Journal of Biblical Literature* 72 (1953): xii, is too brief to be informative.

46. Morton Smith, "What May Be Hoped For from Modern Greek Manuscripts," *Studia Codicologica,* ed. Kurt Treu et al., Texte und Untersuchungen 124 (Berlin: Akademie-Verlag, 1977), 457–60, see p. 460.

47. See C. Kannengiesser, "Odes of Solomon," *Encyclopedia of the Early Church,* ed. Angelo Di Berardino, trans. Adrian Walford, ed. W. H. C. Frend (New York: Oxford University Press, 1992), 2: 609–10. Robert Murray, *Symbols of Church and Kingdom: A Study in Early Syriac Tradition* (Piscataway, N.J.: Gorgias Press, 2004), 24–25, 384. J. H. Charlesworth, ed., *The Old Testament Pseudepigrapha* 2 (Garden City, N.Y.: Doubleday, 1985), 725–71.

48. Shaye J. D. Cohen, "In Memoriam Morton Smith: Morton Smith and His Scholarly Achievement," *Josephus and the History of the Greco-Roman Period: Essays in Memory of Morton Smith,* ed. Fausto Parente and Joseph Sievers, Studia Post-Biblica 41 (Leiden:

Brill, 1994): 1–8, see p. 3; the same article without the subtitle in *Studies in the Cult of Yahweh* (1996) 2: 279–85, see p. 280. See also Smith, "Symmeikta," 389.

49. Morton Smith, "The Manuscript Tradition of Isidore of Pelusium," *Harvard Theological Review* 47 (1954): 205–10, see p. 210.

50. Smith, "What May Be Hoped," 459. A similar list is in Smith, "Monasteries," 175.

51. Smith, "Monasteries" 173.

52. MS no. 21 in Smith, "Hellēnika," 118. See also Morton Smith, "New Fragments of Scholia on Sophocles' Ajax," *Greek, Roman and Byzantine Studies* 3 (1960): 40–42, but a better photograph is in Smith, "Monasteries," 175.

53. The author of these writings is not known by his true name, but his historical and cultural background are better understood now than in Smith's day. According to Columba Stewart, *"Working the Earth of the Heart": The Messalian Controversy in History, Texts, and Language to AD 431*, Oxford Theological Monographs (Oxford: Clarendon Press, 1991), 234, 236, "Macarius" seems to have been part of "an irruption into the Hellenistic world of ascetical practices and imagistic language far more characteristic of Syriac Christianity than of the imperial [Greek] Church centred on Constantinople. . . . The poetic, symbolic world of Syriac Christianity somehow came to influence this Christian author writing in Greek." See also the preface and introduction to *Pseudo-Macarius: The Fifty Spiritual Homilies and the Great Letter*, trans. and ed. George A. Maloney, preface by Kallistos Ware, The Classics of Western Spirituality: A Library of the Great Spiritual Masters (New York: Paulist Press, 1992).

54. Smith, *Secret Gospel*, 13. No. 75 in Smith, "Hellēnika," 254. In Smith, "Monasteries," 174; however, Smith called it "a twelfth-century manuscript of the sermons of St. Macarius." On the confused state of the textual tradition see J. Gribomont, "Macarius/ Simeon," *Encyclopedia of the Early Church*, 1: 514.

55. Smith, "Monasteries," 177.

56. See also Smith, *Secret Gospel*, 18–19.

57. Ibid., 12.

58. Ibid., 12–13.

59. Bruce M. Metzger, *The Text of the New Testament: Its Transmission, Corruption, and Restoration*, 3rd enlarged ed. (Oxford: Oxford University Press, 1992), 42–45.

60. Eligius Dekkers, *Clavis Patrum Latinorum*, 3rd ed., Corpus Christianorum Series Latina (Steenbrugge: Abbatia Sancti Petri, 1995), 105 no. 262a, 123 no. 288. Henry Chadwick, "New Sermons of St. Augustine," *Journal of Theological Studies* n.s. 47 (1996): 69–91. Henry Chadwick, "New Letters of St. Augustine," *Journal of Theological Studies* n.s. 34 (1983): 425–52.

61. Smith, *Secret Gospel*, 18.

62. Cohen, "In Memoriam."

63. Philip Jenkins, *Hidden Gospels: How the Search for Jesus Lost Its Way* (Oxford: Oxford University Press, 2001), 101–2, 181, confesses to "serious and enduring doubts" about the text's authenticity and notes a certain similarity to a novel published shortly before Smith's original visit: James Hogg Hunter, *The Mystery of Mar Saba* (Toronto: Evangelical Publishers, 1940; repr. Grand Rapids, Mich.: Zondervan, various dates).

64. In particular Quentin Quesnell, "The Mar Saba Clementine: A Question of Evidence," *Catholic Biblical Quarterly* 37 (1975): 48–67, with a response by Smith in 38

(1976): 196–99, and reply by Quesnell in 38 (1976): 200–3. More recently, Jacob Neusner, originally a Smith supporter (he edited a four-volume Festschrift for Smith at the relatively young age of sixty), has called Smith's *Clement* "an outright fraud," in his foreword to Birger Gerhardsson, *Memory and Manuscript: Oral Tradition and Written Transmission in Rabbinic Judaism and Early Christianity, with Tradition and Transmission in Early Christianity* (Grand Rapids, Mich.: Eerdmans, and Livonia, Mich.: Dove, 1994), xxvi.

65. *Manuscript Material from the Monastery of Mar Saba, Discovered, Transcribed and Translated by Morton Smith* (New York: privately published, 1958). This citation is taken from the bibliography of Smith's publications in Smith, *Studies in the Cult of Yahweh* 2: 260. No doubt this ten-page publication included photographs of the manuscript as well.

66. Smith, *Secret Gospel,* 27–28. Ten experts are cited on the eighteenth-century dating of the script in Smith, "Hellēnika," 251–52, MS no. 65, though Smith did not require such assistance for dating any of the other manuscripts.

67. Smith, *Secret Gospel,* 30. The early scholarly reaction to, and journalistic coverage of, Smith's papers and publications are described in John Dart, *Decoding Mark* (Harrisburg, Pa.: Trinity Press International, 2003), 5–16.

68. For full bibliographical information, see note 23 of this chapter.

69. Smith, *Clement,* 144, 351–52, 370–79. Smith, *Secret Gospel,* 67.

70. William M. Calder, "Smith, Morton," *Biographical Dictionary of North American Classicists,* ed. Ward W. Briggs (Westport, Conn.: Greenwood Press, 1994), 600–2, see p. 602.

71. For full bibliographical information, see the unnumbered note of this chapter.

72. See Smith, *Secret Gospel,* 3, 4, 146.

73. Ibid., 76–77. Smith, *Clement,* 96–97, 167, 194. *Secret Gospel* was actually the first to become available, according to Guy G. Stroumsa, "Comments on Charles Hedrick's Article: A Testimony," *Journal of Early Christian Studies* 11 (2003): 147–53, see p. 152.

74. Smith, *Clement,* 448–53, facing facsimiles of the original manuscript.

75. Ibid., 446–47. Smith, *Secret Gospel,* 14–17. The text is also given in the appendix to the present volume. The Greek text and an emended translation are now also published in Scott G. Brown, *Mark's Other Gospel: Rethinking Morton Smith's Controversial Discovery,* Studies in Christianity and Judaism 15 (Waterloo, Ontario: Wilfrid Laurier University Press for the Canadian Corporation for Studies in Religion, 2005): xvii–xxiii.

76. It is easier to omit nouns in Greek than it is in English because Greek articles, adjectives, and participles indicate the number and gender of whatever is being referred to; in English one can get this information only from the noun. Thus the Greek adjective *gymnos* ("naked"), since it has a masculine singular ending, implies a noun like "man" or "male," which therefore may not need to be specified.

77. *Stromateis,* the title of Clement's longest extant work, is not italicized in Smith, *Clement,* 446. The word "author" has "the" in front of it, ibid.

78. Ibid., has "what" instead of "those."

79. Ibid., omits the word "as."

80. Ibid., has "prepared" instead of "prearranged." This is the most substantive difference in wording between the two translations.

81. Ibid., 447, has a semicolon instead of a comma.

82. Philo Judaeus Alexandrinus, *Questions on Genesis* 4.67, see Philo, *Questions and Answers on Genesis,* trans. Ralph Marcus, Loeb Classical Library 380 [= Philo Supplement I] (Cambridge, Mass.: Harvard University Press, 1953), 346, and Philo, *Questions and Answers on Exodus,* trans. Ralph Marcus, Loeb Classical Library 401 [= Philo Supplement II] (Cambridge, Mass.: Harvard University Press, 1953), 219.

83. Smith, *Clement,* 447, does not capitalize the word "spirit" here, though it does elsewhere.

84. In ibid., this is punctuated, "And they come into Bethany. And a certain woman whose brother had died was there."

85. For some concise descriptions from early sources, see Thomas M. Finn, *From Death to Rebirth: Ritual and Conversion in Antiquity* (Mahwah, N.J.: Paulist Press, 1997), 163–238.

Chapter 2. Questions

Epigraph. Smith, *Secret Gospel,* 18–19.

1. *Clemens Alexandrinus* 1, ed. Otto Stählin, 3rd ed., ed. Ursula Treu, Die griechischen christlichen Schriftsteller (Berlin: Akademie Verlag, 1972), XVI–LXIV.

2. Smith, *Clement,* 1–4, 454, quotation from p. 3.

3. Peristeris, "Literary," 176.

4. Johannes Quasten, *Patrology* 1: *The Beginnings of Patristic Literature* (Westminster, Md.: Newman Press, 1950; repr. Christian Classics, 1992), 197. Maurice Geerard, *Clavis Patrum Graecorum* 3, Corpus Christianorum (Turnhout: Brepols, 1979), 1: 30.

5. L. D. Reynolds and N. G. Wilson, *Scribes and Scholars: A Guide to the Transmission of Greek and Latin Literature,* 3rd ed. (Oxford: Clarendon Press, 1991), 32, 109, 139–40, 181, 218, plate XIV.

6. Tacitus, *Germania,* trans. J. B. Rives, Clarendon Ancient History Series (Oxford: Clarendon Press, 1999), 66–70.

7. Aubrey Burl, *Catullus: A Poet in the Rome of Julius Caesar* (London: Constable, 2004), 259–66, 282. Julia Haig Gaisser, *Catullus and His Renaissance Readers* (Oxford: Clarendon Press, 1993), 2–25.

8. George K. Anderson, *The Literature of the Anglo-Saxons* (Oxford: Oxford University Press, 1957; repr. n.p.: Sandpiper Books, 1997), 86–89.

9. See the prefaces to the various volumes of Max Müller, ed., *Rig-Veda-Sanhita: The Sacred Hymns of the Brahmans; Together with the Commentary of Sayanacharya,* 7 vols. (London: W. H. Allen, 1849–74). The text was probably transmitted orally for many centuries before it was written down. See Nilanjana Sikdar Datta, *The Ṛgveda as Oral Literature* (New Delhi: Harman Publishing House, 1999).

10. *Clemens Alexandrinus* 3, ed. Otto Stählin, 2nd ed., ed. Ludwig Früchtel and Ursula Treu (Berlin: Akademie Verlag, 1970), 223–24, 227–29.

11. Smith, *Clement,* 6. Smith, *Secret Gospel,* 143–44. On *Sacra Parallela,* see Maurice Geerard, *Clavis,* 517 no. 8056; M. Geerard and J. Noret et al., *Clavis Patrum Graecorum: Supplementum,* Corpus Christianorum (Turnhout: Brepols, 1998), 464 no. 8056.

12. Smith, *Secret Gospel,* 147–48. Smith, *Clement,* 6, 285–86, 288.

13. Smith, *Secret Gospel,* 146. Smith, *Clement,* 288–89.

14. A summary list of the known depredations is given in G. Heydock, "Mar Saba," *Dizionario degli Istituiti di Perfezione,* ed. Guerrino Pelliccia and Giancarlo Rocca, vol. 5 (Rome: Edizioni Paoline, 1978), 1016–18. See also Smith, *Secret Gospel,* 4. Other earthquakes, famines, plagues, massacres, bankruptcies, and so on are mentioned in John Thomas, Angela Constantinides Hero, and Giles Constable, eds., *Byzantine Monastic Foundation Documents: A Complete Translation of the Founders' Typika and Testaments,* Dumbarton Oaks Studies 35, part 1 (Washington, D.C.: Dumbarton Oaks, 2000), 1311–18, excerpted at http://www.doaks.org/typikaPDF/typo55.pdf (accessed July 2005).

15. See his epic poem *Clarel: A Poem and Pilgrimage in the Holy Land,* ed. Harrison Hayford et al., *The Writings of Herman Melville* 12 (Evanston, Ill.: Northwestern University Press, and Chicago: Newberry Library, 1991), lines 3.81–166 and 12.150–168, pp. 291–93, 310. Melville's journal is much more terse, see *Journals,* ed. Howard C. Horsford and Lynn Horth, *The Writings of Herman Melville* 15 (1989), 84, 430–31.

16. Mark Twain [Samuel L. Clemens], *The Innocents Abroad or The New Pilgrims' Progress* (Hartford, Conn.: American Publishing, 1869), reprinted in The Oxford Mark Twain series, ed. Shelley Fisher Fishkin (New York: Oxford University Press, 1996), chapter 55, pp. 586–603.

17. Emma Raymond Pitman, *Mission Life in Greece and Palestine: Memorials of Mary Briscoe Baldwin, Missionary to Athens and Joppa* (London: Cassell, Petter, Galpin, n.d. [ca. 1882]), 354.

18. Neophytos, *Annals of Palestine* 27, 31, 36, 44–47, 48, 88 (fund drives); 33, 48, 57 n. 2, 64 and 64 n. 1, 80 (raids).

19. B. de Khitrowo, *Itinéraires russes en orient traduits pour la Société de l'Orient latin* 1/1 (Geneva: Jules-Guillaume Fick, 1889), 274. This was written by the Sabaite monk Sophronius to the metropolitan of Moscow in 1547. He was following the old Russian practice of dating from the creation of the world, which was believed to have taken place in 5508 BCE. Thus Sophronius wrote in the year 7055 (= 1547), stating that the year of resettlement was 7048 (= 1540). Smith, *Clement,* 288. Smith, *Secret Gospel,* 146.

20. Smith, *Secret Gospel,* 2 n. 1, and Smith, *Clement,* 288, following Ioannes Phokylides, *Hē Hiera Laura Sava tou Hēgiasmenou: ētoi Historia tēs Lauras apo tēs hidryseos autēs mechri tēs kath' ēmas chronon kai historia pantōn tōn en autē diaprepsantōn patērōn meta anagraphēs tōn ergōn autōn* [The Sacred Laura of the Most Holy Sabas: that is, History of the Laura from its establishment to our time, and history of all the fathers who were eminent in it, with a list of their works; in Greek] (Alexandria: Patriarchikon Typographeion, 1927). See also Thomas, "The Imprint," 82. Yehoshu'a Frenkel, "Mar Saba During the Mamluk and Ottoman Periods," *The Sabaite Heritage,* 111–16, see p. 115.

21. Smith, *Secret Gospel,* 147. Smith, *Clement,* 286–90.

22. Smith, *Clement,* 283.

23. Smith, *Secret Gospel,* 148, italics in original. Compare Smith, *Clement,* 289–90.

24. Morton Smith, "Clement of Alexandria and Secret Mark: The Score at the End of the First Decade," *Harvard Theological Review* 75 (1982): 449–61.

25. Morton Smith, *The Secret Gospel: The Discovery and Interpretation of the Secret Gospel According to Mark* (Clear Lake, Calif.: The Dawn Horse Press, 1982), 155–57.

26. Smith, "Clement . . . The Score," 450–51.

27. Smith, *Secret Gospel* (1982), 149 n. 2, 150 n. 7, 151 n. 8.

28. Birger A. Pearson, *Gnosticism and Christianity in Roman and Coptic Egypt*, Studies in Antiquity and Christianity (New York: T & T Clark, 2004), 43–44.

29. Bart D. Ehrman, "Response to Charles Hedrick's Stalemate," *Journal of Early Christian Studies* 11 (2003): 155–63, see p. 161.

30. Werner Georg Kümmel, "Ein Jahrzehnt Jesusforschung (1965–1975)," *Theologische Rundschau* n.s. 40 (1975): 302, as translated in Wilhelm Schneemelcher, ed., *New Testament Apocrypha* 1: *Gospels and Related Writings,* rev. ed., trans. R. McL. Wilson (Cambridge, U.K.: James Clarke; Louisville, Ky.: Westminster/John Knox, 1991), 108 n. 5.

31. H. Merkel in Schneemelcher, ed. *New Testament Apocrypha* 1: 108 n. 5. Compare Attila Jakab, *Ecclesia alexandrina: Evolution social et institutionelle du christianisme alexandrin (IIᵉ et IIIᵉ siècles),* Christianismes anciens 1 (Bern: Peter Lang, 2001), 131–33, 179–85. A. Jakab, "Une letter 'perdue' de Clément d'Alexandrie? (Morton Smith et l'Evangile secret de Marc)," *Apocrypha* 10 (1999): 7–15.

32. Robert L. Wilken, "Alexandria: A School for Training in Virtue," *Schools of Thought in the Christian Tradition,* ed. Patrick Henry (Philadelphia: Fortress, 1984), 15–30. Rosemary Radford Ruether, *Women and Redemption: A Theological History* (Minneapolis: Fortress, 1998), 59. See also Clemens Scholten, "Die alexandrinische Katechetenschule," *Jahrbuch für Antike und Christentum* 38 (1995): 16–37. Roelof van den Broek, "The Christian 'School' of Alexandria in the Second and Third Centuries," *Studies in Gnosticism and Alexandrian Christianity,* Nag Hammadi and Manichaean Studies 39 (Leiden: Brill, 1996), 197–205.

33. *Clemens Alexandrinus,* 4: *Register* 1, ed. Otto Stählin, 2nd ed., ed. Ursula Treu, Die griechische christlichen Schriftsteller der ersten Jahrhunderte 39 (Berlin: Akademie Verlag, 1980), XVII–XVIII, quotation from p. VIII. Cf. Smith, "Clement . . . The Score," 452.

34. Maurice Geerard, *Clavis Patrum Graecorum* 1: *Patres Antenicaeni,* Corpus Christianorum (Turnhout: Brepols, 1983), 140 no. 1397.

35. Ron Cameron, *The Other Gospels: Non-Canonical Gospel Texts* (Philadelphia: Westminster, 1982), 67–71. John Dominic Crossan, *Four Other Gospels: Shadows on the Contours of Canon* (Minneapolis: Winston Press, 1985), 89–110 citable disc. 111–21. Schneemelcher, ed., *New Testament Apocrypha* 1: 106–9 (but as an "appendix"). Robert J. Miller, ed., *The Complete Gospels: Annotated Scholars Version,* rev. ed. (Sonoma, Calif.: Polebridge Press, 1992), 408–13. J. K. Elliot, ed. *The Apocryphal New Testament: A Collection of Apocryphal Christian Literature in an English Translation* (Oxford: Clarendon Press, 1993), 148–49. Bart Ehrman, *Lost Scriptures: Books That Did Not Make It into the New Testament* (Oxford: Oxford University Press, 2003), 87–89.

36. Smith, *Secret Gospel,* 12, 14.

37. *Adversus Haereses* 1.25.45. Translation from *St Irenaeus of Lyons Against the Heresies* 1, trans. Dominic J. Unger, rev. John J. Dillon, *Ancient Christian Writers* 55 (New York, and Mahwah, N.J.: Paulist Press, 1992), 88–89.

38. Cyril C. Richardson's review of Smith's two books in *Theological Studies* 35 (1974): 571–77, see p. 573.

39. For a bibliography on the varying points of view, see F. Neirynck et al., *The Gospel of Mark: A Cumulative Bibliography 1950–90*, Bibliotheca Ephemeridum Theologicarum Lovaniensium 102 (Leuven: University Press, Peeters, 1992), 644–45.

40. C. M. Tuckett, "Synoptic Problem"; David L. Dungan, "Two-Gospel Hypothesis"; M.-É. Boismard, "Two-Source Hypothesis," *The Anchor Bible Dictionary*, ed. David Noel Freedman et al. (New York: Doubleday, 1992), 6: 263–70, 671–79, 679–82. Joseph A. Fitzmyer, ed., *The Gospel According to Luke (I–IX)*, The Anchor Bible 28 (Garden City, N.Y.: Doubleday, 1981), 63–106. Helmut Koester, *Ancient Christian Gospels: Their History and Development* (London: SCM, and Philadelphia: Trinity Press International, 1990), 275–86. Robert L. Thomas, ed., *Three Views on the Origins of the Synoptic Gospels* (Grand Rapids, Mich.: Kregel, 2002).

41. On this figure see Raymond E. Brown, *The Death of the Messiah: From Gethsemane to the Grave: A Commentary on the Passion Narratives in the Four Gospels*, Anchor Bible Reference Library, 2 vols. (New York: Doubleday, 1994), 1: 294–304, with bibliography, pp. 238–39. For the opinion that the story was "omitted by Matt[hew] and Luke as too harsh for their outlook on the followers of Jesus," see p. 309. A possible interpretation of the story is given in Adela Yarbro Collins, "Mysteries in the Gospel of Mark," *Mighty Minorities: Minorities in Early Christianity—Positions and Strategies: Essays in Honour of Jacob Jervell on His 70th Birthday*, ed. David Hellholm, Halvor Moxnes, and Turid Karlsen Seim (Oslo, Copenhagen, Stockholm: Scandinavian University Press, 1995), 11–23, especially pp. 19–20. For further discussion, see the forthcoming commentary by Adela Yarbro Collins, *Mark: A Commentary on the Gospel According to Mark*, Hermeneia (Minneapolis: Fortress, forthcoming).

42. Koester, *Ancient Christian Gospels*, 295–303, quotation from p. 302, italics in original.

43. Scott G. Brown, "On the Composition History of the Longer ('Secret') Gospel of Mark," *Journal of Biblical Literature* 122 (2003), 110. See also Scott G. Brown, "Bethany Beyond the Jordan: John 1:28 and the Longer Gospel of Mark," *Revue Biblique* 110 (2003): 497–516, popularized in Scott Brown, "The Secret Gospel of Mark: Is It Real? And Does It Identify 'Bethany beyond the Jordan'?" *Biblical Archaeology Review* 31/1 (January/February 2005): 44–49, 60–61. Scott G. Brown's views are now fully available in his book *Mark's Other Gospel*.

44. Smith, *Clement*, 92 and throughout.

45. Hans-Josef Klauck, *Apocryphal Gospels*, trans. Brian McNeil (London: T & T Clark International, 2003), 35.

46. All this is summarized at the beginning of Brown, "On the Composition History," 89–110, see pp. 90–101. See also Marvin Mayer, *Secret Gospels: Essays on Thomas and the Secret Gospel of Mark* (Harrisburg, Pa.: Trinity Press International, 2003), 114–19.

47. Smith, "Clement . . . The Score," 456.

48. Ibid., 452–53.

49. Ibid., 453 n. 7.

50. Ibid., 452.

51. Smith, *Secret Gospel*, 61.

52. Ibid., 71.

53. Smith, *Clement*, 96.

54. Smith, "Clement . . . The Score," 452.

55. Smith, *Clement,* 145.

56. Smith, *Secret Gospel* (1982), 152.

57. The letters of Paul (written in the 50s of the first century?) are usually taken to be the earliest New Testament writings; see Raymond E. Brown, *An Introduction to the New Testament,* Anchor Bible Reference Library (New York: Doubleday, 1997), 428–29.

58. Smith, *Secret Gospel,* 61.

59. Smith, *Clement,* 196.

60. Ibid., 266.

61. Smith, *Secret Gospel,* 18.

62. Smith, *Secret Gospel* (1982), 149.

63. C. H. Dodd, *Historical Tradition in the Fourth Gospel* (Cambridge, U.K.: Cambridge University Press, 1963), 8, quoted in Smith, *Clement,* 96.

64. Brown, *An Introduction,* 107–9.

65. Ibid., 110.

66. Matthew 10:17–20, 26–27, 28:18–20; Mark 9:9–10, 16:20; Luke 1:1–2, 12:11–12, 24:8, 44–48; John 2:17, 16:12–15; Acts 1:8.

67. Jan Hendrik Walgrave, *Unfolding Revelation: The Nature of Doctrinal Development, Theological Resources* (Philadelphia: Westminster, 1972). Jaroslav Pelikan, *The Christian Tradition: A History of the Development of Doctrine 5: Christian Doctrine and Modern Culture (Since 1700)* (Chicago: University of Chicago Press, 1989), 261–64, 273–81, 322–23.

68. Albert Schweitzer, *The Quest of the Historical Jesus,* 1st complete ed., ed. John Bowden (London: SCM Press, 2000). The original German title was a bit less catchy: *Von Reimarus zu Wrede: eine Geschichte der Leben-Jesu-Forschung* (Tübingen: Mohr [P. Siebeck], 1906). For a more recent perspective see Brown, *An Introduction,* 817–30.

69. Smith, "Clement . . . The Score," 455.

70. I.e., "the devout." Here Smith named two Roman Catholic scholars (Fitzmyer and Skehan) who had written very negative reviews of his books.

71. Smith, "Clement . . . The Score," 455. For concise definitions of "form criticism" and other technical terms from biblical studies, see Richard N. Soulen and R. Kendall Soulen, *Handbook of Biblical Criticism,* 3rd expanded ed. (Louisville, Ky.: Westminster John Knox, 2001). For more extended treatments see David Noel Freedman et al., eds., *The Anchor Bible Dictionary,* 6 vols. (New York: Doubleday, 1992).

72. Smith, "Clement . . . The Score," 456–57.

73. Morton Smith, *Jesus the Magician* (San Francisco: Harper & Row, 1978, 1981); repr. (with different pagination and no endnotes), with introduction by Russell Shorto (Berkeley, Calif.: Seastone/Ulysses Press, 1998). The book barely mentions the Secret Gospel, but the paperback edition of 1981 makes a visual link with a picture of the raising of Lazarus on the cover (another such image between pp. 61 and 62).

74. Marvin Meyer, *Secret Gospels: Essays on Thomas and the Secret Gospel of Mark* (Harrisburg, Pa.: Trinity Press International, 2003), 119, 115, 120.

75. Ibid., 147.

76. Ibid., 149–67.

77. Theodore W. Jennings, *The Man Jesus Loved: Homoerotic Narratives from the New Testament* (Cleveland: Pilgrim Press, 2003), 6–7, 8.

78. Ibid., 124.

79. Ibid., 125.

80. Brown, *Mark's Other Gospel,* 221, 225, 227, 228.

81. Ibid., 28–48.

82. Ibid., 49–59, quotation from p. 53.

83. Ehrman, "Response," 155.

84. Smith, "Clement . . . The Score," 455.

85. Shawn Eyer, "The Strange Case of the Secret Gospel According to Mark: How Morton Smith's Discovery of a Lost Letter by Clement of Alexandria Scandalized Biblical Scholarship," *Alexandria: The Journal of the Western Cosmological Traditions* 3 (1995): 103–19 (quotation from p. 119), which in June 2004 was also available at www.spiritre storation.org/Church/All%20About%20Church%20Articles/The-Strange-Case-of-the-Secret-Gospel-of-Mark.htm.

86. Klauck, *Apocryphal Gospels,* 211–20. Roland H. Worth, Jr., *Alternative Lives of Jesus: Noncanonical Accounts Through the Early Middle Ages* (Jefferson, N.C.: McFarland, 2003), 49–50. See also Edmondo Lupieri, *The Mandaeans: The Last Gnostics,* trans. Charles Hindley (Grand Rapids, Mich.: Eerdmans, 2002), 240–53.

87. See below; also "The Docetic Jesus: Some Interconnections Between Marcionism, Manichaeism and Mandaeism," in Iain Gardner, *Coptic Theological Papyri* II: *Edition, Commentary, Translation,* Mitteilungen aus der Papyrussammlung der Österreichischen Nationalbibliothek (Papyrus Erzherzog Rainer) n.s. 21 (Vienna: Brüder Hollinek, 1988), Textband pp. 57–85.

88. Neal Robinson, *Christ in Islam and Christianity: The Representation of Jesus in the Qur'ān and the Classical Muslim Commentaries* (London: Macmillan, 1991). Brannon M. Wheeler, ed., *Prophets in the Quran: An Introduction to the Quran and Muslim Exegesis* (London: Continuum, 2002), 297–320. Annemarie Schimmel, *Jesus und Maria in der Islamischen Mystik* (Munich: Kösel, 1996). Neal Robinson, "Jesus," in *Encyclopedia of the Qur'ān,* ed. Jane Dammen McAuliffe (Leiden: Brill, 2003), 3: 7–20.

89. Roman Catholic Church, Vatican Council II, Dogmatic Constitution on Divine Revelation *(Dei verbum)* 11, trans. Norman P. Tanner, ed., *Decrees of the Ecumenical Councils* 2: *Trent to Vatican II* (London: Sheed & Ward; Washington, D.C.: Georgetown University Press, 1990), 975.

90. Ibid., 975–76. For comparable statements by other Christian denominations, see the "Comparative Creedal Syndogmaticon" Index 8.11–8.15 in Jaroslav Pelikan, *Creeds & Confessions of Faith in the Christian Tradition* (New Haven, Conn.: Yale University Press, 2003), 1: 920–21, 2: 960–61, 3: 974–75, and Pelikan, *Credo: Historical and Theological Guide to Creeds and Confessions of Faith in the Christian Tradition* (New Haven, Conn.: Yale University Press, 2003), 558–60.

91. Bruce M. Metzger, *The Canon of the New Testament: Its Origin, Development, and Significance* (Oxford: Clarendon Press, 1987), especially pp. 271–75. For how it got that way and whether it can be opened again, see especially James A. Sanders, "The Issue of Closure in the Canonical Process"; Everett Ferguson, "Factors Leading to the Selection and Closure of the New Testament Canon"; Robert W. Funk, "The Once and Future New Testament," and other essays in *The Canon Debate,* ed. Lee Martin McDonald and James A. Sanders (Peabody, Mass.: Hendrickson, 2002), 252–63, 295–320, 541–57.

92. Luke 1:1–4, John 20:30, 21:25.

93. This religion is particularly difficult to research because both the leader and his organizations change names frequently. But see the following: Bob Larson, *Larson's New Book of Cults,* rev. ed. (Wheaton, Ill.: Tyndale House, 1989), 196–99 (includes a bibliography); Texe W. Marrs, *New Age Cults and Religions,* 2nd ed. (Austin, Tex.: Living Truth Publishers, 1996), 195–97, 217; Elisabeth Arweck and Peter B. Clarke, *New Religious Movements in Western Europe: An Annotated Bibliography, Bibliographies and Indexes in Religious Studies* 41 (Westport, Conn.: Greenwood Press, 1997), p. 172 no. 939, p. 216 no. 1205; Benjamin Beit-Hallahmi, *The Illustrated Encyclopedia of Active New Religions, Sects, and Cults,* rev. ed. (New York: Rosen Publishing Group, 1998), 146; George D. Chryssides, *Historical Dictionary of New Religious Movements, Historical Dictionaries of Religions, Philosophies, and Movements* 42 (Lanham, Md.: Scarecrow Press, 2001), 46–48.

94. For full bibliographical information, see note 25 of this chapter. Except for the Foreword (pp. ix–xi), Preface (p. xii), Postscript (pp. 149–57), and advertising (pp. 158–62), the pagination is the same as in the 1973 Harper edition. See the citation in Smith, "Clement . . . The Score," 449 n. 1.

95. Smith, *Secret Gospel* (1982), 158.

96. The term was introduced in Alan Dundes and Carl R. Pagter, *Urban Folklore from the Paperwork Empire,* Publications of the American Folklore Society: Memoir Series 62 (Austin, Tex.: American Folklore Society, 1975), repr. as *Work Hard and You Shall Be Rewarded: Urban Folklore from the Paperwork Empire* (Bloomington: Indiana University Press, 1978), 198. This is their definition: "A double entendre is, of course, a word or expression with two meanings, one of which is usually risqué. By extended double entendre, we refer to whole stories rather than single words or expressions." See also Dundes and Pagter, *When You're Up To Your Ass in Alligators . . . : More Urban Folklore from the Paperwork Empire* (Detroit, Mich.: Wayne State University Press, 1987), 215–16.

97. Charles W. Hedrick, "The Secret Gospel of Mark: Stalemate in the Academy," *Journal of Early Christian Studies* 11 (2003): 133–45, see p. 145.

98. Hedrick, "The Secret Gospel," 135–36.

99. Ibid., 140.

100. Ibid., 142–43.

101. Ibid., 143.

102. Ibid., 144.

103. Guy G. Stroumsa, "Comments on Charles Hedrick's Article: A Testimony," *Journal of Early Christian Studies* 11 (2003): 147–53, see p. 148.

104. Ibid., 148.

105. Ibid., 151–52, 153. Cf. Smith, *Secret Gospel,* 8, 14.

106. Bart D. Ehrman, "Response to Charles Hedrick's Stalemate," *Journal of Early Christian Studies* 11 (2003): 155–63, see p. 159.

107. Ibid., 159–60, italics in original.

108. Stroumsa, "Comments," 147–48. Hedrick, "The Secret Gospel," 140. The photographs were published in Charles W. Hedrick, "Secret Mark: New Photographs, New Witnesses," *The Fourth R* 13.5 (2000): 3–11, 141–46 [I have not seen this publication], and in Brown, "The Secret Gospel," 46–47.

109. Hedrick, "The Secret Gospel," 136.

110. Ehrman, "Response," 160–61, following Eric Osborn, "Clement of Alexandria: A Review of Research, 1958–1982," *Second Century* 3 (1983): 223–25, citing p. 222 (erroneously: 224 is meant).

111. Ehrman, "Response," 161 (italics in original), following A. H. Criddle, "On the Mar Saba Letter Attributed to Clement of Alexandria," *Journal of Early Christian Studies* 3 (1995): 215–20.

112. Ehrman, "Response," 161, following Charles Murgia, "Secret Mark: Real or Fake?" in *Longer Mark: Forgery, Interpolation, or Old Tradition,* ed. Reginald Fuller (Berkeley, Calif.: Center for Hermeneutical Studies, 1976), 35–40.

113. Ehrman, "Response," 162.

114. Ibid. Smith, *Secret Gospel,* 23–25, 65–67. Smith, "Clement . . . The Score," 450.

115. Smith, *Secret Gospel,* v. See Ehrman, "Response," 162.

116. Donald Harman Akenson, *Saint Saul: A Skeleton Key to the Historical Jesus* (Oxford: Oxford University Press, 2000), 87–88, italics in original.

117. After I had finished the manuscript of this book, I was generously offered a prepublication copy of Stephen C. Carlson, *The Gospel Hoax: Morton Smith's Invention of Secret Mark* (Waco, Tex.: Baylor University Press, 2005), for which I gratefully thank the author. Carlson, who is evidently an attorney by profession, begins by arguing from forensic methods that the handwriting of the Mar Saba document belongs to Morton Smith, then proceeds to identify anachronisms and jokes in the text that also point to Smith as the author. My own views on the application of police science to the authentication of handwriting in historical manuscripts are described in my dissertation, "The Autograph Manuscripts of Francesco Cavalli, (1602–1676)" (Ph.D. dissertation, Princeton University, 1980), 47–80. I have not followed Carlson's distinctions between "hoax" and "forgery" (his pp. xii, 15–16, 97) mainly because my book was already written, but also because the difference hinges (as it would in a court of law) on the falsifier's intent or motive. While I don't deny the motives that Carlson ascribes to Smith (pp. 78–86), I think there were more compelling motivations, which I identify in Chapter 11.

118. The story is fully documented at www.the-shipman-inquiry.org.uk and www .guardian.co.uk/shipman (both accessed July 2005). No doubt somebody somewhere is writing a book about this case.

119. Anthony Grafton, *Forgers and Critics: Creativity and Duplicity in Western Scholarship* (Princeton, N.J.: Princeton University Press, 1990), 125.

120. Ibid., 126.

121. A. Q. Morton, *Literary Detection: How to Prove Authorship and Fraud in Literature and Documents* (n.p., United Kingdom: Bowker; [New York:] Charles Scribner's Sons, 1978).

122. An introduction for armchair profilers, but a disturbing read: Katherine Ramsland, *The Criminal Mind: A Writer's Guide to Forensic Psychology* (Cincinnati, Ohio: Writer's Digest, 2002). An actual police manual is John E. Douglas et al., *Crime Classification Manual: A Standard System for Investigating and Classifying Violent Crimes* (San Francisco: Jossey-Bass, 1992).

123. Harold Love, *Attributing Authorship: An Introduction* (Cambridge, U.K.: Cambridge University Press, 2002), 87.

124. Jill M. Farringdon et al., *Analysing for Authorship: A Guide to the Cusum Technique* (Cardiff: University of Wales Press, 1996), 81.

125. "Cidade" is Portuguese for "city," and in fact the document ends with Jesus saying "you are in The City of God, and ye are The City." The word "calentura" would mean a high fever, and the English-looking *-ixness* might be derived from "sickness," a topic of central importance to Christian Science.

126. The *Cidade* "is said to be recorded in a (non-existent) Latin document in the British Museum, and which is, in fact, concocted by the forger from translations of ancient sources and his own imagination," according to British Museum, *An Exhibition of Forgeries and Deceptive Copies Held in the Department of Prints and Drawings* ([London:] British Museum, 1961), 24, and similarly Gerald Bonner, "Literary Forgery," *Encyclopaedia Britannica* (Chicago: William Benton, 1965), 14: 104–6, see p. 105. The text can be found conveniently at www.christianscience.org/Jesus2John.html. The web site makes reference to the article "Recently Discovered Sayings of Jesus," *The Christian Science Journal* 21 (1903–4), 649–55; however, this article is about the Greek fragments of the Gospel of Thomas discovered at Oxyrhynchus and does not mention the *Cidade Calenixness*. On the much-translated Gospel of Thomas see *The Nag Hammadi Library in English*, 4th ed., ed. James M. Robinson and Richard Smith (Leiden: Brill, 1996), 124–38; J. K. Elliott, *The Apocryphal New Testament* (Oxford: Clarendon Press, 1993), 123–47; Marvin Meyer, *The Gospel of Thomas: The Hidden Sayings of Jesus* (San Francisco: Harper, 1992); Schneemelcher, ed., *New Testament Apocrypha* 1: 110–33; Bentley Layton, *The Gnostic Scriptures: A New Translation*, The Anchor Bible Reference Library (New York: Doubleday, 1987), 376–99.

127. Dan Brown, *The Da Vinci Code: A Novel* (New York: Doubleday, 2003). For the book's misrepresentations of early Christian history, see Bart D. Ehrman, *Truth and Fiction in* The Da Vinci Code: *A Historian Reveals What We Really Know About Jesus, Mary Magdalene, and Constantine* (Oxford: Oxford University Press, 2004). The Priory of Sion is debunked at priory-of-sion.com.

128. See Lotte Motz, *The Faces of the Goddess* (New York: Oxford University Press, 1997). On Mary Magdalene, see Victor Saxer, *Le culte de Marie Madeleine en occident des origines à la fin du moyen âge*, Cahiers d'Archéologie et d'Histoire 3 (Auxerre: Société des Fouilles Archéologiques and Paris: Clavreuil, 1959); Saxer, *Le Dossier vézelien de Marie Madeleine: Invention et translation des reliques en 1265–1267*, Subsidia Hagiographica 57 (Brussells: Société des Bollandistes, 1975); Renate Schmid, *Maria Magdalena in gnostischen Schriften*, Material-Edition 29 (Munich: Arbeitsgemeinschaft für Religions- und Weltanschauungen, 1990); Eva M. Synek, " 'Die andere Maria': Zum Bild der Maria von Magdala in den östlichen Kirchentraditionen," *Oriens Christianus* 79 (1995): 181–96; Jane Schaberg, *The Resurrection of Mary Magdalene: Legends, Apocrypha, and the Christian Testament* (New York: Continuum, 2002); Holly Hearon, *The Mary Magdalene Tradition: Witness and Counter-Witness in Early Christian Communities* (Collegeville, Minn.: Liturgical Press, 2004).

129. The term arose in the context of form criticism, where it applied to textual genres, not to individual texts. From that perspective it is correct to say "The Sitz im Leben must be carefully distinguished from the *historical* occasion that may have led to the production of any particular text" (John Barton, "Form Criticism: Old Testament," *Anchor*

Bible Dictionary 2: 838–41). But it has since begun to be applied more broadly, see *Ze hove und an der strâzen: Die deutsche Literatur des Mittelalters und ihr "Sitz im Leben": Festschrift für Volker Schupp zum 65. Geburtstag,* ed. Anna Keck and Theodor Nolte (Stuttgart: S. Hirzel, 1999), XI–XIV; Alan James Beagley, *The "Sitz im Leben" of the Apocalypse with Particular Reference to the Role of the Church's Enemies* (Berlin: Walter de Gruyter, 1987).

130. I am following Raymond E. Brown, *The Community of the Beloved Disciple* (New York: Paulist Press, 1979). However, an alternative reconstruction has been put forward in Allen Dwight Callahan, *A Love Supreme: A History of the Johannine Tradition* (Minneapolis: Augsburg, 2005).

131. David E. Aune, *Word Biblical Commentary 52: Revelation 1–5* (Dallas, Tex.: Word Books, 1997), xlvii–lxx.

132. Acts of John 93, 101. Wilhelm Schneemelcher, ed., *New Testament Apocrypha 2: Writings Related to the Apostles, Apocalypses and Related Subjects,* trans. R. McL. Wilson (Cambridge, U.K.: James Clarke; Louisville, Ky.: Westminster/John Knox, 1992), 181, 185–86. Elliott, *Apocryphal New Testament,* 318, 321.

133. Translations in *The Nag Hammadi Library,* 104–23. Marvin Meyer, *The Gnostic Gospels of Jesus: The Definitive Collection of Mystical Gospels and Secret Books About Jesus of Nazareth* (San Francisco: Harper San Francisco, 2005), 143–83.

134. Andrew Welburn, *Mani, the Angel and the Column of Glory: An Anthology of Manichaean Texts* (Edinburgh: Floris Books, 1998), 259, with a translation of the Secret Book of John on pp. 260–76.

135. Hedrick, "The Secret Gospel," 142.

136. Ehrman, "Response," 157.

137. Examples from a variety of cultures: Robert I. Levy, *Tahitians: Mind and Experience in the Society Islands* (Chicago: University of Chicago Press, 1973); Alan P. Bell and Martin W. Weinberg, *Homosexualities: A Study of Diversity Among Men and Women* (New York: Simon and Schuster, 1978); Walter Williams, *The Spirit and the Flesh: Sexual Diversity in American Indian Culture* (Boston: Beacon, 1986); David F. Greenberg, *Constructions of Homosexuality* (Chicago: University of Chicago Press, 1988); Gilbert H. Herdt and Robert J. Stoller, *Intimate Communications: Erotics and the Study of a Culture* (New York: Columbia University Press, 1990); Gilbert Herdt, *Same Sex, Different Cultures: Gays and Lesbians Across Cultures* (Boulder, Colo.: Westview Press, 1997); Craig A. Williams, *Roman Homosexuality: Ideologies of Masculinity in Classical Antiquity* (New York: Oxford University Press, 1999); David M. Halperin, *How to Do the History of Homosexuality* (Chicago: University of Chicago Press, 2002), 106–37.

138. Hedrick, "The Secret Gospel," 143.

139. All quotations from Smith, *Secret Gospel,* 14–17.

140. The Greek word for "things not to be uttered," *aporrhēta* (ἀπόῤῥητα), is one we will need toward the end of this book.

141. Smith, *Clement,* 38.

142. Everett Procter, *Christian Controversy in Alexandria: Clement's Polemic Against the Basilideans and Valentinians,* American University Studies series 7: Theology and Religion 172 (New York: Peter Lang, 1995), 99–103.

Chapter 3. The Secret Gospel and the Origins of Christian Liturgy

Epigraph. Smith, *Secret Gospel,* 72–73, 76, 96.

1. For an example of ritual writing from the Christian tradition, see the Benedictine Rule 58: 17–23, as translated in *RB 1980,* 269.

2. Lawrence A. Hoffman, *Beyond the Text: A Holistic Approach to Liturgy* (Bloomington: Indiana University Press, 1987).

3. D. H. Tripp, "The Letter of Pliny," *The Study of Liturgy,* rev. ed., ed. Cheslyn Jones et al. (London: SPCK, and New York: Oxford University Press, 1992), 80–81.

4. The term was invented in Eric Hobsbawm and Terence Ranger, eds., *The Invention of Tradition* (Cambridge, U.K.: Cambridge University Press 1983).

5. Ronald L. Grimes, *Ritual Criticism: Case Studies in Its Practice, Essays on Its Theory* (Columbia: University of South Carolina Press, 1990).

6. Paul F. Bradshaw, "Ancient Church Orders: A Continuing Enigma," *Fountain of Life: In Memory of Niels K. Rasmussen, O.P.* (Washington, D.C.: Pastoral Press, 1991), 3–22.

7. Edward Yarnold, *The Awe-Inspiring Rites of Initiation: The Origins of the R.C.I.A.* [Rite of Christian Initiation of Adults], 2nd ed., (Collegeville, Minn.: Liturgical Press, 1994).

8. Milton McC. Gatch, "Old English Literature and the Liturgy: Problems and Potential," *Anglo-Saxon England* 6 (Cambridge University Press, 1977), 237–47, quotation from p. 238.

9. For a stab I once took along these lines see Peter Jeffery, *Re-Envisioning Past Musical Cultures: Ethnomusicology in the Study of Gregorian Chant* (Chicago: University of Chicago Press, 1992).

10. I deal with a current controversy of this sort in *Translating Tradition: A Chant Historian Reads* Liturgiam Authenticam (Collegeville, Minn.: Liturgical Press, 2005).

11. Cohen, "In Memoriam," (1994) 6, 8; (1996) 283, 285.

12. Smith, *Clement,* 163, 193.

13. Recent studies of the early initiation liturgy include Enrico Mazza, *Mystagogy: A Theology of Liturgy in the Patristic Age,* trans. Matthew J. O'Connell (New York: Pueblo Publishing, 1989); Yarnold, *Awe-Inspiring Rites;* William Harmless, *Augustine and the Catechumenate* (Collegeville, Minn.: Liturgical Press, 1995); Maxwell E. Johnson, *The Rites of Christian Initiation: Their Evolution and Interpretation* (Collegeville, Minn.: Liturgical Press, 1999); E. C. Whitaker, *Documents of the Baptismal Liturgy,* 3rd ed., rev. and expanded by Maxwell E. Johnson (Collegeville, Minn.: Liturgical Press, 2003).

14. See, for example, Gabriele Winkler, *Das armenische Initiationsrituale: Entwicklungsgeschichte und liturgievergleichende Untersuchung der Quellen des 3. bis 10. Jahrhunderts,* Orientalia Christiana Analecta 217 (Rome: Pont. Institutum Studiorum Orientalium, 1982), 95–96, 132–56, 166–67, 170–75.

15. The first ecumenical council of Nicea (325 CE) marks the beginning of the process by which the Roman Empire became officially Christian. Christian worship changed dramatically at that point (at least in some respects) because it went from being a secret, persecuted activity to a public, imperial ceremony. Documentation of liturgical practices also improves dramatically in the fourth century. Thus the council of Nicea is an impor-

tant watershed in Christian liturgical history, dividing it into pre-Nicene and post-Nicene periods.

16. John Evangelist Walsh, *Unraveling Piltdown: The Science Fraud of the Century and Its Solution* (New York: Random House, 1996), 6–7, 9, 31, 77, 122–23. Winifred McCulloch, *Teilhard de Chardin and the Piltdown Hoax*, Teilhard Studies 33 (Spring 1996). Some scientists believed at the time that the brain would have been the first structure to evolve to a fully human state, producing a creature who had the intelligence to speak but not the anatomical equipment. But it is now beyond question that, even from the earliest times, the human capacity for speech has always outpaced the human capacity for thought.

17. I happen to be quoting from the American edition (1928 revision) that would have been most familiar to Morton Smith, but the English and most other national editions of the period would be the same: *The Book of Common Prayer and Administration of the Sacraments and Other Rites and Ceremonies of the Church, According to the Use of the Protestant Episcopal Church in the United States of America, Together with The Psalter or Psalms of David* (New York: The Church Pension Fund, 1945), 161–62.

18. Charles Wheatly, *A Rational Illustration of the Book of Common Prayer of the Church of England* (London: Thomas Tegg, 1842), 222–23. John Henry Blunt, ed., *The Annotated Book of Common Prayer, Being an Historical, Ritual, and Theological Commentary on the Devotional System of the Church of England* (New York: E. P. Dutton, 1916), 287–88. Massey Hamilton Shepherd, Jr., *The Oxford American Prayer Book Commentary* (New York: Oxford University Press, 1955), 161–62.

19. Robert N. Swanson, "Medieval English Liturgy: What's the Use?" *Studia Liturgica* 29 (1999): 159–90.

20. Robert Amiet, *La veillée pascale dans l'église latine* 1: *Le rite romain, Histoire et liturgie*, Liturgie 11 (Paris: Cerf, 1999). Actually, from some point in the early Middle Ages the vigil was actually celebrated in the daytime on Saturday morning. It was restored to its original evening placement in 1951, the first major event in the liturgical renewal that transformed the Catholic and most Protestant worship traditions in the last decades of the twentieth century.

21. Before the liturgical renewal movement that began in the 1970s, the official Prayer Books used in most branches of the Anglican Communion did not contain any sort of Paschal Vigil for the night of Holy Saturday, though the American edition of 1928 included an additional set of collect and readings for churches that celebrated an early morning Easter Eucharist preceding the regular one. Neither was the white robe mentioned. One does, however, find fully developed Easter vigils based on the Roman Missal in unofficial publications used in "high-church" congregations, such as *The People's Anglican Missal in the American Edition, Containing the Liturgy from the Book of Common Prayer According to the Use of the Church in the United States of America, Together with Other Devotions and with Liturgical and Ceremonial Notes* (Mount Sinai, N.Y.: The Frank Gavin Liturgical Foundation, 1944), A182–A199. See also K. D. Mackenzie, "Anglican Adaptations of Some Latin Rites and Ceremonies," *Liturgy and Worship: A Companion to the Prayer Books of the Anglican Communion,* ed. W. K. Lowther Clarke and Charles Harris (London: Society for Promoting Christian Knowledge, 1932; repr. 1943), 729–48, especially pp. 738–40. The Paschal Vigil was officially restored

during the reforms of the 1970s; see Marion J. Hatchett, *Commentary on the American Prayer Book* (n.p.: Seabury Press, 1980), 238–50.

22. The white robes were also worn for a week in medieval Coptic baptism; see Reginald Maxwell Woolley, *Coptic Offices* (London: Society for Promoting Christian Knowledge, 1930), 49. Thus it is possible that this practice was known in Alexandria centuries earlier.

23. John Milton, *Animadversions Upon the Remonstrants Defence, against Smectymnuus* (London: Thomas Underhill, 1641), as printed in *Complete Prose Works of John Milton* 1: *1624–1642,* ed. Don M. Wolfe et al. (New Haven, Conn.: Yale University Press, 1953), 683, 686, 688, 730.

24. As regards the rites of initiation, see, for example the articles "Holy Baptism" and "Confirmation" in *Liturgy and Worship,* 410–28, 443–57; J. W. Tyrer, "Baptismal Offices," *The Prayer Book Dictionary,* ed. George Harford, Morely Stevenson, and J. W. Tyrer (London: Waverley Book, n.d. [1918]), 84–92, especially pp. 90–91.

25. Gregory Dix, *The Shape of the Liturgy,* 2nd ed. (London: Dacre Press, Adam & Charles Black, 1945), xi–xii. There have been numerous reprints.

26. The text survives in multiple recensions in several languages; the whole transmission is best presented in Paul F. Bradshaw, Maxwell E. Johnson, and L. Edward Phillips, *The Apostolic Tradition: A Commentary,* ed. Harold W. Attridge, Hermeneia (Minneapolis: Fortress, 2002).

27. There is growing uncertainty, however, about both the identity of Hippolytus and the origins and textual history of *The Apostolic Tradition.* John Baldovin, "Hippolytus and the *Apostolic Tradition:* Recent Research and Commentary," *Theological Studies* 64 (2003): 520–42. Christoph Markschies, "Neue Forschungen zur sogenannten 'Traditio Apostolica,'" and Paul F. Bradshaw, "The Problems of a New Edition of the *Apostolic Tradition,*" in *Comparative Liturgy Fifty Years After Anton Baumstark (1872–1948): Acts of the International Congress, Rome, 25–29 September 1998,* ed. Robert F. Taft and Gabriele Winkler, Orientalia Christiana Analecta 265 (Rome: Pontificio Istituto Orientale, 2001), 583–98, 613–22.

28. Dix, *Shape,* 157. As one can see from the cross-references on pp. 758 and 762, *The Apostolic Tradition* is treated throughout as an early source of the Roman practice.

29. Massey H. Shepherd, *The Paschal Liturgy and the Apocalypse,* Ecumenical Studies in Worship 6 (London: Lutterworth Press, 1960), 79.

30. Shepherd, *Paschal Liturgy,* 79, 77, 83.

31. Gregory Dix, ed., *The Treatise on the Apostolic Tradition of St Hippolytus of Rome, Bishop and Martyr* (1933), reissued with corrections, preface, and bibliography by Henry Chadwick (London: The Alban Press; Ridgefield, Conn.: Morehouse Publishing, 1992).

32. Dix, *Apostolic Tradition,* 31–33. Compare Bradshaw et al., *Apostolic Tradition,* 104–7, 110–12.

33. Dix, *Apostolic Tradition,* 28. Bradshaw et al., *Apostolic Tradition,* 96–98.

34. Dix, *Shape,* 337–41, 348–57.

35. Ibid., 338–40.

36. Bradshaw et al., *Apostolic Tradition,* 118–19.

37. Yarnold, *Awe-Inspiring,* 31–33. Mazza, *Mystagogy,* 57–58, 129–31. Harmless,

Augustine, 311–14. Whitaker, *Documents,* rev. Johnson, 211, 251. Winkler, *Das armenische Initiationsrituale* 166; on the date of the Acts of John see p. 96.

38. For example, in the Armenian rite, Charles Renoux, *Initiation chrétienne* 1. *Rituels arméniens du baptême,* Sources liturgiques 1 (Paris: Cerf, 1997), 156–57. For the Roman rite before it was reformed after Vatican II, see *Rituale Romanum* Titulus II, Caput 1, paragraph 64 and II.2.24; translated, for example, in Philip T. Weller, *The Roman Ritual: Complete Edition* (Milwaukee: Bruce, 1964), 42, 60.

39. Shepherd, *Paschal Liturgy,* 89–91. For another early example of white clothing in the context of a "sealing" ceremony, see 2 Esdras (= 4 Esdras) 2:38–40, 45.

40. Dix, *Shape,* 23, where Revelation 7:14 is also cited, cf. p. 339.

41. Oscar Cullmann, *Baptism in the New Testament,* trans. J. K. S. Reid, Studies in Biblical Theology 1 (Chicago: Alec R. Allenson, 1950), 9, 71–80, especially p. 75.

42. See Avery Dulles, *Models of Revelation* (Garden City, N.Y.: Doubleday, 1983; repr. Maryknoll, N.Y.: Orbis, 1992), 45, 212, 223.

43. Roman Catholic Church, Council of Trent, Sessio 7, 3. Mart. 1547, see Tanner, *Decrees* 2: 684.

44. L. Duchesne, *Christian Worship: Its Origin and Evolution: A Study of the Latin Liturgy Up to the Time of Charlemagne,* 5th ed., trans. M. L. McClure (London: Society for Promoting Christian Knowledge, 1927), 331–38, especially p. 333.

45. Paul Bradshaw, *The Search for the Origins of Christian Worship: Sources and Methods for the Study of Early Liturgy,* 2nd ed. (Oxford: Oxford University Press, 2002), 144–70. See also Bryan D. Spinks, "Baptismal Patterns in Early Syria: Another Reading," *Studia Liturgica Diversa: Essays in Honor of Paul F. Bradshaw,* ed. Maxwell E. Johnson and L. Edward Phillips, Studies in Church Music and Liturgy (Portland, Ore.: Pastoral Press, 2004), 45–52; Paul F. Bradshaw, "Liturgy in the Absence of Hippolytus," *Yale Institute of Sacred Music Colloquium: Music, Worship, Arts* 1 (2004): 1–10.

46. Willy Rordorf, "The Bible in the Teaching and the Liturgy of Early Christian Communities," *The Bible in Greek Christian Antiquity,* ed. and trans. Paul M. Blowers, The Bible Through the Ages 1 (Notre Dame, Ind.: University of Notre Dame Press, 1997), 69–102, quotation from p. 87. The first scholar to document this extensively was André Benoît, *Le Baptême chrétien au second siècle: La théologie des Pères,* Études d'histoire et de philosophie religieuses de l'Université de Strasbourg 43 (Paris: Presses Universitaires de France, 1953), 227–30; see also the pages listed under "Paulinisme" in the index, p. 241. See now André Benoît and Charles Munier, *Le Baptême dans l'Eglise ancienne (Ier– IIIe siècles),* Traditio Christiana 9 (Bern: Peter Lang, 1994).

47. Maxwell E. Johnson, "Tertullian's '*Diem baptismo sollemniorem*' Revisited: A Tentative Hypothesis on Baptism at Pentecost," *Studia Liturgica Diversa: Essays in Honor of Paul F. Bradshaw,* ed. Maxwell E. Johnson and L. Edward Phillips, Studies in Church Music and Liturgy (Portland, Ore.: Pastoral Press, 2004), 31–44.

48. Johnson, *Rites,* 168, 382–83. For Syrian examples see "Epiphany" in the index to Thomas M. Finn, *Early Christian Baptism and the Catechumenate: West and East Syria,* Message of the Fathers of the Church 5 (Collegeville, Minn.: Liturgical Press, 1992), 214. According to Finn (p. 9), "Origen, who appears to have retrieved it from the Gnostics, is the first Church Father to bring Paul's doctrine of symbolic participation in the death and resurrection of Christ (see Rom 6:1–11) to bear on baptism." It was only in the West that

Epiphany was associated with the arrival of the Magi. On Jesus' baptism as a liturgical model, contrasted with the Passover/Easter model, see Johnson, *Rites,* 9–19, 31, 47–50, 53, 56–59, 107–9, 119, 190–91.

49. Gabriele Winkler, "Die Licht-Erscheinung bei der Taufe Jesu und der Ursprung des Epiphaniefestes: Eine Untersuchung griechischer, syrischer, armenischer und lateinischer Quellen," *Oriens Christianus* 78 (1994): 177–229. Merja Merras, *The Origins of the Celebration of the Christian Feast of Epiphany: An Ideological, Cultural, and Historical Study,* University of Joensuu Publications in the Humanities 16 (Joensuu, Finland: Joensuu University Press, 1995), reviewed by Gabriele Winkler in *Oriens Christianus* 81 (1997): 271–75, *Orientalia Christiana Periodica* 63 (1997): 226–30, *Theologische Quartalschrift* 177 (1997): 59–60.

50. *Protrepticus* 9, trans. G. W. Butterworth, Loeb Classical Library 92 (Cambridge: Harvard University Press, 1919; repr. 1982), 182–95. *Paedagogus* 1.6, translated in *The Ante-Nicene Fathers,* ed. Alexander Roberts et al., American ed. (New York: Christian Literature, 1893; many reprints), 2: 215–22; see also the quotations in Benoît and Munier, *Le Baptême,* 98–119.

51. For example Maxwell E. Johnson, *The Prayers of Sarapion of Thmuis: A Literary, Liturgical, and Theological Analysis,* Orientalia Christiana Analecta 249 (Rome: Pontificio Istituto Orientale, 1995), 54–59; Johnson, *Rites,* 119; Maxwell E. Johnson, *Liturgy in Early Christian Egypt,* Alcuin/GROW Joint Liturgical Studies 33 (Cambridge, U.K.: Grove Books, 1995), 7–16; A. Salles, ed., *Trois antiques rituels du baptême,* Sources Chrétiennes 59 (Paris: Cerf, 1958), 16–17; Woolley, *Coptic Offices,* 20–58; Heinrich Denzinger, *Ritus Orientalium Coptorum, Syrorum et Armenorum in Administrandis Sacramentis, ex Assemanis, Renaudotio, Trombellio aliisque fontibus authenticis collectos,* 2 vols. (Würzburg: Stähelin, 1863–64), 1: 192–248.

52. The Ethiopian blessing published in Klaus Gamber, *Liturgische Texte aus der Kirche Äthiopiens,* Studia Patristica et Liturgica, Beiheft 13 (Regensburg: Pustet 1984), 53–69, does utilize Exodus themes (pp. 57, 66) but also themes from the first psalm (p. 56), light and fire and creation (pp. 57, 61, 64), the Jordan and the Holy Spirit (p. 65), as well as healing and delivery from evil. The Byzantine rite blessing published in Isabel Florence Hapgood, ed., *Service Book of the Holy Orthodox-Catholic Apostolic Church,* 4th ed. (Brooklyn: Syrian Antiochian Orthodox Archdiocese of New York and All North America, 1965), 189–97, emphasizes John the Baptist, his Old Testament background of water in the desert (Isaiah 12, 35, 55), creation and the blessing of waters (p. 194), light (pp. 189, 191, 192), and the pairing of water with spirit (p. 189). By contrast, the blessing of water for the Vigil of Epiphany found in the *Rituale Romanum* titulus IX, caput 9, no. 28 (any edition between 1890 and 1962), which is not a survival of ancient Roman practice, is concerned almost exclusively with exorcising evil spirits.

53. Clemente Alessandrino, *Estratti profetici: Eclogae Propheticae,* ed. Carlo Nardi (Florence: Nardini Editore, Centro Internazionale del Libro, 1985). Carlo Nardi, *Il Battesimo in Clemente Alessandrino: Interpretazione di Eclogae propheticae 1–26,* Studia Ephemeridis "Augustinianum" 19 (Rome: Institutum Patristicum "Augustinianum," 1984).

54. Paul F. Bradshaw, "'Diem baptismo sollemniorem': Initiation and Easter in Christian Antiquity," Εὐλόγημα: *Studies in Honor of Robert Taft,* ed. E. Carr et al., Studia

Anselmiana 110, Analecta Liturgica 17 (Rome: Pontificio Ateneo S. Anselmo, 1993), 41–51, especially pp. 42–43; reprinted in *Living Water, Sealing Spirit: Readings on Christian Initiation,* ed. Maxwell E. Johnson (Collegeville, Minn.: Liturgical Press, 1995), 137–47, see p. 139. Bradshaw, "Baptismal Practice in the Alexandrian Tradition, Eastern or Western?" in Bradshaw, *Essays in Early Christian Initiation,* Alcuin/GROW Joint Liturgical Study 8 (Nottingham: Grove, 1988), 5–17, reprinted in *Living Water,* 82–100.

55. *Stromata* 4.22.140, translated in *Ante-Nicene Fathers,* 2: 435.

56. *Stromata* 1.21.146.2, trans. John Ferguson, The Fathers of the Church 85 (Washington, D.C.: Catholic University of America Press, 1991), 132–33. See Thomas J. Talley, *The Origins of the Liturgical Year,* 2nd emended ed. (Collegeville, Minn.: Liturgical Press, 1991), 119–21.

57. Athanase Renoux, ed., *Le codex arménien Jérusalem 121 2: Édition comparée du texte et de deux autres manuscrits,* Patrologia Orientalis 168 [= 36/2] (Turnhout: Brepols, 1971), 210–15, 294–311. Michel Tarchnischvili, *Le grand lectionnaire de l'église de Jérusalem (V^e–VIIIe siècle)* 1, Corpus Scriptorum Christianorum Orientalium 189 [= Scriptores Iberici 10] (Louvain: Secrétariat du CorpusSCO, 1959), 9–13, 19–25, 107–14.

58. Alexis Kniazeff, "La lecture de l'ancien et du nouveau testament dans le rite byzantin," *La prière des heures,* ed. Cassien [Bezobrazov] and Bernard Botte, Lex Orandi 35 (Paris: Cerf, 1963), 201–51, especially pp. 218–26. Gabriel Bertonière, *The Historical Development of the Easter Vigil and Related Services in the Greek Church,* Orientalia Christiana Analecta 193 (Rome: Pontificium Institutum Studiorum Orientalium, 1972).

59. Carlo Marcora, *La vigilia nella liturgia: Ricerche sulle origini e sui primi sviluppi (sec. I–VI),* Archivio Ambrosiano 6 (Milan: [no publisher], 1954). Anton Baumstark, *Nocturna Laus: Typen frühchristlicher Vigilienfeier und ihr Fortleben vor allem im römischen und monastischen Ritus,* ed. Odilo Heiming, Liturgiewissenschaftliche Quellen und Forschungen 32 (Münster: Aschendorff, 1957; repr. 1967).

60. Peter Jeffery, *They Saw His Glory: How Judaism and Christianity Grew Apart, as Told in Their Most Ancient Hymns* (forthcoming).

61. Peter Jeffery, "Philo's Impact on Christian Psalmody," *Psalms in Community: Jewish and Christian Textual, Liturgical, and Artistic Traditions,* ed. Harold W. Attridge and Margot E. Fassler, Society of Biblical Literature Symposium Series 25 (Atlanta, Ga.: Society of Biblical Literature, 2003), 147–87.

Chapter 4. The Secret Gospel and the Alexandrian Lectionaries

Epigraph. Smith, *Secret Gospel,* 70–71. Note that Smith attributes the alleged ritual to Mark's church, not Clement's — another expression of his belief that the Secret Gospel preserves a very early tradition.

1. Paul F. Bradshaw, "The Gospel and the Catechumenate in the Third Century," *Journal of Theological Studies* n.s. 50 (1999): 143–52. Marcia L. Colish, *Ambrose's Patriarchs: Ethics for the Common Man* (Notre Dame, Ind.: University of Notre Dame Press, 2005).

2. Renoux, *Codex,* 232–37.

3. Johnson, *Rites,* 181. Enzo Lodi, "Signification théologique des trois catéchèses

homilétiques du sacramentaire Gélasien," *La prédication liturgique et les commentaires de la liturgie: Conférences Saint-Serge, XXXVIIIe semaine d'études liturgiques, Paris, 25–28 juin 1990,* ed. A. M. Triacca and A. Pistoia, Bibliotheca "Ephemerides Liturgicae" "Subsidia" 65 (Rome: Edizioni Liturgiche, 1992), 105–30, especially pp. 107–14.

4. Talley, *Origins,* 203–14, quotation from p. 206.

5. Juan Mateos, ed., *Le Typicon de la Grande Église: Ms. Saint-Croix n° 40, Xe siècle 2: Le cycle des fêtes mobiles,* Orientalia Christiana Analecta 166 (Rome: Pontificium Institutum Orientalium Studiorum, 1963), 62–65.

6. The practices are spelled out in canons 52, 55, and 56 of the "Quinisext" Council "in Trullo," held at Constantinople in 691 or 692. See George Neundgatt and Michael Featherstone, eds., *The Council in Trullo Revisited,* Kanonika 6 (Rome: Pontificio Istituto Orientale, 1995), 133, 136–38. See also *The Lenten Triodion Translated from the Original Greek,* ed. Mother Mary [Sonia Hambourg Bessarab] and Kallistos Ware (London: Faber and Faber 1977), 28–64.

7. Mateos, *Le Typicon,* 223–27. See also Kniazeff, "La lecture," 209–15, 226–31.

8. As briefly outlined in Taft, *The Byzantine Rite.*

9. Renoux, *Codex.* For the influence of the Jerusalem lectionary on the traditions of other places, see Rolf Zerfass, *Die Schriftlesung im Kathedraloffiizium Jerusalems,* Liturgiewissenschaftliche Quellen und Forschungen 48 (Münster: Aschendorffsche Verlagsbuchhandlung, 1968).

10. However, the reading of Romans 12:1–5, 6–16, 16–21, 13:8–10 on the first four Sundays after Epiphany, and of Matthew 8:1–13, 23–27, 13:24–30, 31–35 on the third through sixth Sundays looks like vestiges of an old course reading system for the Mass that survived in the Roman Missal up to Vatican II.

11. Thus Egeria wrote of the Jerusalem liturgy she witnessed in the 380s: "And what I admire and value most is that all the hymns and antiphons and readings they have, and all the prayers the bishop says, are always relevant to the day which is being observed and to the place in which they are used" (47.5). See John Wilkinson, *Egeria's Travels,* 3rd ed. (Warminster: Aris & Phillips, 1999), 163; on the date see pp. 169–71.

12. Renoux, *Codex,* 254–57, 220–21.

13. Talley, *Origins,* 176–83, 213. The relationship between Jerusalem and Constantinople might have to be reconsidered in light of John F. Baldovin, "A Lenten Sunday Lectionary in Fourth Century Jerusalem," *Time and Community: In Honor of Thomas Julian Talley,* ed. J. Neil Alexander, NPM [National Association of Pastoral Musicians] Studies in Church Music and Liturgy (Washington, D.C.: Pastoral Press, 1990), 115–22. What Baldovin actually brings forward is evidence that Jerusalem had a Lenten course reading from the epistle to the Hebrews. "Given the later association of Hebrews and Mark as Lenten readings in the Byzantine tradition," he writes, "it seems to me that a case could be made for supposing that Mark was read [in Jerusalem] as well" (p. 119).

14. René-Georges Coquin, "Les origines de l'Épiphanie en Égypte," *Noël — Épiphanie, retour du Christ: Semaine liturgique de l'Institut Saint-Serge,* Lex Orandi 40 (Paris: Cerf, 1967), 139–70. Talley, *Origins,* 189–203.

15. Coquin, "Les origines," 140–46. Waiting until Passover was finished before celebrating Easter, so that the two could never coincide, has been a common practice for much of Christian history; see Bonnie Blackburn and Leofranc Holford-Stevens, *The Oxford Companion to the Year* (Oxford: Oxford University Press, 1999), 791–92, 797–98.

16. Coquin, "Les origines," 141–43.

17. The ecumenical council of Chalcedon (451), which defined that Christ was one person in two natures (divine and human), provoked the most serious split in Eastern Christianity. Many Christians whose first language was not Greek rejected the council and thus are traditionally known by the pejorative term "Monophysite" (one-naturist), or the more ecumenical modern expression "non-Chalcedonian." Those who did accept the council and became Greek Orthodox were sometimes called "Melkites" (royalists) after the Syriac word for "king," because they were perceived by the Monophysites as siding with the Byzantine emperor.

18. Coquin, "Les origines," 143–44.

19. Ibid., 149–54. A good introduction to these letters is Charles Kannengiesser, "The Homiletic Festal Letters of Athanasius," *Preaching in the Patristic Age: Studies in Honor of Walter J. Burghardt, S. J.,* ed. David Hunter (Mahwah, N.J.: Paulist Press, 1989), 73–100.

20. For more information on this practice and on Macarius, see Heinzgerd Brakmann, "La 'Mystagogie' de la liturgie alexandrine et copte," *Mystagogie: Pensée liturgique d'aujourd'hui et liturgie ancienne: Conférences Saint-Serge, XXXIXe semaine d'études liturgiques, Paris, 30 juin–3 juillet 1992,* ed. A. M. Triacca and A. Pistoia, Bibliotheca "Ephemerides Liturgicae" "Subsidia" 70 (Rome: Edizioni Liturgiche, 1993), 54–65, especially pp. 61–63.

21. Coquin, "Les origines," 146–47.

22. Talley, *Origins,* 204.

23. Thomas J. Talley, "Afterthoughts on the Origins of the Liturgical Year," *Western Plainchant in the First Millennium: Studies in the Medieval Liturgy and Its Music in Memory of James W. McKinnon,* ed. Sean Gallagher, James Haar, John Nádas, and Timothy Striplin (Aldershot: Ashgate, 2003), 1–10, quotation from p. 8. See Talley, *Origins,* 203–14.

24. Talley, *Origins,* 194–203.

25. See also Smith, *Clement,* 175.

26. Alberto Camplani, "Sull'Origine della Quaresima in Egitto," International Association for Coptic Studies, *Acts of the Fifth International Congress of Coptic Studies: Washington, 12–15 August 1992 2/1: Papers from the Sections 1,* ed. David W. Johnson (Rome: C.I.M., 1993), 105–21, quotation from p. 105. Camplani, *Le Lettere festali di Atanasio di Alessandria: Studio storico-critico* (Rome: C.I.M., 1989).

27. Camplani, "Sull'Origine," 116.

28. Cyril, *Lives,* 103, 115, 117, 119.

29. For some of it, see Peter Jeffery, "Eastern and Western Elements in the Irish Monastic Prayer of the Hours," *The Divine Office in the Latin Middle Ages: Methodology and Source Studies, Regional Developments, Hagiography, Written in Honor of Professor Ruth Steiner,* ed. Margot E. Fassler and Rebecca A. Baltzer (New York: Oxford University Press, 2000), 99–143, see pp. 131 and 141–42 n. 88.

30. Peter Jeffery, "The Earliest Christian Chant Repertory Recovered: The Georgian Witnesses to Jerusalem Chant," *Journal of the American Musicological Society* 47 (1994): 1–39. Jeffery, "The Lost Chant Tradition of Early Christian Jerusalem: Some Possible Melodic Survivals in the Byzantine and Latin Chant Repertories," *Early Music History* 11 (1992): 151–90. Jeffery, "Monastic Reading and the Emerging Roman Chant Repertory," *Western Plainchant in the First Millennium,* 45–104.

31. Jakab, *Ecclesia alexandrina,* 45–49. Smith, *Clement,* 20–21.

32. Other bibliography on the origins of Epiphany: Martin F. Connell, "Did Ambrose's Sister Become a Virgin on December 25 or January 6? The Earliest Western Evidence for Christmas and Epiphany Outside Rome," *Studia Liturgica* 29 (1999): 145–58.

33. An interesting second- or third-century letter from a non-Christian hierophant is compared with the Christian practices regarding the Nile in Kurt Treu, "Liturgische Traditionen in Ägypten (Zu P. Oxy. 2782)," *Studia Coptica,* ed. Peter Nagel, Berliner byzantinische Arbeiten 45 (Berlin: Akademie-Verlag, 1974), 43–66. Little specific importance is given to January 6, but see p. 51. See also Myriam Wissa, "Le Calendrier copte, héritage du calendrier pharaonique," and Heinzgerd Brakmann, "Neue Funde und Forschungen zur Liturgie der Kopten," *Actes du IVᵉ congrès copte: Louvain-la-Neuve, 5–10 septembre 1988* 2, ed. Marguerite Rassart-Debergh and Julien Ries, Publications de l'Institut Orientaliste de Louvain 41 (Louvain-la-Neuve: Université Catholique de Louvain, Institut Orientaliste, 1992), 163–77 and 419–35, especially pp. 423–24.

34. Peter Jeffery, "The Liturgical Year in the Ethiopian Deggʷā (Chantbook)," Εὐλόγημα, 199–234, see pp. 225–26. One early source is a papyrus fragment from the White Monastery published in Ugo Zanetti, "Un index liturgique du Monastère Blanc," *Christianisme d'Égypte: Hommages à René-Georges Coquin,* Cahiers de la Bibliothèque Copte 9 (Paris-Leuven: Éditions Peeters, 1995), 55–75.

35. See, for example, Matta el-Meskeen, "The Wedding in Cana of Galilee," *Coptic Church Review* 16 (1995): 99–107; Maged S. A. Mikhail, "On Cana of Galilee: A Sermon by Coptic Patriarch Benjamin I," *Coptic Church Review* 23 (2002): 66–93. Benjamin I reigned 622–661 CE. For a twelfth-century miniature see Massimo Capuani et al., *Egitto Copto* (Milan: Jaca Book, 1999), 253.

36. Robert A. Wild, *Water in the Cultic Worship of Isis and Sarapis,* Études préliminaires aux religions orientales dans l'empire romain 87 (Leiden: Brill, 1981), 90–92, cf. pp. 50–51.

37. The singular of this word is *tarh.* See O. H. E. Burmester, "The Ṭuruḥāt of the Coptic Church," *Orientalia Christiana Periodica* (1937): 78–109. A less fragmentary and much later lectionary of this kind was published in S. C. Malan, "The Gospel and Versicles for Every Sunday in the Year; as used in the Coptic Church" in S. C. Malan, *Original Documents of the Coptic Church, Translated from Coptic and Arabic Originals* 4 (London: D. Nutt, 1874), though Malan uses the word "versicle" for the chant texts.

38. A possible echo of such an arrangement occurs in an early thirteenth-century guide to the churches of Egypt. It describes a church dedicated to St. John the Baptist, which was located near a lake and had a large second-story area that was originally "prepared for the assembling of the novices." A festival was kept there on the *second* day of Epiphany (when the Cana story was read?), and it was customary for "a great number" to assemble there "on the Monday of the second week of the Great Fast . . . to hear the Lenten charge, and the instructions which are given them as to what must be done during that season." Since this author knew the first week of Lent as "White Week," when fish and white meats were still allowed, it is possible that the second week was the beginning of the full fast, or of Lent proper. B. T. A. Evetts, ed. and trans., *The Churches and Monasteries of Egypt and Some Neighbouring Countries Attributed to Abû Ṣâliḥ, the Armenian,* Anecdota Oxoniensia: Semitic Series 1/7 (Oxford: Clarendon Press, 1895), 129, 152, see also p. 39.

39. The epileptic demoniac (Luke 9:39–42), the calming of the storm (Matthew 8:23–26), the Gerasene demoniac (Matthew 8:28), where the fragment ends. Mario Geymonat, "Un antico lezionario della chiesa di Alessandria," *Laurea Corona: Studies in Honour of Edward Coleiro*, ed. Anthony Bonanno and H. C. R. Vella (Amsterdam: B. R. Grüner, 1987), 186–96, see pp. 188–93.

40. Talley, *Origins*, 85–103. Susan K. Roll, "The Debate on the Origins of Christmas," *Archiv für Liturgiewissenschaft* 40 (1998): 1–16.

41. Harry A. Echle, "The Baptism of the Apostles: A Fragment of Clement of Alexandria's Lost Work Ὑποτυπώσεις in the *Pratum Spirituale* of John Moschus," *Traditio* 3 (1945): 365–68. *Clemens Alexandrinus* 3, ed. Otto Stählin, 2nd ed., ed. Ludwig Früchtel and Ursula Treu (Berlin: Akademie-Verlag, 1970), 196.

42. Coquin, "Les origines," 141.

43. Camplani, "Sull'Origine," 112.

44. Now being reedited in Cyrille d'Alexandrie, *Lettres festales*, ed. W. H. Burns et al. in *Sources Chrétiennes* 372, 392, 434 etc. (Paris: Cerf, 1991, 1993, 1998). Each letter ends by announcing the dates of the Monday on which the forty-day fast began, the Monday that Paschal week (i.e., Holy Week) began, the date the fast ended (Holy Saturday), and the date of Easter itself, according to the Egyptian calendar in which every month has thirty days. The introduction by Pierre Évieux in the first volume includes a discussion of the date of Easter (pp. 73–94), but not of the structure of Lent.

45. Camplani, "Sull'Origine," 118, 120.

46. Ibid., 111–12. Alberto Camplani, "La Quaresima egiziana nel VII secolo: note di cronologia su Mon. Epiph. 77, Manchester Ryland Suppl. 47–48, P. Grenf. II 112, P. Berol. 10677, P. Köln 215 e un'omelia copta," *Augustinianum* 32 (1992): 423–32. A fragment that Camplani would date to 596 still has the six-week Lent: Camplani, "Coptic Fragments from a Festal Letter of the Late Sixth Century (John Rylands Library, Coptic Suppl. N. 47–48): Damian or Eulogius?" *Coptic Studies on the Threshold of a New Millennium: Proceedings of the Seventh International Congress of Coptic Studies, Leiden, 27 August–2 September 2000*, ed. Mat Immerzeel, Jacques van der Vliet et al., 2 vols. (Leuven: Peeters, 2004), 1: 317–27.

47. O. H. E. KHS-Burmester, "The Baptismal Rite of the Coptic Church (A Critical Study)," *Bulletin de la Société d'Archéologie Copte* 11 (1945): 27–86, see pp. 82–84.

48. Talley claimed to find support for part of his hypothesis in "some old Coptic lectionaries" (*Origins*, p. 212), but he did not identify them. Possibly he was referring to the occurrence of Mark 115–117 (Egyptian numbering, equivalent to Mark 10:46–52) at Matins on the Saturday of Lazarus, as found in what became the standard lectionary (Table 4.5) and in manuscripts of the type published in Malan, "The Gospel and Versicles," 4: 52–53.

49. Diliana Atanassova, "Zu den sahidischen Pascha-Lektionaren," *Coptic Studies on the Threshold of a New Millennium* 1 (2004): 607–20.

50. Sources for the Coptic Bible are being catalogued in Karlheinz Schüssler, ed., *Biblia Coptica: Die koptischen Bibeltexte* (Wiesbaden: Harrassowitz, 1995–). But the focus of attention is biblical content, not liturgical arrangement. See also Schüssler, "Das Projekt 'Biblia Coptica Patristica,'" *Oriens Christianus* 79 (1995): 224–28.

51. For the Coptic and Arabic a beginning has been made in Ugo Zanetti, "Premières recherches sur les lectionnaires coptes," *Ephemerides Liturgicae* 98 (1984): 3–34;

Zanetti, *Les lectionnaires coptes annuels: Basse-Égypte,* Publications de l'Institut Orientaliste de Louvain 33 (Louvain-la-Neuve: Université Catholique de Louvain, Institut Orientaliste, 1985); Zanetti, "Abû-l-Barakât et les lectionnaires de Haute-Égypte," *Actes du IVe congrès copte* 450–62. On the meaning of the word *Katameros* see Zanetti, *Les lectionnaires,* 6–8.

52. H. Steneker, ΠΕΙΘΟΥΣ ΔΗΜΙΟΥΡΓΙΑ: *Observations sur la fonction du style dans le Protreptique de Clément d'Alexandrie,* Graecitas Christianorum Primaeva 3 (Nijmegen: Dekker & Van de Vegt, 1967), 104–7. M. Mees, *Die Zitate aus dem Neuen Testament bei Clemens von Alexandrien* (Rome: Typis Pontificiae Universitatis Gregorianae, 1970).

53. Rodolphe Kasser, "Lazare conté en un lyco-diospolitain d'aspect fort étrange (Jean 10,7–13,38)," *Christianisme d'Égypte: Hommages à René-Georges Coquin,* ed. Jean-Marc Rosenstiehl, Cahiers de la Bibliothèque Copte 9 (Paris, Leuven: Peeters, 1994), 21–54, see p. 27. Cf. Rodolphe Kasser, *L'Évangile selon saint Jean et les versions coptes de la Bible,* Bibliothèque théologique (Neuchâtel: Éditions Delachaux et Niestlé, 1966).

54. Zanetti, "Un index liturgique." The eighteenth-century codex Vatican Copt. 29, ff. 406–17, marks Epiphany with Matthew's (3:1–12) and Mark's (1:1–11) accounts of Jesus' baptism at Vespers and the morning office, with John's (1:18–34) at the Eucharist, while the fourteenth-century Codex 93, ff. 33–36, evidently expands this arrangement with further readings. Adolphe Hebbelynck and Arnold van Lantschoot, *Codices Coptici Vaticani, Barberiniani, Borgiani, Rossiani* 1 (Vatican City: Bibliotheca Vaticana, 1937), 111, 637.

55. H. J. M. Milne, "Early Psalms and Lections for Lent," *The Journal of Egyptian Archaeology* 10 (1924): 278–82.

56. New York, Morgan Library, MS M 573, echoed in MS 615. Leo Depuydt, *Catalogue of Coptic Manuscripts in the Pierpont Morgan Library,* 2 vols., Corpus of Illuminated Manuscripts 4–5, Oriental Series 1–2 (Leuven: Peeters, 1993), 1: 73–76, 90–92. See also Karlheinz Schüssler, "Analyse der Lektionarhandschrift sa 530^L," *Journal of Coptic Studies* 4 (2002): 133–66. Zanetti, *Les lectionnaires,* 15, 18.

57. Jeffery, "The Liturgical Year," 223.

58. Morgan MS 669(4), see Depuydt, *Catalogue* 1: 517. The same tradition in Göttingen, Universitätsbibliothek, Orientalis 125, 9, according to Paul de Lagarde, "Die koptischen handschriften der goettinger bibliothek," *Abhandlungen der historisch-philosophischen Classe der königlichen Gesellschaft der Wissenschaften zu Göttingen* 24 (Göttingen: Dieter, 1879), 1–62, see p. 14. See also Vatican MS Borgia copt. 21, f. 252, and Borgia copt. 31, f. 179 in Arnold van Lantschoot, *Codices Coptici Vaticani, Barberiniani, Borgiani, Rossiani* 2/1 (Vatican City: Bibliotheca Vaticana, 1947), 95, 142. Hamburg MSS in Lothar Störk, *Koptische Handschriften 2: Die Handschriften der Staats- und Universitätsbibliothek Hamburg,* Teil 2: *Die Handschriften aus Dair Anbā Maqār,* Verzeichnis der orientalischen Handschriften in Deutschland 21/2 (Stuttgart: Franz Steiner, 1995), 169.

59. Waheed Hassab Alla, *Le Baptême des enfants dans la tradition de l'église copte d'Alexandrie* (Fribourg: Éditions Universitaires, [1985]), 138. In the course of defending infant baptism against Protestant objections, the author has produced a very useful compilation of statements on baptism by Egyptian theological writers, from the earliest fathers to the fifteenth century. See also Brakmann, "La 'Mystagogie,'" 63. John 3:5 and

the baptism of Jesus are also prominent themes in a book for popular instruction: Sami R. Hanna, *The Holy Sacraments of the Coptic Orthodox Church,* ed. Peter Brownfield and Mikhail Meleka (Los Angeles: St. Fam Orthodox Publications, 1985), 8–17.

60. Pauly Kannookadan, *The East Syrian Lectionary: An Historico-Liturgical Study* (Rome: Mar Thoma Yogam, 1991), 42, 94, 144, 186.

61. Cairo, Coptic Museum J42572 (also Lib. 3805), published in J. Drescher, "A Coptic Lectionary Fragment," *Annales du Service des Antiquités de l'Égypte* 51 (1951), 247–56 and plates I–IV, see pp. 252–55. See also Klaus Gamber, "Fragmente eines griechischen Perikopenbuches des 5. Jh. aus Ägypten," *Oriens Christianus* 44 [ser. 4 no. 8] (1960): 75–87, see pp. 82–83.

62. Göttingen, Orientalis 125,7 and 125,9 in Lagarde, "Die koptischen handschriften," 7, 13–16. Malan, "The Gospel and Versicles," 46–58 (excerpts from all four gospels on Palm Sunday, p. 54). Hamburg MSS in Oswald Hugh Ewart KHS-Burmester, *Koptische Handschriften* 1: *Die Handschriftenfragmente der Staats- und Universitätsbibliothek Hamburg* Teil 1, Verzeichnis der orientalischen Handschriften in Deutschland 21/1 (Wiesbaden: Franz Steiner, 1975), 70, and in Störk, *Koptische Handschriften* 2/2, 124–25, 146. These manuscripts give the three Johannine readings (i.e., John 4, 5, 9) on the fourth, fifth, and sixth Sundays, with John 11 (Lazarus) and John 12 (triumphal entry) on Saturday and Sunday of the seventh week, except those manuscripts that contain only the Sunday gospels, which therefore omit the Saturday Lazarus reading. A sixteenth-century fragment that had this arrangement is described in J. E. Gilmore, "Manuscript Portions of Three Coptic Lectionaries," *Proceedings of the Society for Biblical Archaeology* 24 (1902): 186–91, see p. 188.

63. The inclusion of John 8:1–11 (the adulterous woman), an unusual item in such lists, is of particular interest because it seems to owe something to the baptismal interpretation presented in the commentary on Daniel ascribed to Hippolytus, 1.17. See Hippolyte, *Commentaire sur Daniel,* ed. Maurice Lefèvre, Sources Chrétiennes 14 (Paris: Cerf, 1947), 100–01. This raises an unexplored perspective on the question of Hippolytus's relationship to the liturgical tradition of the city of Rome. On the stational calendar, see Hartmann Grisar, *Das Missale im Lichte römischer Stadtgeschichte: Stationen, Perikopen, Gebräuche* (Freiburg: Herder, 1925).

64. There was considerable interest in this series in the mid-twentieth century, but it has since largely disappeared from liturgiological discussion. Not all the evidence has been fully discussed in print, especially for the non-Roman Latin rites. The large bibliography is summarized in Hermann Schmidt, *Introductio in Liturgiam Occidentalem* (Rome: Herder, 1960; repr. 1962), 287–91, 516–18. Thierry Maertens, "History and Function of the Three Great Pericopes: *The Samaritan Woman, The Man Born Blind, The Raising of Lazarus,*" trans. P. J. Hepburn-Scott, *Adult Baptism and the Catechumenate,* ed. Johannes Wagner, Concilium: Theology in the Age of Renewal 22 (New York: Paulist Press, 1967), 51–56. Adrian Nocent, *The Liturgical Year* 2: *Lent,* trans. Matthew J. O'Connell (Collegeville, Minn.: Liturgical Press, 1977), 92–130, 221–36. Maxwell E. Johnson, "From Three Weeks to Forty Days: Baptismal Preparation and the Origins of Lent," *Living Water,* 118–36.

65. See the Hamburg manuscript described in Störk, *Koptische Handschriften* 2/2, 126, 134. Zanetti, *Les lectionnaires,* 39–40.

66. Kniazeff, "La lecture," 230–33. I. Karabinov, *Постная Тріодь: Историческій обзоръ ея плана, состава, редакцій и славянскихъ переводовъ* [*Lenten Triodion: Historical Survey of Its Plan, Composition, Redaction and Slavonic Translation;* in Russian] (St. Petersburg: В. Д. Смирновъ, 1910), 25–31. Slavonic sources often preserve archaic elements of the Byzantine liturgy that were dropped from the Greek textual tradition. Nicolas Schidlovsky is working on an annotated translation of Karabinov's rare and valuable book.

67. Raymond E. Brown, "The Johannine Sacramentary," *New Testament Essays* (Milwaukee: Bruce, 1965), 51–76, see pp. 71, 76.

68. Oscar Cullmann, *Early Christian Worship,* trans. A. Stewart Todd and James B. Torrance (Philadelphia: Westminster Press, 1953), 37.

69. "In Quatriduanum Lazarum," in *Patrologia Graeca,* ed. J.-P. Migne, vol. 48 (Paris: J.-P. Migne, 1863), 779–84.

70. Allen Wikgren, "Chicago Studies in the Greek Lectionary of the New Testament," *Biblical and Patristic Studies in Memory of Robert Pierce Casey,* ed. J. Neville Birdsall and Robert W. Thomson (Freiburg: Herder, 1963), 96–121.

71. Gabriel Bertonière, *The Sundays of Lent in the Tridion* [sic]: *The Sundays Without a Commemoration,* Orientalia Christiana Analecta 253 (Rome: Pontificio Istituto Orientale, 1997), 65–78. Talley, *Origins,* 226 n. 29. Anton Baumstark, "Die sonntägliche Evangelienlesung im vorbyzantinischen Jerusalem," *Byzantinische Zeitschrift* 30 (1929–30): 350–9. G. Garitte, "Un évangéliaire grec-arabe du Xᵉ siècle (cod. Sin. ar. 116)," *Studia Codicologica,* ed. Kurt Treu et al., Texte und Untersuchungen 124 (Berlin: Akademie-Verlag, 1977), 207–25, see pp. 218–20.

72. Bertonière, *Sundays,* 34, see also pp. 29–30.

Chapter 5. A Gospel in Fragments

Epigraph. Preface to *What the Bible Really Says,* ed. Morton Smith and R. Joseph Hoffmann (1989; repr. San Francisco: Harper Collins, 1993), 7–10, quotation from pp. 8–9.

1. Raymond E. Brown, "The Relation of 'The Secret Gospel of Mark' to the Fourth Gospel," *Catholic Biblical Quarterly* 36 (1974): 466–85, quoting pp. 469, 484, 480.

2. *Theological Dictionary of the New Testament,* ed. Gerhard Friedrich, trans. Geoffrey W. Bromiley, vol. 6 (Grand Rapids, Mich.: Eerdmans, 1968), 758–59. Brown, "The Relation," 481 n. 41, notes that this is not the usual Marcan word for adoration. He speculates that it was used "probably because *proskynein* . . . fitted better the ritual, initiatory atmosphere of the SGM fragment."

3. J. E. Lighter, J. Ball, J. O'Connor, eds., *Random House Historical Dictionary of American Slang* 1: *A–G* (New York: Random House, 1994), 459. The documentation shows that this meaning has been in British usage since at least 1600. Sixteenth-century attestations are discussed in Gordon Williams, *A Dictionary of Sexual Language and Imagery in Shakespearean and Stuart Literature* (London: Athlone Press, 1994), 1: 277.

4. See Chapter 2, n. 96. Also Richard A. Waterman, "The Role of Obscenity in the Folk Tales of the 'Intellectual' Stratum of Our Society," *Journal of American Folklore* 62 (1949): 162–65, especially pp. 164–65. Alan Dundes, "Here I Sit — A Study of American

Latrinalia," *The Kroeber Anthropological Society Papers* 34 (Spring 1966): 91–105; reprinted in Alan Dundes, *Analytic Essays in Folklore, Studies in Folklore* 2, 2nd printing (The Hague: Mouton, 1979), 177–91. Shirley Leone, "Associational-Metaphorical Activity: Another View of Language and Mind," *American Anthropologist,* new series 75 (1973): 1276–81, especially pp. 1278–79. Gary Alan Fine, "Obscene Joking Across Cultures," *Journal of Communication* 26/3 (September 1976): 134–40, especially pp. 138–39. Finnegan Alford and Richard Alford, "A Holo-Cultural Study of Humor," *Ethos* 9 (1981): 149–64, especially pp. 155, 159. W. D. Redfern, "Guano of the Mind: Puns in Advertising," *Language and Communication* 2 (1982): 269–76, especially pp. 270–72. Walter Redfern, *Puns* (Oxford: Basil Blackwell, 1984), 132–35. Women take longer than men to recognize sexual double entendres, according to James H. Geer and Jeffrey S. Melton, "Sexual Content–Induced Delay with Double-Entendre Words," *Archives of Sexual Behavior* 26 (1997): 295–316.

5. Bradshaw et al., *Apostolic Tradition,* 114.

6. Kurt Rudolph, *Gnosis: The Nature and History of Gnosticism,* trans. Robert McLachlan Wilson (San Francisco: Harper, 1987), 188–89, 226–28, 360–62.

7. Ibid., 361.

8. Eric Segelberg, *Maṣbūtā: Studies in the Ritual of the Mandaean Baptism* (Uppsala: Almqvist & Wiksell, 1958), 63–65. Segelberg, "The Baptismal Rite According to Some of the Coptic-Gnostic Texts of Nag-Hammadi," *Studia Patristica* 5: *Papers Presented to the Third International Conference on Patristic Studies Held at Christ Church, Oxford, 1959* 3: *Liturgica, Monastica et Ascetica, Philosophica,* ed. F. L. Cross (Berlin: Akademie-Verlag, 1962), 117–28, see p. 121.

9. Translation from *The Gospel of Truth: A Valentinian Meditation on the Gospel,* trans. Kendrick Grobel (London: Adam & Charles Black, 1960), 120.

10. Harold Attridge et al., eds., *Nag Hammadi Codex I (The Jung Codex),* 2 vols., The Coptic Gnostic Library, Nag Hammadi Studies 22–23 (Leiden: Brill, 1985), 1: 100–01, 2: 86.

11. *The Nag Hammadi Library,* 488. See also Jacques É. Ménard, "Termes et thèmes valentiniens de l'exposé valentinien (ExpVal) et des fragments du baptême et de l'Eucharistie du codex XI de Nag Hammadi," *Deuxième journée d'études coptes, Strasbourg 25 mai 1984,* Cahiers de la Bibliothèque Copte 3 (Louvain: Peeters, 1986), 161–68.

12. Victor Saxer, *Les rites de l'initiation chrétienne du IIe au VIe siècle: Esquisse historique et signification d'après leurs principaux témoins,* Centro Italiano di Studi sull'Alto Medioevo 7 (Spoleto: Centro Italiano di Studi sull'Alto Medioevo, 1988), 67–71.

13. E. S. Drower, *The Canonical Prayerbook of the Mandaeans* (Leiden: Brill, 1959), 2 n. 1, 27, see also the many references to "kušta" in the index, pp. 319–20.

14. Edwin M. Yamauchi, *Gnostic Ethics and Mandaean Origins* (Piscataway, N.J.: Gorgias Press, 2004), finds that the Mandaean religion is essentially a Mesopotamian fertility worship that absorbed Gnostic mythology and cult practices but retained a very un-Gnostic emphasis on the goodness of marriage and reproduction. Thus practices like the ritual handshake cannot simply be assumed to be legacies from ancient Gnosticism.

15. C. R. C. Allberry, ed., *A Manichaean Psalm-Book, Part II,* Manichaean Manuscripts in the Chester Beatty Collection 2 (Stuttgart: W. Kohlhammer, 1938), 94 line 2, similarly p. 108 line 18.

16. Since writing this, I've discovered that the Sipsey River Primitive Baptist Association in Eutaw, Alabama, does have a hand-grasping ritual but does not sing the hymn genres to which the Dorsey and MacLellan examples belong. Instead they preserve a more archaic musical tradition, on which see http://www.yale.edu/music/linesinging/ (accessed July 2005).

17. Smith, *Clement*, 110.

18. Ibid.

19. The evidence cited in John Boswell, *Same-Sex Unions in Premodern Europe* (New York: Villard Books, 1994), 211–17 and Figs. 14–15, 17–19, shows that joining hands was not limited to sexual unions, whatever Boswell himself thought. On the whole, Boswell's thesis that Byzantine brotherhood rituals amounted to homosexual marriages is a misconstrual. See Elizabeth A. R. Brown, Claudia Rapp, and Brent D. Shaw, "Ritual Brotherhood in Ancient and Medieval Europe: A Symposium," *Traditio* 52 (1997): 259–381.

20. Marvin H. Pope, *Song of Songs: A New Translation with Introduction and Commentary,* Anchor Bible 7/4 (Garden City, N.Y.: Doubleday, 1977), 517–18 and plate V. William Loader, *Sexuality and the Jesus Tradition* (Grand Rapids, Mich.: Eerdmans, 2005), 24, 28–29.

21. For representations see Michael B. Poliakoff, *Combat Sports in the Ancient World: Competition, Violence, and Culture* (New Haven, Conn.: Yale University Press, 1987), 5, 13, 14, 26, 35–40; K. J. Dover, *Greek Homosexuality,* 2nd ed. (Cambridge, Mass.: Harvard University Press, 1989), 54–57; Thomas Schäfer, *Imperii Insignia: Sella curulis und Fasces: Zur Repräsentation römischer Magistrate,* Mitteilungen des Deutschen archaeologischen Instituts: roemische Abteilung, Ergänzungsheft 29 (Mainz: Philipp von Zabern, 1989), Tafel 4.3; Thomas F. Scanlon, *Eros & Greek Athletics* (Oxford: Oxford University Press, 2002), with depictions of wrestlers holding hands on pp. 186–88, 241, wrestling Erotes on pp. 261–62.

22. On the two different kinds of wrestling see Plato, *Alcibiades,* ed. Nicholas Denyer, Cambridge Greek and Latin Classics (Cambridge, U.K.: Cambridge University Press, 2001), 110 on 107e5–107e6.

23. The risen Jesus' words to Mary, "Do not cling to me," are not about gender differences according to Raymond Brown, *The Gospel According to John (xiii–xxi),* Anchor Bible 29A (Garden City, N.Y.: Doubleday, 1970), 992–93, 1011–17.

24. *Paedagogus* 1.4, *Stromata* 4.8, translated in *Ante-Nicene Fathers,* 2: 211, 419. See also Denise Kimber Buell, *Making Christians: Clement of Alexandria and the Rhetoric of Legitimacy* (Princeton, N.J.: Princeton University Press, 1999), 47–48, 64, 130.

25. Kathleen E. Corley, "Salome and Jesus at Table in the Gospel of Thomas," *Semeia* 86 (1999): 85–97.

26. Smith proposed that something had been deliberately excised, perhaps by Clement himself, in *Clement,* 121–22, *Secret Gospel,* 69.

27. Smith, *Clement,* 89.

28. Ibid., 121.

29. "The case for abbreviation [of Mark's expanded text] is further strengthened by the fact that the omitted material mentions Salome. . . . The presumption is that Salome was eliminated [from Matthew and Luke] because persons of whom the canonical evangelists

disapproved were appealing to her as an authority. . . . Since the Carpocratians who appealed to Salome's authority . . . also maintained that Jesus was a natural man, the son of Joseph, and since Salome in orthodox material was cursed for her denial of the virgin birth, it would seem that she had figured as an authority for esoteric traditions allied with a naturalistic account of Jesus' birth. . . . There must have been other early traditions about Salome to explain the later developments. The later developments, in turn, suggest reasons for the suppression of the early material." Smith, *Clement*, 189, 190, 191–92.

30. "unverständlich und problematisch . . . unplausibel"; Silke Petersen, *"Zerstört die Werke der Weiblichkeit!": Maria Magdalena, Salome und andere Jüngerinnen Jesu in christlich-gnostischen Schriften*, Nag Hammadi and Manichaean Studies 48 (Leiden: Brill, 1999), 229.

31. Richard Bauckham, "Salome the Sister of Jesus, Salome the Disciple of Jesus, and the Secret Gospel of Mark," *Novum Testamentum* 33 (1991): 245–75, quotations from pp. 245, 268, 272.

32. Smith, *Clement*, 192–94.

33. Bauckham, "Salome," 272–75, quotations from p. 274.

34. Smith, *Clement*, 190.

35. Smith cited M. R. James, ed., *The Apocryphal New Testament* (Oxford: Clarendon Press, 1924), 183. One could now cite Elliott, *Apocryphal New Testament*, 669. The original Coptic word in this and another source correspond to the Greek word *peirázein* (πειράζειν), according to Petersen, *"Zerstört,"* 233 n. 170. This word can be used of a man who "tests" a woman's virtue.

36. Bauckham "Salome," 251–52.

37. The relevant passages are excerpted and translated in Andrew Barker, *Greek Musical Writings* 1: *The Musician and His Art*, Cambridge Readings in the Literature of Music (Cambridge, U.K.: Cambridge University Press, 1984), 117–23. A relatively new translation of the entire text, with commentary, is Xenophon, *Symposium*, ed. A. J. Bowen (Warminster: Aris & Phillips, 1998).

38. Eva Cantarella, *Bisexuality in the Ancient World*, 2nd ed., trans. Cormac Ó Cuilleanáin (New Haven, Conn.: Yale University Press, 2002), 86–88.

39. *Paedagogus* 2.7, see also 2.1, 2.4–5, translated in *Ante-Nicene Fathers*, 2: 251–52, 236–42, 248–50.

40. Corley, "Salome," 86, 89. Bentley Layton translated similarly: "Who are you, O man? Like a stranger (?) you have gotten upon my couch and you have eaten from my table." See *The Gnostic Scriptures: A New Translation*, The Anchor Bible Reference Library (New York: Doubleday, 1987), 391. Petersen, *"Zerstört,"* 198–99, translates: "Wer bist du, Mensch, als aus wem bist du gestiegen auf mein Bett und hast gegessen von meinem Tisch?"

41. Smith, *Secret Gospel*, 69–70; much more tentatively in Smith, *Clement*, 121–22.

42. Smith, *Clement*, 101–2.

43. A. H. Criddle, "On the Mar Saba Letter Attributed to Clement of Alexandria," *Journal of Early Christian Studies* 3 (1995): 215–20, quotation from p. 218.

44. Smith, *Clement*, 251.

45. Compare the lists of early theological themes in Maxwell E. Johnson, *The Rites of Christian Initiation: Their Evolution and Interpretation* (Collegeville, Minn.: Liturgical

Press, 1999), 30–31. Saxer, *Les rites,* 647–49. Smith could have consulted J. Ysebaert, *Greek Baptismal Terminology: Its Origins and Early Development,* Graecitas Christianorum Primaeva 1 (Nijmegen: Dekker and Van de Vegt, 1962); his bibliography does not cite it.

46. See "Esprit Saint" in the index to Benoît and Munier, *Le Baptême,* 275.

47. Thus baptism is scarcely mentioned in Martha Himmelfarb, *Ascent to Heaven in Jewish and Christian Apocalypses* (New York: Oxford University Press, 1993) — only pp. 129 n. 35 and 130 n. 50, where more could have been said about the place of anointing in Christian initiation rites.

48. For a fictional evocation of a time close to the period in which Smith was writing, see Dan Wakefield's novel *Going All the Way* (New York: Delacorte, 1970), which is set in the year 1954. Sara Davidson adds a female perspective in her Introduction to one of the reprint editions (New York: E. P. Dutton, 1989). A sociological study of a more recent generation is Sharon Thompson, *Going All the Way: Teenage Girls' Tales of Sex, Romance and Pregnancy* (New York: Hill and Wang, 1995).

49. Smith, *Secret Gospel,* 113–14.

50. Ibid., 113 n. 12.

51. Morton Smith, "Pauline Worship as Seen by Pagans," *Harvard Theological Review* 73 (1980): 241–49, reprinted in *Studies in the Cult of Yahweh* 2: 95–102, see p. 96. Smith, *Clement,* 221.

52. Smith, *Clement,* 224–27, 64.

53. Smith, "Pauline Worship," 96; Smith, "Two Ascended to Heaven — Jesus and the Author of 4Q491" (1992), reprinted in *Studies in the Cult of Yahweh* 2: 73. On sexual charms in the papyri see Dominic Montserrat, *Sex and Society in Graeco-Roman Egypt* (London: Kegan Paul International, 1996), 180–209. Andrzej Wypustek, "Un aspect ignoré des persécutions des chrétiens dans l'antiquité: Les accusations de magie érotique imputées aux chrétiens aux IIᵉ et IIIᵉ siècles," *Jahrbuch für Antike und Christentum* 42 (1999): 50–71.

54. Ian Moyer, "The Initiation of the Magician: Transition and Power in Graeco-Egyptian Ritual," *Initiation in Ancient Greek Rituals and Narratives: New Critical Perspectives* (London and New York: Routledge, 2003), 219–38, especially p. 230. On the survival of Pharaonic funeral practices in Coptic Christianity see Otto F. A. Meinardus, "Modern Coptic Survivals of Pharaonic Funerary Customs," *Studia Orientalia Christiana: Collectanea* 35–36 (2002–03): 125–36.

55. The relevant passages (Babylonian Talmud Shabbat 104b and Tosefta Shabbat 11.15) are translated in R. Travers Herford, *Christianity in Talmud and Midrash* (London: Williams & Norgate, 1903; repr. New York: Ktav [1975]), 35–41, 54–56. That we have a confusion between two different people is proposed in Asher Finkel, "Yavneh's Liturgy and Early Christianity," *Journal of Ecumenical Studies* 18 (1981): 231–50, see pp. 248–49.

56. There is a brief mention in Smith, *Clement,* 269. See also Smith, *Jesus the Magician,* 47, 178 (1998 reprint, p. 62).

57. Smith, "Two Ascended," 68–78, see p. 73. See also Smith, *Clement,* 181, 221, 225–26. The text is papyrus IV.475–834, published in Karl Preisendanz et al., *Papyri Graecae*

Magicae: Die griechischen Zauberpapyri I (Leipzig: Teubner, 1928), 88–101; translated in Hans Dieter Betz, ed., *The Greek Magical Papyri in Translation Including the Demotic Spells* I, 2nd ed. (Chicago: University of Chicago Press, 1992), 48–54. We now have, however, Hans Dieter Betz, *The "Mithras Liturgy": Text, Translation, and Commentary* (Tübingen: Mohr Siebeck, 2003).

58. Betz, *The "Mithras Liturgy,"* 57 line 735, and commentary pp. 199–200.

59. Smith did recognize a connection to Hermeticism in "Transformation by Burial (1 Cor 15:35–49; Rom 6:3–5 and 8:9–11)" (1983), reprinted in *Studies in the Cult of Yahweh* 2: 110–20, see p. 127. Betz sees the ritual as a Stoic philosophical reinterpretation of "traditional Egyptian religion" that "seems to reflect an early or nascent Hermeticism," *The "Mithras Liturgy,"* 37.

60. Garth Fowden, *The Egyptian Hermes: A Historical Approach to the Late Pagan Mind* (Princeton, N.J.: Princeton University Press, 1986), 146, see also pp. 82–87.

61. Brian P. Copenhaver, trans. and ed., *Hermetica: The Greek Corpus Hermeticum and the Latin Asclepius in a New English Translation with Notes and Introduction* (Cambridge, U.K.: Cambridge University Press, 1992), 44, 82–86.

62. Ibid., 34–35, see also pp. 82–86.

63. Morton Smith, "Prolegomena to a Discussion of Aretalogies, Divine Men, the Gospels and Jesus" (1971), reprinted in *Studies in the Cult of Yahweh* 2: 3–27, quotation from p. 18.

64. Smith, *Clement*, 181, 240, 242. He had originally made this argument in "Observations on Hekhalot Rabbati," *Biblical and Other Studies,* ed. Alexander Altmann, Philip W. Lown Institute of Advanced Judaic Studies, Brandeis University, Studies and Texts 1 (Cambridge, Mass.: Harvard University Press, 1963), 142–60. However, the similarities listed on p. 159 ("The contrast between mortal and immortal beings . . .") are the kinds of things any mystical tradition might come up with on its own—for the most part they are too general to sustain a claim that the magical papyri and the Hekhalot are so closely interrelated as to be effectively the same, even if there may have been borrowings or points of contact. It is also not irrelevant that Smith dated the *Hekhalot Rabbati* to the fourth century CE, p. 148.

65. Rachel Elior, *The Three Temples: On the Emergence of Jewish Mysticism,* trans. David Louvish (Oxford: The Littman Library of Jewish Civilization, 2004), especially pp. 250–52, 257.

66. Smith, "Observations," 159. A good introduction to this literature is Peter Schäfer, *The Hidden and Manifest God: Some Major Themes in Early Jewish Mysticism,* trans. Aubrey Pomerance (Albany: State University of New York Press, 1992).

67. Radcliffe G. Edmonds, "The Faces of the Moon: Cosmology, Genesis, and the *Mithras Liturgy,"* *Heavenly Realms and Earthly Realities in Late Antique Religions,* ed. Ra'anan S. Boustan and Annette Yoshiko Reed (Cambridge, U.K.: Cambridge University Press, 2004), 275–95, quotations from pp. 278, 293.

68. Peter Shäfer, "In Heaven As It Is in Hell: The Cosmology of *Seder Rabbah di-Bereshit,"* *Heavenly Realms,* 233–74, quotation from p. 272.

69. James R. Davila, "Shamanic Initiatory Death and Resurrection in the *Hekhalot* Literature," *Magic and Ritual in the Ancient World,* ed. Paul Mirecki and Marvin Meyer,

Religions in the Graeco-Roman World 141 (Leiden: Brill, 2002), 283–302. James R. Davila, *Descenders to the Chariot: The People Behind the Hekhalot Literature,* Supplements to the Journal for the Study of Judaism 70 (Leiden: Brill, 2001).

70. See now Ra'anan S. Boustan, "Angels in the Architecture: Temple Art and the Poetics of Praise in the *Songs of the Sabbath Sacrifice,*" *Heavenly Realms,* 195–212.

71. Michael D. Swartz, *Mystical Prayer in Ancient Judaism: An Analysis of Ma'aseh Merkavah* (Tübingen: J. C. B. Mohr [Paul Siebeck], 1992), 222.

72. According to Michael Wise, "In the original Hebrew, the syllables and long, drawn-out phrases tumble over one another in an almost hypnotic cadence. We encounter a constant rotation of synonyms that follow one another to numbing effect." See Michael Wise, Martin Abegg, Jr., and Edward Cook, eds., *The Dead Sea Scrolls: A New Translation* (San Francisco: Harper, 1996), 365.

73. *The Dead Sea Scrolls: Hebrew, Aramaic, and Greek Texts with English Translations 4B: Angelic Liturgy: Songs of the Sabbath Sacrifice,* ed. James H. Charlesworth, Carol A. Newsom et al., The Princeton Theological Seminary Dead Sea Scrolls Project (Tübingen: Mohr Siebeck; Louisville, Ky.: John Knox, 1999), 10.

74. A classic exploration of John's relationship to the Essenes was W. H. Brownlee, "John the Baptist in the New Light of Ancient Scrolls," *The Scrolls and the New Testament,* ed. Krister Stendahl (New York: Harper, 1957), repr. with new material by James H. Charlesworth (New York: Crossroad, 1992), 33–53. For a more up-to-date view see Joan E. Taylor, *The Immerser: John the Baptist Within Second Temple Judaism* (Grand Rapids, Mich.: Eerdmans, 1997), 15–48. The most relevant Qumran texts are conveniently collected in Benoît and Munier, *Le Baptême,* 2–11.

75. Smith, *Secret Gospel,* 119.

76. Thus *Union Hymnal for Jewish Worship,* 2nd ed. (n.p.: Central Conference of American Rabbis, 1914), includes "O God Our Help in Ages Past" by Isaac Watts, "O Worship the King" by Robert Grant, other psalm paraphrases by Watts, John Milton, Tate and Brady, and the "Scottish Version" (a metrical paraphrase of the Psalter), as well as other texts by Rudyard Kipling, James Russell Lowell, Walter Scott, John Greenleaf Whittier, and other Christian authors. The 3rd revised edition, *Union Hymnal: Songs and Prayers for Jewish Worship* (1940), drops some of these and has proportionally fewer hymns of Christian origin despite a larger overall repertory. But it adds D. C. Roberts's "God of Our Fathers" and C. F. Alexander's "All Things Bright and Beautiful."

77. Karen L. King, *What Is Gnosticism?* (Cambridge, Mass.: The Belknap Press of Harvard University Press, 2003).

78. Morton Smith, "The History of the Term 'Gnostikos' " (1981), reprinted in *Studies in the Cult of Yahweh* 2: 183–93.

79. Michael Allen Williams, *Rethinking "Gnosticism": An Argument for Dismantling a Dubious Category* (Princeton, N.J.: Princeton University Press, 1996), 265.

80. April D. DeConick, *Seek to See Him: Ascent and Vision Mysticism in the Gospel of Thomas,* Supplements to Vigiliae Christianae 33 (Leiden: Brill, 1996).

81. April D. DeConick, *Voices of the Mystics: Early Christian Discourse in the Gospels of John and Thomas and Other Ancient Christian Literature,* Journal for the Study of the New Testament Supplement Series 157 (Sheffield: Sheffield Academic Press, 2001), 128–31.

82. Saxer, *Les rites,* 67. Robert Pierce Casey, ed. and trans., *The Excerpta ex Theodoto of Clement of Alexandria,* Studies and Documents 1 (London: Christophers, 1934), 88–89. DeConick, *Seek,* 43–96.

83. Compare Eckhard Rau, "Zwischen Gemeindechristentum und christlichen Gnosis: Das geheimen Markusevangelium und das Geheimnis des Reiches Gottes," *New Testament Studies* 51 (2005): 482–504.

84. See Marvin W. Meyer, "Gospel of Thomas Logion 114 Revisited," in *For the Children, Perfect Instruction: Studies in Honor of Hans-Martin Schenke on the Occasion of the Berliner Arbeitskreis für koptisch-gnostische Schriften's Thirtieth Year,* ed. Hans-Gebhard Bethge, Stephen Emmel, Karen L. King, and Imke Schletterer, Nag Hammadi and Manichaean Studies 54 (Leiden: Brill, 2002), 101–11.

85. Rudolph, *Gnosis,* 171. The text known as *Treatise on the Resurrection* also teaches that "since the Elect knows himself to be already dead, he should recognize that 'in Christ' . . . he is already resurrected and in rest." Malcolm Peel in Attridge et al., *Nag Hammadi Codex I* 2: 142, see also 1: 148–57.

86. Layton, *Gnostic Scriptures,* 332, quotation from p. 345. See also Hans-Martin Schenke, "Zur Exegese des Philippus-Evangeliums," *Coptology: Past, Present, and Future: Studies in Honour of Rodolphe Kasser,* ed. S. Giversen, M. Krause, and P. Nagel, Orientalia Lovaniensia Analecta 61 (Leuven: Peeters, 1994), 23–37, especially pp. 128–31.

87. Gospel According to Philip, 52–53, 60, 66, 68, 70, 83, 105. See Layton, *Gnostic Scriptures,* 326, 339–43, 346, 352.

88. On the other hand, Williams argues in *Rethinking,* 147–50, that this refers to "spiritual marriage," in which a man and woman who are married to each other make a joint commitment to renounce sexual intercourse. Irenaeus also says that some groups practice "spiritual marriage" in place of baptism (*Adversus Haereses* 1.21.3, trans. Unger, 28), but he does not describe the ceremony very clearly.

89. *Zostrianos,* trans. John N. Sieber, *The Nag Hammadi Library,* 402–30. Smith certainly knew this text; he mentioned it briefly in "History of the Term," 2: 192.

90. The subject was long ignored, but recent research has found "that youths (particularly male youths) who have a self-declared or perceived homosexual orientation or activity have a rate of suicidal behavior that is between two and eight times greater than in others," according to Christopher Bagley and Pierre Tremblay, "Elevated Rates of Suicidal Behavior in Gay, Lesbian, and Bisexual Youth," *Crisis: The Journal of Crisis Intervention and Suicide Prevention* 21 (2000): 111–17. The college Morton Smith attended has been described as an environment in which many people "saw a logical link between homosexuality and suicide"; see William Wright, *Harvard's Secret Court: The Savage 1920 Purge of Campus Homosexuals* (New York: St. Martin's Press, 2005), 9–25, 66, 101, 136, 144–50, 189, 200–1, 259, quotation from p. 25. For more, including a high Anglican literature professor who taught while Smith was there, see Douglass Shand-Tucci, *The Crimson Letter: Harvard, Homosexuality, and the Shaping of American Culture* (New York: St. Martin's Press, 2003), 128–29, 144, 149–55.

91. *Zostrianos* 3–5, pp. 404–5.

92. *Zostrianos* 57–60, p. 418.

93. See, for example, Woolley, *Coptic Offices,* 46, 75–82.

94. *Zostrianos* 130:23, 131:5–10, p. 430.

95. John N. Sieber's introduction in *The Nag Hammadi Library*, 402–3. On the other hand, John D. Turner would connect *Zostrianos* with the Sethian tradition of Gnosticism, based partly on its cosmology. It is nonetheless somewhat divorced from "an explicit ritual setting" and perhaps represents "the terminus of a process of development in which a traditional practice of visionary ascent that originally arose in the context of Sethian baptismal practice . . . was subsequently transformed . . . into a self-contained and self-performable contemplative practice." Turner, "Ritual in Gnosticism," *Gnosticism and Later Platonism: Themes, Figures, and Texts,* ed. John D. Turner and Ruth Majercik, Society of Biblical Literature Symposium Series 12 (Atlanta: Society of Biblical Literature, 2000), 83–139, quotations from 96–97.

96. Smith, *Clement*, 264, italics in original. Smith was trying to explain away the "second-century silence about Paul's doctrine of baptism" revealed in Benoît, *Le Baptême chrétien*, 228, one of the few books on early Christian liturgy that Smith did read.

97. Smith, *Clement*, 265.

98. Morton Smith, "The Origin and History of the Transfiguration Story" (1980), reprinted in *Studies in the Cult of Yahweh* 2: 79–86, see p. 84.

99. Morton Smith, "The Reason for the Persecution of Paul and the Obscurity of Acts" (1967), reprinted in *Studies in the Cult of Yahweh* 2: 87–94, see pp. 88 and 89–90.

100. Morton Smith, "Ascent to the Heavens and the Beginning of Christianity" (1981), reprinted in *Studies in the Cult of Yahweh* 2: 47–67.

101. Smith, *Clement*, 277.

102. For what follows, see Smith, *Clement*, 175–78.

103. It is not at all clear that Jewish proselyte baptism antedates Christianity; see Adela Yarbro Collins, "The Origin of Christian Baptism," *Living Water*, 35–57, especially pp. 41–46. Smith himself acknowledged this problem in *Secret Gospel*, 92.

104. A. F. J. Klijn, ed., *The Acts of Thomas: Introduction, Text, and Commentary,* 2nd rev. ed., Supplements to Novum Testamentum 108 (Leiden: Brill, 2003), 206–7, 10–11.

105. Robert Cabié, *Les sacrements de l'initiation chrétienne (Baptême, confirmation, première communion),* Bibliothèque d'histoire du christianisme 32 ([Tournai:] Desclée, 1994), 36.

106. Thus in one of the Latin texts, the apostle does have the neophyte put on "new and white garments," but not a sindōn. See Klaus Zelzer, ed., *Die alten lateinischen Thomasakten,* Texte und Untersuchungen 122 (Berlin: Akademie-Verlag, 1977), 32. On the Greek and Syriac differences, see Klijn, *Acts of Thomas,* 12–14; Spinks, "Baptismal Patterns," 45–52. On the Armenian, Louis Leloir, "Le Baptême du roi Gundaphor," *Le Muséon* 100 (1987): 225–33.

107. I assume Smith was consulting Richard Adelbert Lipsius and Max Bonnet, eds., *Acta Apostolorum Apocrypha,* 2 vols. in 3 (Leipzig: Hermann Mendelssohn, 1891–1903; repr. Hildesheim: Georg Olms, 1972, 1990), 2/2 p. 297 and 2/1 p. 257.

108. The sentence "And let them stand in the water naked" (21.11) actually isn't in *AT* but in the fifth-century Syriac text known as *Testamentum Domini,* which is derived from *AT*. See Bradshaw et al., *Apostolic Tradition,* 115. However, one cannot tell this from Dix's translation (*Apostolic Tradition,* 35). It is not clear that "them" refers to both "the initiate and the presbyter who is baptizing him," as Smith says (*Clement,* 91). But if it

does this is a peculiarity of the *Testamentum* and not part of the main tradition of the text. On the origin of the *Testamentum* see Michael Kohlbacher, "Wessen Kirche ordnete das Testamentum Domini Nostri Jesu Christi? Anmerkungen zum historischen Kontext von CPG 1743," *Zu Geschichte, Theologie, Liturgie and Gegenwartslage der syrischen Kirchen: Ausgewählte Vorträge des deutschen Syrologen-Symposiums vom 2.–4. Oktober 1998 in Hermannsburg,* ed. Martin Tamcke and Andreas Heinz, Studien zur Orientalischen Kirchengeschichte 9 (Hamburg: LIT Verlag, 2000), 55–137.

109. Colossians 2:11, Galatians 3:27, 1 Corinthians 15:33 as reinterpreted in *Odes of Solomon* 15:8, 2 Corinthians 5:2, without asking whether Colossians actually dates from "Paul's time."

110. Quoted from Schneemelcher, ed., *New Testament Apocrypha* 1: 123, 211.

111. Jonathan Z. Smith, "The Garments of Shame," *History of Religions* 5 (1965–66): 217–38, quotation from p. 236. It is hard to believe that Morton Smith was unaware of this article, for he published an obituary in the next issue: "Erwin Ramsdell Goodenough (1893–1965)," pp. 351–52. More recently Loader, *Sexuality,* 193–207, has placed the *Thomas* and *Egyptians* logia in the context of a larger group of texts on the theme of celibacy as overcoming gender boundaries.

112. Smith cites by volume and page of the critical edition, but they are translated into title and chapter numbers as *Excerpta* 80 (III.131.25ff), *Eclogae* 12 and 25 (III.140.6ff, 143.24ff).

113. This interpretation is more broadly hinted in Smith, *Secret Gospel,* 78–81.

114. Saxer, *Les rites,* 191–92, 206–7, 262, 281, 315, 321–22, 324–27, etc.

115. Ante Crnčević, *Induere Christum: Rito e linguaggio simbolico-teologico della vestizione battesimale,* Bibliotheca "Ephemerides Liturgicae" "Subsidia" 108 (Rome: CLV Edizioni Liturgiche, 2000), 179.

116. Mark Pierce, "Themes in the 'Odes of Solomon' and Other Early Christian Writings and Their Baptismal Character," *Ephemerides Liturgicae* 98 (1984): 35–59, especially p. 48. The garment in the Hymn of the Pearl is resplendent but not necessarily white; it is not interpreted as a baptismal garment in Paul-Hubert Poirier, *L'Hymne de la Perle des Actes de Thomas: Introduction, Texte-Traduction, Commentaire,* Homo Religiosus 8 (Louvain-la-Neuve: Institut Orientaliste de l'Université Catholique, 1981), 413–15, 422–23, 430–36. For the Odes of Solomon see Charlesworth, *Old Testament Pseudepigrapha,* 2: 754. For the Hymn of the Pearl see Elliott, *Apocryphal New Testament,* 488–91; Layton, *Gnostic Scriptures,* 366–75; Schneemelcher, *New Testament Apocrypha* 2: 380–85. For the Acts of Peter and the Twelve Apostles see Schneemelcher, *New Testament Apocrypha* 2: 420–25.

117. See Benoît and Munier, *Le Baptême,* 72–73, 78–79.

118. Eibert J. C. Tigchelaar, "The White Dress of the Essenes and the Pythagoreans," *Jerusalem, Alexandria, Rome: Studies in Ancient Cultural Interaction in Honour of A. Hilhorst,* ed. Florentino García Martínez and Gerard P. Luttikhuizen (Leiden: Brill, 2003), 301–21. Interestingly, white clothes were for men, colored clothes for women, see pp. 313, 315, 319.

119. Schneemelcher, ed., *New Testament Apocrypha* 2: 187. Elliott, ed., *Apocryphal New Testament,* 322.

120. Betz, *The "Mithras Liturgy,"* 55.

121. Following the terms used in the Jewish Publication Society translation, 2nd ed. See, for example, *The Jewish Study Bible,* ed. Adele Berlin and Marc Zvi Brettler (Oxford: Oxford University Press, 2004), 244.

122. Mary Dean-Otting, *Heavenly Journeys: A Study of the Motif in Hellenistic Jewish Literature,* Judentum und Umwelt 8 (Frankfurt am Main, Bern: Peter Lang, 1984), 285 (shining garments), 279 (water above the heavens), 287 (anointing). Michael D. Swartz, "The Semiotics of the Priestly Vestments in Ancient Judaism," *Sacrifice in Religious Experience,* ed. Albert I. Baumgarten, Numen Book Series: Studies in the History of Religions 93 (Leiden: Brill, 2002), 57–80, especially pp. 64–65, 69, 76–77.

123. John 7:2, 37, on which see Joel Marcus, "Rivers of Living Water from Jesus' Belly (John 7:38)," *Journal of Biblical Literature* 117 (1998): 328–30. Louis Jacobs, "Sukkot in Rabbinic Literature," *Encyclopaedia Judaica* (Jerusalem: Keter, 1971), 15: 498–99.

124. Clement of Alexandria also seems to have combined priestly symbolism with baptismal symbolism, see Annewies van den Hoek, *Clement of Alexandria and His Use of Philo in the Stromateis: An Early Christian Reshaping of a Jewish Model,* Supplements to Vigiliae Christianae 3 (Leiden: Brill, 1988), 142–43.

125. R. J. Zwi Werblowsky and Geoffrey Wigoder, eds., *The Oxford Dictionary of the Jewish Religion* (New York: Oxford University Press, 1997), 402. See also "Kitel" in *Encyclopaedia Judaica* 10: 1079; Louis Jacobs, *The Jewish Religion: A Companion* (Oxford: Oxford University Press, 1995), 306; Geoffrey Wigoder et al., *The New Encyclopedia of Judaism* (New York: New York University Press, 2002), 460–41. See Ronald L. Eisenberg, *The JPS Guide to Jewish Traditions* (Philadelphia: Jewish Publication Society, 2004), 619.

126. Talmud Yerushalmi, *Rosh Hashanah* 1.3. For translation and commentary, see *The Talmud of the Land of Israel: A Preliminary Translation and Explanation 16: Rosh Hashanah,* trans. Edward A. Goldman, Chicago Studies in the History of Judaism (Chicago: University of Chicago Press, 1988), 44. Jacob Neusner, *The Talmud of the Land of Israel: An Academic Commentary to the Second, Third, and Fourth Divisions 10: Yerushalmi Tractate Rosh Hashanah,* South Florida Academic Commentary Series 119 (Atlanta, Ga.: Scholars Press, 1998), 20.

127. Ellen Frankel and Betsy Platking Teutsch, *The Encyclopedia of Jewish Symbols* (Northvale, N.J.: Jason Aronson, 1992), 91–92, which includes a drawing. For a photograph, see Philip R. Davies et al., *The Complete World of the Dead Sea Scrolls* (London: Thames and Hudson, 2002), 138. A Polish silver belt buckle from 1821 is pictured in *Encyclopedia Judaica* 5: 1381.

128. Schneemelcher, ed., *New Testament Apocrypha* 2: 194–201. This text uses an unusual word for "undergarment," see pp. 196, 208 n. 67. Elliott, ed., *Apocryphal New Testament,* 328–35.

129. Jodi Magness, *The Archaeology of Qumran and the Dead Sea Scrolls* (Grand Rapids, Mich.: Eerdmans, 2002), 168.

130. Minna Lönnqvist and Kenneth Lönnqvist, *Archaeology of the Hidden Qumran: The New Paradigm* (Helsinki: Helsinki University Press, 2002), 241–72, 292–96.

131. Rachel Hachlili, *Jewish Funerary Customs, Practices and Rites in the Second Temple Period,* supplements to the Journal for the Study of Judaism 94 (Leiden: Brill, 2005), 13, 385, 444, 475, 480–81, on leather shrouds see pp. 18–19.

132. Numerous writings have made such claims, for example Kenneth E. Stevenson and Gary R. Habermas, *The Shroud and the Controversy* (Nashville, Tenn.: Thomas Nelson, 1990), 149–52. On the other hand, see Raymond E. Brown, "Appended Notes on the Shroud of Turin," *Biblical Exegesis and Church Doctrine* (Mahwah, N.J.: Paulist Press, 1985), 147–55; Giuseppe Ghiberti, "The Gospels and the Shroud," *The Turin Shroud: Past, Present and Future: International Scientific Symposium, Torino 2.–5. March 2000*, ed. Silvano Scannerini and Piero Savarino (Turin: Effatà Editrice, 2000), 273–84; Hachlili, *Jewish Funerary Customs*, 442–43.

133. Osborn, "Clement," 224.

Chapter 6. Hypnotic Hymns

Epigraph. Smith, *Secret Gospel*, 118–19.

1. Ibid., 1–2.

2. I.e., the morning service, which ran from midnight to 6 a.m., see ibid., 4.

3. Ibid., 5–6.

4. Smith, *Secret Gospel*, 113 n. 12.

5. See the chronology of Smith's career at the beginning of the next chapter.

6. There are, of course, people for whom just being at Harvard is a religious experience, a subject that endlessly fascinates Harvard-connected authors. See, for example, Ari L. Goldman, *The Search for God at Harvard* (New York: Times Books/Random House, 1991); Kelly Monroe, *Finding God at Harvard: Spiritual Journeys of Christian Thinkers* (Grand Rapids, Mich.: Zondervan, 1996); Harvey Cox, *When Jesus Came to Harvard: Making Moral Choices Today* (New York: Houghton Mifflin, 2004); "Fear of God at Harvard" at http://www.boundless.org/1999/regulars/kaufman/a0000095.html; "God and Mammon at Harvard" at http://www.fastcompany.com/magazine/94/god-and-mammon.html; "God and Man at Harvard" at http://www.theatlantic.com/doc/prem/200502u/int2005-02-10; "Meeting God at Harvard" at http://www.aish.com/spirituality/odysseys/Meeting_God_at_Harvard.asp (all web sites accessed July 2005).

7. Smith, *Secret Gospel*, 5, 113 with n. 12, 6, 113–14. Smith, *Clement*, 265. Smith, "The Reason," 89–90. Smith, *Secret Gospel*, 6.

8. Waterman, "The Role of Obscenity," 162. For an exceptional genre involving written transmission see Dundes, "Here I Sit."

9. Charles Winick, "A Content Analysis of Orally Communicated Jokes," *The American Imago* 20 (1963): 271–91, quotation from p. 291. Also Winick, "The Social Contexts of Humor," *Journal of Communication* 26/3 (September 1976): 124–28. Ronald L. Baker, *Jokelore: Humorous Folktales from Indiana* (Bloomington: Indiana University Press, 1986). The internet, of course, opens up all kinds of exciting new possibilities for collecting oral jokes, as evidenced by http://www.laughlab.co.uk/.

10. In 1988, Indiana University basketball coach Bobby Knight, whose outbursts of rage were legendary, told the joke to interviewer Connie Chung when she asked him how he handled stress, see http://espn.go.com/classic/biography/s/Knight_Bob.html (accessed April 2006). More recently, Clayton Williams lost the race for governor of Texas after telling a version of the joke, see Roberto Suro, "Texan Hunkers Down After Stumbling on Tongue," *New York Times* 139/48,240 (May 19, 1990), 7. On May 24–25,

2004, it was widely reported in Asian news media that a Malaysian politician named Haji Roselan Johar Mohamed had told the joke at a "legal literacy seminar for women" — thereby managing to offend not only women but people who actually knew something about Confucius. In April of 2005 some of these stories could still be accessed at http:// osabah.tblog.com/, http://www.onlinewomeninpolitics.org/archives/04_0524_my_ vaw.htm, http://www.mca.org.my/services/printerfriendly.asp?file=/articles/news/2004/ 5 /25/24922.html&lg=1, and elsewhere. For the 1954 Georgia criminal case (*Smith v. The State* 18569 [210 Ga. 713] [82 SE2d 507]), see www.lawskills.com/case/ga/id/ 18745/ (accessed July 2005); "Lie Back and Enjoy It" was the title of the 1970 album by the rock band Juicy Lucy, see *The Encyclopedia of Popular Music,* 3rd ed., ed. Colin Larkin (New York: MUZE UK, 1998), 4: 2909–10; for the New York City incident, see "WABC Suspends Tex Antoine After a Flippant Remark on Rape," *New York Times* 126/43,405 (November 25, 1976), 58, and subsequent stories through December 18. Although not many folklorists have studied the Confucius joke cycle, see www.uta.fi/ FAST/US7/FOLK/confuci.html (accessed July 2005). The folklorist's difficulties in collecting oral obscene jokes are illustrated by the fact that this one is not found in G. Legman, *No Laughing Matter: An Analysis of Sexual Humor,* 2 vols. (Bloomington: Indiana University Press, 1968, 1975), 1: 256–65, though a similar statement is attributed to Confucius on p. 262.

11. Smith, *Secret Gospel,* 6–7.

12. Harold Leitenberg and Kris Henning, "Sexual Fantasy," *Psychological Bulletin* 117 (1995): 469–96, especially pp. 480, 482–84, 490–91.

13. Karen Franklin, "Enacting Masculinity: Antigay Violence and Group Rape as Participatory Theater," *Sexuality Research & Social Policy* 1/2 (April 2004): 25–40, quotation from p. 35. See also Alan Dundes with Lauren Dundes, "The Elephant Walk and Other Amazing Hazing: Male Fraternity Initiation Through Infantilization and Feminization," in Alan Dundes, *Bloody Mary in the Mirror: Essays in Psychoanalytic Folkloristics* (Jackson: University Press of Mississippi, 2002), 95–121. Alan Dundes, "The American Game of 'Smear the Queer' and the Homosexual Component of Male Competitive Sport and Warfare," in Dundes, *Parsing Through Customs: Essays by a Freudian Folklorist* (Madison: University of Wisconsin Press, 1987), 178–94. Dundes, *From Game to War and Other Psychoanalytic Essays on Folklore* (Lexington: University Press of Kentucky, 1997), 25–45. Paul Ruffins, "The Persistent Madness of Greek Hazing: Psychologists Provide Insight on Why Hazing Persists Among Black Greeks," *Black Issues in Higher Education* 15/9 (June 25, 1998): 14–16. Michael Scarce, *Male on Male Rape: The Hidden Toll of Stigma and Shame* (New York: Plenum Press, 1997), 51–56. Peter M. Sheridan and Steven Hucker, "Rape and Sadomasochistic Paraphilias," *The Handbook of Forensic Sexology: Biomedical & Criminological Perspectives,* ed. James J. Krivacska and John Money (Amherst, N.Y.: Prometheus Books, 1994), 104–25, especially pp. 109–111. Damon Mitchell, Richard Hirschman, and Gordon C. Nagayama Hall, "Attributions of Victim Responsibility, Pleasure, and Trauma in Male Rape," *Journal of Sex Research* 36/4 (November 1999): 369–73. Seven percent of male college athletes reported being subjected to initiatory hazing rituals that included "engaging in or simulating sexual acts," according to Nadine C. Hoover et al., "National Survey: Initiation Rites and Athletics for NCAA [National Collegiate Athletic Association] Sports

Teams" (Alfred University, August 30, 1999), p. 10, available at http://www.alfred.edu/
sports_hazing/docs/hazing.pdf. See also http://www.alfred.edu/sports_hazing/initia
tionrites.html (accessed March 2006). I am unaware of reliable statistics for fraternities,
where such practices are often alleged to be common.

14. *The Philokalia: The Complete Text Compiled by St Nikodimos of the Holy Mountain and St Makarios of Corinth,* trans. G. E. H. Palmer et al., vol. 2 (London: Faber and
Faber, 1981), 346, 352, 346, 354.

15. For these hymn quotations see Robert F. Taft, *The Great Entrance: A History of the
Transfer of Gifts and other Pre-Anaphoral Rites of the Liturgy of St. John Chrysostom,*
2nd ed., Orientalia Christiana Analecta 200 (Rome: Pont. Institutum Studiorum Orientalium, 1978), 54–55.

16. John Climacus, *The Ladder of Divine Ascent,* trans. Colm Luibheid and Norman
Russell, The Classics of Western Spirituality (New York: Paulist Press, 1982), 276.

17. Hilarion Alfeyev, *St. Symeon the New Theologian and Orthodox Tradition,* Oxford Early Christian Studies (Oxford: Oxford University Press, 2000), 79–80. For further
bibliography see Steven Payne, "Attention, Attentiveness," *The New Dictionary of Catholic Spirituality,* ed. Michael Downey (Collegeville, Minn.: Liturgical Press, 1993), 65–
66; R. Vernay, "Attention," *Dictionnaire de spiritualité* 1/4 (Paris: Beauchesne, 1935),
1058–77.

18. Archimandrite Sophrony, *The Monk of Mount Athos: Staretz Silouan 1866–1938,*
trans. Rosemary Edmonds (London: Mowbray, 1973 [many reprint editions]), 25.

19. Smith, *Secret Gospel,* 7.

20. Introductions to the major issues and thinkers include John Middleton, "Magic:
Theories of Magic," *Encyclopedia of Religion,* 2nd ed., ed. Lindsay Jones et al. (Detroit,
Mich.: Thomson Gale, 2005), 8: 5562–69; Mary R. O'Neil, "Superstition," Ibid., 13:
8864–67; Jeffrey Burton Russell and Sabina Magliocco, "Witchcraft: Concepts of Witch-
craft," Ibid., 14: 9768–76; Phillips Stevens, "Magic," "Religion," and "Sorcery and
Witchcraft," *Encyclopedia of Cultural Anthropology,* ed. David Levinson and Melvin
Ember (New York: Henry Holt, 1996), 3: 721–26, 3: 1088–1100, 4: 1225–32; Nancey
Murphy, "Religion and Science," *Routledge Encyclopedia of Philosophy,* ed. Edward
Craig (London: Routledge, 1998), 8: 230–36; Diane Ciekawy, "Magic" and "Witch-
craft," *New Dictionary of the History of Ideas,* ed. Maryanne Cline Horowitz (Detroit:
Thomson Gale, 2005), 4: 1330–34, 6: 2476–79; Christopher Southgate, "Religion and
Science," Ibid., 5: 2072–75; William E. Burns, "Superstition," Ibid., 5: 2272–76; Gilbert
Lewis, "Magic, Religion and the Rationality of Belief," *Companion Encyclopedia of
Anthropology,* ed. Tim Ingold (London: Routledge, 1994; repr. 2000), 563–90.

21. Sophrony, *The Monk,* 75.

22. Ibid., 75–76.

23. St. Isaac the Syrian, *Homily 22 (23),* quoted in Kallistos Ware, *The Inner Kingdom,*
Collected Works 1 (Crestwood, N.Y.: St. Vladimir's Seminary Press, 2000), 14. The
following essays in Ware's volume are also highly relevant to the present discussion: "The
Orthodox Experience of Repentance," 43–57; "The Theology of Worship," 59–68; "A
Sense of Wonder," 69–74; "Pray Without Ceasing: The Ideal of Continual Prayer in
Eastern Monasticism," 75–87; "Silence in Prayer: The Meaning of Hesychia" 89–110.

24. The hymn of the Great Entrance for the Liturgy of St. Basil on Holy Saturday, in the

poetic paraphrase by Gerard Moultrie (1829–85), cited from *The Hymnal of the Protestant Episcopal Church in the United States of America 1940* (New York: Church Pension Fund, 1943) no. 197. Prose translations will be found in Mary and Ware, *The Lenten Triodion*, p. 659, and Taft, *The Great Entrance*, 55. The text is also frequently associated with the Liturgy of St. James, the original Eucharistic rite of Jerusalem — which, however, is rarely celebrated in the modern Greek Orthodox Church; see Albert Edward Bailey, *The Gospel in Hymns: Backgrounds and Interpretations* (New York: Charles Scribner's Sons, 1950), 287–88.

25. S. L. Davies, *Jesus the Healer: Possession, Trance, and the Origins of Christianity* (New York: Continuum, 1995); John J. Pilch, *Visions and Healing in the Acts of the Apostles: How the Early Believers Experienced God* (Collegeville, Minn.: Liturgical Press, 2004). Bernhard Lang, *Sacred Games: A History of Christian Worship* (New Haven, Conn.: Yale University Press, 1997), acknowledges a debt to Smith (pp. xi, 468 n. 15 and n. 16). His chapter on "Paul the Possessed" (which begins p. 372) has the same title as the book Smith was working on when he died, according to Cohen, "In Memoriam" (1994) 3; (1996) 281.

26. Smith, *Clement,* 251.

27. Thus one of the earliest serious researchers on rock music mentioned "the monotony of the rhythm which, even in the course of a slight ritard, might induce a kind of hypnotic climax." Mantle Hood, *The Ethnomusicologist* (New York: McGraw-Hill, 1971), 18. Hood, "The Consensus Makers of Asian Music," *Perspectives in Musicology: The Inaugural Lectures of the Ph.D. Program in Music at the City University of New York,* ed. Barry S. Brook, Edward O. D. Downes, and Sherman Van Solkema (New York: W. W. Norton, 1972), 290–306, see pp. 292–96, quotation from p. 294.

28. Notably in the songs that end each of the two acts: "Be In/Hare Krishna" and "Let the Sun Shine In." See Barbara Lee Horn, *The Age of Hair: Evolution and Impact of Broadway's First Rock Musical,* Contributions in Drama and Theatre Studies 42 (Westport, Conn.: Greenwood Press, 1991), 73–74, 79–80.

29. Barbara W. Lex, "The Neurobiology of Ritual Trance," *The Spectrum of Ritual: A Biogenetic Structural Analysis,* ed. Eugene G. d'Aquili et al. (New York: Columbia University Press, 1979), 117–51. Lex depends in part on two articles by Andrew Neher: "Auditory Driving Observed with Scalp Electrodes in Normal Subjects," *Electroencephalography and Clinical Neurophysiology* 13 (1961): 449–51, and "A Physiological Explanation of Unusual Behavior in Ceremonies Involving Drums," *Human Biology* 34/2 (1962): 151–60. But more recent writers have rejected Neher's views: Gilbert Rouget, *Music and Trance: A Theory of the Relations Between Music and Possession,* trans. and rev. by Brunhilde Biebuyck (Chicago: University of Chicago, 1985), 169–76; Marina Roseman, *Healing Sounds from the Malaysian Rain Forest: Temiar Music and Medicine,* Comparative Studies of Health Systems and Medical Care (Berkeley: University of California Press, 1991), 171–73; Judith Becker, *Deep Listeners: Music, Emotion, and Trancing* (Bloomington: Indiana University Press, 2004), 37, 122, 127–29 with footnote at p. 164; the CD accompanying this book illustrates the wide variety of music that can be associated with trance experiences.

30. Smith, *Secret Gospel,* 102 n. 4.

31. Douglas O. Linder, "The Chicago Seven Conspiracy Trial," at http://www.law

.umkc.edu/faculty/projects/ftrials/Chicago7/Account.html (accessed July 2005). The best evocation of the Yippie spirit is Abbie Hoffman's prison classic *Steal This Book* ([New York:] Pirate Editions, 1971; repr. New York: Four Walls Eight Windows, 2002). Illegal copies are available (as of March 2006) at http://www.tenant.net/Community/steal/steal.html and http://www.mindmined.com/public_library/nonfiction/abbie_hoffman_steal_this_book.html.

32. The most famous example is the so-called "Family" of Charles Manson, whose horrific 1969 murders included the writing of Beatles lyrics on the walls of the victims' homes and may have been motivated by Manson's rage at his failure to obtain a recording contract. On their music, still available and often recorded by other artists, see http://www.charliemanson.com/music.htm; general information at http://en.wikipedia.org/wiki/Manson_Family (both accessed July 2005). Green Beret Jeffrey MacDonald, who was convicted of murdering his wife and children in 1970, was widely believed when he blamed the murders on a group of chanting hippies; the veracity of his story is still being debated. See Joe McGinniss, *Fatal Vision* (New York: Penguin, 1983, 1985, 1989); Janet Malcolm, *The Journalist and the Murderer* (New York: Vintage, 1990); Jerry Allen Potter and Fred Bost, *Fatal Justice: Reinvestigating the MacDonald Murders* (New York: Norton, 1997). The text of the alleged chant, "Acid is groovy kill the pigs" [*sic*] was made the title of a (by all accounts unmemorable) 1993 movie short by Joe Christ.

33. Gilbert Rouget, *La musique et la transe: Esquisse d'une théorie générale des relations de la musique et de la possession* (Paris: Gallimard, 1980).

34. According to psychiatrist Marlene Steinberg and her coauthor Maxine Schnall, *The Stranger in the Mirror: Dissociation, the Hidden Epidemic* (New York: Cliff Street Books, 2000), dissociative experiences can include anything from "getting lost in a good book" to the conviction that one has been abducted by space aliens. The latter can at times be a disguised memory of sexual abuse (pp. 275–93), which brings us back to Morton Smith . . .

35. Thus Robin Sylvan sees "a strong current of the West African religious sensibility in popular music," specifically the rock-related categories of the Grateful Dead, Rave and "Electronic Dance Music," Heavy Metal, and Rap music. But he locates this primarily in cultural attitudes rather than specific musical characteristics such as repetitiveness: "The power of music to deeply affect people, the central importance of experiential states, and the crucial role of the body are all features that West African possession religion and contemporary Western musical subcultures have in common, and they demonstrate significant continuities." Robin Sylvan, *Traces of the Spirit: The Religious Dimensions of Popular Music* (New York: New York University Press, 2002), 5, 218.

36. Rouget, *Music and Trance*, 325–26, cf. pp. 167–69.

37. Eugene G. d'Aquili and Charles D. Laughlin, Jr., "The Neurobiology of Myth and Ritual," *The Spectrum of Ritual*, 152–82.

38. Becker, *Deep Listeners*, 60–67, 100–07, 163–64. I. M. Lewis, *Ecstatic Religion: A Study of Shamanism and Spirit Possession*, 3rd ed. (London: Routledge, 2003), 52–56, 82–83, 170–71. On Sufi song and dance see William C. Chittick, *Sufism: A Short Introduction* (Oxford: Oneworld, 2000), 61–96. Pnina Werbner and Helene Basu, *Embodying Charisma: Modernity, Locality and the Performance of Emotion in Sufi Cults* (London: Routledge, 1998). Michael A. Sells, ed., *Early Islamic Mysticism: Sufi, Qur'an,*

Mi'raj, Poetic and Theological Writings, The Classics of Western Spirituality (Mahwah, N.J.: Paulist Press, 1996), 56–74. See also *The Collected Works of St. John of the Cross,* rev. ed., ed. and trans. Kieran Kavanaugh and Otilio Rodriguez (Washington, D.C.: ICS Publications, Institute of Carmelite Studies, 1991), 41–80.

39. Brian W. Sturm, "The 'Storylistening' Trance Experience," *Journal of American Folklore* 113 (2000): 287–304, especially pp. 292–93.

40. Lewis, *Ecstatic Religion,* 26–27, 67–89 etc. (see "women" in the index, p. 200). J. Ricardo Alviso, "Feel the Power: Music in a Spanish-Language Pentecostal Church," *Pacific Review of Ethnomusicology* 10 (2001–02): 62–79. Joel Robbins, "The Globalization of Pentecostal and Charismatic Christianity," *Annual Review of Anthropology* 33 (2004): 117–43, especially pp. 16–37, 125–28, 132–34.

41. Janice Boddy, *Wombs and Alien Spirits: Women, Men, and the Zār Cult in Northern Sudan* (Madison: University of Wisconsin Press, 1989), 306–08.

42. Isabelle Nabokov, *Religion Against the Self: An Ethnography of Tamil Rituals* (Oxford: Oxford University Press, 2000), 70–99.

43. See Becker, *Deep Listeners,* 40–44.

44. Jeff Todd Titon, "Bi-musicality as Metaphor," *Journal of American Folklore* 108 (1995): 287–97, quotation from pp. 287–88.

45. Colin Turnbull, "Liminality: A Synthesis of Subjective and Objective Experience," *By Means of Performance: Intercultural Studies of Theatre and Ritual,* ed. Richard Shechner and Willa Appel (Cambridge: Cambridge University Press, 1990), 50–81, quotation from p. 55.

46. Ibid., 56.

47. Ibid., 61.

48. Ibid., 64.

49. Much of the story is told in his classic work: Colin M. Turnbull, *The Forest People: A Study of the Pygmies of the Congo* (New York: Simon & Schuster, 1961 [numerous reprints]). His recordings of Mbuti music are available on *Mbuti Pygmies of the Ituri Rainforest, Recorded by Colin Turnbull and Francis S. Chapman* (Smithsonian Folkways CD SF 40401).

50. Titon, "Bi-musicality," 296.

51. The story is summarized by David Pultz at http://www.fpcnyc.org/fosdick.html (accessed July 2005).

52. Harry Emerson Fosdick, *A Pilgrimage to Palestine* (New York: Macmillan, 1927), 252–53. The text "Art thou weary" is actually by John Mason Neale, first published in his *Hymns for the Eastern Church* (1st ed. 1862), but I am citing J. M. Neale, *Hymns of the Eastern Church* (London: J. T. Hayes, 1876), 154–58. However, Neale's text is an adaptation of a Byzantine idiomelon of the *Oktoechos,* in the first plagal tone, ascribed to Stephen of Mar Saba. Bailey, *The Gospel in Hymns,* 288–99, especially pp. 290–92.

53. Robert Guy McCutchan, *Our Hymnody: A Manual of the Methodist Hymnal,* 2nd ed. (Nashville: Abingdon Press, 1937), 240.

54. See the next chapter.

55. Not far from Smith's office at Columbia, there were liturgical scholars at St. Vladimir's Orthodox Theological Seminary who would have been glad to assist an inquirer with his command of Greek.

56. Mircea Eliade, *Le Chamanisme et les techniques archaïques de l'extase* (Paris: Payot, 1951). Eliade, *Shamanism: Archaic Techniques of Ecstasy,* trans. Willard R. Trask, Bollingen Series 76 (Princeton, N.J.: Princeton University Press, 1964, 1972, 1974).

57. For the continuing discussion of the meaning of the term and its associated phenomena, see Graham Harvey, ed., *Shamanism: A Reader* (London: Routledge, 2003).

58. Smith, *The Secret Gospel,* 105–6, 110.

59. In *Jesus the Magician* Smith did cite Eliade (pp. 77, 104, 186, 194; 1998 reprint, pp. 102, 137), but not enough; he simply lifted two scattered indications and went on his way.

60. Eliade, *Shamanism,* 5.

61. Ibid., 5–6.

62. Ibid., 110–44.

63. Note: Smith had just denied this in the previous paragraph, where he said the story of Acts 2 (the first Pentecost) was an "imagined miracle," "a late reflection of reports" from Paul's churches. He can't have it both ways.

64. Smith, *Secret Gospel,* 116–17.

65. Cohen, "In Memoriam," (1994) 3; (1996) 281. See also Lang, *Sacred Games,* xi, 295, 468 n. 15–16, 372 ff.

66. The debate then was (as I believe it still is) about the relative impacts of heredity and environment, as illustrated by *The Transmission of Schizophrenia: Proceedings of the Second Research Conference of the Foundation's Fund for Research in Psychiatry, Dorado, Puerto Rico, June 26 to July 1, 1967,* ed. David Rosenthal and Seymour S. Kety (Oxford: Pergamon Press, 1968; repr. 1969). Smith would have enjoyed reading H. B. M. Murphy, "Cultural Factors in the Genesis of Schizophrenia," 137–53, which speculates that Roman Catholic attitudes toward marriage and celibacy contribute to a higher incidence of schizophrenia in certain populations.

67. Eliade, *Shamanism,* 26–27. There is an entire chapter on "Possession and Psychiatry" in Lewis, *Ecstatic Religion,* 160–84.

68. R. A. Knox, *Enthusiasm: A Chapter in the History of Religion, with Special Reference to the XVII and XVIII Centuries* (Oxford: Oxford University Press, 1950, corrected 1962), 8.

Chapter 7. The Happiness of the Dead

Epigraph. Book review of Smith, *Jesus the Magician* in *Anglican Theological Review* 61 (1979): 515–17, quotation from p. 517. For the quotation see Schweitzer, *The Quest,* 16.

Epigraph. Smith, *Secret Gospel,* 77, quoting Pontius Pilate on Jesus' death warrant (John 19:22).

1. *The Living Church Annual: Yearbook of the Episcopal Church,* known as the *Episcopal Church Annual* from 1953 (New York: Morehouse; from 1990 Harrisburg, Pa.), is arranged by diocese, but Smith is listed also in the "General Clergy List" in the back as "Smith, Robert M." *Stowe's Clerical Directory* (New York: Church Hymnal Corporation), which went through a number of name changes from 1956 to 1972, but finally

settled on *Episcopal Clerical Directory* in 1975, is organized by individual and gives much more information. There Smith is listed variously as "Smith, Morton" or "Smith, Robert Morton."

2. William M. Calder, "Morton Smith+," *Gnomon* 64 (1992): 382–84, adapted in Calder, "Smith, Morton," *Biographical Dictionary of North American Classicists*, ed. Ward W. Briggs (Westport, Conn.: Greenwood Press, 1994), 600–2. Cohen, "In Memoriam."

3. Jacob Neusner, "Foreword," *Christianity, Judaism and Other Greco-Roman Cults: Studies for Morton Smith at Sixty* 1: *New Testament*, ed. Jacob Neusner (Leiden: Brill, 1975), IX–XI, see p. IX.

4. He is first listed as nonparochial in the *Episcopal Church Annual* 1956 (p. 218), which probably means the status was granted in 1955. The *Episcopal Clergy Directory* says, beginning in 1972, that he had been nonparochial since 1957, but in 1983 this was corrected to 1955.

5. *Annotated Constitution and Canons for the Government of the Protestant Episcopal Church in the United States of America: Adopted in General Conventions 1789–1952*, 2 vols., 2nd ed. rev., ed. Edwin Augustine White and Jackson A. Dykman (Greenwich, Conn.: Seabury Press, 1954). See Canons 60, 62, 63 in vol. 2: 359–74, 380–86, 386–91.

6. Morton Smith, "Psychiatric Practice and Christian Dogma," *The Journal of Pastoral Care* 3 (1949): 12–20.

7. In the following series of quotations from Smith, "Psychiatric," rearranged in what I consider a more logical order, the pages quoted are identified at the end of each excerpt.

8. A paraphrase of the Anglican burial anthem "In the midst of life we are in death," based on the medieval Gregorian chant *Media vita in morte sumus*. See Blunt et al., ed., *The Annotated Book of Common Prayer*, 480–81.

9. Thus St. Sabbas was remembered as "gentle towards men although a fighter against demons." Cyril, *Lives*, 127–28.

10. The fact that Smith made use of auricular confession is one indication that he identified with the "high-church" branch of Anglicanism — the branch where liturgical matters, and the writings of people like Gregory Dix, were taken most seriously. We will encounter it again.

11. There is no mention of such a concept, for example, in the very thorough book Edwin F. Healy, *Marriage Guidance: A Study of the Problems of the Married and of Those Contemplating Marriage* (Chicago: Loyola University Press, 1948; repr. 1958), 148–55, 190–92.

12. For the current ecclesiastical law of the time see the discussions of Canons 17 and 18 in *Annotated Constitution and Canons*, 354–87.

13. I agree that we need more research on and analysis of the history of Christian opposition to homosexuality, and the experiences of individual Christians, of the sort that John Boswell attempted in his *Christianity, Social Tolerance, and Homosexuality: Gay People in Western Europe from the Beginning of the Christian Era to the Fourteenth Century* (Chicago: University of Chicago Press, 1980). However, I have to agree with Boswell's best-informed reviewers that his main argument — that Christianity was relatively tolerant of homosexuality before the thirteenth century — remains unproved. For despite Boswell's impressive erudition, he deals with many topics inadequately or too

impressionistically. These include biblical exegesis and the history of ecclesiastical law (J. Robert Wright, "Boswell on Homosexuality: A Case Undemonstrated," *Anglican Theological Review* 66 [1984]: 79–94), the medieval theology of natural law (Glenn W. Olsen, "The Gay Middle Ages: A Response to Professor Boswell," *Communio* 8 [1981]: 119–38; Jeremy duQ. Adams in *Speculum* 56 [1981]: 350–55; Stanley Hauerwas in *The Saint Luke's Journal of Theology* 28 [1984–85]: 228–32), and the sociology of "the urban/rural dichotomy" on which he lays much weight (Nicholas A. Patricca in *American Journal of Sociology* 88 [1982–83]: 1333–36).

14. As one traditional source put it, "concupiscence, or the fuel of sin . . . does not constitute sin, for . . . [it] is nothing more than an appetite of the soul in itself repugnant to reason. But if it is not accompanied by the consent of the will or by negligence, it is very far from being sin. . . . Sins against God are committed by thought, by word and by deed." *Catechism of the Council of Trent for Parish Priests, Issued by Order of Pope Pius V,* trans. John A. McHugh and Charles J. Callan (New York: Joseph F. Wagner, 1934; repr. 1952), 183–84, 273.

15. A convenient contemporary summary of traditional doctrine, citing sources from all periods in Christian history, is *Catechism of the Catholic Church* (many editions, 1994), paragraphs 1699–1802, 1846–76, 2357–59. Modern statements by a wide range of Christian, Jewish, and humanist groups, some of which cite traditional arguments and sources, are collected in J. Gordon Melton, *The Churches Speak on: Homosexuality: Official Statements from Religious Bodies and Ecumenical Organizations* (Detroit, Mich.: Gale Research, 1991). See also Jeffrey S. Siker, ed., *Homosexuality in the Church: Both Sides of the Debate* (Louisville, Ky.: Westminster John Knox Press, 1994).

16. James H. VanderVeldt and Robert P. Odenwald, *Psychiatry and Catholicism* (New York: McGraw-Hill, 1952), 392–93. For those interested in the legal issues, the authors close with "We may add that the Church has laid down the canonical regulations and penal laws concerning homosexuals and other sexual delinquents in Canons 2357 to 2359 of the Codex Juris Canonici."

17. *Summa Theologica* II-II q. 154 art. 12 Resp. For English translation see St. Thomas Aquinas, *Summa Theologica: First Complete American Edition in Three Volumes, Literally Translated by Fathers of the English Dominican Province* (New York: Benziger Brothers, 1947), 2: 1826.

18. Ibid. art. 11 Resp. In the English translation (op. cit.), 2: 1825.

19. 1879 was the date of the encyclical *Aeterni Patris* of Pope Leo XIII, which aimed at "the restoration of Christian philosophy according to the mind of St. Thomas Aquinas, the Angelic Doctor."

20. Jeremy Taylor, *The Rules and Exercises of Holy Dying,* Chapter 4, Section 8, VII Commandment. I happen to be citing the 25th ed. (London 1739), p. 170.

21. Sheila Kaye-Smith, *Anglo-Catholicism* (London: Chapman and Hall, 1925), 169. This ecclesiology was originally worked out in William Palmer, *A Treatise on the Church of Christ: Designed Chiefly for the Use of Students in Theology,* 2 vols. (London: J. G. & F. Rivington, 1838; New York: D. Appleton, 1841). A good book-length account of Anglo-Catholic ecclesiology as it was commonly accepted in Smith's time (though it does not use the term "branch theory") is Wilfred L. Knox, *The Catholic Movement in the Church of England* (New York: Edwin S. Gorham, 1923).

22. Smith, "Psychiatric Practice," 13. Smith did describe himself as "from the Protestant tradition" in *Secret Gospel,* 2. But his denomination was officially called the Protestant Episcopal Church, he was talking about music, and he was writing from his 1973 perspective, estranged from his religious past.

23. *Catechism of the Council of Trent,* 248, citing Session xiii, Chapter 7, Canon II.

24. Stated, for example, by Aquinas in *Summa Theologica* III, q. 6 Resp. In the translation (op. cit.), 2: 2492.

25. For the Catholic law in force in 1949 see Canon 855 of *Codex Iuris Canonici Pii X Pontificis Maximi iussu digestus Benedicti Papae XV auctoritate promulgatus* (Rome: Typis Polyglottis Vaticanis, 1917 [many other editions with varying pagination]), 246. For the Episcopal Church of the time see Canon 16 in *Annotated Constitution and Canons,* 1: 338–54, quotation from p. 339.

26. *The Book of Common Prayer and Administration of the Sacraments and Other Rites and Ceremonies of the Church, According to the Use of the Protestant Episcopal Church in the United States of America, Together with the Psalter or Psalms of David* [small pocket-size edition] (New York: The Church Pension Fund 1945; repr. 1966); 84–85. For the more ancient wording that would have been used in Kirk's English edition, see Blunt et al., ed., *The Annotated Book of Common Prayer,* 369–70.

27. Kenneth E. Kirk, *Conscience and Its Problems: An Introduction to Casuistry* (London: Longmans, Green, 1927), 242.

28. Kenneth E. Kirk, *Some Principles of Moral Theology and their Application* (London: Longmans, Green, 1920), 256.

29. Ibid., 257.

30. Ibid., 252, 259.

31. Ibid., 263 (italics in original) citing Thomas Aquinas, *Quodl.* V. a. 18.

32. David E. Roberts, *Psychotherapy and a Christian View of Man* (New York: Charles Scribner's Sons, 1950), 33, 95.

33. K. E. Kirk, "Marriage," in *Personal Ethics,* ed. Kenneth E. Kirk (Oxford: Clarendon Press, 1934), 25–49. " 'Birth-Control,' " in Kirk, *Conscience and Its Problems,* 290–306.

34. This interpretation arose mostly after the biblical period. When Sodom is mentioned in the Bible, a variety of reasons are given for its destruction: Mark D. Jordan, *The Invention of Sodomy in Christian Theology* (Chicago: University of Chicago Press, 1997), 29–37. Samuel Terrien, *Till the Heart Sings: A Biblical Theology of Manhood and Womanhood* (Grand Rapids, Mich.: Eerdmans, 2004), 168. For some modern interpretations of the Sodom story see Robert Alter, "Sodom as Nexus: The Web of Design in Biblical Narrative," *Reclaiming Sodom,* ed. Jonathan Goldberg (New York: Routledge, 1994), 28–42; John McNeill, *The Church and the Homosexual,* 4th ed. (Boston: Beacon Press, 1993), 42–50, 68–76.

35. T. W. Pym, *Our Personal Ministry: A Book for the Clergy as Consultants and Advisers* (London: Student Christian Movement Press, 1935), 36–38.

36. T. W. Pym, *Psychology and the Christian Life* (London: Student Christian Movement, 1921), 67–68.

37. Lindsay Dewar and Cyril E. Hudson, *Psychology for Religious Workers* (New York: Ray Long & Richard R. Smith, 1932).

38. I'm using the second edition: Anomaly, *The Invert and His Social Adjustment, To Which Is Added a Sequel by the Same Author,* 2nd ed. (Baltimore, Md.: Williams and Wilkins, 1948). However, Dewar and Hudson were using the first edition of 1927, repr. 1929; see Dewar and Hudson, *Psychology,* 133 n. 40.

39. Dewar and Hudson, *Psychology,* 185–86, based on Anomaly, *The Invert,* 134, 154, 157, 118–19, etc.

40. Anomaly, *The Invert,* 129, 136.

41. Dewar and Hudson, *Psychology,* 187–88, citing Anomaly, *The Invert,* 135–37. The author himself described his list of "don'ts" as "somewhat priggish" in the Sequel, p. 268.

42. I do not know this man's identity, though he says that his book was actually a collaboration (pp. 107, 163). The 1927 first edition was published "twenty years since the stress of adolescence" (p. xiii, see also p. 12), indicating he was born in the 1890s. He was evidently a British officer during World War I (pp. 65–66, 71, 173, 181) but had moved to Canada by 1935 (pp. v, 175).

43. For example, it is described as "that remarkable book . . . (which should be on every counsellor's shelf)" in George Hagmaier and Robert W. Gleason, *Moral Problems Now: Modern Techniques and Emotional Conflicts* (London: Sheed and Ward, 1960), 101. See also Gene D. Phillips, "Hope for the Homosexual," *Homiletic and Pastoral Review* 66 (1966): 1002–7, especially pp. 1003, 1005.

44. Anomaly, *The Invert,* 75–76.

45. Ibid., 84–85.

46. Ibid., 130. "The Cities of the Plain" are Sodom and Gomorrah (Genesis 13:12, 19:17, 25).

47. Ibid., 10–11.

48. Ibid., 11.

49. Ibid., 51–53. On the traditional classification of "sins that cry to heaven for vengeance," see *Catechism of the Catholic Church,* 1867.

50. Ibid., 101–2, 152–53.

51. Ibid., 153–54.

52. Ibid., 154–57.

53. Ibid., 156.

54. Ibid., 158–59.

55. Ibid., 160. Compare his reflections on this optimism in the Sequel, p. 271.

56. See Mark F. Williams, *Aelred of Rievaulx's Spiritual Friendship: A New Translation* (Scranton, Pa.: University of Scranton Press, 1994), with a discussion of Aelred's alleged homosexuality pp. 91–103. A priest of Smith's generation might have learned about Aelred from the life by John Dobree Dalgairns in *The Lives of the English Saints, Written by Various Hands at the Suggestion of John Henry Newman Afterwards Cardinal,* ed. Arthur Wollaston Hutton, 6 vols. (New York: Scott-Thaw, 1903), 5: 51–210. Chapter III, "The Struggle," shows Aelred striving to overcome intense personal friendships, "inordinate affection," "vile bodily habit," and so on (pp. 99, 110), but without venturing to be overly specific about what exactly the problem was.

57. Smith, "Psychiatric Practice," 12–13.

58. While cultural factors certainly play a role in definitions of illness, anyone who

thinks insanity is purely a social construct should read the introduction to T. M. Luhr-mann, *Of Two Minds: An Anthropologist Looks at American Psychiatry* (New York: Vintage Books, 2000), 3–24.

59. [Reginald Somerset Ward,] *A Guide for Spiritual Directors by the Author of "The Way"* (London: A. R. Mowbray, 1958), 126–27. Ward also recommended daily prayer, weekly communion, and confession every two months. His conditions for granting absolution included a promise not be alone with a boy for a year, to return to confession in two months, and (if the penitent is in Holy Orders) to inform his bishop.

60. Smith, "Psychiatric Practice," 19.

61. John A. O'Brien, ed., *Winning Converts: A Symposium on Methods of Convert Making for Priests and Lay People: A Companion to The White Harvest* (New York: P. J. Kenedy & Sons, 1948).

62. Smith, "Psychiatric Practice," 19.

63. John Henry Newman, *Apologia pro Vita Sua,* ed. David J. DeLaura (New York: W. W. Norton, 1968). I am using the Norton edition because it includes the earlier documents of the controversy that led up to the book.

64. Walter E. Houghton, "The Issue Between Kingsley and Newman," *Theology Today* 4 (1947): 81–101, reprinted in ibid., 390–409.

65. Newman, *Apologia,* 297–98.

66. Ibid., 299–300.

67. See Martin J. Svaglic, "Why Newman Wrote the *Apologia,*" in ibid., 374.

68. Newman, *Apologia,* 303.

69. Kingsley, "What, Then, Does Dr. Newman Mean?" in ibid., 327, quoting Newman's 1850 sermon "The Social State of Catholic Countries No Prejudice to the Sanctity of the Church," Sermon 8, part 4, in *Certain Difficulties Felt by Anglicans in Catholic Teaching Considered* 1: *In Twelve Lectures Addressed in 1850 to the Party of the Religious Movement of 1833,* new impression (London: Longmans, Green, 1901), 229–60, quotation from p. 240. Cf. *Apologia,* 190. I cite the new impression of 1901 because it is available on the Internet at http://www.newmanreader.org/works/anglicans/volume1/index.html (accessed July 2005).

70. Kingsley, "What, Then," 327, 328.

71. Walgrave, *Unfolding,* 299.

72. For an informed consideration of the concept from a modern perspective, see Karl Rahner, *On Heresy,* Quaestiones Disputatae 11 (New York: Herder and Herder, 1964). For history see Harold O. J. Brown, *Heresies: The Image of Christ in the Mirror of Heresy and Orthodoxy from the Apostles to the Present* (Garden City, N.Y.: Doubleday, 1984); Walter Bauer, *Orthodoxy and Heresy in Earliest Christianity,* ed. Robert A. Kraft and Gerhard Krodel (Philadelphia: Fortress, 1971).

73. Kingsley, "What, Then," in Newman, *Apologia,* 333, citing Newman's "On the Theory of Developments in Religious Doctrine" in "Chiefly on the Theory of Religious Belief," p. 343.

74. Ibid., 334, citing Newman's "On the Theory," p. 342, quoting Clement of Alexandria *Stromata* 7.9, see *Ante-Nicene Fathers,* 2: 538.

75. Ibid., 334.

76. See the editorial comments to the translation in *Ante-Nicene Fathers,* 2: 537 n. 9, 538 n. 1, 556–57, 567–68.

77. Newman, *Apologia,* xvii.

78. Ibid., 208–15.

79. Newman, "The Social State," in *Certain Difficulties,* 1: 239–40 (http://www.new manreader.org/works/anglicans/volume1/lecture8.html).

80. Joe Holland, *Modern Catholic Social Teaching: The Popes Confront the Industrial Age 1740–1958* (New York: Paulist Press, 2003). Edward P. De Berri, James E. Hug et al., *Catholic Social Teaching: Our Best Kept Secret,* 4th rev. and expanded ed. (Maryknoll, N.Y.: Orbis Books; Washington, D.C.: Center of Concern, 1992).

81. Not specifically the infallibility of the pope, which was not defined as doctrine until 1870. Newman, *Apologia,* 190.

82. Ibid.

83. See J. M. Harty, "Probabilism," *The Catholic Encyclopaedia* (New York: Robert Appleton, 1911), 12: 441–46, now available on the web at http://www.newadvent.org/cathen/12441a.htm.

84. Smith, "Psychiatric Practice," 19.

85. Ibid., 18, 13.

86. Morton Smith, "Forms, Motives, and Omissions in Mark's Account of the Teaching of Jesus," *Understanding the Sacred Text: Essays in Honor of Morton S. Enslin on the Hebrew Bible and Christian Beginnings,* ed. John Reumann (Valley Forge, Pa.: Judson Press, 1972), 153–64, quotation from p. 158.

87. Smith, "Forms," 158, 163.

Chapter 8. Hellenistic Homosexualities

Epigraph. Smith, *Secret Gospel,* 80, referring to Mark 14:12–16 and Luke 22:3–6. The fact that the parallel passage in Matthew (16:17–19) omits the pitcher of water could be consistent with Smith's opinion that evidence of Jesus' homosexuality was suppressed by later generations of Christians. See also the remarks of Smith's Columbia colleague, Gilbert Highet, in *The Immortal Profession: The Joys of Teaching and Learning* (New York: Weybright and Talley, 1976), 210 footnote. Jennings, *The Man,* 160–61.

1. Dover, *Greek Homosexuality,* updated with a new postscript (Cambridge, Mass.: Harvard University Press, 1989).

2. Dover responded to his early critics in "Greek Homosexuality and Initiation," in Dover, *The Greeks and Their Legacy: Collected Papers* 2: *Prose, Literature, History, Society, Transmission, Influence* (Oxford: Basil Blackwell, 1988), 115–34. On the other hand, "Whenever a myth is ancient or there are good reasons for assuming it is, it always connotes an initiation," according to Bernard Sergent, *Homosexuality in Greek Myth,* trans. Arthur Goldhammer (Boston: Beacon Press, 1986), 261. See also William Armstrong Percy III, *Pederasty and Pedagogy in Archaic Greece* (Urbana and Chicago: University of Illinois Press, 1996), especially pp. 10–92; David M. Halperin, *One Hundred Years of Homosexuality and Other Essays on Greek Love* (New York: Routledge, 1990), 54–71; Bernard Sergent, *L'Homosexualité initiatique dans l'Europe ancienne* (Paris: Payot, 1986); Marilyn B. Skinner, *Sexuality in Greek and Roman Culture* (Oxford: Blackwell, 2005), 12–13, 62–67.

3. "wenn darunter eine feste individuelle Triebrichtung zur Erlangung sexueller Befriedigung verstanden wird, weil die Knabenliebe eine gesellschaftliche Institution ist,

deren mögliche Inanspruchnahme durch jedermann allgemein vorausgesetzt ist, weil sie auf Knaben- und Jünglingsalter eingeschränkt ist und auf die Entwicklung dieser Jugendlichen zum erwachsenen Gruppenideal abzielt." Harald Patzer, *Die griechische Knabenliebe,* Sitzungsberichte der Wissenschaftliche Gesellschaft an der Johann Wolfgang Goethe-Universität Frankfurt am Main 19/1 (Wiesbaden: Franz Steiner, 1982), 125.

4. A number of interesting essays on the relationship of the individual to society are published in *Culture Theory: Essays on Mind, Self, and Emotion,* ed. Richard A. Shweder and Robert A. LeVine (Cambridge, U.K.: Cambridge University Press, 1984). Especially relevant, though not particularly focused on homosexuality, are Clifford Geertz, " 'From the Native's Point of View': On the Nature of Anthropological Understanding," 123–36; and Richard A. Shweder and Edmund J. Bourne, "Does the Concept of the Person Vary Cross-Culturally?" 158–99. An attempt to look at the whole question more broadly is Fitz John Porter Poole, "Socialization, Enculturation and the Development of Personal Identity," *Companion Encyclopedia of Anthropology,* 831–60. For an interesting first-person account of a Ghanaian Hausa prince who "discovered individualism" in the United States, but still accepted a marriage arranged by his king father, see Mohammed Naseehu Ali, "Summer of My Discontent," *New York Times* (September 17, 2005), A15.

5. Alan Macfarlane, *Marriage and Love in England: Modes of Reproduction 1300–1840* (Oxford: Basil Blackwell, 1986), 119–21.

6. Lawrence Stone, *The Family, Sex and Marriage in England 1500–1800* (New York: Harper & Row, 1977), 221–69.

7. Rodger Doyle, "Leveling the Playing Field: Economic Development Helps Women Pull Even with Men," *Scientific American* 292/6 (June 2005), 32.

8. See Carol Dougherty and Leslie Kurke, eds. *The Cultures Within Ancient Greek Culture: Contact, Conflict, Collaboration* (Cambridge, U.K.: Cambridge University Press, 2003).

9. Werner Jaeger, *Paideia: The Ideals of Greek Culture* 1: *Archaic Greece, The Mind of Athens,* 2nd ed., trans. Gilbert Highet (New York: Oxford University Press, 1967), 117.

10. *Diagnostic and Statistical Manual of Mental Disorders,* 4th ed., 6th printing (Washington, D.C.: American Psychiatric Association, 1997), 527. An extended attempt to provide ancient Greek justification for the modern paederast's view that his attentions are helpful to the child is J. Z. Eglinton, *Greek Love* (New York: Oliver Layton Press, 1964), which includes a rebuttal by psychologist Albert Ellis, pp. 429–38.

11. For the typologies, see David F. Greenberg, *The Construction of Homosexuality* (Chicago: University of Chicago Press, 1988), 26–40; Stephen O. Murray, *Homosexualities* (Chicago: University of Chicago Press, 2000), 2–3. Obviously, what people actually do, and what cultures accept, may resist both sociological and ethical classification. But the implicit and explicit cultural assumptions are what can be useful for dating and authenticating historical and literary texts, not the endless possibilities that may or may not have occurred in what might whimsically be called "real life."

12. For example, see Gilbert H. Herdt, ed., *Ritualized Homosexuality in Melanesia* (Berkeley and Los Angeles: University of California Press, 1984).

13. Scanlon, *Eros,* 77–83, who gets much of his information from Nigel M. Kennell, *The Gymnasium of Virtue: Education and Culture in Ancient Sparta* (Chapel Hill: University of North Carolina Press, 1995). Percy, *Pederasty,* 73–92.

14. Sergent, *Homosexuality,* 40–48 (on parallels in other cultures). Percy, *Pederasty,* 59–72. Walter Burkert, "Initiation," *Thesaurus Cultus et Rituum Antiquorum (Thes-CRA)* 2 (Los Angeles: J. Paul Getty Museum, 2004), 91–124, lists the major literary, epigraphic, and iconographic sources for Crete and Sparta, pp. 121–23. On initiations and rites of passage more generally, see Ronald L. Grimes, *Deeply into the Bone: Re-Inventing Rites of Passage* (Berkeley: University of California Press, 2000), 100–21; Fritz Graf, "Initiation: A Concept with a Troubled History," and Bruce Lincoln, "The Initiatory Paradigm in Anthropology, Folklore, and History of Religions," in *Initiation in Ancient Greek Rituals,* 3–24, 241–54.

15. Scanlon, *Eros* 74–77. Cantarella, *Bisexuality,* 7. Thomas K. Hubbard, *Homosexuality in Greece and Rome: A Sourcebook of Basic Documents* (Berkeley and Los Angeles: University of California Press, 2003), 72–73. For a study of one of these drinking cups, see Robert B. Koehl, "Ephoros and Ritualized Homosexuality in Bronze Age Crete," *Queer Representations: Reading Lives, Reading Cultures,* ed. Martin Duberman (New York: New York University Press, 1997), 7–13.

16. Murray, *Homosexualities,* 34–43, 99–111.

17. Quote from Cantarella, *Bisexuality,* xviii. See also Dover, *Greek Homosexuality,* 16.

18. Cantarella, *Bisexuality,* 27–34.

19. 183a. Translation from R. E. Allen, *The Dialogues of Plato 2: The Symposium* (New Haven, Conn.: Yale University Press, 1991), 123.

20. 184a. Translation from Plato, *The Symposium,* trans. Christopher Gill (London: Penguin Books, 1999), 16.

21. 184d–e, ibid., 17.

22. Plato, *Phaedrus,* 231a, 231d, 233a, trans. Alexander Nehamas and Paul Woodruff in Plato, *Complete Works,* ed. John M. Cooper and D. S. Hutchinson (Indianapolis, Ind.: Hackett, 1997), 511–12.

23. David M. Halperin, "Why Is Diotima a Woman? Platonic Erōs and the Figuration of Gender," *Before Sexuality: The Construction of Erotic Experience in the Ancient World,* ed. David M. Halperin, John J. Winkler, and Froma I. Zeitlin (Princeton, N.J.: Princeton University Press, 1990), 257–308, see pp. 272–74.

24. See Hubbard, *Homosexuality,* 76.

25. Dover, *Greek Homosexuality,* 53, 91–100.

26. See Daniel B. McGlathery, "Reversals of Platonic Love in Petronius' *Satyricon,*" *Rethinking Sexuality: Foucault and Classical Antiquity,* ed. David H. J. Larmour, Paul Allen Miller, and Charles Platter (Princeton, N.J.: Princeton University Press, 1998), 204–27.

27. Keith DeVries, "The 'Frigid Eromenoi' and their Wooers Revisited: A Closer Look at Greek Homosexuality in Vase Painting," in *Queer Representations,* 14–24, with response by David M. Halperin, pp. 45–53.

28. A modern person may wonder how a homosexual relationship could teach virtue. Plato's *Laches* discusses the training of boys who dine in a group that includes their fathers. Other sources show that dinners and symposia, like the gymnasia, were often seen as opportunities for the education—and sexual pursuit—of boys. See Percy, *Pederasty,* 95–121

29. For some more recent attempts to interpret ancient Greek imagery, see Robert F. Sutton, Jr., "Pornography and Persuasion on Attic Pottery," and H. A. Shapiro, "Eros in Love: Pederasty and Pornography in Greece," *Pornography and Representation in Greece and Rome* (New York: Oxford University Press, 1992), 3–35, 53–72. Martin Kilmer, " 'Rape' in Early Red-Figure Pottery: Violence and Threat in Homo-erotic and Hetero-erotic Contexts," *Rape in Antiquity,* ed. Susan Deacy and Karen F. Pierce (London: Duckworth; Swansea: The Classical Press of Wales, 1997), with the bibliography cited therein. Skinner, *Sexuality,* 79–111.

30. David Cohen, *Law, Sexuality, and Society: The Enforcement of Morals in Classical Athens* (Cambridge, U.K.: Cambridge University Press, 1991), 183, 240.

31. Ibid., 175–77.

32. Ibid., 183.

33. David M. Halperin, "Homosexuality," *The Oxford Classical Dictionary,* 3rd ed. (Oxford: Oxford University Press, 1996), 720–23, quotation from p. 722. For more detail, see John J. Winkler, "Laying Down the Law: The Oversight of Men's Sexual Behavior in Classical Athens," *Before Sexuality,* 171–209. Halperin, *How to Do the History,* 32–38, 71–73. Socrates holds forth on the boy's responsibilities in Xenophon, *Symposium,* 8.12–27.

34. Cantarella, *Bisexuality,* 36–53.

35. The speech provides the structure for most of Dover's book *Greek Homosexuality,* but see especially pp. 13–14, 19–42.

36. David M. Halperin, "Is There a History of Sexuality?" *History and Theory* 28 (1989): 257–74, quotation from p. 260.

37. Cohen, *Law,* 197.

38. *Symposium* 181b, trans. Gill, 13.

39. For example "The Ladder of Love" in the commentary of R. E. Allen in Allen, *Dialogues of Plato,* 154–55; Allan Bloom, "The Ladder of Love" in *Plato's "Symposium,"* trans. Seth Benardete (Chicago: University of Chicago Press, 2001), 55–177.

40. Carl Kerényi, *Eleusis: Archetypal Image of Mother and Daughter,* trans. Ralph Manheim, Bollingen Series 65/4 (Princeton, N.J.: Princeton University Press, 1967), 45–47. The major literary, epigraphic, iconographic, and archaeological sources for the Eleusinian Mysteries are listed in Burkert, "Initiation," pp. 92–96 and plate 15.

41. *Symposium* 210b, trans. Gill, 48.

42. *Phaedrus* 252d, trans. Nehamas and Woodruff, 530.

43. *Phaedrus* 256a–b, trans. Nehamas and Woodruff, 532–33.

44. David M. Halperin, "Plato and Erotic Reciprocity," *Classical Antiquity* 5 (1986): 60–80, especially pp. 77–79.

45. From the commentary in Allen, *Dialogues of Plato,* 82

46. Kevin Clinton, "The Sacred Officials of the Eleusinian Mysteries," *Transactions of the American Philosophical Society* new series 64/3 (June 1974): 116.

47. 211b, as translated in Robin Waterfield, *Plato: Symposium: A New Translation,* Oxford World's Classics (Oxford: Oxford University Press, 1994), 55.

48. Amy DeRogatis, "What Would Jesus Do? Sexuality and Salvation in Protestant Evangelical Sex Manuals, 1950s to the Present," *Church History: Studies in Christianity & Culture* 74 (2005): 97–137, quotation from p. 132. It is taken for granted, of course, that such a "godly person" would be a married heterosexual.

49. 175e, cf. William S. Cobb, *The Symposium and The Phaedrus: Plato's Erotic Dialogues* (Albany: State University of New York Press, 1993), 18, 180 nn. 13–14.

50. Smith, *Clement*, 64, 186.

51. It is hard to say what age Alcibiades is represented as being. The *Symposium* was composed between 384 and 379 BCE, according to K. J. Dover, "The Date of Plato's *Symposium*," in Dover, *The Greeks and Their Legacy*, 86–101, especially p. 98. That would be well after Alcibiades' death around 404 BCE. Moreover, the entire dialogue is narrated many years later by someone who wasn't actually present. In *Protagoras* 309a Alcibiades has just begun to grow a beard, which makes him about the right age to have been Socrates' erōmenos. In *Gorgias* 481d, Socrates says he loves both Alcibiades and philosophy.

52. *Symposium* 217c–d, trans. Gill, 56.

53. Ibid., 218d, 58.

54. Ibid., 222b, 62.

55. Xenophon, *Memorabilia* 1.2, translated in Xenophon, *Conversations of Socrates*, trans. Hugh Tredennick and Robin Waterfield, ed. Robin Waterfield (London: Penguin Books, 1990), 74–75. "His entire life may be explained as hybristic insolence, in which conceit led to a self-destructive combination of daring and insolence," according to Stanley Rosen, *Plato's Symposium*, 2nd ed. (New Haven, Conn.: Yale University Press, 1987), 281.

56. Plutarch, *Greek Lives: A Selection of Nine Greek Lives*, trans. Robin Waterfield, ed. Philip. A. Stadter (Oxford: Oxford University Press, 1998), 218–59, quotations from pp. 254, 242, 255. See also Debra Nails, *The People of Plato: A Prosopography of Plato and Other Socratics* (Indianapolis, Ind.: Hackett, 2002), 10–20. Mark Munn, *The School of History: Athens in the Age of Socrates* (Berkeley: University of California Press, 2000), contains multiple discussions of Alcibiades' activities and reputation.

57. *Symposium* 213c and 217e are cited at *Alcibiades I* 104e. Socrates has not spoken for some time to Alcibiades (103a), who is not yet twenty years old and is "completely uneducated" (123e, 127e).

58. Ralf Krumeich, Nikolaus Pechstein, Bernd Seidensticker et al., eds. *Das griechische Satyrspiel*, Texte zur Forschung 72 (Darmstadt: Wissenschaftliche Buchgesellschaft, 1999). Ian C. Storey and Arlene Allan, *A Guide to Ancient Greek Drama* (Oxford: Blackwell, 2005), 156–68.

59. Ehrman, "Response," 159.

60. Diogenes Laertius, *Vitae Philosophorum*, 6.96–98.

61. K. J. Dover, "Classical Greek Attitudes to Sexual Behaviour," *Sexuality and Gender in the Classical World: Readings and Sources*, ed. Laura McClure (Oxford: Blackwell, 2002), 19–33, see p. 22.

62. Murray, *Homosexualities*, 39–40, 109.

63. Cantarella, *Bisexuality*, 216. See also Plato, *Symposium* 192b.

64. Cantarella, *Bisexuality*, 41–42.

65. On the contrary, in New Testament times "a new model of the family was emerging" that forbade the husband to have sex partners of any kind beyond his wife, according to William R. Schoedel, "Same-Sex Eros: Paul and the Greco-Roman Tradition," *Homosexuality, Science, and the "Plain Sense" of Scripture* (Grand Rapids, Mich.: Eerdmans, 2000), 43–72, see p. 72.

66. Halperin, *How to Do the History*, 24–47, especially pp. 160–62 n. 11. *Rethinking Sexuality*, ed. Larmour et al., is an entire volume of critical essays on Foucault's *The History of Sexuality* 1: *An Introduction*, trans. Robert Hurley (New York: Vintage, 1980). Both Foucault and Dover are engaged in many of the essays in *The Sleep of Reason: Erotic Experience and Sexual Ethics in Ancient Greece and Rome*, ed. Martha C. Nussbaum and Juha Sihvola (Chicago: University of Chicago Press, 2002).

67. Thus Rictor Norton accuses "social constructionist" historians of "fail[ure] to appreciate that homosexuals existed before 1869" in his book *The Myth of the Modern Homosexual: Queer History and the Search for Cultural Unity* (London: Cassell, 1997), 8. But even he acknowledges that "queer desire . . . expresses itself in sexual or social actions and (sub)cultures that may reflect to a greater or lesser degree the time and place in which they occur" (p. 13). Indeed he regrets the loss of many (sub)cultural traditions as a uniform modern construction of homosexuality becomes more widespread throughout the world. This kind of variation is all we need to place the Mar Saba document in its correct context, without solving the question of to what degree homosexuality is inborn and thus impervious to cultural manipulation.

68. Bernadette J. Brooten, *Love Between Women: Early Christian Responses to Female Homoeroticism* (Chicago: University of Chicago Press, 1996).

69. Andrie B. du Toit, "Paul, Homosexuality, and Christian Ethics," *Neotestamentica et Philonica: Studies in Honor of Peder Borgen,* ed. David E. Aune et al. (Leiden: Brill, 2003), 92–107.

70. Philo, *De Specialibus Legibus,* 3.7.37–42, *De Vita Contemplativa,* 6.48–52, 7.57–63. Josephus, *Contra Ap.,* 2.25.199.

71. It is not known if any Jewish court ever actually imposed a death penalty for sex between men, but courts in Christian societies certainly have. For a few random examples see Richard Sherr, "A Canon, a Choirboy, and Homosexuality in Late Sixteenth-Century Italy: A Case Study," *Journal of Homosexuality* 21/3 (March 31, 1991): 1–22; Helmut Puff, *Sodomy in Reformation Germany and Switzerland, 1400–1600* (Chicago: University of Chicago Press, 2003).

72. It is obviously beyond my present scope to consider whether the Leviticus passages were originally meant to be taken literally, or what we should make of them today. A range of viewpoints on such questions will be found in Pim Pronk, *Against Nature? Types of Moral Argumentation Regarding Homosexuality,* trans. John Vriend (Grand Rapids, Mich.: Eerdmans, 1993), 265–301; Martti Nissinen, *Homoeroticism in the Biblical World: A Historical Perspective* (Minneapolis: Fortress, 1998), 37–44, 93–97, 103–22; James B. De Young, *Homosexuality: Contemporary Claims Examined in Light of the Bible and Other Ancient Literature and Law* (Grand Rapids, Mich.: Kregel, 2000), 23–68, 139–231; David L. Balch, ed., *Homosexuality, Science, and the "Plain Sense" of Scripture* (Grand Rapids, Mich.: Eerdmans, 2000). Robert A. J. Gagnon, *The Bible and Homosexual Practice: Texts and Hermeneutics* (Nashville, Tenn.: Abingdon Press, 2001), 111–20, 185–339; Steven Greenberg, *Wrestling with God and Men: Homosexuality in the Jewish Tradition* (Madison: University of Wisconsin Press, 2004), 147–214. The oft-expressed notion that biblical proscriptions of homosexuality had something to do with Canaanite fertility rituals involving sacred prostitution is not easily confirmed; see Richard A. Henshaw, *Female and Male: The Cultic Personnel: The Bible and the Rest*

of the Ancient Near East, Princeton Theological Monograph Series 31 (Allison Park, Pa.: Pickwick Publications, 1994), 191–280, especially p. 256.

73. Murray, *Homosexualities,* 373–78. Gagnon, *The Bible,* 347–61.

74. In *Phaedo* 60a, Xanthippe visits Socrates in prison the morning of his execution, bringing their little boy. But she is so emotional and distraught (which is perceived as typical female behavior) that Socrates has her sent home. Later (116a) all the women of his household appear with all three of his sons, but they are sent home again. Later tradition gave Socrates a second wife, Myrto. She is mentioned, for example, in the pseudo-Platonic *Halcyon* 8. See the translation by Brad Inwood in Plato, *Complete Works,* 1714, 1717.

75. Ovid, *Metamorphoses,* 10.110–23, 11.1–117. Fritz Graf, "Orfeo, un poeta tra gli uomini," *Musica e mito nella Grecia antica,* ed. Donatella Restani (Bologna: Il Mulino, 1995), 303–20, especially pp. 310–11. A different explanation is given in *Symposium* 179d: The gods punished Orpheus for being "soft" and unmanly (he was a musician, after all!) by having him killed by women.

76. *Protrepticus* 1.1, 1.3, 2.17, 2.21, 7.74, trans. Butterworth, 3, 9, 37, 43, 167. Thomas Halton, "Clement's Lyre: A Broken String, a New Song," *The Second Century* 3 (1983): 177–99

77. Robert A. Skeris, Χρῶμα Θεοῦ: *On the Origins and Theological Interpretation of the Musical Imagery Used by the Ecclesiastical Writers of the First Three Centuries, with Special Reference to the Image of Orpheus,* Musicae Sacrae Melethmata 1, Publications of Catholic Church Music Associates 1 (Altötting: Alfred Coppenrath, 1976), especially pp. 146–56. Mario Naldini, "I Miti di Orfeo e di Eracle nell'Interpretazione Patristica," *Civiltà Classica e Cristiana* 14 (1993): 331–43.

78. *Nicomachean Ethics,* 7.5.3 (1148b).

79. Achilles Tatius, *Leucippe and Clitophon,* trans. with notes by Tim Whitmarsh, with introduction by Helen Morales (Oxford: Oxford University Press, 2001), 9.

80. Ibid., 11.

81. The quotations that follow are from the translation by Donald Russell in Plutarch, *Selected Essays and Dialogues: A New Translation* (Oxford: Oxford University Press, 1993), 246–83.

82. Ibid., *Eroticus* 753, 254.

83. Ibid., *Eroticus* 749, 248.

84. Ibid., *Eroticus* 752, 253.

85. Ibid., *Eroticus* 750 and 751, 249 and 250.

86. Ibid., *Eroticus* 751, 251.

87. Ibid., *Eroticus* 749, 248–49.

88. Ibid., *Eroticus* 750, 250.

89. Although there are ancient references to marriages between men, see Williams, *Roman Homosexuality,* 245–52.

90. Plutarch *Eroticus* 771, trans. Russell, 283.

91. Tatius, *Leucippe,* 40.

92. Translated as "Affairs of the Heart" in *Lucian* 8, trans. M. D. Macleod, Loeb Classical Library 432 (Cambridge, Mass.: Harvard University Press, 1967), 150–235.

93. *Amores* 31, trans. Macleod, 198–99.

94. Ibid., *Amores* 35, 204–5.

95. Ibid., *Amores* 41, 213.

96. Ibid., *Amores* 45, 218–19.

97. Ibid., *Amores* 49, 226–27.

98. Ibid., *Amores* 51, 228–29.

99. Ibid., *Amores* 54, 234–35, italics in original. Achilles and Patroclus, of course, are the warrior pair in the Iliad, though Achilles, the older man, had also acquired the Trojan woman Briseis as war booty.

100. Michael Allen Williams, *Rethinking "Gnosticism": An Argument for Dismantling a Dubious Category* (Princeton, N.J.: Princeton University Press, 1996), 169.

101. Winrich A. Löhr, "Karpokratianisches," *Vigiliae Christianae* 49 (1995): 23–48, see pp. 25, 26, 35. Paul Corby Finney, "Did Gnostics Make Pictures?" *The Rediscovery of Gnosticism: Proceedings of the International Conference on Gnosticism at Yale, New Haven, Connecticut, March 28–31, 1978* 1: *The School of Valentinus*, ed. Bentley Layton, Studies in the History of Religions 41 (Leiden: Brill, 1980), 434–54.

102. Löhr, "Karpokratianisches," 34–35, 44–45 n. 56. *Stromata* 3.2.10.2., trans. Ferguson, 263.

103. *Stromata* 3.2.5.2, trans. Ferguson, 259.

104. Kathy L. Gaca, *The Making of Fornication: Eros, Ethics, and Political Reform in Greek Philosophy and Early Christianity* (Berkeley: University of California Press, 2003), 277, 278, 279.

105. Christoph Riedweg, *Pythagoras: His Life, Teaching, and Influence*, trans. Steven Rendall (Ithaca, N.Y.: Cornell University Press, 2005), 55–56, 62–63.

106. Gaca, *The Making of Fornication*, 270, 96, 299.

107. Gaca, *The Making of Fornication*, 302.

108. Smith, *Clement*, 84, 88–89, 92, 283–84, 275–76.

109. Irenaeus, *Against the Heresies* 1.25.1, trans. Unger, 87.

110. Smith, "Two Ascended," 70.

111. Sigmund Freud, *The Joke and Its Relation to the Unconscious*, trans. Joyce Crick (New York: Penguin Books, 2002), 97–98, italics in original. For a more up-to-date view, see Kathryn M. Ryan and Jeanne Kanjorski, "The Enjoyment of Sexist Humor, Rape Attitudes, and Relationship Aggression in College Students," *Sex Roles* 38 (1998): 743–55. On satire as ritual aggression see George A. Test, *Satire: Spirit and Art* (Tampa: University of South Florida Press, 1991). On the differences between satire and parody see Margaret A. Rose, *Parody: Ancient, Modern, and Post-Modern* (Cambridge, U.K.: Cambridge University Press, 1993), 80–86.

Chapter 9. Uranian Venus

Epigraph. Smith, *Secret Gospel*, 73.

1. J. N. Adams, *The Latin Sexual Vocabulary* (Baltimore, Md.: Johns Hopkins University Press, 1982), 123, 202, 228. Philo, *De Vita Contemplativa* 6.48–49. But see also Williams, *Roman Homosexuality,* 64–72.

2. Dennis Altman, *Global Sex* (Chicago: University of Chicago Press, 2001), 144–45, 88–100.

3. Paul Henry Lang, *George Frideric Handel* (New York: W. W. Norton, 1966), 543–46.

4. Ellen T. Harris, *Handel as Orpheus: Voice and Desire in the Chamber Cantatas* (Cambridge, Mass.: Harvard University Press, 2001), 25–48, 240–65, and throughout. This period is covered more generally, without reference to Handel, in Rictor Norton, *Mother Clap's Molly House: The Gay Subculture in England 1700–1830* (London: GMP, 1992), especially p. 76.

5. John Addington Symonds, *A Problem in Greek Ethics, Being an Inquiry into the Phenomenon of Sexual Inversion, Addressed Especially to Medical Psychologists and Jurists,* privately printed in ten copies (1873); privately reprinted in one hundred copies (London 1901); reprinted in John Addington Symonds, *Male Love: A Problem in Greek Ethics and Other Writings,* foreword by Robert Peters, ed. John Lauritsen (New York: Pagan Press, 1983), xix–73.

6. The term is enshrined in the title of Havelock Ellis's monumental book *Sexual Inversion* (London: Wilson and Macmillan, 1897). See Joseph Bristow, "Symond's History, Ellis's Heredity: *Sexual Inversion,*" *Sexology in Culture: Labelling Bodies and Desires,* ed. Lucy Bland and Laura Doan (Cambridge, U.K.: Polity Press, 1998), 79–99. For excerpts from this and other sources of the period, see Lucy Bland and Laura Doan, *Sexology Uncensored: The Documents of Sexual Science* (Cambridge, U.K.: Polity Press, 1998), 41–72.

7. An early use of the term is in Alfred Tennyson's 1847 poem *The Princess: A Medley,* canto 1, line 239. It is used at the point in the story where the hero disguises himself as a girl in order to rescue his betrothed from an all-female university, where she is being indoctrinated to despise marriage. Heterosexuality triumphs in the end, of course, but the story helps to illustrate the conception of homosexuality as gender "inversion."

8. For example, Linda Dowling, *Hellenism and Homosexuality in Victorian Oxford* (Ithaca, N.Y.: Cornell University Press, 1994).

9. See Karl Beckson, *The Oscar Wilde Encyclopedia* (New York: AMS Press, 1998), 391–93.

10. Halperin, *One Hundred Years,* 1, 153, quoting E. M. Forster, *Goldsworthy Lowes Dickinson* (1934; repr. New York, n.d.), 46. The novel itself is E. M. Forster, *Maurice: A Novel* (New York: W. W. Norton, 1971).

11. Symonds, *A Problem,* reprinted in Symonds, *Male Love,* 48–55.

12. John Addington Symonds, *Studies of the Greek Poets* (London: Smith, Elder, 1873), 416–17, reprinted in Symonds, *Male Love,* 138–39; 3rd ed. (London: Adam and Charles Black, 1893), 2: 379–80.

13. John Addington Symonds, *The Life of Michelangelo Buonarotti, Based on Studies in the Archives of the Buonarotti Family at Florence,* 2 vols., 3rd ed. (London: John C. Nimmo; New York: Charles Scribner's Sons, 1899), 2: 177. The first editor, Michelangelo's grandnephew, had changed the masculine word "friends" (*amici*) in the last line to "souls" (*animi*).

14. A. C. Benson, *Walter Pater* (London: Macmillan, 1906), 163–64.

15. Ibid., 164–66.

16. Walter Pater, *The Renaissance: Studies in Art and Poetry* (originally 1873; London: Macmillan, 1922), 24.

17. Ibid., 56–57, 60.

18. Ibid., 236. This epilogue was removed from the second edition because of objections but was restored in the third.

19. Denis Donoghue, *Walter Pater: Lover of Strange Souls* (New York: Alfred A. Knopf, 1995), 66–69.

20. Thomas Wright, *The Life of Walter Pater*, 2 vols. (1907; repr. New York: Haskell House Publishers, 1969), 2: 130–31.

21. Pater, *The Renaissance*, 80–81.

22. Ibid., 81, 82, 86.

23. Ibid., 123, 124–25.

24. Morton Smith, *Hope and History: An Exploration*, World Perspectives 54 (New York: Harper & Row, 1980), 90–91. It is interesting to compare this with his much earlier account: Morton Smith, *The Ancient Greeks*, The Development of Civilization (Ithaca, N.Y.: Cornell University Press, 1960), 27.

25. On the other hand, we do find this notion advocated in Anomaly, *The Invert*, 8–9. It derives from Otto Weininger, *Geschlecht und Charakter; eine prinzipielle Untersuchung* (Vienna: Leipzig, 1903). English translations include *Sex and Character: An Investigation of Fundamental Principles*, trans. Ladislaus Löb, ed. Daniel Steuer with Laura Marcus (Bloomington: Indiana University Press, 2005). Other translations are available at http://www.theabsolute.net/ottow/ (accessed January 2006).

26. Smith, *Hope*, 185.

27. Joseph Bristow, "*Fratrum Societati*: Forster's Apostolic Dedications," *Queer Forster*, ed. Robert K. Martin and George Piggford (Chicago: University of Chicago Press, 1997), 113–36, quotation from pp. 114–15.

28. See, for example, A. L. Rowse, *Homosexuals in History: A Study of Ambivalence in Society, Literature and the Arts* (New York: Macmillan, 1977), 271–87.

29. Thus neither of the following books has an index entry for "homosexuality": Peter Allen, *The Cambridge Apostles: The Early Years* (Cambridge, U.K.: Cambridge University Press, 1978); W. C. Lubenow, *The Cambridge Apostles, 1820–1914: Liberalism, Imagination, and Friendship in British Intellectual and Professional Life* (Cambridge, U.K.: Cambridge University Press, 1998).

30. Christopher Lane, *The Ruling Passion: British Colonial Allegory and the Paradox of Homosexual Desire* (Durham, N.C.: Duke University Press, 1995), 170.

31. *Marius the Epicurean: His Sensations and Ideas*, 2 vols. (London: Macmillan 1885), reprinted in the series Victorian Fiction: Novels of Faith and Doubt (New York: Garland 1975), 1: 121–29.

32. *Marius the Epicurean*, Chapter 23, 2: 144–57.

33. Compare Pater's description of the Kyrie eleison (*Marius the Epicurean*, 2: 148) with Égérie, *Journal de Voyage (Itinéraire)*, ed. Pierre Maraval, Sources Chrétiennes 296 (Paris: Cerf, 1982), 240–41; John Wilkinson, ed., *Egeria's Travels*, 3rd ed. (Warminster: Aris & Phillips, 1999), 52, 143, 176–77; and Michel Andrieu, *Les Ordines Romani du haut moyen age 2: Les textes (Ordines I–XIII)*, (Louvain: Spicilegium Sacrum Lovaniense, 1948), 84. I am working on a translation and illustrated commentary on the Ordo Romanus.

34. Pater's description on p. 149 (*Marius the Epicurean* 2) alludes to Pliny's letter to

Trajan 10.96, *The Letters of the Younger Pliny,* trans. Betty Radice (Baltimore, Md.: Penguin, 1963), 293–95. The phrase "cum grandi affectu et compunctione dicatur" comes from the Council of Vaison (529 CE), see Charles de Clercq, ed., *Concilia Galliae A. 511–A. 695,* Corpus Christianorum Series Latina 148A (Turnhout: Brepols, 1963), 79.

35. Psalms 84:2 [85:1], 109:1 [110:1] (*Marius the Epicurean,* 2: 149), 132:2 [133:2] (p. 152). The text *Astiterunt reges terrae,* described as a "sequence" (a type of hymn), is actually a paraphrase of Acts 4:25–26, which is itself a paraphrase of Psalm 2:1–2 (p. 151). *Adoramus te Christe* is a Gregorian chant antiphon for feasts of the Holy Cross (p. 155).

36. The *Sursum corda* dialogue that begins the Preface (*Marius the Epicurean,* 2: 154), *Dominus vobiscum* (p. 155), *Ite missa est* (p. 157). The phrase "perducat vos ad vitam aeternam" (p. 156) comes from the prayer *Misereatur vestri,* said by the priest after the *Confiteor,* which the congregation recited as a preparation for communion. Pater seems to have confused it with the wording used at the actual distribution of communion: "Corpus Domini nostri Jesu Christi custodiat animam tuam in vitam aeternam. Amen."

37. Wright, *The Life of Walter Pater,* 2: 31–42, 84–85. Kenneth Hylson-Smith, *High Churchmanship in the Church of England from the Sixteenth Century to the Late Twentieth Century* (Edinburgh: T & T Clark, 1993), 219–22. Some were of the opinion that the Ritualist movement attracted more than its fair share of homosexuals. On the other hand, its revival of lacy vestments, liturgical kisses, auricular confession, and other popish customs offered easy targets to those who perceived the movement as betraying the Reformation. See David Hilliard, "Unenglish and Unmanly: Anglo-Catholicism and Homosexuality," *Victorian Studies* 25 (1981–82): 181–210, especially p. 193; G. I. T. Machin, "The Last Victorian Anti-Ritualist Campaign, 1895–1906," *Victorian Studies* 25 (1982): 277–302; W. S. F. Pickering, *Anglo-Catholicism: A Study in Religious Ambiguity* (London: Routledge, 1989), 184–206.

38. Richard Ellmann, *Oscar Wilde* (New York: Alfred A. Knopf, 1988), 30, 358. A chreia or chria is a narrative that climaxes in a humorous or thought-provoking saying, usually spoken by a well-known figure; see Soulen and Soulen, *Handbook,* 33.

39. Wilfred Owen, *Collected Letters,* ed. Harold Owen and John Bell (London: Oxford University Press, 1967), 459–60. The biblical sources include Judges 4:19, Luke 13:11, Matthew 19:22, Psalm 137:1, Exodus 7:21, Genesis 1:26 and elsewhere, 2 Kings 5:10, 14; Job 2:7, Luke 10:34, 1 Timothy 5:23, John 2:6–7, Revelation 8:1, Luke 24:12 or John 20:5, Mark 1:7, Matthew 9:17, Matthew 27:51, 2 Samuel 16:5, Revelation 6:8, Matthew 8:6, Matthew 13:45, Genesis 38:16, Luke 10:35, Ruth 1:16, Matthew 4:5, Luke 6:48, Mark 2:4, Luke 19:40.

40. Ibid., 460–61.

41. Noel Annan, "The Cult of Homosexuality in England 1850–1950," *Biography: An Interdisciplinary Quarterly* 13 (1990): 189–202, quotation from p. 192.

42. Louis Crompton, *Byron and Greek Love: Homophobia in 19th-Century England* (Berkeley: University of California Press, 1985), 281–83. Bentham seems to have been referring to a note in "Extracts from the Portfolio of a Man of Letters," *The Monthly Magazine* 32/2 No. 217 (September 1, 1811): 143, which objects to the translation "lay hold on him" in Mark 14:51, favoring "layed hold of him." The unnamed "man of

letters" referred to this verse as "the anecdote of the cinaedus" (i.e., the word *kinaidos* respelled in Latin) without further explanation, as if this were a well-known way of designating it. The "Extracts" was a regular column in this periodical, but its author was not identified. Elsewhere in the same issue, an unsigned letter to the editor (pp. 117–19) refers in a footnote (p. 118) to a *cinaedus* at the court of King James I, but does not mention the Mark passage. Bentham's remarks occur in the draft of a book titled "Not Paul but Jesus," which he did not actually publish but evidently made available for like-minded people to read (Crompton, *Byron*, 269, 385).

43. Constance Brown Kuriyama, *Christopher Marlowe: A Renaissance Life* (Ithaca, N.Y.: Cornell University Press, 2002), 221. See also Norton, *Mother Clap's*, 21.

44. Halperin, *One Hundred Years*, 1–2, italics in original.

45. There has not been a lot of study of fantasy or invented rituals, but see Grimes, *Deeply into the Bone*, 111–21.

Chapter 10. The Wisdom of Salome

Epigraph. Smith, *Secret Gospel*, 70 and n. 8.

1. Josephus, *Jewish Antiquities* 18.5.4.136, trans. Louis H. Feldman in *Josephus* 9, Loeb Classical Library (Cambridge, Mass.: Harvard University Press, 1965), 93.

2. On the ethical issues see Ben Witherington, "Herodias," *The Anchor Bible Dictionary* (New York: Doubleday, 1992), 3: 174–76. The genealogical issues, however, are summarized differently by Witherington and by John P. Meier, *A Marginal Jew: Rethinking the Historical Jesus* 2: *Mentor, Message, and Miracles,* The Anchor Bible Reference Library (New York: Doubleday, 1994), 172. The historical issues are explored in Nikos Kokkinos, "Which Salome Did Aristobulus Marry?" *Palestine Exploration Quarterly* 118 (1986): 33–50.

3. Indeed, an argument can be made that the preferred reading in the gospel of Mark itself is the one that says the dancing daughter was also named Herodias like her mother. See Meier, *Marginal Jew* 2: 228 n. 230.

4. Patricia Kellogg-Dennis, "Oscar Wilde's *Salomé:* Symbolist Princess," in *Rediscovering Oscar Wilde,* ed. C. George Sandulescu, Princess Grace Irish Library 8 (Gerrards Cross, U.K.: Colin Smythe, 1994), 224–31, quotation from p. 224. For more on Salome see Anne Hudson Jones and Karen Kingsley, "Salome in Late Nineteenth-Century French Art and Literature," *Studies in Iconography* 9 (1983): 107–27; Kerry Powell, *Oscar Wilde and the Theatre of the 1890s* (Cambridge, U.K.: Cambridge University Press, 1990), 33–54; Eleonora Bairati, *Salomè: immagini di un mito* (Nuoro: Ilisso, 1998); Linda Gertner Zatlin, "Wilde, Beardsley, and the Making of Salome," *Journal of Victorian Culture* 5 (2000): 341–57.

5. Robert C. Schweik, "Oscar Wilde's *Salome,* the Salome Theme in Late European Art, and a Problem of Method in Cultural History," *Twilight of Dawn: Studies in English Literature in Transition,* ed. O. M. Brack, Jr. (Tucson: University of Arizona Press, 1987), 123–36, quotation from p. 124.

6. Lionel Lambourne, *The Aesthetic Movement* (London: Phaidon, 1996), 198–200. Gérard-Georges Lemaires, *The Orient in Western Art* (Cologne: Könemann, 2001), 252–55.

7. See Jason Paul Mitchell, "A Source Victorian or Biblical?: The Integration of Biblical Diction and Symbolism in Oscar Wilde's Salome," available at http://home.olemiss.edu/~jmitchel/oscar.htm (accessed June 2003).

8. Tanya Touwen, "Salome: The Music and Language of Oscar Wilde and Richard Strauss," *Irish Studies Review* 11 (Summer 1995): 20–23, quotation from p. 20.

9. Ellmann, *Oscar Wilde*, 376. For an assessment of Wilde's use of prior material, see Josephine M. Guy and Ian Small, *Oscar Wilde's Profession: Writing and the Culture Industry in the Late Nineteenth Century* (Oxford: Oxford University Press, 2000), 226–27, 258–80.

10. Derrick Puffett, ed., *Richard Strauss: Salome,* Cambridge Opera Handbooks (Cambridge, U.K.: Cambridge University Press, 1989), includes the article by Mario Praz, "Salome in Literary Tradition," 11–20; and Richard Ellman, "Overtures to Wilde's Salome," 21–35.

11. *A Full Moon in March* and *The King of the Great Clock Tower.*

12. For a chronology of productions, adaptations, operas, and films, see Robert Tanitch, *Oscar Wilde on Stage and Screen* (London: Methuen, 1999), 134–90.

13. Gaylyn Studlar, "'Out-Salomeing Salome': Dance, the New Woman, and Fan Magazine Orientalism," *Visions of the East: Orientalism in Film,* ed. Matthew Bernstein and Gaylyn Studlar (London: I. B. Tauris, 1997), 99–129. Richard Bizot, "The Turn-of-the-Century Salome Era: High- and Pop-Culture Variations on the Dance of the Seven Veils," *Choreography and Dance: An International Journal* 2/3 (1992): 71–87.

14. Puffett, *Richard Strauss,* 167, 196 n. 9. For more on Strauss's musical conception, see Patricia Coleman Tate, "'The Dance of the Seven Veils:' A Historical and Descriptive Analysis," (D.A. dissertation, University of Northern Colorado, 1985).

15. Eva Maria Fischer, "Salome — Femme fatale des Neuen Testaments? Ein Streifzug durch die Rezeptions- und Wirkungsgeschichte," *Steht nicht geschrieben? Studien zur Bibel und ihrer Wirkungsgeschichte: Festschrift für Georg Schmuttermayr,* ed. Johannes Frühwald-König et al. (Regensburg: Friedrich Pustet, 2001), 383–401, quotation from p. 383: "Personifikation von Eros und Thanatos, Lust und tödlicher Grausamkeit." See also Franz Meier, "Oscar Wilde and the Myth of the Femme Fatale in Fin-de-Siècle Culture," *The Importance of Reinventing Oscar: Versions of Wilde During the Last 100 Years,* ed. Uwe Böker et al. (Amsterdam: Rodopi, 2002), 117–34.

16. Lawrence Kramer, "Culture and Musical Hermeneutics: The Salome Complex," *Cambridge Opera Journal* 2/3 (1990): 269–94, see p. 271.

17. Carolyn Abbate, "Opera; or, the Envoicing of Women," *Musicology and Difference: Gender and Sexuality in Music Scholarship,* ed. Ruth A. Solie (Berkeley: University of California Press, 1993), 225–58, see p. 238.

18. Ellmann, *Oscar Wilde,* 339–45. The plate facing p. 429 shows a photograph of Wilde costumed as Salome.

19. Ibid., 340, 341.

20. The Greek might literally be translated "the innermost sanctuary of the sevenfold veiled truth." Smith's translation "that truth hidden by seven veils" seems to point a little too boldly to Wilde's Salomé; he evidently tried to muffle this cue in his second book, by adding the brackets around the word "[veils]."

21. Smith, *Clement,* 40–41, assembles a number of passages and variant readings to

show that Clement wrote elsewhere of innermost sanctuaries and veiled truths, and that he was aware of a tradition of seven walls or precincts around the Temple. One Jewish text refers to seven veiled gates around the Temple, but not the Holy of Holies. What the cited texts do *not* say is that the seven veils covered the "innermost sanctuary," as in the Mar Saba text. Thus Smith adduces no direct support for the proposition that Clement (or any other ancient writer) actually used a metaphor of seven veils hiding an innermost sanctuary. For some Jewish traditions on the number and locations of veils in the Temple see C. R. A. Morray-Jones, *A Transparent Illusion: The Dangerous Vision of Water in Hekhalot Mysticism: A Source-Critical and Tradition-Historical Inquiry,* supplements to the Journal for the Study of Judaism 59 (Leiden: Brill, 2002), 153–72. Clement's understanding of the Temple was based on Philo's allegorical account; on the veil see Hoek, *Clement of Alexandria,* 120–23.

22. Smith, *Clement,* 191, citing Allberry, *Manichaean Psalm-Book,* 222–23.

23. Smith, *Clement,* 55.

24. Although represented in the King James Version as Solomon and the Shulamite, Shlomo and Shulamit can be read as masculine and feminine forms of the same name, like John and Joan. In that case the characters can be read as Everyman and Everywoman, and the Song of Songs as a celebration of all monogamous heterosexual love.

25. The law was passed May 16, 1559; see E. K. Chambers, *The Elizabethan Stage* 1 (Oxford: Clarendon Press, 1923), 276.

26. Ellman, *Oscar Wilde,* 348.

27. This is the final sentence in Stephen Wayne Foster, "Wilde, Oscar F. O. W. (1856–1900)," *Encyclopedia of Homosexuality,* ed. Wayne R. Dynes et al. (New York: Garland, 1990), 2: 1389–91.

28. "Introduction" to Oscar Wilde, *The Importance of Being Earnest and Other Plays,* ed. Richard Allen Cave (New York: Penguin Books, 2000), vii.

29. See Michael Patrick Gillespie, *Oscar Wilde and the Poetics of Ambiguity* (Gainesville: University Press of Florida, 1996), 137.

30. See the play *Saint Oscar* by Terry Eagleton (Derry, Ireland: Field Day, 1989), reprinted in Eagleton, *Saint Oscar and Other Plays* (Oxford: Blackwell, 1997), 11–63, quotation from p. 5.

31. Ian Bradley, ed., *The Complete Annotated Gilbert and Sullivan* (Oxford: Oxford University Press, 1996), 292–93; on the other nineteenth-century figures who are satirized by the character, see pp. 267–69, 290. I find the commentary more à propos of our issues in *Asimov's Annotated Gilbert & Sullivan,* ed. Isaac Asimov (New York: Doubleday, 1988), 299.

32. Bradley, *Complete Annotated,* 268.

33. See Guy Willoughby, *Art and Christhood: The Aesthetics of Oscar Wilde* (Rutherford/Madison/Teaneck: Fairleigh Dickinson University Press, 1993), 103–34. John Albert, "The Christ of Oscar Wilde," *Critical Essays on Oscar Wilde,* ed. Regenia Gagnier (New York: G. K. Hall, 1991), 241–57.

34. G. K. Chesterton, "Oscar Wilde," from the London *Daily News* (1909), reprinted in *The Bodley Head G. K. Chesterton,* ed. P. J. Kavanagh (London: The Bodley Head, 1985), 251–53, quotation from p. 251. Chesterton, who had recently published his book *Orthodoxy* (London: John Lane, 1909), was an Anglican at the time; only in 1922 did he become Roman Catholic.

35. From the London *Evening News,* quoted in H. Montgomery Hyde, *The Trials of Oscar Wilde,* 2nd ed. (New York: Dover, 1973), 18.

36. There had already been a private performance about 1905, according to Matt Cook, *London and the Culture of Homosexuality, 1885–1914* (Cambridge, U.K.: Cambridge University Press, 2003), 35, 166.

37. Philip Hoare, *Oscar Wilde's Last Stand: Decadence, Conspiracy, and the Most Outrageous Trial of the Century* (New York: Arcade, 1998), especially pp. 57–59, 91, 115, 198. Billing's remarkable exploits as a pioneering aviator, disgruntled minor war hero, sometime playwright, and hapless inventor are summarized in G. R. Searle, "Billing, Noel Pemberton," *The Dictionary of National Biography: Missing Persons,* ed. C. S. Nicholls et al. (Oxford: Oxford University Press, 1993), 67, revised in *Oxford Dictionary of National Biography,* ed. H. C. G. Matthew and Brian Harrison (Oxford: Oxford University Press, 2004), 5: 721–22.

38. Hoare, *Oscar Wilde's Last Stand,* 106–8, 120, 193–94, 199–201.

39. Ibid., 118–19, 122–30, 193–94, 213.

40. Ibid., 214–15.

41. Ibid., 171–72. Hoare's sources (pp. 232 n.3, 235 n. 59) include the *Vigilante*'s own published account and Michael Kettle, *Salome's Last Veil* (London: Hart-Davis/ Granada, 1977). See also Lucy Bland, "Trial by Sexology?: Maud Allan, *Salome* and the 'Cult of the Clitoris' Case," *Sexology in Culture,* 183–98.

42. Hoare, *Oscar Wilde's Last Stand,* 58.

43. Ibid., 189. The book has since been reprinted: A. T. Fitzroy, *Despised and Rejected* (London: C. W. Daniel, [1918]; repr. New York: Arno, 1975; London: Gay Men's Press, 1988). On *Messiah* see Ruth Smith, *Handel's Oratorios and Eighteenth-Century Thought* (Cambridge, U.K.: Cambridge University Press, 1995), 148–52.

44. Hoare, *Oscar Wilde's Last Stand,* 194–97, 210.

45. See Stephen O. Murray, *American Gay* (Chicago: University of Chicago Press, 1996). 2.

46. Ira L. Reiss and Albert Ellis, *At the Dawn of the Sexual Revolution: Reflections on a Dialogue* (Walnut Creek, Calif.: Alta Mira Press, 2002), xi.

47. Akenson, *Saint Saul,* 88.

48. Ibid., 89.

49. For some less successful examples see Edgar J. Goodspeed, *Modern Apocrypha* (Boston: Beacon Press, 1956).

50. Indeed, a fascinating history of this modern notion could be written, with Jesus as the blank screen on which a long succession of self-identifications was projected, from the "similisexual" of yesteryear to the metrosexual of today. Early examples would include the following (asterisks indicate items I have not seen): Xavier Mayne [Edward I. Prime-Stevenson], *The Intersexes: A History of Similisexualism as a Problem in Social Life* (n.p. [Florence or Rome]: privately printed, 1908; repr. New York: Arno, 1975), 46, 258–60; C. J. Bulliet, *Venus Castina: Famous Female Impersonators Celestial and Human* (New York: Covici, Friede, 1928; repr. 1933), 33–37; Edgar Lee Masters, *Whitman* (New York: Charles Scribner's Sons, 1937), 139–41; *Robert Wood, *Christ and the Homosexual* (New York: Vantage Press, 1960), 169, 176; Noel I. Garde [Edgar Leoni], *Jonathan to Gide: The Homosexual in History* (New York: Vantage, 1964), 122–29; H. W. Montefiore, "Jesus, the Revelation of God," *Christ for Us Today: Papers Read at the Con-*

ference of Modern Churchmen, ed. Norman Pittenger (London: SCM, 1968), 101–16, see pp. 108–10; *Mikhail Itkin, *The Radical Jesus & Gay Consciousness: Notes for a Theology of Gay Liberation* (n.p.: Communiversity West, 1972); John A. T. Robinson, *The Human Face of God* (London: SCM, 1973), 63, 68, 70. James Kirkup's poem "The Love That Dares to Speak Its Name," published in London's *Gay News* in 1976, was the subject of a blasphemy trial the following year, and thus is widely available on the Internet. More recent examples include Tom Horner, *Jonathan Loved David: Homosexuality in Biblical Times* (Philadelphia: Westminster, 1978), 117–25; *Malcolm Boyd, "Was Jesus Gay?" *The Advocate* 565 (December 4, 1990), 90; *Gore Vidal, *Live from Golgotha* (New York: Random House, 1992); Robert Williams, *Just As I Am: A Practical Guide to Being Out, Proud, and Christian* (New York: Crown Publishers, 1992), 116–22; Robert Goss, *Jesus Acted Up: A Gay and Lesbian Manifesto* (San Francisco: Harper, 1993), 81–85; Goss, *Queering Christ: Beyond Jesus Acted Up* (Cleveland: The Pilgrim Press, 2002), 134–35, 137, 163–64, 175; Terence McNally, *Corpus Christi: A Play* (New York: Grove Press, 1998); Nancy L. Wilson, *Our Tribe: Queer Folks, God, Jesus, and the Bible* (San Francisco: Harper, 1995), 140–47, omitted from the rev. ed. (Tajique, N.M.: Alamo Square Press, 2000); Stephen D. Moore, *God's Beauty Parlor, and Other Queer Spaces In and Around the Bible* (Palo Alto, Calif.: Stanford University Press, 2001); Rollan McCleary, *Signs for a Messiah: The First and Last Evidence for Jesus* (Christchurch, New Zealand: Hazard Press, 2003). On the relatively less popular idea that Jesus was heterosexual, see William E. Phipps, *The Sexuality of Jesus: Theological and Literary Perspectives* (New York: Harper & Row, 1973), 2nd ed. (Cleveland, Ohio: Pilgrim Press, 1996); Barbara Thiering, *Jesus the Man: A New Interpretation from the Dead Sea Scrolls* (Sydney: Doubleday, 1992), 87–89, 100.

51. Ehrman, "Response," 161, italics in original. C. C. Richardson, quoted in Schneemelcher, ed., *New Testament Apocrypha* 1: 107.

52. Smith, *Clement,* 6, 285–86, 288.

53. Plures enim paginas nugis istis implerat impudentissimus iste nebulo. . . . Tu vale lector, si quis unquam futurus sis, & properanti si quae exciderunt, ignosce." For the facing page see Smith, *Secret Gospel,* plate facing p. 39.

54. William Blackstone, *Commentaries on the Laws of England* (Oxford: Clarendon Press, 1765), Book 4, Chapter 15, available at http://www.lonang.com/exlibris/blackstone/index.html (June 2003).

55. Michael Goodich, *The Unmentionable Vice: Homosexuality in the Middle Ages* (Santa Barbara, Calif.: ABC-Clio, 1979).

56. See Alexander Souter, ed., *Pelagius's Exposition of Thirteen Epistles of St Paul* 2: *Text and Apparatus Criticus,* Texts and Studies 9/2 (Cambridge, U.K.: Cambridge University Press, 1926), 374 line 8. See Theodore de Bruyn, *Pelagius's Commentary on St Paul's Epistle to the Romans* (Oxford: Clarendon Press, 1993), 27–28, 30–31. For some roughly contemporary exegesis that does not mention Sodom at this point, see Ronald E. Heine, *The Commentaries of Origen and Jerome on St Paul's Epistle to the Ephesians,* Oxford Early Christian Studies (Oxford: Oxford University Press, 2002), 209–17. Although Pelagius himself was regarded as a heretic, adaptations of his commentary that included the Sodom passage circulated in the Middle Ages under the names of Cassiodorus and Hrabanus Maurus: see David W. Johnson, "Purging the Poison: The Revi-

sion of Pelagius' Pauline Commentaries by Cassiodorus and His Students" (Ph.D. dissertation, Princeton Theological Seminary, 1989).

57. This Pelagius is the British-born, early-fifth-century controversialist who sparred with Augustine in the Pelagian controversy; see V. Grossi, "Pelagius-Pelagians-Pelagianism," *Encyclopedia of the Early Church*, 2: 665–66. He should not be confused with the Pelagius of Galicia described in Boswell, *Christianity*, 198–200.

58. Thus a modern Greek study of ancient Greek obscenities is Euios Lēnaios [Chariton Charalampous Charitōnidēs], Ἀπόρρητα (Thessaloniki: Mich. Triantaphullos, 1935).

59. See Eve Kosofsky Sedgwick, *Between Men: English Literature and Male Homosexual Desire* (New York: Columbia University Press, 1985), 94–95; H. G. Cocks, *Nameless Offences: Homosexual Desire in the Nineteenth Century* (London: I. B. Tauris, 2003).

60. Byrne R. S. Fone, *The Columbia Anthology of Gay Literature: Readings from Western Antiquity to the Present Day* (New York: Columbia University Press, 1998), 295–97.

61. Rumors that the received account of the trial has been embellished by later hagiographers are hard to prove, but the original stenographer's shorthand account of the first trial has recently turned up and been published: Merlin Holland, *Irish Peacock & Scarlet Marquess: The Real Trial of Oscar Wilde* (London: Fourth Estate, 2003).

62. Hyde, *The Trials*, 201. Excerpted in Fone, *The Columbia Anthology*, 339–41; Ellmann, *Oscar Wilde*, 463.

Chapter 11. The One Who Knows

Epigraph. Smith, "On the Authenticity of the Mar Saba Letter of Clement," *The Catholic Biblical Quarterly* 38 (1976): 196–99, quotation from p. 197 and n. 7.

Epigraph. Quentin Quesnell, "A Reply to Morton Smith," *The Catholic Biblical Quarterly* 38 (1976): 200–03, quotation from p. 202.

1. Indeed Salomé seems to have had some sort of iconic or folk status in the secretive homosexual culture at Harvard, according to Wright, *Harvard's Secret Court*, 21, cf. p. 149.

2. Alan Dundes, "The Fabrication of Fakelore," in Dundes, *Folklore Matters* (Knoxville: University of Tennessee Press, 1989). Marshall W. Fishwick, "Sons of Paul: Folklore or Fakelore?" *Western Folklore* 18 (1959): 277–86.

3. Quentin Quesnell, "The Mar Saba Clementine: A Question of Evidence," *The Catholic Biblical Quarterly* 37 (1975): 48–67, quotation from p. 66. See also Ehrman, "Response," 162.

4. Quesnell, "The Mar Saba Clementine," 65, 60.

5. Ibid., 60–61.

6. Lawrence A. Hoffman, *Beyond the Text: A Holistic Approach to Liturgy* (Bloomington: Indiana University Press, 1989), 172, quoting Clifford Geertz, *The Interpretation of Cultures* (New York: Basic Books, 1973), 126–27.

7. Mark Goodale, "Ethical Theory as Social Practice," *American Anthropologist* 108 (2006): 25–37. For an example see Richard Taruskin, *Defining Russia Musically: Historical and Hermeneutical Essays* (Princeton, N.J.: Princeton University Press, 1997), xxix.

8. Roman Catholic Church, Second Vatican Council, Pastoral Constitution on the Church in the Modern World *(Gaudium et spes)* 52, trans. Tanner, *Decrees* 2: 1105.

9. Georges Florovsky, *Ways of Russian Theology* 2, ed. Richard S. Haugh, trans. Robert L. Nichols, *Collected Works of Georges Florovsky,* 6 vols. (Belmont, Mass.: Nordland, Büchervertriebsanstalt, 1987), 27–38.

10. Simon Karlinsky, *The Sexual Labyrinth of Nikolai Gogol* (Cambridge, Mass.: Harvard University Press, 1976).

11. N. B. [*sic*] Gogol, *Meditations on the Divine Liturgy: A Mystical Interpretation of the Rite of the Holy Eucharist as Celebrated in the Eastern Orthodox Churches,* new ed., trans. L. Aléxeyev (London: Anglican and Eastern Churches Association, 1926), 97–98. According to the translator, pp. v–vi, one edition of the Russian text was published by the Holy Synod, which would indicate that the Russian Orthodox hierarchy approved of what the text says. For comment see Florovsky, *Ways,* 31, 326 nn. 137–38; also Lorenz Amberg, *Kirche, Liturgie und Frömmigkeit im Schaffen von N. V. Gogol',* Slavica Helvetica 24 (Bern: Peter Lang, 1986).

Index of Ancient and Medieval Writings

APOCRYPHA, PSEUDEPIGRAPHA, GNOSTIC WRITINGS

TALMUDIC AND OTHER JEWISH WRITINGS

GREEK AND LATIN AUTHORS

General Index

Acts of Thomas, 112–13, 114
Aelred of Rievaulx, 172
Aiskhines, 191–92
Akenson, Donald Harman, 42
Alcibiades, 195–98
Alexandria, 53; Epiphany at, 78–80, 82; initiation liturgy, 53; Lent at, 73–77, 79–89; liturgical lectionaries, 71, 82–89
Anglican Communion, 62–65, 149–51, 248; apologetics, 176–78; Book of Common Prayer, 159, 245, 275nn17–18, 275n21, 304n8; "high church," 144, 157–58, 221, 224, 231, 293n90, 304n10; moral theology, 155–74, 175–80; sacraments, 158–62; spirituality, 173–74
Anomaly (pseudonym), 165–72
Antiphons: communion, 87–88; gospel, 78–79; introit, 63
Apostolic Tradition, 65–67, 111, 113
Armenian rite, 277n38, 294n106
Athanasius, St., Festal Letters, 75–76, 82

baptism, 17, 127–28; of the apostles, 81; at Constantinople, 72–74; dates of, 72, 74, 75–77, 81–82; at Easter, 63–69; at Epiphany, 68–69, 82; Lazarus and, 88–90; in Lent, 72, 82; nudity in, 111–15, 127–28; at Pentecost, 68; and resurrection, 61–62, 64, 66–67; water symbolism, 78; white garments, 61, 63, 67, 115–19. See also initiation rites
Beloved Disciple, 33, 47, 223, 241
Bentham, Jeremy, 223
Billing, Noel Pemberton, 232–34
Book of Common Prayer, 63–65, 90, 159
Boswell, John, 288n19, 304–5n13
Brown, Raymond E., 30, 89, 91–92
Brown, Scott G., 34
Buckham, Richard, 96–97, 99
burial practices, 114–15, 118
Byzantine rite, 8, 249–51, 299n15, 299–300nn23–24; hymns, 2, 101, 124–27, 130, 131–36, 142, 143; lectionaries,